Statistics   Statistique
Canada   Canada

canada handbook

The 46th annual handbook
of present conditions
and recent progress

Prepared in the
Publishing Section
Information Division
Statistics Canada

Published under the authority of the
Minister of Industry, Trade and Commerce

preface

This is the 46th edition of the *Canada Handbook*. It presents a view of life in this country and a summary of recent social, cultural and economic developments. Textual and statistical material has been provided by various divisions of Statistics Canada, by other government departments and by special contributors. A feature of this edition is the article describing the 1976 Olympic Games held in Montreal. Illustrations have been selected from a wide range of government, commercial, press and private sources.

Canada is now in the process of converting to the SI (Système Internationale) metric system. In support of this movement all relevant amounts in the text of *Canada Handbook* are expressed in SI only; however, tables are stated in both SI and Imperial (inch-pound) units where applicable. A table giving conversion of selected metric figures into the traditional Canadian units is printed on page 365.

Canada Handbook was planned and produced by Sandra Smart, Editor, and Margaret Johnstone, Assistant Editor, with the assistance of the staff of the Publishing Section, Information Division.

Peter G. Kirkham
Chief Statistician of Canada

December 1976

contents

The Environment viii

   The Land 4
   The Climate 17

The People and Their Heritage .. 26

   History 27
   Population 36
   Religion 57
   Arts and Culture 61
   Education 96
   Leisure 112
   Science and Technology 125
   Communications 146
   The Olympics 152
   External Relations 162

The Economy 172

   Economic Trends in Canada,
     1975-76 173
   Natural Wealth 177
   Employment 211
   Industry 216
   Trade 238
   Finance 262
   Transportation 279

Governments and Their Services 290

   Government 291
   The Legal System 299
   Citizenship 306
   Manpower and Immigration .. 308
   Labour 312
   Industry, Trade and
     Commerce 319
   Regional Economic Expansion 321
   Consumer and Corporate
     Affairs 323
   Urban Affairs 327
   Veterans Affairs 331
   Health and Welfare 334
   Environment 347
   Agriculture 352
   External Affairs 356
   National Defence 363

**Common Conversion Factors
from SI Metric to Canadian
Imperial Units** 365

Acknowledgements 367

Index 373

the environment

Canadians like to boast that Canada is the second largest country in the world, with an area of almost 10 million square kilometres. With this in mind, we tend to assume that Canada will never have problems of crowding. Unfortunately, relatively little of that area is easily habitable for those living average southern Canadian lifestyles, and only about 7 per cent of the land is presently economically viable for farming. Recent years have seen increased concern about how we use or abuse this environment and how Canadians can better adapt to their demanding climate while making much more efficient use of finite resources.

Rapid population growth has been concentrated mainly in cities. Growing cities increasingly threaten surrounding agricultural lands with demands for more land for housing, transportation systems, etc.; this is especially obvious in the Windsor–Quebec City corridor and the lower BC mainland. Since Canadian cities tend to develop where climate and landscape are gentlest, the land they and their spreading suburbs use tends also to be the most productive farm land. At the same time, population growth, both locally and world-wide, demands increasing food production, and in the light of those demands the loss of any good agricultural land becomes a very high price to pay for continuing urbanization and industrialization.

As population has grown, so has dependency on the goods and services provided by more and more large-scale technology. Non-renewable resources are consumed at an accelerated rate, both as raw materials and as energy to keep the machinery of transport and production going. While concern about continued supply of these resources rises, growing quantities of solid wastes accumulate and pollution threatens the air, land and water which support all life. One result of such overuse and abuse of the environment is a growing scarcity of resources and resulting higher costs for food, energy, housing and other human needs. Another is the fear that the quality of life in Canada must deteriorate under such pressures.

In the past the availability of unexploited agricultural land, of readily accessible renewable and non-renewable resources, and of cheap and abundant energy have allowed Canadians to avoid the problem of finite resources. When the resource on which a community's economy was based was used up, there seemed to be plenty of unexploited resources elsewhere to move on to. At a time when people were few and far between, most of the pollution they generated could be tolerated by the natural environment. Some communities did suffer severely from changes in the resource base; trappers, the native peoples, farmers, miners, fishermen and lumberjacks have all faced drastic changes when the resources they had built their lives on were depleted. But the country as a whole still seemed to offer unlimited new resources.

The Canadian economy and society were founded upon cheap, abundant resources and limitless horizons. However, the realities which must now govern policies, lifestyles and designs are finite and increasingly expensive resources, and social and environmental conditions that can no longer tolerate abuses.

The Canadian climate has to be given much more consideration by policy makers, resource managers, planners and designers. Canada's long non-growing season, the distribution of water resources and such specific problems as permafrost in the North all limit food production, and mean that renewable resources take longer to renew, wastes take longer to decay, and flora and fauna are under greater stresses than in milder climates. Alternating extremes of hot and cold temperatures create special design and medical problems. Common building materials like steel and plastics don't stand up well. Existing Canadian buildings were built on the basis of cheap energy or mild-climate designs; they need renovation to conserve energy and save on heating and cooling costs, while efforts continue to develop designs for new structures and arrangements of buildings that will suit the climatic extremes prevailing in most of the country. People too are stressed, both physically and emotionally, by extreme temperatures, especially by the combination of cold and increasing periods of darkness in winter.

The use of Canada's 10 million square kilometres is also limited by physiography and the general environment. Permafrost, ice, muskeg, slope and unstable soils produce particular problems for constructing and maintaining buildings and transportation systems. Lack of suitable soils, or soils that require expensive drainage and fertilization, limits agriculture and forestry. Shortages of rock (gravel) in other areas make construction difficult and expensive. Much of British Columbia is just too high and/or too steep for development.

The very large distances between settlements throughout most of Canada introduce problems of energy consumption for transportation, high costs for transporta-

Midnight sun over Eureka Sound and Axel Heiberg Island, NWT.

tion systems, due to both distances and difficulties of construction, and the cultural and psychological effects of isolation. The costs associated with these problems are borne by all Canadians, as government and industry subsidize development so that it might some day become profitable.

Biting insects in the North are both a source of food in one part of the ecological web and a check on mammal populations on the other because their large numbers can fatally weaken the sick, infirm and very young; if man were to use insecticides to make areas comfortably habitable for him and his livestock the insecticides and the absence of the insects would both have serious repercussions.

The alternative to stumbling into a future dominated by forces beyond our control, such as climate, resource-base changes or the changing policies of other nations that now fill the gaps in Canadian production, is to consciously and conscientiously redesign our physical systems and social institutions and to adapt our lifestyles to the physical realities. Canadians can develop a society that strikes a better balance between what we demand of our resources and environment and what nature is able to provide over the long term, and they can do it without drastic changes in their way of life.

The following descriptions of Canada's climate and physiography provide an introduction to the necessary self-knowledge.

DIXON THOMPSON

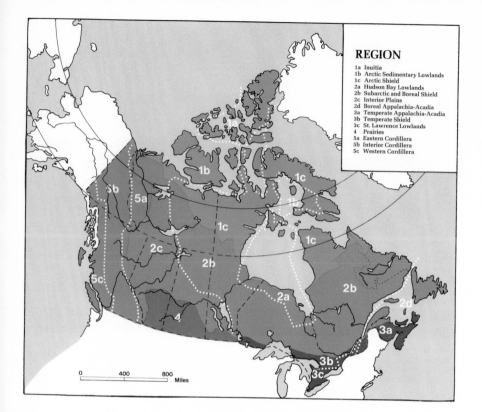

The Land

Canada's borders encompass 9 977 000 km² (square kilometres), yet the country's over-all pattern of relief is simple. The interior is a plain-like surface bounded on the east, west and north by a highland rim but open to our American neighbours to the south. This low-relief area is 3 200 km (kilometres) wide at its widest in the south and narrows to about 1 600 km in the north. On the western side the Cordilleran region is an almost unbroken mountain chain extending from the American border to the Beaufort Sea. On the eastern side, the Appalachian Mountain system forms the Atlantic provinces. On the northern side, the Torngat Mountains of Labrador and the Baffin, Axel Heiberg and Ellesmere Island mountains form a more broken barrier.

In any analysis of Canada's physical geography the fact that up to 97 per cent of its surface has been repeatedly covered by glacier ice within the last million years is of fundamental importance, in that the surface features of both mountains and plains have been extensively modified. Only the central part of the Yukon Territory and minor parts of the Northwest Territories escaped glaciation. About 2 per cent of Canada is still covered by glacier ice, but its distribution is so restricted that probably two thirds of the Inuit (Eskimo) population, for example, has never seen a glacier. About 155 000 km² of ice remain in the Arctic islands and 52 000 km² remain on the mainland.

Four major vegetation zones and five major landform regions of Canada are used as a basis for the discussion that follows. In general, the vegetation zones provide a convenient basis for regional description; only in the case of the Cordilleran region are landforms considered more useful for this purpose. Accordingly, the regions are described under the five major headings of: 1. The Arctic Tundra; 2. The Subarctic Parkland and Boreal Forest; 3. The Eastern Temperate Forest; 4. The Prairies; and 5. The Cordillera. An attempt has also been made to identify the distinctive natural hazards associated with each of these regions, where natural hazard is defined as "an interaction of people and nature governed by the co-existent state of adjustment in the human use system and the state of nature in the natural events system. Extreme events which exceed the normal capacity of the human system to reflect, absorb or buffer them are inherent in hazard."[1]

1. The Arctic Tundra Region

The Arctic Tundra corresponds closely to that region which lies north of the southern limit of continuous permafrost. Permafrost is the thermal condition in earth materials that remain below 0°C for two years or more. Approximately 26 per cent of the world's land surface is underlain by permafrost, and distinctive landforms and engineering problems are associated with its occurrence. The tundra vegetation that is characteristic of this region shows considerable variety, and is discussed under each sub-region.

[1]G.F. White, *Natural Hazards* (Oxford University Press, 1974), p 4.

Arctic tundra vegetation on Baffin Island, NWT.

This region has generally been regarded as comparatively free from natural hazards. Nevertheless, a number of potential environmental problems can be identified, such as building and highway construction, sewage disposal, water supply and hot-oil pipelines. In each case the problem results from a disturbance of surface conditions, whereby there is an increase in summer thawing and a consequent thickening of the active layer. Insulation of the ground surface needs to be maintained by not removing the vegetation mat or by adding coarse gravel fill.

(a) The Inuitian Sub-region (378 000 km²)

This is the northernmost part of Canada, north of Parry Channel (74°N). Included are Ellesmere, Axel Heiberg, Parry and Queen Elizabeth islands. One third of Ellesmere and Axel Heiberg are covered with ice (about 96 000 km²) and this includes 12 ice caps, each with an area of more than 2 500 km². Local relief up to 1 200 m (metres), with the highest summits around 2 500 m, provide the setting for some of the harshest environments on earth. In this high Arctic polar desert, vegetation may be completely absent except for crustaceous lichens. "In its variety, its aridity and its glaciers, and above all its potential for petroleum development, it is perhaps the most fascinating of all the regions of northern Canada."[2]

(b) Arctic Sedimentary Lowlands Sub-region (409 000 km²)

Included in this category are: most of the Arctic islands south of Parry Channel, such as Banks, Victoria, Prince of Wales, Somerset and Southampton islands; low-lying parts of Devon, Ellesmere and Baffin islands; and the Arctic Coastal Plain, including the Mackenzie River Delta. They form low coastal plains and plateaus underlain by horizontally bedded sedimentary strata covered by a variable depth of drift sediments or, in the case of the Mackenzie Delta, of fluvial sediments. Although underlain by continuous permafrost, the land surface shows a markedly richer tundra vegetation than the Inuitian sub-region. Lichen moss tundra, including reindeer moss in the drier sites and wet tundra with grasses and sedges, provide an almost continuous vegetation cover. The Mackenzie Delta has exceptionally rich vegetation, including stands of white and black spruce on the higher parts of stable river island bars. Rock deserts and peat-covered tundra plains are also present and are especially well developed on Southampton, Coats and Mansel islands in Hudson Bay.

Of particular interest in this sub-region are the distinctive landforms that have developed under the influence of periglacial processes. Spectacular conical hills called pingos develop in drained lake bottoms along the Arctic Coastal Plain; polygon-patterned ground is common; mounds, hollows and mud circles are widespread; and solifluction terraces — resulting from the saturation of the soils and frost action—are here classically developed. All this over a depth of permafrost that reaches 400 m in the delta and 490 m on the islands, and also on massive layers of ice up to 30 m thick.

[2]J.B. Bird in W.C. Wonders, The North (Toronto, 1972), p 24.

With twenty hours a day of daylight in mid-summer, a gardener in Pine Point, NWT, can produce a flourishing crop.

(c) Arctic Shield Sub-region (1 412 000 km²)

Included in this part of the Arctic tundra are 20 per cent of the Mackenzie District, 80 per cent of the Keewatin District, 35 per cent of the Franklin District (including most of Baffin Island) — all in the Northwest Terrritories — and 15 per cent of Quebec. At least two rather distinct landscapes are evident. There is the spectacular eastern highland rim, which includes the southeastern corner of Ellesmere Island, the eastern end of Devon Island, Bylot Island, eastern Baffin Island and the Torngat Mountains of Quebec, with local relief in the Baffin fiords as high as 1 830 m; some of the most remarkable glaciated-erosional topography of the North American continent is found on Baffin Island's east coast. The remainder of the sub-region is commonly known as Canada's Barren Grounds, and is characterized by uplands, hills and rocky lowlands.

The most luxuriant tundra vegetation is known as bush tundra, with willow and alder bushes and dense undergrowth, and occurs locally in the Barren Grounds, especially on the south side of Amundsen and Coronation gulfs. Wet tundra is more common in the eastern part of the sub-region, where the environment is generally more humid. While the eastern rim may have long periods of cold, cloudy, damp weather in summer, the western shield has weeks of warm, dry, cloudless weather.

In spite of this poor climate the fiord lands of Baffin Island support the widest variety of arctic ecosystems. Cliffs and talus slopes, gravel outwash plains, coastal sedge and grass marshes, and permanent ice caps, in addition to the standard wet tundra, give variety to the landscape.

2. The Subarctic Parkland and Boreal Forest Region

This is a region underlain by discontinuous permafrost in the north and totally free of permafrost in the south. It cuts a swath through Mackenzie, western Keewatin, northeastern British Columbia, northern Alberta and Saskatchewan, almost the whole of Manitoba, Ontario, Quebec and Newfoundland. The distinctive zones of vegetation which give character to this region are discussed under the Shield sub-region.

Here, as in the first region, natural hazards have not been generally recognized or adequately investigated. Perhaps the most severe hazard faced by agents of economic development in this region is the vast expanse of muskeg that is characteristic of the surface cover. "Movement by foot in summer is exhausting and often impossible, as one sinks into the saturated moss and peat."[3]

[3]J.B. Bird, *The Natural Landscapes of Canada.* (John Wiley, 1972), p 165.

The Spotted Lake in southern BC; formed by heavy mineral deposits, it was once valued by Indians for its medicinal properties.

(a) Hudson Bay Lowland Sub-region (303 000 km²)

Although continuous permafrost is present in the narrow strip along the Hudson Bay coast where the mean annual air temperature is less than −4°C, the significant difference that characterizes this sub-region is that some areas of it do not have permafrost. In the southernmost part of the lowland there is no permafrost at all; at the southern fringe of the discontinuous permafrost zone (53¹/₂°N is the southernmost occurrence of permafrost in Canada outside the Cordillera), permafrost islands vary from less than 15 m² to several hectares in extent and a few centimetres to 60 cm (centimetres) in depth. At Churchill the permafrost is continuous and 60 m deep.

Physiographic uniformity derives from horizontally bedded sedimentary strata covered by a varying depth of drift, but this sub-region contrasts with the surrounding Shield sub-region most markedly in the nearly universal presence of organic terrain and the absence of bedrock outcrops.

Tamarack and scattered-to-dense spruce stands, ranging in height from less than one metre to more than 12 m, are dominant. Alder and willow form the undergrowth. Sphagnum, feather and other mosses, Labrador tea, grass and marsh sedge form the ground vegetation.

Microrelief of hummocks, peat plateaus and palsas up to 6 m in height is characteristic. It is estimated that peat is accumulating at a rate of 2.5 cm (centimetres) every 20 years.

(b) Subarctic and Boreal Shield Sub-region (3 354 000 km²)

Covering 40 per cent of Mackenzie, 10 per cent of Keewatin, 35 per cent of Saskatchewan, 60 per cent of Manitoba, 80 per cent of Quebec and 55 per cent of Ontario, this represents the largest single sub-region described. The Precambrian bedrock of the Shield gives subdued relief, and extensive drift areas are preserved. Fluvioglacial deposits in the form of eskers are particularly well expressed in the Keewatin and eastern Mackenzie districts. Another noteworthy feature is the recentness of the massive post-glacial uplift of land; for example, on the east side of Hudson Bay post-glacial marine features are found as high as 270 m above the present sea level.

Three major vegetation associations occur in this sub-region: the forest-tundra, the northern woodland and the closed boreal forest (or Canadian forest). The major part of the sub-region is underlain by discontinuous permafrost.

The forest-tundra zone varies from 48 km wide in Mackenzie to 160 km wide in Keewatin and Quebec. Islands or strips of white or black spruce or (in Quebec) larch are restricted to sheltered areas but become progressively more dominant southwards.

The northern woodland zone has the appearance of an open parkland and is best developed in Quebec, where widely separate candelabra spruce stand on a deep lichen floor. Along the banks of the major rivers and in sheltered areas, full boreal forest is developed.

The boreal forest of spruce, fir, larch, hemlock and pine extends across the whole of Canada from Newfoundland to British Columbia. The eastern half of this zone has a smaller number of species than the western half, but there is remarkable similarity in over-all structure.

The clay belts of the Shield (especially the great clay belt of Ontario) stand out because of the general absence of rock outcrop and because agricultural development is leading to extensive modification of the boreal forest.

(c) Interior Plains Sub-region (1 479 000 km²)

This sub-region covers 25 per cent of Mackenzie, 10 per cent of British Columbia, 80 per cent of Alberta, 30 per cent of Saskatchewan and 30 per cent of Manitoba. With the same three major vegetation associations as the Shield immediately to the east, it differs from the Shield mainly in its physiography. Major hills, plateaus and escarpments are formed by outcrops of gently dipping sedimentary rocks (limestone, sandstone and shale) which contrast with the Precambrian rocks of the Shield. On the other hand, the details of the landscape are a product of glaciation and particularly extensive areas are occupied by meltwater channels from proglacial lakes, and by extensive lake-bed materials. The sub-region is about 960 km wide in the south. It narrows to 320 km wide east of the Franklin Mountains, and widens to 800 km again in western Mackenzie. The scenery consists of wide vistas of undulating plains, the occasional valley cut deep below the general surface and the distant lines of hills and escarpment.

There are no mountain barriers to provide protection from cold air moving south from the Arctic or from warm air from the Gulf of Mexico. Consequently the widest variation of temperature between summer and winter tends to occur and day-to-day changes are frequent. Those areas within 160 km or so of the Rocky Mountain foothills experience Chinook winds that can raise temperatures from $-29°$ to $+2°C$ in a few hours.

(d) The Boreal Appalachian—Acadian Sub-region (155 000 km²)

This area includes Newfoundland and the Gaspé Peninsula of Quebec. It is moderately rugged country reaching its highest elevation of over 1 200 m in the Shickshock Mountains of the Gaspé. Newfoundland has an extremely varied physiography and as a result there are considerable limitations to agriculture. About 50 per cent of the province is classified as bedrock outcrop, some thinly mantled with stony till; 25 per cent is classified as ground moraine; 10 per cent is end moraine; 10 per cent is organic terrain or sphagnum peat in morainic depressions; the remaining 5 per cent is glaciofluvial, marine sediment and recent alluvium, which has some agricultural potential.

3. The Eastern Temperate Forest Region

The eastern temperate forest includes a deciduous forest zone in southwestern Ontario, a Great Lakes—St. Lawrence forest zone north and northeast of the deciduous forest, and an Acadian forest zone characteristic of the Maritime provinces. Although there are conifers in this region, deciduous trees are progressively more important toward the southwest.

The most widely recognized natural hazard in this region is that of earthflows associated with a marine clay that was deposited in the post-glacial Champlain Sea.

Apple blossoms in the Annapolis Valley, NS.

In the St. Lawrence and Saguenay Lowlands of Quebec this clay is found in a relatively densely settled agricultural area; on May 4, 1971, 40 houses were destroyed and 31 people killed by an earthflow at St. Jean Vianney, Quebec. Over 700 earthflow locations have been mapped in this region.

There is also an area of major earthquake activity in the St. Lawrence Valley but, because historically there have been few damaging events, there is a low level of public awareness of the hazard. In September 1944, at Cornwall, Ontario, an estimated million dollars' worth of damage occurred from earthquake activity, but there was no loss of life.

(a) Temperate Appalachian–Acadian Sub-region (210 000 km²)

This area includes New Brunswick, Nova Scotia, Prince Edward Island and the Eastern Townships of Quebec. The uplands are arranged in two linear belts—one across southern New Brunswick and northern Nova Scotia and the other over peninsular Nova Scotia and Cape Breton Island. Further, the Eastern Townships are located on the Eastern Quebec uplands, a southwesterly extension of the Notre Dame Mountains. The Acadian forest zone is most typical here. Red spruce, balsam

fir, yellow birch, sugar maple and beech are common. Also present is the Great
Lakes – St. Lawrence forest with red and white pine, eastern hemlock, yellow birch,
sugar maple, red oak, basswood and white elm.

(b) Temperate Shield Sub-region (161 000 km²)

Fifteen per cent of Ontario between Sault Ste Marie and Ottawa, including
Sudbury, North Bay and Algonquin Park, is dominated by sugar maple, aspen,
yellow birch, hemlock and red and white pine (Great Lakes – St. Lawrence forest).
This Shield area, with its protruding rock knobs and intervening pockets of sand,
silt and clay, is primarily a forested area. With its varying combination of trees,
lakes, rivers, hills and animal life, located close to the major urban centres of
Canada and the northeastern United States, it is a favourite recreational area.

(c) St. Lawrence Lowlands Sub-region (181 000 km²)

Ten per cent of Ontario and 5 per cent of Quebec are included in this small
sub-region. It contains Canada's two largest cities, Toronto and Montreal, and its St.
Lawrence Seaway connects the heart of Canada to the Atlantic Ocean. Located
between the Appalachians and the Shield, these lowlands are formed of very gently
dipping Palaeozoic sedimentary rocks. West of the Thousand Islands they are
240 km wide; east they are never more than 125 km wide. Most of the land is
undulating and less than 150 m above sea level, but in the Bruce Peninsula, above
the Niagara Escarpment, the plain reaches 550 m. In detail, the lowland has a varied
terrain that has been investigated more comprehensively than any other landform
region of Canada. Glacial depositional features predominate. Till plains are extensive, and there are recurring end moraines, drumlins, clay plains and sand plains.
Beech-maple forest is the dominant vegetation with admixtures of white oak,
hickory, walnut, basswood and black cherry. In terms of heat and sunshine or
growing days a year the southwestern corner is by far the most favourable area for
agriculture in Canada. The presence of deciduous forest is evidence of that preferred environment. The influence of the Great Lakes reduces the range in temperature from winter to summer by as much as 9°C compared with parts of Minnesota in
equivalent latitudes.

4. The Prairie Region (337 000 km²)

Ten per cent of Alberta, 35 per cent of Saskatchewan and 5 per cent of Manitoba
form a southern extension of the Interior Lowlands, discussed earlier. The distinctiveness of this region lies in the absence of forest vegetation in the so-called
Canadian Grassland and the associated aspen parkland immediately to the north.
Most of the primeval grassland (needlegrass, gramagrass, wheat grass, dropseed
and fescue) has been ploughed.

Tall, short and mixed grass prairie form the core of the region. The tall grass
prairie, typical of the Lake Agassiz plain west of Red River, Manitoba, is the result of
an abundant supply of moisture. The short grass prairie (notably blue grama, June
grass, wheat grass and spear grasses) has a moisture deficit of 200 to 300 mm

(millimetres). But there are many complex associations relating to particular drainage, soil and topographic conditions. The mixed grass prairie has a denser, taller and more diverse cover. It is transitional between both long and short grass prairie to parkland.

The parkland areas are a mixture of grassland and woodland cover. Aspen poplar predominates in most parkland groves but bur oak and other Great Lakes Forest species are present in Manitoba, and various mountain and subalpine species occur in the Rocky Mountain Foothills.

Hummocky moraine, end moraine, ground moraine and lake beds are the major landform features. Some semi-arid areas occur in southern Alberta and southwestern Saskatchewan. A number of badland areas have developed in Alberta where spectacular surface erosion has occurred.

The major natural hazard in this region is climatically induced and is that of floods and droughts. The Red River flood of 1950 and many subsequent lesser floods have been well documented, as have the droughts of the 1930s and 1950s. A feature of these natural hazards is that loss of life tends to be small, but economic costs are continuing to increase in spite of extensive flood protection works.

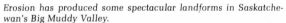

Erosion has produced some spectacular landforms in Saskatchewan's Big Muddy Valley.

5. The Cordilleran Region

The Cordilleran region is part of one of the major mountain systems of the world. Five of the eight major forest zones of Canada (not to mention the Alpine tundra zone) are represented: the boreal, subalpine, montane, coast and Columbia forest zones. The boreal forest zone has already been described and is well developed in the Cordillera in northern British Columbia, southern Yukon Territory and southern Mackenzie district. The subalpine forest is a coniferous forest found on the higher slopes of the mountains east of the Coast Mountains; typical species are Engelmann spruce, alpine fir and lodgepole pine. The montane forest, with Ponderosa pine, Douglas fir, lodgepole pine, aspen (in the north) and sagebrush (in the southern valleys), is extensive in the interior plateau of British Columbia and a small area on the east side of the Rockies. The Columbia forest is characteristic of the southeastern part of the interior system of British Columbia, with western red cedar and western hemlock the typical trees. Finally, the coast forest, on the west-facing slopes of the Coast Mountains and the western islands, is the finest forest in Canada; towering stands of western red cedar, western hemlock, Douglas fir (south) and Sitka spruce (north) are extensively exploited commercially.

The Cordillera experiences the greatest variety of natural hazards of any region in Canada. Snow avalanche hazard is typified by the Rogers Pass area in the Selkirk Mountains of British Columbia; earth slide hazard is illustrated by the 1903 Frank Slide in Alberta, where 70 people were killed; earthquake hazard is important, as the Yukon Territory and coastal British Columbia are in a major earthquake activity zone; tsunami (or tidal wave) hazard is high on the west coast of Vancouver Island; and flood hazard in the Lower Fraser Valley has been well documented. Even drought hazard in the Interior Sub-region of the Cordillera should be considered. Nevertheless, the level of awareness of natural hazards, even in the heavily populated Fraser Valley, is remarkably low.[4]

[4]W.D.F. Sewell, *Water Management and Floods in the Fraser River Basin* (University of Chicago, Department of Geography, Research Paper 100, 1964).

Rugged Prince Edward Island coastline.

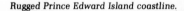

Rose Blanche, Nfld., hugs the island's rocky shore.

(a) Eastern Sub-region (458 000 km²)

This area is 60 per cent rugged mountains (Mackenzie, Richardson and Rocky mountains), 30 per cent plateaus and foothills (Porcupine and Liard plateaus and Rocky Mountain Foothills) and 10 per cent plains (Old Crow, Eagle and Mackenzie plains). The highest peak is Mt. Robson, at 3 954 m. One of the most characteristic features of this landscape is the impressive cliffs in near-horizontally bedded sedimentary strata, which have been carved by glaciation. The Rockies are seldom more than 100 km wide but together with the Mackenzie and Richardson mountains they form an almost continuous series of ranges from the 49th parallel to the Arctic.

A complex succession of vegetation zones occurs with elevation. Above the boreal forest is a sub-alpine parkland and above this, a dense scrub where stunted spruces and pines are common. Beyond this timberline, alpine tundra, moss campion, saxifrage, sandworts, sedges and bilberries are common. Summer days are warmer than in the Arctic, soils are deeper and vegetation is lusher than its Arctic equivalent.

(b) Interior Sub-region (821 000 km²)

Approximately 55 per cent of this sub-region is plateaus (Interior, Stikine, Hyland and Yukon), 40 per cent true mountains (British, Ogilvie, Selwyn, Cassiar, Omineca, Skeena, Hazelton and Columbia) and 5 per cent lowlands (Rocky Mountain, Tintina and Shakwak trenches). This extremely complex region is characterized by lesser local relief and a drier climate than the surrounding mountains. A considerable number of the peaks of the Columbia Mountains exceed 3 000 m. The interior plateau ranges from 600 to 1 500 m in elevation, with local relief from 90 to 150 m and deeply entrenched valleys to 900 m deep. The plateau is narrowest and highest in the south, where it narrows to less than 48 km between the Cascade and

A fall scene in the Rocky Mountains in Alberta.

Monashee mountains. It broadens to 320 km in the Nechako—Prince George area. Here the plateau is lower, the valleys are less deeply incised and low hills form the scenery. There is also a change in vegetation from the mixed forests in the north to the mountain woodland, grassland and arid sagebrush country to the south.

(c) Western Sub-region (313 000 km²)

The Western System is formed of massive plutonic rock bodies or, less commonly, by volcanic and folded sedimentary strata, intruded by scattered plutons, all of which have produced high-relief, high-altitude terrain. These plutons are masses of coarse-grained igneous rock, such as granite.

Longitudinally, the system is divided into three: the Coast Mountains of the mainland; the outer mountains forming the Queen Charlotte and Vancouver islands and the St. Elias Mountains; and between the three a series of lowlands. The Coast Mountains and the St. Elias Mountains contain the bulk of the 52 000 km² of glacier ice on the Canadian mainland. Mt. Waddington, over 3 900 m, is the highest peak in the Coast Mountains and Mt. Logan, at 6050 m, is the highest in the St. Elias Mountains. Along the coast for nearly 2 400 km from Vancouver to Alaska there are major fiords.

The treeline declines from 1 800 m on Vancouver Island to 900 m in the northern Coast Mountains. Over the same distance the level of glacier snouts declines from 2 400 m to sea level. This means that in the northern Coast Mountains, glaciers and forests are juxtaposed. The heavy snow accumulation is perhaps the most distinctive hydrologic feature of this sub-region.

OLAV SLAYMAKER

The Climate

Canadians have tended to accept their climate fatalistically. However, the desire to remain both a consumer society and a custodian of ecological values poses a need for skill, efficiency and prudence with respect to using and living with climate. Sustained economic development is essential to providing an increasing population with desired consumer goods, and this demands greater efficiencies and effectiveness in the use of our limited resources. On the other hand, the desire for a sustained high environmental quality demands that commerce, industry and social practices be within the restraints imposed by our climatically controlled ecosystem. Failure to do so for the sake of short-term benefits may require very costly corrective measures in the future, or create irremediable problems.

Climate and the Economy

Climate is both a resource and a liability. As a resource, it provides the heat and moisture that are essential for life. It is a basis for agriculture, it provides warm lakes for swimmers and snow for skiing, and it drives ocean currents. Drought, floods and hurricanes are among its hazards. These destroy life, damage property and inconvenience people, often stopping all normal economic activity within a community. Climatic change can drastically alter the regional economy by altering the ecosystems which are fundamental to our way of life.

Economic activity serves social goals and must usually be considered in the light of social desires and needs. Conversely, the need and desire to maintain unique landscapes, to reduce travel time between functional areas or to reduce the cost of public service are basically social, but they have great economic implications. Accordingly, many environmental and social issues are referred to in this article because, like climate, they too shape the Canadian economy and must be considered in the evaluation and use of climatic resources.

Climate as a Resource

It has been pointed out that "in general the centre of active progress in civilization has migrated from relatively unstimulating warm regions with few storms, where the winter is the most comfortable season, to stimulating regions with many storms, where the summer is the most comfortable period."[1] This has been made possible by the development of housing and buildings that provide a suitable indoor climate, and transportation systems that withstand the rigours of temperate-zone winters. That our climate is economically stimulating is attested to by our Gross National Product compared to those of low-energy-consumption countries of the tropics.

But our weather is much more than stimulating. Our heat and cold, rain, snow and wind are exploitable resources. Definition of the nature of climatic resources has been a major occupation over the past century in the planning of land use (particularly for agriculture), the development of water supplies and the development of drainage and irrigation systems, etc. The trend to optimal productivity

[1]Ellsworth Huntington, *Mainsprings of Civilization* (John Wiley and Sons, Inc., New York, 1945).

through fuller exploitation of climatic energy, light and moisture sources is increasing as natural resource supplies become more stringent.

Renewable resources are the basis of much of Canada's industry; they provide the necessities of life—food, drink and shelter—and earn about one half of our export dollars. These resources depend primarily on climate. Resource management and use must therefore be based on climatological knowledge and the use of weather forecasts for optimal productivity.

The extraction and use of other resources are also highly climate-dependent. A major use of oil and gas, for example, is to offset cold, heat and snow. Climate-dependent ice fields and weather control the economics of arctic development. Much of our industrial energy is generated from climate-dependent water resources, and water is used extensively in processing — for example, 22 m³ (cubic metres) to refine one cubic metre of petroleum and 3 000 m³ to make one tonne (metric tonne) of synthetic rubber.

On the other hand, the impact of industry, cities and people on the atmospheric environment places an upper limit to certain types of economic endeavour. Economic activity must therefore be tailored in the light of understanding of the environment, man's influence thereon and the capacity of the atmosphere to safely disperse industrial effluents. The interactions of weather, ecology and economy are an area that demands understanding.

Climate as a Liability

Climatic hazards stand out in our memory because of their great impact on society and their newsworthiness. Canada, like most countries in temperate and polar regions, has a fluctuating climate which has caused crises from the times of early settlement.

The Atmospheric Environment Service's Upper Air Station at Alert, NWT.

Direct economic losses caused by some of the more notable weather events in Canada are noted in Table 1. Included in the list are events which are recognized historically as major disasters, but for which there was no available estimate of the direct economic effect.

Table 1. Selected weather events, and some losses directly caused by them, 1868-1973

Year	Event	Estimated losses	
		Life	$'000,000
1868	Drought at the Red River Settlement		
1860s	Storms on the Great Lakes		
1885-96	Drought on the Prairies		
1912	Tornado at Regina, Sask.	30	4
1917-21	Drought on the Prairies		
1930-36	Drought on the Prairies		
1935	Snow-storm at Vancouver, BC		
1944	Tornado at Kamsack, Sask.	(2,000 homeless)	2
1945	Low temperatures in Nova Scotia		4
1949	Drought in Ontario		100
1950	Red River flood		100
1953	Tornado at Sarnia, Ont.		5
1954	Hurricane Hazel, Ontario	100	252
1954	Wheat rust on the Prairies		33
1955	Drought in Ontario		85
1957	Hail storm in Saskatchewan		17
1959	Wet weather in Saskatchewan (harvest lost)		12.5
1959	Snow-storm in Ontario		
1967	Snow-storm in Alberta		10
1969	Glaze storm near Quebec City, Que.		30
1967-68	Forest fires—all of Canada		100
1973	Drought in British Columbia		
1973	Glaze storm at Sept-Îles, Que.		10

Losses due to storms are rarely easy to express. The dollar value of cattle lost in a snowstorm may be easy to define within certain limits, but it is difficult to place a dollar value on the weakened state of the remaining herd. The $2.2 million loss in the Quebec City ice storm of 1973 does not disclose the fact that 250,000 people were deprived of electricity, heat and drinking water; freezers stopped operating; fire protection facilities were impotent during a period when the hazard was greatly increased by the use of camp stoves and other makeshift equipment.

Defending Against Loss. People have five, not necessarily mutually exclusive, ways of facing up to weather, namely: "1. passive acceptance; 2. avoidance of areas and actions unfavourable to effective use of resource conditions; 3. current operational and defensive actions based on assessment of meteorological information; 4. modification and direct control of the weather/climate; and 5. structural and mechanical defenses—i.e. capitalizing on climatological knowledge."[2] We do not need to take our losses passively; there are alternatives, one of which is insurance.

[2]J.R. Hibbs, "Evaluation of weather and climate by socio-economic sensitivity indices," *Human Dimensions of Weather Modification* (University of Chicago, Department of Geography, Research Paper No. 105, 1966).

Typical of our defensive actions are salting programs for highways, switching from carbon to steel trolleys by transit systems, the operation of frost protection devices and evacuation of areas likely to be flooded. These actions are frequently based on weather forecasts, and their basis is climatology. For example, the design of a dam and the operational program for a reservoir are based on long-term climatological and related information, which ensures the operator that the stored waters will serve all reasonable demands during the lifetime of the reservoir, including periods of drought, and will also withstand floods and minimize their effects downstream. Weather forecasts are necessary in the operational phase to ensure that the system functions safely and in the best interests of the public.

. The Atmospheric Environment Service of Environment Canada has responded with foresight to changing and increasing societal demand. Its service horizon has been broadened and adapted to meet the special needs, both national and regional. New technology has been exploited to improve services and to achieve greater efficiency. This has enabled meteorologists to apply their science in the resolution of important socio-economic issues in which weather is a factor.

The Applications of Climatology

Agriculture and Forestry

Agriculture and Forestry are among those activities which are highly exposed and sensitive to weather. Weather forecasts and planning information are therefore essential in combatting the recognized major hazards, such as drought, frost, hail, excessive rainfall, flood, wind, snow and winterkill, as well as climatically influenced diseases, epidemics and insect infestations. Forest fire losses average about $23 million per annum, and have been as high as $83 million in one year. Recent major losses, based on federal assistance payments, are identified in Table 2; they provide an indication of the potential economic benefits of accurate forecasts.

Table 2. Crop losses as identified by assistance payments

Year	Cause	Location	Estimated loss $'000,000
1945	Low temperatures	Nova Scotia	4.0
1954	Wheat rust	Prairies	33.0
1959	Wet harvest	Prairies	12.5
1964-65	Wet weather	Quebec	1.5
1965	Drought	Eastern Canada	5.5

The production of rapeseed, a $100 million business in 1971, illustrates again the importance of climate in the agricultural economy. Rapeseed crops thrive in the prairie climate of hot, sunny days and cool nights, and production is unique to this area. To the south, the percentage of oil contained in the seed drops off so that it becomes uneconomic as far north as Minneapolis. Delineation of the area where the climate is suitable for such crops has obvious economic value.

Fall foliage near Edson, Alta.

The weather must be suitable not only for growing, but also for seeding, cultivating, spraying and harvesting operations. Both weather forecasts and climatological statistics have been used extensively by farmers in overcoming the problem of unfavourable weather (during haying, for example) or in assessing the chances of getting favourable drying weather as the harvest season advances toward winter.

Water Resources

Precipitation is the primary source of surface water supplies, and evaporation the major consumer. Planning, public and political conviction, and economic decisions as to the viability of a hydrologic system are therefore frequently dependent on climatology. The magnitude and reliability of supplies is dictated by rainfall and snowfall characteristics. Design flood, irrigation need, urban demand, storm-sewer capacity and culvert size are all functions of climate, and the operation of water control systems for flood control and conserving water in times of drought is often highly dependent on forecasts.

Annual expenditures on water control and conveyance structures, designed in whole or in part on the basis of rainfall, snow melt and evaporation data or analysis, are probably about $1 billion. Benefit-cost data for hydrometeorological studies in Canada are not readily obtainable, but it has been estimated that a one per cent improvement in the spring flow forecast to the Portage Mountain Reservoir will yield $1 million a year in reduced operational costs.[3]

[3]J.P. Bruce, personal communication.

Logging in New Brunswick.

Use of water resources by towns, cities, industry and agriculture, as well as natural losses through evaporation, must be understood in terms of probability and seasonality to enable the design of supply systems that will serve all reasonable requirements. They are predictable, using meteorological forecasts and information directly and in relation to industrial, social and biological activities.

Resource Development

Development of Canada's resources in hinterland and frontier areas poses major environmental problems in which climatology must play a dominant role. For example, sulphur dioxide releases from refineries in the tar sands of Alberta could destroy vegetation over vast areas of land if improperly controlled; the capacity of the atmosphere to disperse this contaminant is therefore a major concern. Should coal come back into prominence, then the dispersal of sulphur dioxide and particulate could be a major problem. Gasification and cooling towers may release great amounts of thermal energy and moisture into the atmosphere. Safety and security from natural hazards are major factors to be considered in off-shore drilling, pipelining (river crossings), the transmission of electrical energy and the operation of nuclear generating stations.

Topoclimatology and air quality studies must play a significant role in the placement of refineries, conversion systems, infrastructures, etc. Marine climatology and weather forecasts are highly involved in problems of off-shore drilling, shipping in ice-congested waters, oil storage at sea to allow for interruptions of shipments from drilling sites by fog, and the placement of facilities for deep-sea harbours.

Environmental concerns should force greater use of renewable energy resources, which in turn would require much improved interpretation and understanding of the space and time variations of solar energy, wind and their by-products, such as waves, currents and thermal gradients.

Land Use Planning

Resource development, industrialization, the trend to urbanization, growing population, limited resources and moral responsibilities make necessary a rational approach to land use in Canada.

Intensified resource use and exploration is linked with affluence and a desire for urban life. Not only are Canadians leaving the farms for the towns, but they are abandoning the towns to concentrate in a few large industrialized urban centres. It is estimated that, by the year 2000, 20 million Canadians (60 per cent of our population) may live in 15 centres with populations over 300,000, 17 million of these in centres of about 1,000,000 or more population.

These trends are of major socio-economic importance, and among the problems created are formidable and complex land use problems. The potential roles climatology will play in dealing with them are equally numerous and complex.

The luxuriant Butchart Gardens thrive in the mild climate of Victoria, BC.

Construction

Construction is Canada's largest industry, grossing about $18 billion in 1973. Highly exposed and weather-sensitive, it qualifies as a prime area for meteorological support. The use of meteorology in the engineering of structures has included the problems of snow loads, wind loads, ice accretion, drainage, rain penetration and weathering of materials. The prediction of construction weather—weather for setting concrete, for earthwork and for the operation of cranes — is of major importance to the industry.

Transportation

Aviation has grown exponentially. Airport capacities have been exceeded repeatedly within short periods after their construction, and the noise created by modern aircraft has been of increasing concern. To alleviate this growing problem, new airports have been developed in areas removed from the large cities. This has required the determination of locations having the most favourable take-off and landing weather, and whose runway orientations would not cause conflict with established traffic patterns.

Pipelines, ships and tractor trains are an important part of the arctic transportation scene; their supporting infrastructure requires compressor stations, harbours and towns. Topography-climate relationships are the basis of arctic site selection, and are therefore an important factor in northern resource development. Shoreline and inland installations have been blown away or badly damaged by arctic winds; shelter is all-important. On the other hand, unventilated areas pose the hazard of air pollution and ice fog under conditions of persistent cold and airmass inversion. The study of air drainage and wind is, therefore, most important in the collocation of facilities and residential areas.

Tourism and Recreation

For most Canadians recreation is an outdoor activity, and weather dictates whether or not the outdoors experience is enjoyable. Recreation is highly oriented to renewable natural resources, and the state of the resources is climate-dependent. In some cases climate is the resource.

Tourist spending is of great significance to national, provincial and local economies, and governments have immediate interests in the development of parks, lodges and other recreation areas. A rational approach to development requires climatic inputs—even the Niagara Falls are unimpressive when they are enshrouded by fog. Methods of getting optimal recreational value on the basis of climate have been developed, and climatic studies of national parks have been undertaken to provide a basis for the placing of facilities and roads, and the development of operational programs.

Environmental Impact Assessment

Environmental impact assessments are an essential defence against undesirable environmental effects of man's activities, both deliberate and inadvertent. In undertaking an assessment planners are forced to consider the side-effects of their

A bolt of lightning in a summer storm.

proposals over the short, medium and long ranges, and also of possible alternatives, one of which is always not to proceed. A decision is ultimately reached to stop the program or approve the most acceptable alternative in its actual, or in a modified, form. A surveillance program is established to ensure desired conditions are met.

The climatological aspects of assessment do not reside only in air quality. They may start with the evaluation of the engineer's design—will a tower fail under ice and wind loads, for example? Changes in land use, such as extending agricultural area, installing pipelines and creating new lakes, may also alter climate. Such alterations are usually small in scale, but there is concern that the aggregated sum of a large number of inconsequential projects might be critical. Small changes in temperature, precipitation or fog might not significantly influence a region's climate, but perhaps these conditions could create new extremes which would place an intolerable stress on certain species. Or perhaps they are involved in a non-obvious feedback mechanism that would suffer significant consequences. Broad, positive understanding of interdisciplinary relationships is extremely important in these matters.

There is a need to distinguish between what should be done and what can be done. The potential for applying meteorology in economic decisions is virtually infinite. Some applications have a high payoff, others a low payoff. In still other cases, the payoff may not be clearly definable because it is indirect. Naturally, the high-return activities will have precedence, but not always; the application may be part of a greater integrated or comprehensive plan of which it is an essential component. The social issues that merit our response cannot be evaluated in economic terms; they will presumably be self-evident, such as those now posed by famine in many areas of the world, and dwindling global food reserves.

GORDON MCKAY

the people and their heritage

History

Canada is an independent nation in North America composed of two predominant linguistic and cultural groups: French and English. To these two major groups, and to the small native population of Indians and Inuit, have been added over the last hundred years many thousands of immigrants representing the major European cultures. For the most part these immigrant groups have associated themselves with the English-speaking community, though maintaining many aspects of their mother cultures. The country has thus never been a homogeneous melting pot, but has rather had the aspect of a cultural mosaic in which the major pattern is traced in the colours of the French and English cultures.

Much of the country's history can be viewed as a continuing search for accommodation and co-operation between the two major cultural communities, and the integration of newcomers into the basic pattern. At the same time as this internal accommodation has been working itself out, the country has passed through a dual process of self-definition in relation to the outside world. The first of these processes has been the evolution of the country from the status of a colony within the

British Empire to the stature of independent nationhood within the Commonwealth. The second, more subtle and often more difficult process has been in
defining and defending its independence in relation to the power and prestige of its
enormous neighbour, the United States. These two themes of internal bicultural
accommodation and external self-definition underlie and affect nearly every other
development in the Canadian past: patterns of settlement, institutional growth,
economic development, foreign policy and cultural evolution.

The interior of an early settler's home, reconstructed in the Museum of Man and Nature, Winnipeg, Man.

Labelling bones at an Indian grave site at Selkirk, Man.

The exploration and settlement of North America by Europeans began seriously at the beginning of the 17th century. There had, of course, been earlier voyages dating back as far as the Norsemen, but concentrated efforts had to await the emergence of the powerful nation states of Europe. From the earliest beginnings the French and English established competitive settlements and trading centres. The English moved in from the north through Hudson Bay in the 1670s but the French had already penetrated the continent through the vast St. Lawrence River more than half a century earlier. To the south were the Dutch on the Hudson, soon to be pushed out by the British, and the Puritan settlements in New England. As these colonies grew, so did competition for the hinterlands. The French pressed north and westward to challenge the English on Hudson Bay. And traders from the two communities, with the aid of their Indian allies, struggled for control of the rich Ohio valley. It was this competition, and the rivalry of France and Britain in Europe, which ultimately brought war and the downfall of the French empire in North America. But before that event took place New France had sunk deep roots along the banks of the St. Lawrence and in Acadia.

The first half century of New France's existence, down to 1663, had been characterized by near failure on all fronts: settlement, missionary activity and trade. Yet it was this struggling period that provided later generations with a sense of an heroic past when the tiny colony struggled for survival against the elements, the Iroquois and the English. From these years came the heroes and martyrs, both religious and secular: Brébeuf and his brethren, who died in their effort to bring Christianity to the Indians; Dollard and his young companions, who died defending the colony and its trade at the Long Sault in 1660.

By 1663 the colonists numbered fewer than 2,500 and the future was bleak. It was saved only by the decision of Louis XIV to assume direct control of his North American possessions. The establishment of royal government was accompanied by an infusion of new settlers, trained civil servants with plans for economic development and troops to defend the colony. Though the colony's economy became somewhat more diversified, it remained dependent upon France on the one hand and the fur trade on the other. By the 1740s French-English rivalry in Europe, North America and elsewhere in the world brought the beginnings of the war that was to spell the end of New France. The final phase of that war began in 1754 and was concluded by the Treaty of Paris in 1763 when France's major North American possessions were ceded to the British.

The British conquest of Canada, a major event in the country's history, temporarily united North America under the British flag. Within two decades that unity was permanently destroyed by the success of the American War of Independence. Yet in the intervening period the French-speaking inhabitants of Canada, numbering about 70,000 at the time of the conquest, had continued to exhibit their capacity to survive. Faced with growing unrest in the 13 colonies, the British authorities in Canada gave up an early attempt to assimilate their new subjects and granted recognition, in the Quebec Act of 1774, to the major institutions of the French-speaking community: its civil laws, its seigneurial system and its Roman Catholic religious organization. The efforts of the revolting colonies to add Canada and Nova Scotia to their cause failed. But during and after the war thousands of Loyalists fled northward, settling in Nova Scotia, in what was later to become New Brunswick, and in Canada in both the Eastern Townships and the western region of the colony north of Lake Ontario. It was in this fashion that the first substantial group of English-speaking settlers established themselves in the predominantly French-speaking British colony. Here was the beginning of the pattern of Canada's future development.

The coming of the Loyalists required new constitutional arrangements. The Constitutional Act of 1791 divided the old province of Quebec into two colonies, Upper and Lower Canada, and granted each its first representative assembly, an institution which had existed in Nova Scotia since 1758. It was within the context of this constitution that the colony began to grow economically and demographically. It was also within this context that a struggle took place for internal self-government or responsible government. That was achieved in 1849, but only after abortive rebellions in the two Canadas in 1837 and the reunification of the two colonies in 1841.

By the middle of the 19th century the British colonies in North America — Canada, Nova Scotia, New Brunswick, Prince Edward Island and Newfoundland — were ready to move haltingly toward a new stage in their constitutional development. Each colony separately faced an increasing burden of public expenditure in the age of canal and railway building. Each, too, was faced with limited markets, since the coming of free trade in Britain had ended their preferential treatment within the Empire. In the Canadas there was the additional problem of growing political deadlock and threatening cultural conflict in a union based upon equality of representation for each of the two sections. And finally, in the 1860s, there was the threat of an increasingly hostile US just emerging from its bloody civil war.

Black Creek Village, Toronto, Ont.

These events, plus the encouragement of a Britain anxious to reduce its commitments in North America, resulted in a decision in 1865 to move toward a federation of all British North America.

That federation was partially achieved on July 1, 1867, when the Canadas, Nova Scotia and New Brunswick joined together in Confederation under the British North America Act. This constitution was the work of an energetic group of British North American politicians including John A. Macdonald, George Brown, Georges Étienne Cartier, Alexander Galt of Canada, Charles Tupper of Nova Scotia and Leonard Tilley of New Brunswick. Their combined political skills and legal talents were severely tested in the foundation of "the new nationality." The constitution was a highly centralized federal scheme which made the central government clearly dominant, but left to the provinces those matters which they considered to be of purely local concern. The French and English languages were established as official in the federal Parliament, its records and its courts, and the province of Quebec was also recognized as an officially bilingual province. The new nation was a parliamentary monarchy operating according to the well-understood principles of cabinet government. The Parliament of Canada at Ottawa was composed of the Crown's representative, the Governor General and a bicameral legislature, the House of Commons and the Senate.

At the outset the plan was incomplete, for it was intended that the territory of the new nation should stretch from coast to coast. The first step was the acquisition of the lands owned by the Hudson's Bay Company in the west. This was quickly achieved, but the first new province, Manitoba, was established only after a rebellion in Red River led by a young Métis, Louis Riel, was defeated; the province was established in 1870. A year later the Pacific Coast province of British Columbia entered the union on the promise that a transcontinental railway would be built. Two years later Prince Edward Island was added. In 1874 the extensive lands between Manitoba and British Columbia were organized as the Northwest Territories. This area, in 1885, was the scene of a second uprising of Métis and Indians, again led by Louis Riel. The completion of the Canadian Pacific Railway in that same year made it possible for the Canadian authorities to defeat the rebels, and this time Riel was captured, tried and hanged for treason. Twenty years later, in 1905, the provinces of Saskatchewan and Alberta were added to the union. The last of the 10 provinces to join Canada was Newfoundland in 1949.

Once the basic structure had been established, the federal Conservative government, led by Sir John A. Macdonald, proceeded to develop policies to fill out the skeleton. The railway, binding together the various far-flung sections, was the first developmental policy. But along with it were immigration programs to populate the open spaces with agricultural settlers, and a policy of tariff protection, announced in 1879, to develop a Canadian industrial system. It was the Macdonald government's determination to build a national economy on an east-west axis independent of the US.

Though the Liberal opposition had been critical of many of these policies, when they came to power under Wilfrid Laurier in 1896 they continued them with few modifications. The major difference was that under Laurier the policies experienced greater success because prosperous world economic conditions provided investment funds for Canadian development, markets for the country's growing grain and mineral production, and thousands of new immigrants from Great Britain, the US and Europe. By the outbreak of World War I Canada was well on its way to fulfilling the destiny which the Fathers of Confederation had predicted.

The Laurier years, for all of their prosperity, witnessed the beginnings of serious cultural, sectional and class conflicts. Relations between English- and French-speaking Canadians had been worsened by the hanging of Louis Riel, with whom the French Canadian identified. Then came attacks upon the French language and Catholic separate schools in Manitoba and the Northwest in the 1890s. Laurier successfully smoothed over this latter crisis, but cultural relations were also strained by Canadian involvement in the Boer War and the long prewar debate over the country's place in Imperial affairs. French Canadians, on the whole, were reluctant to be involved in Imperial affairs, while many English Canadians identified Canadian interests with those of the Empire — especially since the Empire provided a protective umbrella against the US. This development reached its culmination in 1917 when the country, which had entered the war united, was split culturally over the issue of conscription for overseas service.

Sectional discontents were also present, especially in the Prairies. This region, almost exclusively agricultural, felt the national economic policies were designed primarily for the industrial areas of central Canada. The defeat of a proposed reciprocity arrangement with the US in the election of 1911 left the West in a mood of discontent that manifested itself after the war in the form of the farmers' Progressive Party. Class tensions were apparent in the growth of labour organization under

Fort Prince of Wales, once the stronghold of the Hudson's Bay Company, near Churchill, Man.

the leadership of the Trades and Labour Council of Canada. The end of the war also saw labour conflict flare in a general strike in Winnipeg in the spring of 1919.

Canada emerged from the war, in which she had played a substantial part, with a new sense of national pride. That pride was transformed in the postwar years into a quest for a status of equality within the new British Commonwealth. Sir Robert Borden, the wartime Prime Minister, set this development in motion and it was continued by the Liberal and Conservative governments under W. L. Mackenzie King and R. B. Bennett. The Statute of Westminster in 1931 provided the legal definition of Canadian autonomy.

The Great Depression brought serious dislocation of the Canadian economy, heavy unemployment and new movements of social protest. In Quebec this discontent expressed itself in a new party called the Union nationale while elsewhere in Canada, especially in the West, the Social Credit and Co-Operative Commonwealth Federation parties made a marked impact. The federal government's major problem in these years was its weakened constitutional position, the provinces having been given or having won control over such matters as social welfare and natural resource development. A federal Royal Commission in 1940 recommended that the constitutional arrangements should be revised to give the federal government authority over major economic, social and tax policies. The recommendations were never implemented, but the exigencies of the war once more placed the federal government in a predominant position.

The schooner Bluenose II *sailing off the coast of Nova Scotia.*

The war and postwar years were a period of great prosperity and economic growth for Canadians. Again Canada played an important part in the war and its unity was only briefly threatened, again over the conscription issue. W. L. Mackenzie King's retirement in 1949 and his replacement by Louis St. Laurent marked an easy transition to postwar prosperity. Much of this new growth was financed by American direct investment, so that prosperity was bought at the price of increasing American control of the Canadian economy. Since this came at a time when Canada was moving into closer European (NATO) and North American (NORAD) military alliances with the US, some Canadians began to worry about the country's future. It was this concern, added to a growing dissatisfaction in several of the provinces over Ottawa's centralist policies, that brought the Conservative John Diefenbaker to power in 1957.

The Diefenbaker years were marked by a growing debate over Canada—US relations and, more particularly, the revival of nationalism in Quebec in the guise of a "quiet revolution". This latter event included a whole series of measures meant to modernize a Quebec society now transformed by accelerated industrialism. With increasing frequency and intensity many prominent French Canadians expressed dissatisfaction with their status within Confederation and began asking that Quebec be given more autonomy as a province and that French be given greater recognition throughout Canada. In 1963 Lester Pearson's minority Liberal government established a Royal Commission on Bilingualism and Biculturalism to examine this question. Four years later, after the Centennial celebrations, Mr. Pearson proposed a series of federal-provincial discussions to examine and reform the constitution in general. This task was continued under the direction of his successor, Pierre Elliott Trudeau, whose Liberal party was given a majority in the general election of 1968.

The first four years of the Trudeau government saw continued, but ultimately unsuccessful, constitutional negotiations. In October 1970 the government responded to the kidnapping of a British diplomat, and the kidnapping and murder of a Quebec Cabinet Minister, by the Front de la Libération de Québec by proclaiming the War Measures Act. Some changes in foreign policy were designed to affirm

The Royal Newfoundland Regiment Military Tattoo on Signal Hill in St. John's, Nfld.

Canadian sovereignty and reduce the country's military commitment in Europe. Increasingly, however, economic problems took precedence over all others, with inflation and unemployment creating serious difficulties. In October 1972 the electorate returned a minority government. During the next 18 months the Trudeau government managed to remain in power, generally supported by the New Democratic Party. It attempted to reduce US influence on many aspects of Canadian life, evolve new fiscal and social policies and, perhaps above all, to grapple with the domestic implications of the world energy crisis. In July 1974 the voters returned a majority Liberal government, still led by Pierre Elliott Trudeau.

With the Liberals returned to power, each of the major opposition parties moved to elect new leaders. The New Democratic Party chose Ed Broadbent, an Ontario Member of Parliament. Early in 1976 the Progressive Conservative leadership convention selected Joe Clark, an Alberta MP for High River, Alberta. Both expressed determination to focus the country's attention on economic issues.

Management of the economy, especially the problem of inflation, had become a central issue of public debate even before the 1974 election. During that campaign the Progressive Conservative Party had advocated a scheme of wage and price controls. Though the Liberals had rejected that proposal during the election campaign, continuing inflation and increasing public pressure resulted in a decision in October 1975 to implement a three-year anti-inflation program.

On November 15, 1976, the future status of Quebec once again became the dominating issue in Canadian public life. On that date the Parti Québécois was elected as the government of Quebec and its leader, René Lévesque, was sworn in as Prime Minister of the province on November 25. Although the Parti Québécois campaigned on issues of the economy, social welfare and the management of public business, it is nevertheless a party whose platform commits it to working toward the establishment of a sovereign Quebec. Pierre Trudeau stated shortly after the election that, as Prime Minister of Canada, he had no mandate to negotiate separation with the province of Quebec, while Mr. Lévesque repeated his election pledge that independence would take place only after the people of Quebec had expressed their desire for it in a referendum. A date has not yet been set for that referendum.

RAMSAY COOK

Population

The total population of Canada in 1975 was estimated to be 22,800,000, an increase of 25.0 per cent over the total population count of 18,238,247 reported in the 1961 Census.

In spite of this over-all increase, Canada has actually experienced declining population growth rates during this period. The census figures presented in Table 1 show a mean annual increase of 1.9 per cent in the period 1961-66, falling to 1.6 per cent in the years 1966-71. Estimates suggest that the mean annual increase for the four-year period 1971-75 was 1.4 per cent, which would indicate that the trend toward lower population growth rates has been continuing.

As a result of the different population growth rates for each province, over 80 per cent of Canada's total population is now concentrated in Quebec, Ontario, Alberta and British Columbia. Table 1 shows that British Columbia, Alberta and Ontario were the only provinces whose mean annual increases, of 3.6 per cent, 2.3 per cent and 2.3 per cent, respectively, exceeded the national mean of 1.8 per cent for the period 1961-75. The Yukon Territory and the Northwest Territories, which have relatively small populations compared to the provinces, have also experienced high growth rates over the period, the population of the Northwest Territories having increased by 4.7 per cent and that of the Yukon Territory by 2.9 per cent.

Birth, death, immigration and emigration are the components of population change. The high mean annual birth rate (28.0 per thousand in 1951-56) and mean annual rate of natural increase (19.6 per thousand) are representative of the rapid growth that occurred in the early postwar period, which peaked to record highs in the mid-1950s (Table 2). Lower rates of growth in succeeding years resulted mainly from falling birth rates beginning in the early 1960s and continuing on to 1975. Death rates, though declining slightly, have remained relatively stable compared to other components of growth. Net international migration (total emigration subtracted from total immigration) during the early and mid-1950s (7.9 in the period 1951-56 and 5.6 in 1956-61) has also had a strong influence on Canada's population growth.

Canada had a mean population density of 2.3 persons per square kilometre in 1971; according to estimates this figure had risen to 2.5 in 1975, still one of the lowest population densities in the world. However, this figure takes into account the whole land area of the country, and it should be kept in mind that vast spatial variations exist. For example, some of the larger urban areas have as many as 7,800 persons per square kilometre. Prince Edward Island, Nova Scotia and New Brunswick are the three smallest provinces in terms of land area, but have population densities well above those of other parts of Canada.

Over the years, Canada's population has changed from predominantly rural to predominantly urban. According to the census carried out in 1901, 2,005,080, or only 37.5 per cent of the total population, lived in urban communities. By 1971, 16,410,785 Canadians, or 76.1 per cent of the total population, were located in urban areas; of this urban population, the largest part (62.5 per cent) lived in centres of 100,000 or more, and the remainder in communities ranging from 1,000 to 99,999 inhabitants. The term "urban population", as used in the census, refers to all population living in incorporated cities, towns and villages, and in unincorporated

Table 1. Numerical and percentage distribution of population, Canada and provinces, 1961, 1966, 1971 and 1975

	Population in thousands[1]				Percentage distribution	Mean annual percentage change			
	1961	1966	1971	1975	1975	1961-75	1961-66	1966-71	1971-75
Canada	18,238	20,015	21,568	22,800	100.0	1.8	1.9	1.6	1.4
Newfoundland........	458	493	522	549	2.4	1.4	1.5	1.2	1.3
Prince Edward Island....	105	109	112	119	0.5	1.0	0.8	0.6	1.6
Nova Scotia........	737	756	789	822	3.6	0.8	0.5	0.9	1.0
New Brunswick........	598	617	635	675	3.0	0.9	0.6	0.6	1.6
Quebec........	5,259	5,781	6,028	6,188	27.1	1.3	2.0	0.9	0.7
Ontario........	6,236	6,961	7,703	8,226	36.1	2.3	2.3	2.1	1.7
Manitoba........	922	963	988	1,019	4.5	0.8	0.9	0.5	0.8
Saskatchewan........	925	955	926	918	4.0	0.1	0.6	− 0.6	− 0.2
Alberta........	1,332	1,463	1,628	1,768	7.8	2.3	2.0	2.3	2.2
British Columbia........	1,629	1,874	2,185	2,457	10.8	3.6	3.0	3.3	3.1
Yukon Territory........	15	14	18	21	0.1	2.9	− 1.3	5.7	4.2
Northwest Territories....	23	29	35	38	0.2	4.7	5.2	4.1	2.2

[1] Based on census data for 1961, 1966 and 1971, and on estimates for 1975.

Table 2. Components of population change, 1951-56, 1956-61, 1961-66, 1966-71 and 1971-75

Date	Births	Deaths	Natural increase	Immigration	Emigration	Net international migration	Total change %
	Rate per thousand[1]						%
1951-56	28.0	8.4	19.6	10.4	2.5	7.9	27.5
1956-61	27.5	8.0	19.5	8.8	3.2	5.6	25.1
1961-66	23.5	7.6	15.9	5.6	2.9	2.7	18.6
1966-71	17.8	7.4	10.5	8.6	4.1	4.5	14.9
1971-75	15.6	7.4	8.2	7.6	2.1	5.5	13.7

[1] Mean rate per one thousand people, for each time interval indicated.

Table 3. Population of census metropolitan areas (CMAs), 1971 and 1974[1]

	1971	1974	Percentage change
Canada	21,569	22,446	4.1
Total CMAs	11,876	12,335	3.8
Percentage of total population	55.1	55.0	− 0.1
Percentage of urban population	72.4	...	...
Montreal	2,743	2,798	2.0
Toronto	2,628	2,741	4.3
Vancouver	1,082	1,137	5.1
Ottawa – Hull	603	626	3.8
Ontario portion	453	...	...
Quebec portion	149	...	...
Winnipeg	540	570	5.6
Hamilton	449	520	4.2
Edmonton	496	529	6.7
Quebec City	481	499	3.7
Calgary	403	444	10.2
St. Catharines – Niagara	303	311	2.6
London	286	296	3.5
Windsor	259	266	2.7
Kitchener	227	238	4.8
Halifax	223	224	0.4
Victoria	196	208	6.1
Sudbury	155	154	− 0.6
Regina	141	151	7.1
Chicoutimi – Jonquière	134	137	2.2
St. John's	132	132	—
Saskatoon	126	130	3.2
Thunder Bay	112	112	—
Saint John	107	112	4.7

[1] Based on census data for 1971 and estimates for 1974.
... Not available.
— Nil or zero.

places with population densities of 390 or more people per square kilometre. The population in the built-up fringes of these places is also considered to be urban if the population density is 390 or more persons per square kilometre.

Of the 5,157,525 persons making up Canada's rural population in 1971, 1,419,796 (27.5 per cent) lived on farms, while 3,737,730 (72.5 per cent) did not. The term "farm population", as used in the census, includes all of the population living in dwellings situated on farms in the rural areas. For census purposes up to and including 1976, a farm has been considered to be an agricultural holding of one or more acres, with sales of agricultural products of $50 or more in the previous year.

Ontario, Quebec and British Columbia had the largest proportions of their total populations living in the urban areas, the percentages being 82.4 per cent, 80.6 per cent and 75.7 per cent respectively. Prince Edward Island, the Northwest Territories and Saskatchewan had the largest proportions of their populations classified as rural, 61.7 per cent, 51.7 per cent and 47.0 per cent respectively, with the remaining Atlantic provinces following closely in this category. Alberta and Saskatchewan reported the largest proportions of rural farm population relative to the total rural population, 54.7 per cent and 53.6 per cent respectively.

In 1974 over 50 per cent of Canada's total population resided in 22 census metropolitan areas (CMAs), as shown in Table 3. According to the census definition, these major urban agglomerations each contain the main labour-force market for a continuous built-up area having a population of 100,000 or more.

Population estimates for 1974 show that Montreal and Toronto were Canada's largest metropolitan areas, each having over 2.5 million inhabitants, while Vancouver had grown to over a million. In terms of proportionate growth, however, Calgary and Edmonton had developed most rapidly in recent years, Calgary having increased its total population by 10.2 per cent in the period 1971-74, and Edmonton by 6.7 per cent. In contrast, the population of Sudbury actually declined slightly over this time interval, while the populations of Halifax, Montreal and Chicoutimi—Jonquière experienced relatively small increases.

The age structure of a population is of vital interest to all levels of government involved in the designing of social and economic programs for their constituents. Educational planners, for example, have noted a sharp drop in school enrolment rates at the elementary and secondary school levels as a result of the declining proportions of the population in the younger age groups. Table 4 shows that the proportion of Canada's population under 15 years of age declined by 3.2 per cent in the five-year period 1966-71, and by 4.1 per cent in the four-year period 1971-74. This was the result mainly of the declining birth rates in previous years, a fact

Table 4. Population by age groups, 1966, 1971 and 1974[1]

Age group	Population in thousands			Percentage distribution			Percentage change	
	1966	1971	1974	1966	1971	1974	1966-71	1971-74
Total	20,015	21,568	22,446	100.0	100.0	100.0	7.8	4.1
Under 15	6,592	6,381	6,097	32.9	29.6	27.2	−3.2	−4.4
0-4	2,197	1,816	1,766	11.0	8.4	7.9	−17.5	−2.8
5-9	2,301	2,254	1,979	11.5	10.4	8.8	−2.0	−12.2
10-14	2,093	2,311	2,352	10.5	10.7	10.5	10.4	1.8
15-64	11,884	13,443	14,466	59.4	62.3	64.4	13.1	7.6
15-19	1,838	2,114	2,277	9.2	9.8	10.1	15.1	7.7
20-24	1,461	1,889	2,033	7.3	8.8	9.1	29.3	7.6
25-34	2,483	2,889	3,362	12.4	13.4	15.0	16.4	16.4
35-44	2,543	2,526	2,549	12.7	11.7	11.4	−0.7	0.9
45-54	2,078	2,291	2,423	10.4	10.6	10.8	10.3	5.8
55-64	1,480	1,732	1,822	7.4	8.0	8.1	17.0	5.2
65 +	1,540	1,744	1,883	7.7	8.1	8.4	13.3	7.9

[1] Based on census data for 1966 and 1971 and on estimates for 1974.

Art exhibits in front of Toronto City Hall draw a crowd.

clearly indicated by the decrease of 17.5 per cent in the number of children 0-4 years of age in the period 1966-71.

As the population "bulge" resulting from high birth rates in the 1950s has moved into early adulthood, the working age group (15-64 years of age) has increased rapidly. The proportion of the total population between the ages of 15 and 64 years increased by 13.1 per cent during the period 1966-71 and by 7.6 per cent in 1971-74. In addition to birth and death rates, immigration has a strong influence on the growth of this broad working age group, especially at the younger age levels. In the period from January 1969 to May 1971, for example, 47.8 per cent of the population arriving from foreign lands were 20-34 years of age, and 57.8 per cent were 20-44.

The changing proportion of the population in the older age groups is of particular interest to those planning facilities for the care of the elderly and determining future pension needs. This segment of the population has been characterized by rapid growth in recent years, increasing by 13.3 per cent in the period 1966-71 and by 7.9 per cent in 1971-74; the total population increased by 7.8 per cent and 4.1 per cent, respectively, during the same periods. Declining birth rates and an increased life expectancy are the two major causative factors in the growth in the proportion of the population 65 years of age and over.

Of the 15,187,415 persons 15 years of age and over in Canada in 1971, 4,290,675, or 28.2 per cent, were single (never married); this represented an increase of 525,842, or 14.0 per cent, over the five-year period 1966-71. The figures in Table 5 also show that 31.6 per cent of the adult male population and 25.0 per cent of the adult female population were single; this differential is caused mainly by the fact that men tend to remain single longer than women. In the 1971 Census, for example, 67.3 per cent of the male population 20-24 years of age were reported as single, compared to 43.5 per cent of the female population in that age group.

In 1971, 9,777,605 (65.0 per cent of the total population 15 years of age and over) were married, the number of married persons having increased by 1,054,388 over the period 1966-71. However, the proportion of the population who were married fell slightly during the same period, from 65.0 per cent in 1966 to 64.4 per cent in

Table 5. Numerical and percentage distribution of population 15 years of age and over, by marital status, 1966 and 1971

Marital status	Population in thousands						Percentage distribution						Percentage change, 1966-71		
	1966			1971			1966			1971					
	Total	Male	Female	Total	Male	Female	Total	Male	Female	Total	Male	Female	Total	Male	Female
Total	13,423	6,681	6,742	15,187	7,532	7,655	100.0	100.0	100.0	100.0	100.0	100.0	13.1	12.7	13.6
Single	3,765	2,101	1,664	4,291	2,378	1,913	28.0	31.4	24.7	28.2	31.6	25.0	14.0	13.2	15.0
Married¹	8,723	4,359	4,364	9,778	4,889	4,889	65.0	65.2	64.7	64.4	64.9	63.9	12.1	12.1	12.0
Widowed	870	196	675	944	191	753	6.5	2.9	10.0	6.2	2.5	9.8	8.5	- 2.3	11.6
Divorced	65	25	39	175	74	101	0.5	0.4	0.6	1.1	1.0	1.3	170.3	193.0	155.8

¹Includes separated persons not having obtained a divorce.

Table 6. Ten vocational training courses¹ most commonly reported by men and by women, 1971

Course	Reported by men		Course	Reported by women	
	Number	%		Number	%
All kinds	1,143,270	100.0	All kinds	828,235	100.0
Auto mechanics and repair	89,060	7.8	Typing, shorthand and secretarial sciences	190,350	23.0
Electrical equipment installation and repair	70,500	6.2	Registered nursing and nursing assistant	140,215	16.9
Tool, die-making and machinists	53,220	4.7	Barbering and hairdressing	77,435	9.3
Technology (architectural, engineering, mathematical and pure sciences)	49,600	4.3	Elementary and secondary school teaching	31,435	3.8
Welding	47,520	4.2	Medical and dental technology	18,185	2.2
Radio, TV and other electronic equipment repair	47,300	4.1	Garment making and repair	17,620	2.1
Accounting and auditing	37,985	3.3	Fine and applied arts	16,820	2.0
Drafting	36,995	3.2	Bookkeeping and account recording	14,150	1.7
Carpentry	36,165	3.2	Accounting and auditing	14,125	1.7
Pipe trades	34,985	3.1	Power sewing	12,065	1.5
All other	639,940	56.0	All other	295,835	35.7

¹ Includes vocational, trade and apprenticeship training.

1971; this may be attributed to demographic factors such as the changing age structure and the changing nuptiality patterns.

In 1966, there were 64,776 divorced persons in Canada; by 1971 this figure had risen to 175,115, an increase of 170.3 per cent. While the general trend over the years has been toward higher divorce rates and toward a drop in the age of persons obtaining divorces, the marked increase between 1966 and 1971 may be attributed directly to new legislation passed in 1968 making divorces easier to obtain.

One of the most striking features of marital status statistics is the larger proportion of widows over widowers. In 1971, 191,125 men (2.5 per cent of the adult male population) were widowed, in contrast to 752,895 women (9.8 per cent of the adult female population). This wide difference is attributed to higher death rates of males and to higher probability of remarriage of widowers.

Of the people in Canada who were 15 years of age or over in 1971 and had, to all intents and purposes, completed their full-time formal education, 4,899,350 (37.2 per cent) had obtained only an elementary school education and 6,976,440 (53.0 per cent) had terminated their education at the secondary level. However, these figures take into account only formal academic education in the elementary and secondary school systems of the provinces and territories; about 10 per cent of all Canadians with this level of education would have obtained, in addition, some form of vocational trade or apprenticeship training.

In the same age group, 1,292,235 (9.9 per cent) of those who no longer attended school on a full-time basis had obtained one or more years of education at the university level. Of these, 613,785 (4.7 per cent of the total population) had obtained a university degree, and the remaining 678,450 (5.2 per cent) had one or more years of university but had not obtained a degree. British Columbia led the provinces, with 163,690 (11.8 per cent of its total population) having attained education at the university level; it was closely followed by Alberta, with 106,270 (11.1 per cent), and Ontario, with 482,700 (10.1 per cent) in this category.

Educators at all levels have been striving to satisfy the needs not only of the university-bound, but also of the great majority who require adequate preparation for early entry into the labour force. This has become particularly important as Canada has grown industrially and the need for unskilled and semi-skilled workers has diminished. In 1971, 1,971,510 (13.0 per cent of Canada's total population 15 years of age and over) had completed some form of apprenticeship, trade or vocational training. Foremost among the provinces was again British Columbia, where 260,275 (16.5 per cent of the total population) had completed training courses in 1971; Alberta and Manitoba followed closely, Alberta reporting 174,130 (15.6 per cent) and Manitoba, 92,275 (13.2 per cent) of their total populations in this category.

Trade and occupational training schools, community colleges, technical institutes and systems of apprenticeship offer a wide variety of courses. Auto mechanics and repair and electrical equipment installation and repair are courses most frequently reported as having been taken by men, while typing, shorthand and secretarial science, and registered nursing and nursing assistant courses have been preferred by women. It is also apparent from the figures of Table 6 that a substantial amount of training taken by women has been concentrated in relatively few fields—those mentioned above, and hairdressing — while training taken by men has been much more widely diversified.

The Native Peoples

Indians

On December 31, 1974, there were 276,436 people registered as Indians under the provisions of the Indian Act of Canada. There were 566 separate Indian bands, for whom 2,216 reserves have been set aside; total reserve area was about 2.5 million hectares. Approximately half of the registered Indians, mainly those living in Ontario and the three Prairie provinces, are entitled to receive treaty payments as a result of treaties between their ancestors and the Crown.

The number of persons of Indian ancestry who are not entitled to be registered under the provisions of the Indian Act is unknown. Included among these people are those Indians who have given up their Indian status and band membership through the legal process known as enfranchisement — Indian women who have married non-Indians, the Métis and the descendants of persons who received land or money-scrip.

There are 54 different languages or dialects in Canada, belonging to 10 major linguistic groups: Algonkian, Iroquoian, Siouan, Athapaskan, Kootenayan, Salishan, Wakashan, Tsimshian, Haida and Tlingit.

Education. Provision of education services to Indians living on reserves is the responsibility of the federal government, which funds a complete range of education services from four-year-old kindergarten to university, professional or technological education and trade training through the Department of Indian and Northern Affairs. Approximately 60 per cent of reserve-based Indian children attend schools operated by the provinces. The remaining 40 per cent attend schools on reserves operated either by the department or by the Indian bands.

This ceremonial Indian house near Terrace, BC, serves as a handicraft shop.

Since the acceptance of the National Indian Brotherhood paper "Indian Control of Indian Education" in 1973, increasing numbers of Indian bands are assuming control of their schools and other educational programs, and a major aim of government involvement in Indian education has been to facilitate the transfer of education programs to Indian bands and to develop appropriate curricula in consultation with them. Almost all of the 270 federal schools operated by the department now offer culturally enriched programs, and many of the provincial schools attended by Indian or Inuit children include language courses or native studies units as part of the regular school program.

Several provinces and universities have designed and conducted special teacher-training courses to encourage natives to enter the teaching profession; paraprofessional courses are also conducted to train Indian teacher aides and social counsellors for federal, provincial and band-operated schools. Vocational training, vocational counselling and employment placement programs have been supported by the Department of Indian and Northern Affairs in co-operation with the Department of Manpower. The Education Branch of the department has also assumed responsibility for training of elected and appointed officials of Indian bands and Inuit settlement councils that is specifically related to their official duties.

Local Government. A policy encouraging the development of local government on Indian reserves began to evolve in 1965 in response to the expressed wishes of the Indian people to assume greater responsibility for the administration of their own affairs. At that time some 26 Indian bands from across Canada assumed responsibility for the administration of specific departmental programs amounting to $66,000. Increased interest since then is reflected by the fact that in 1976 some

An Indian summer camp at Rae, NWT.

545 of the 566 Indian bands in Canada managed departmental programs in excess of $108 million. Government policies will continue to reflect this approach.

Economic Development. The obstacles confronting Indian people in their efforts to achieve economic independence have been their isolated and inaccessible geographical locations and restrictions of the Indian Act that limited investment in Indian reserves. The Indian Economic Development Fund was established in 1970 to provide a source of capital to enable them to overcome these obstacles.

In 1976, the fund had a working capital of $140 million, available for such endeavours as farms, vacation resorts, hotels, motels, shopping centres, contracting businesses, outfitters and pre-fab housing, which provided over 8,500 jobs for Indian people. The bulk of the fund is advanced as direct loans, with repayments along the lines of conventional loans. It also provides guarantees for loans from traditional sources of investment capital, allowing the Indian people to establish themselves as independent businessmen.

Inuit (Eskimos)

During recent years the many changes and developments in the Canadian north have affected almost every aspect of the lives of the more than 19,000 Inuit living there. These northern people have survived for many centuries in spite of the harsh conditions under which they have had to live, and in recent years they have been offered new opportunities and facilities for strengthening their capacity to survive.

Early accounts and archaeological research show that the Canadian Inuit once ranged farther south than they do now, particularly on the Atlantic seaboard. Traditionally, they were mainly a coastal people and they settled by the sea. Fish and sea mammals were their sources of food, fuel and clothing. Centuries ago, however, one group broke away from the others to follow the caribou herds to the interior, where they formed a culture that was much different. They lived on the caribou herds and fish from the inland lakes; they made fires from shrubs instead of blubber and rarely visited the sea.

The early explorers of the Canadian Arctic met Inuit from time to time over a period of some 300 years, but had few dealings with them; development in Arctic Canada came at a much later date than in other arctic lands. However, with the arrival of the whaling ships and the fur traders early in the 19th century changes began to take place. Through their dealings with whalers and traders the Inuit began to move into a position of some dependence upon the white man's goods and supplies. The traditional, nomadic wandering life was becoming less attractive to them.

Trading posts had been built along both shores of Hudson Strait by 1923, down the east coast of Hudson Bay to Port Harrison and up the west coast of Hudson Bay to Repulse Bay; similar development took place in the western Arctic. Today the Hudson's Bay Company has some 30 posts in arctic regions.

With World War II came a rapid development in air travel, and the building of defence installations and of meteorological and radio stations. During the past two decades the reduction of the Inuit's isolation has proceeded apace.

Many of these people have made a difficult and dramatic transition from nomadic hunters to modern urbanized residents. By such means as the Anik communications satellite, telephone, radio and television transmissions are now beamed into the Inuit household.

The sled dogs, long-time companions and necessity to the Inuit, have gone. The motorized toboggan has replaced them, and for longer journeys the airplane is the Arctic taxi. Few communities are without airstrips. Modern technology in the form of STOL (short take-off and landing) and jet aircraft have considerably shrunk the vast spaces of the Inuit domain.

Various programs initiated by the federal government, such as education, social affairs, local government and economic development, have also contributed to the dramatic change in the Inuit way of life. For example, today co-operatives do a total volume of business of over $8 million annually, and to a large extent control the marketing of all Inuit art. Federal schools have been built in every Inuit community. Beyond Grade 6, or 8 in some locations, students attend pre-vocational or secondary schools either in the Arctic or at locations in southern Canada.

Many communities have evolved from having a resident government administrator to becoming incorporated villages, managing their own affairs through elected councils. The Council of the Northwest Territories, a provincial-style body, has six Inuit elected members.

Concern for the survival of Inuit identity and culture resulted in 1971 in the formation of Inuit Tapirisat of Canada (ITC —the Eskimo Brotherhood), an association funded by the Secretary of State in the interest of the Inuit people. In consultation with the Department of Indian and Northern Affairs, ITC has initiated many programs aimed at improving the lot of the Inuit.

Activities of the association and its related Inuit Cultural Institute include a legal service centre to assist Inuit of the eastern Arctic in legal matters, a language commission established to make recommendations relating to the standardization

Inuit hunters from Repulse Bay, NWT, skinning a caribou.

This co-operative at Yellowknife, NWT, is an outlet for Inuit arts and crafts; it is owned and controlled by some 40 Inuit families.

and the implementation of Inuit language orthographies, a communications program aimed at inter-settlement communication through UHF radio, and a special project in International Women's Year entitled the Role of Women in Inuit Society. These programs and activities have been assisted by grants, contributions and loans from the Department of Indian and Northern Affairs and the Secretary of State.

With the spirited search for oil, gas and minerals in the Arctic, much is being done to create and make available opportunities for the employment of Inuit in the petroleum and related industries. However, some adult Inuit still live by their traditional skills of hunting, trapping and fishing. One of the most successful and remarkable revenue-producing pursuits of the Inuit is based on their creative talents, expressed in the media of stone, bone and ivory sculpture and vibrant graphics depicting their lifestyle and culture. This industry is expanding, and local co-operatives ensure the artist a fair return for his works of art.

Native Claims

The question of settling native claims has been before Canadian governments for many years.

As a result of nation-wide consultation on proposed changes to the Indian Act during 1968-69, the National Indian Brotherhood sponsored a National Committee on Rights and Treaties to investigate Indian rights with a view to proposing revisions to the Indian Act, and also to consider how treaty rights had been administered in the past so that Indian claims could be identified and put forward to the government. In addition, a Commissioner for Indian Claims was appointed to examine, classify and propose a means of settlement of claims submitted to him. In 1970 the government began funding native groups to enable them to research rights and treaties.

On August 8, 1973, the Minister of Indian and Northern Affairs announced the federal government's policy on comprehensive claims of Indian and Inuit people.

This policy recognized the existence of native interest in areas of Canada where it had not been properly extinguished by treaty or superseded by law. It stated that claims made by native groups on the basis of this interest — which represented the loss of traditional use and occupancy of land in these areas — must be settled, that the most promising avenue for reaching settlement is through negotiation, and that settlement would extinguish this interest in return for compensation for its loss.

Comprehensive claims were to be settled on the basis of the awareness that such claims involved not only money but also the loss of a way of life, and therefore could include such elements as hunting, fishing and trapping rights, land, resource revenue sharing, participation in local and regional government, and the preservation of cultural identity. The areas in question were taken to be British Columbia, northern Quebec, the Yukon Territory and the Northwest Territories.

Other types of claims recognized by the policy statement were classified as specific claims. These were based on longstanding government policy, reaffirmed in 1969, that lawful obligations must be met. They encompassed those claims relating to the administration of land and other Indian assets under the various Indian Acts and Regulations, and those relating to the actual fulfilment or interpretation of Indian Treaties or Agreements and Proclamations affecting Indians and reserve lands.

In 1974, a native claims office was set up in the Department of Indian and Northern Affairs to be primarily responsible for representing the Minister and the department in negotiations with native groups about their land claims and related grievances. A year later a Special Government Representative was appointed and given a particularly broad mandate to deal with comprehensive native claims, as a further mark of the seriousness that the government attached to the satisfactory settlement of these claims. That year a joint committee of federal cabinet ministers and the executive of the National Indian Brotherhood was also established to provide a forum for the discussion of major problems and issues, chief among which were the revision of the Indian Act and the way in which native claims might best be handled.

As of the end of March 1976, native claims in several areas were being dealt with. A final agreement had been reached with the Cree and Inuit people of northern Quebec (the James Bay Agreement, signed on November 11, 1975, and ratified by the Crees on December 4 and by the Inuit on March 12, 1976), and work is now progressing on the legislation that is required to approve and give effect to the agreement. The national Inuit organization, Inuit Tapirisat of Canada, had presented its claim and a proposal for its settlement to the federal government on behalf of the Inuit people of the Northwest Territories. In the Yukon Territory, the Council for Yukon Indians and federal representatives were close to reaching an agreement in principle that would provide the basis for a final agreement with the native people. In the Mackenzie Valley area of the Northwest Territories, the federal government expected that a claim and a proposal for its settlement would be submitted by the Indian Brotherhood of the Northwest Territories around the beginning of November 1976.

Also as of the end of March 1976, more than $7.5 million had been disbursed by the federal government for research by native groups on treaties and aboriginal rights, and over $9 million for the settlement of native claims.

Official Languages

Throughout Canada's history the existence of two major linguistic groups has been one of the dynamic forces that have shaped the country and contributed much to its unique character. To safeguard this valuable national heritage, the federal government has taken a number of steps to ensure the equal participation of both English-speaking and French-speaking Canadians in Canada's future.

In 1963, it appointed a Royal Commission on Bilingualism and Biculturalism whose purpose was to inquire into a wide range of questions relating to language and culture in Canada. Following the publication of the first volume of the commission's report, the federal government introduced an Official Languages Bill in the House of Commons in October 1968. The Bill was adopted by Parliament in July 1969 and came into force in September of the same year.

The Official Languages Act stipulates that "the English and French languages are the official languages of Canada" and that they "possess and enjoy equality of status and equal rights and privileges as to their use in all the institutions of the Parliament and Government of Canada."

The Act provides three other major sections, under which: all statutory and other government documents directed to or intended for the Canadian public shall be available in both official languages; bilingual districts may be created, and in those areas federal government services shall be available in both official languages; and a Commissioner of Official Languages shall be appointed to ensure compliance with the spirit and intent of the Act.

Responsibility for administering official languages policies and programs is shared by Treasury Board, Department of the Secretary of State, Public Service Commission and National Capital Commission. In addition, the Commissioner of Official Languages is responsible for ensuring recognition of the status of the official languages and general compliance with the spirit and intent of the Act in the administration of the affairs of the institutions of the Parliament and Government of Canada.

Treasury Board

The Treasury Board is responsible for the administration of the government's language policy in federal departments and agencies responsible to it. Agencies for which Treasury Board is not the employer include such Crown corporations as the National Gallery of Canada, Air Canada and the CBC. Also excluded from Treasury Board's mandate are those programs entrusted by Parliament to the Public Service Commission and to the Translation Bureau.

The Official Languages Branch of Treasury Board is responsible for the development, implementation, evaluation and communication of policy.

The Policy and Evaluation Division identifies, develops and recommends policies and guidelines for the implementation of official languages in the federal public service. It also plans, develops and recommends related programs and procedures required to give effect to official languages policy and guidelines. The division is also responsible for establishing a statistical analysis and monitoring system to evaluate progress toward achieving the government's official languages objective and the implementation by departments of recommendations made by the Commissioner of Official Languages.

In full collaboration with departments and agencies, the Operations Division is responsible for implementing official languages programs. It provides interpretation of Treasury Board policies for unique departmental situations, assists in the development of departmental strategies to achieve objectives and overcome particular problems, and administers funds used to assist departments in implementing programs. It also monitors actions taken by departments to ensure their participation in the development of policies and programs, and maintains liaison with staff bargaining agents at the national level. In terms of administrative support, the division develops procedures for official languages programs and ensures that the Official Languages Information System is continuously developed and maintained.

The Information Division ensures the co-ordination, development and provision of information programs, both within and without the Public Service, designed to promote understanding, acceptance and support for the Act, and for the policies and programs related to the official languages in the public service. It also responds to official languages inquiries.

Department of the Secretary of State

The Department of the Secretary of State has a general responsibility for the development of the official languages in education and in the private sector, and a special responsibility, through its Translation Bureau, for meeting the translation, interpretation and terminology requirements of the Government of Canada. The department also has a program of support for minority official language groups, under the direction of the Citizenship Branch. This program is concerned with the linguistic and cultural development of official language communities in areas where they are established as minorities.

Language Programs Branch. A series of programs devoted to the development of the official languages is administered by the Language Programs Branch. Its Federal-Provincial Program for Bilingualism in Education is intended to increase the opportunity for Canadians of the majority official language group in each province to acquire a knowledge of the other official language, and to increase the opportunity for Canadians of the minority official language group in each province to be educated in their own language. Financial aid is offered to the provinces on the basis of the numbers of students engaged in these language programs. Provision is also made for various bursaries, awards and contributions to institutions at post-secondary and teacher-training levels, and for special projects on a cost-shared basis. Assistance is given to provincial governments and municipalities, in agreement with provincial authorities, so they can offer services to the public in both official languages.

In the private sector, various programs have been developed to encourage the adoption of improved methods for acquiring and using both official languages. These include: technical advice to business and industry; assistance to voluntary associations for interpretation and translation; and the dissemination of research results, documents and information on the official languages. In collaboration with other appropriate departments, the Department of the Secretary of State co-operates with other countries and international organizations on problems relating to institutional and individual bilingualism.

Bilingual exchanges sponsored by the school boards of Quebec City and the National Capital Region and by the NCC allow students to learn about each other's language and culture.

The Translation Bureau. The Translation Bureau provides translation and interpretation services in all languages as necessary for the proper functioning of Parliament, the government and its agencies, especially those services required for implementation of the official languages policy. In co-operation with Parliament, the government and its agencies it determines their translation, interpretation and terminology requirements, and arranges to meet them; it also provides simultaneous interpretation of the proceedings of the House of Commons, of the Senate and of Parliamentary committees, and when government departments and agencies require them interpreters are sent to national and international conferences. The Translation Bureau also organizes and encourages terminological projects, in co-operation with specialized institutions in Canada and abroad, in order to establish a bank of equivalent terms to keep abreast of current vocabulary in all disciplines and all relevant languages and to increase the efficiency of translation in the two official languages.

Official Language Minority Groups Directorate. The Official Language Minority Groups Directorate was set up to: assist the official language groups to make use of their language in ways that enable them to contribute their full potential to Canadian society in areas where they constitute minorities; promote their socio-cultural development; and facilitate the harmonious co-operation of the two official language communities in furthering the national goals of the bilingualism development program.

The official language minority groups have several organizations in each province that relate to some facet or other of the social, educational, cultural and economic life. Seven different Official Language Minority Groups Programs are designed to meet the needs of these organizations and their members, as long as the projects presented meet the objectives of the Official Language Minority Groups Directorate.

The Public Service Commission

The Public Service Commission is responsible for: the determination of the level of second-language knowledge required of and possessed by candidates for bilingual positions in the federal public service; provision of language training for public servants; hearing of appeals against the results of language testing and language qualifications required in a competition; and review of the language knowledge of employees to ensure retention of language skills. Under an agreement with the Department of National Defence, the Public Service Commission is also responsible for the language training of Canada's military personnel.

The commission modified its language training system in 1973. The change has involved a greatly increased emphasis on continuous language training, under which the public servants concerned can spend up to 52 weeks at language school without interruption. This change of technique was brought about to increase the effectiveness of language training and also to ensure compatibility with the language requirements of positions. While its main training facilities are in Ottawa and Hull, the Public Service Commission also conducts regional language training operations in language schools in Halifax, Quebec City, Montreal, Winnipeg, Vancouver and Edmonton, and makes language training available to federal public servants through contract arrangements in Saint John, Moncton, Fredericton, Toronto, Sudbury, North Bay, Regina and Banff. The commission also conducts various specialized courses to meet particular needs.

National Capital Commission

With the object of making Canada's National Capital Region a true reflection of the country as a whole, a special program dealing with official languages outside the federal public service is administered by the National Capital Commission.

The commission negotiates with the provinces of Ontario and Quebec with a view to ensuring that the linguistic and cultural values of the Anglophone and Francophone communities are adequately reflected in the region. It pursues this goal by collaborating with the regional and municipal governments and other local public authorities such as school boards to strengthen their bilingual capabilities, and with private business organizations, voluntary associations and individuals to encourage the use of both official languages in various services and activities; it also seeks to inform public opinion and stimulate discussion on such broad questions as bilingual education, the official languages in provincial courts and social services to both linguistic communities.

Commissioner of Official Languages

It is the duty of the Commissioner of Official Languages "to take all actions and measures within his authority with a view to ensuring recognition of the status of each of the official languages and compliance with the spirit and intent of this Act in the administration of the affairs of the institutions of the Parliament and Government of Canada and, for that purpose, to conduct and carry out investigations either on his own initiative or pursuant to any complaint made to him and to report and make recommendations with respect thereto as provided in this Act" (Section 25 of the Official Languages Act).

The commissioner exercises two functions, those of language ombudsman and linguistic auditor general in matters under federal jurisdiction, and reports each year directly to Parliament.

Within practical limits, the Official Languages Act permits everyone to address, in writing or orally, any department or agency of the federal government in English or French, and to receive a response in the same language. Documents or publications printed by these departments or agencies for their public must also appear in both languages.

Parliament has provided the Commissioner of Official Languages as an ombudsman to back up these rights. Appointed by both the House of Commons and the Senate for a seven-year term, the commissioner must investigate all complaints. If a department or agency of the federal government is found to have ignored someone's language rights, the commissioner can and will make recommendations on that person's behalf. The law also requires that all such investigations are conducted in private.

Frequently, if the problem is outside the jurisdiction of the Commissioner of Official Languages, aid may be given in finding the appropriate door to knock on.

Multiculturalism

According to the 1971 Census, 44.6 per cent of Canada's population was of British origin, 28.7 per cent French and the remaining 26.7 per cent of other language origins. The government's multiculturalism policy, announced in October 1971, is a response to recommendations of the report of the Royal Commission on Bilingualism and Biculturalism, which described the status of all the various cultures in Canada. The policy promised support to programs aimed at retaining, developing and sharing these cultures on a larger scale.

Folk dancing by the Polish Podhale, of Montreal, Que.

In November 1972 the position of Minister of State responsible for Multiculturalism was created to give life to the policy, and in May 1973 the Canadian
Consultative Council on Multiculturalism was established to provide a focus for
consultation by the Minister on matters relating to implementation of multiculturalism policy. Regional, national and executive meetings have since been held as
required in order to review policy and evaluate multiculturalism programs. The
CCCM undertook the sponsorship of the 2nd Canadian Conference on Multiculturalism, held in February 1976; it discussed Multiculturalism as State Policy.

Multiculturalism Programs

Implementation of the government's multiculturalism policy is carried out by the
Multiculturalism Directorate of the Department of the Secretary of State and by
several federal cultural agencies. One of the cultural agencies, the National Film
Board, is producing a new series of films and multi-media materials on the history,
culture and lifestyles of ethnocultural groups in Canada and on the inter-cultural
relationship of various groups. The NFB also prepares and distributes ancestral-
language versions of NFB films originally produced in English and French.

The National Museum of Man is actively involved in research, collection, preservation, interpretation and public presentation of various aspects of Canada's cultural heritage. It has accumulated a vast number of artifacts, tape recordings, video
tapes and films reflecting elements of Canadian ethnocultural traditions. The
museum also administers a related program of displays, travelling exhibits, educational kits and publications.

The National Ethnic Archives, a component of the Public Archives of Canada,
collects, catalogues and preserves materials of historical significance relating to
Canada's cultural minorities. It seeks to create a greater awareness among the many
cultural communities of the importance of and need for documenting their heritage
and preserving all types of archival materials in order to ensure that the many facets
of Canadian history be fully recorded.

The Multilingual Biblioservice of the National Library administers a program to
acquire and circulate books in languages other than English and French through the
public library system.

The Multiculturalism Directorate of the Department of the Secretary of State
implements a number of programs which include the following:

The Multicultural Studies Program involves several projects. Visiting Professors
and Visiting Lecturers are available to universities to teach in areas related to
multiculturalism and ethnic studies in Canada. Studies commissioned by the
department on questions related to multiculturalism are monitored. The Ethnic
History Project encourages the writing and publishing of the history of ethnocultural minority groups. The Canadian Ethnic Studies Advisory Committee advises
the department on questions related to multicultural studies in Canada.

The Canadian Identities Program seeks to create an awareness of different lifestyles and traditions within Canadian society and promote inter-group understanding through activities such as theatre, folk arts, publishing, projects to improve
inter-cultural communication and development of informational material.

1. Dancers of the Dutch Community of Ottawa.
2. A Chinese dancer from the Niagara Peninsula performs a traditional fan dance.
3. Dancers from the Armenian Cultural Community of Ottawa.

The Multiculturalism Directorate also provides financial assistance for the development and production of ancestral-language teaching aids and for a wide range of activities initiated by voluntary groups that enable these groups not only to maintain and develop their cultural heritage but to share it with others as well. At the same time, the department continues to carry on liaison work with groups and organizations representing Canada's ethnocultural groups in order to assist them to achieve full participation in society.

Chinese market gardeners on the Fraser River Delta, BC.

Religion

Religion has been an important influence in Canada's history since the earliest days of discovery. Not just the search for riches or the lure of exploration, but a sense of mission, to Christianize the Indians, drew Frenchmen to the New World. Later settlers, both French- and English-speaking, looked to their churches as centres of social stability, of community as well as religious activities, and of the consolations of faith in the face of adversities, sufferings and despair. The institutional church still provides leadership and guidelines for living to many Canadians, and most would agree that the Judaeo-Christian values carried from Europe influence their national life.

Although French Protestants were active in the early fur trade of New France, religious and economic rivalries led to the banning of all but French Roman Catholics from the colony in 1627. Before settlers arrived in any numbers, however, the Roman Catholic Church was already operating schools and hospitals as part of its great missionary effort to convert the Indians. One of the most heroic stories in Canada's past is that of the 17th century mission to the Hurons on Georgian Bay, where Fathers Jean de Brébeuf and Gabriel Lalemant died at the hands of the Iroquois. Five other Jesuits killed in the course of their mission to the Hurons have also been recognized as martyr saints. From similar missionary enterprise in that century grew the great city of Montreal.

When the British acquired Acadia in 1713 and New France in 1763, the new rulers guaranteed to the Roman Catholic population freedom to practise their religion. A policy encouraging a "Canadian" Catholic Church was confirmed by the Quebec Act of 1774, which gave official recognition to that church. This pattern of religious unity inherited from New France was, however, soon altered by the predominantly Protestant Loyalists. Their arrival meant that from that time forward Canada would be religiously pluralistic. This religious diversity and the growing spirit of equality eventually doomed to failure the post-revolutionary plan to make Anglicanism the official religion of the colonies. Vast land endowments and special political and legal privileges for the Church of England had all disappeared before Confederation as voluntaryism — the separation of church and state — became the unwritten law and universal practice in Canada.

Canadians have come literally from a hundred nations, and their different faiths are now represented in this country of their adoption. The larger churches have established "ethnic" parishes where the temporary use of their mother tongue helps ease the immigrants' entrance into Canadian culture, but in ethnic churches such as the Eastern Orthodox community, where the mother language is an essential part of religious services, the cultural transfer from the Old World to the New is sometimes more lengthy and difficult. Historically the churches of England and Scotland too could be considered ethnic churches, but in Canada they have had the advantage of using one of the two "charter" languages.

While the great majority of Canadians are Christian by heritage, and in times past have often referred to Canada as a "Christian nation", other faiths are also represented in the religious mosaic of the country. European Jews have brought both the major Judaic religious traditions with them and are organized in orthodox, conservative and liberal synagogues. Judaism in Canada has remained essentially an urban phenomenon, with 77 per cent of its followers living in Montreal and Toronto alone. Since the 1940s the Canadian Council of Christians and Jews has worked for greater understanding between these two faiths, but it has also promoted civil rights and the end of religious prejudice through education. From Asia other recent immigrants have introduced Islam, Hinduism, Buddhism and Sikhism, and one of Christianity's oldest branches, the Coptic Church of Ethiopia, now has a congregation in Toronto.

Soon after Confederation nationalists like George M. Grant, principal of Queen's University, voiced their dream of reuniting all Christians in a single Canadian church. Their ideal of Protestant-Catholic reunion seemed an impossibility until Vatican II, but in the intervening century Canadian Protestant denominations did take long strides toward church union. In 1875 all Presbyterian bodies in Canada were joined into a single church, and nine years later all Methodist groups were similarly reunited. These denominational unions led immediately to discussion of an interdenominational union of Anglicans, Methodists, Presbyterians, Congregationalists and Baptists. Not until 1925, however, and then only after bitter

The United Church at Williamstown, Ont.

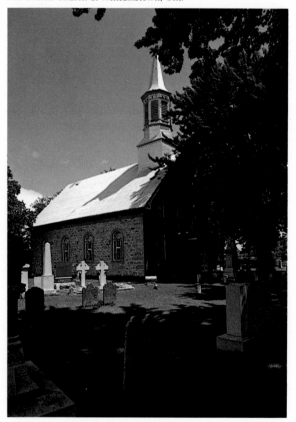

The Polish Roman Catholic Church, Our Lady Queen of Peace, in Calgary, Alta.

controversy divided the Presbyterian Church, was a United Church achieved that included Methodists, Presbyterians and Congregationalists only.

The United Church of Canada, a unique experiment in interdenominationalism and Canada's largest Protestant denomination, has recently merged with the smaller Evangelical United Brethren. From 1944 to 1975 it discussed a union with the Anglican Church and the Disciples of Christ, which would have contained nearly 30 per cent of Canada's population. Roman Catholics make up 46 per cent of the population and the three next largest denominations — Presbyterians, Lutherans and Baptists — claim another 12 per cent of the population. Thus nearly nine of every 10 Canadians are members of just five churches — the remainder are divided among more than 30 other denominations, as well as sects and cults. While the Canadian religious scene is often called pluralistic, there has in fact been an historical trend toward fewer and bigger "mainline" churches.

Members of Canada's larger churches — Roman Catholic, United and Anglican — are found in every province, but the smaller denominations often reflect a regional concentration that stems from the pattern of settlement or from particular religious events in Canada's history. The Presbyterian Church in Canada is predominantly an urban and Ontario institution because of the schism caused by the union of 1925. Canadian Baptists number only 667,000 and are mainly in the Maritimes, where they separated from the Congregationalists as a result of an 18th century religious revival. Over the past two centuries Canada's tradition of religious freedom has attracted many small religious bodies that have suffered persecution in other lands. These have often settled here in close communities to preserve their religious and folk ways. Among the earliest of such groups were the Quakers, Mennonites, Tunkers and Moravians; more recent arrivals are the German-speaking Hutterites and the Doukhobors from Russia.

During the 19th century rapid and widely dispersed settlement absorbed most of the resources of the churches as they tried to reach these scattered flocks. Where the Catholic Church had earlier provided schools, hospitals, orphanages and asylums

Anglican service in the Inuit church at Povungnituk, Que.

in the more compact settlement of New France, it was now left to the state to develop such social agencies in the rest of Canada, so that the work of the churches, particularly the Protestant churches, was largely limited to providing exclusively religious help.

Despite this growth of the welfare state and its separation from the churches, Canadians have always believed that religion and secular life are necessarily connected. The organized churches have acted as the conscience of the state and have lobbied with some success on such issues as temperance, Sunday observance, birth control, abortion, working and living conditions, capital punishment and criminal law reform. They have also attempted to influence Canada's external relations in connection with aid to under-developed countries and the non-recognition of certain foreign governments. In Quebec the Roman Catholic Church continued to play an important role in politics until the Quiet Revolution of the 1960s, whereas the Protestant churches were strongest as social critics in the generation of mass immigration and industrialization immediately before World War I.

Since the early 1960s the relative decline in the influence of the older churches on national life has been complemented by the rise of various sects and cults whose radical beliefs and practices seem to have attracted a sizable following among a restless younger generation. The more traditional forms of religion may yet regain some of their former effectiveness thanks to the revival of religious conservatism that has recently appeared in the United States and Canada in reaction against the uncertainties, confusion and challenges of the previous decade.

JOHN S. MOIR

Arts and Culture

One goal of the artist is to speak to society. In recent years the artists of Canada have discovered that they have a great deal to say to their fellow citizens—and it is usually *about* their fellow citizens. Much of our poetry is an attempt to interpret one part of Canada to another, or to tell us about our past. A large part of our fiction is an attempt to look into our past, describe where we came from, and thereby tell us where we are now. Much of our theatre is an attempt to describe the heroes and villains of Canadian life, to give us the kind of myths that other countries accept as their birthright. Our movies are telling us, haltingly but often with great insight, about the world we have made for ourselves.

These are not small achievements. The films of Claude Jutra or the novels of Mordecai Richler or the poems of Al Purdy or the stories of Jacques Ferron or the paintings of John Boyle—these are objects of great value to Canadian life, and they were not produced without considerable difficulty. They are to be cherished as among the precious possessions of our country. Perhaps our life as a national community will depend in part on whether we cherish them or ignore them, whether we put them at the centre of our national life or assign them to some distant corner of our consciousness.

In Canada the artist's work has traditionally been confined to the edge of society, while the centre has been occupied by other concerns — work, politics, religion, sport. But the period from 1967 to 1977 has been one of enormous change, almost entirely for the better.

In this period, for instance, scores of Canadian playwrights have had their work performed and toured by professional companies—something that was extremely rare in the 1960s. Performing arts companies, most notably those in once-obscure fields like modern dance and mime, are flourishing. Feature films are often made in Canada now, as they seldom were in the 1960s and almost never were in the 1950s. Book publishing has increased enormously and spread geographically, so that now all provinces and many cities have book publishers producing the work of Canadian writers. The articles that follow contain detailed evidence of this activity.

There are some general reasons for this cultural boom. Canadian society has changed in important ways, and nowhere is this more evident than in its appreciation of the arts. Three fundamental changes have altered forever the place of the arts in Canada.

The Economy: From about 1950 to the early 1970s Canada experienced a period of economic growth unparalleled in its history. This made it possible for society to provide money and time for what had once been considered frills. Private citizens found it possible to spend money on everything from books to theatre tickets to paintings. More important, various governments took the view that spending tax money on the arts was justified — hence the Canada Council and similar institutions. These made artistic activity possible on a scale never before approached.

Education: Within this economic context, provincial and federal governments were able to respond to a vastly increased demand for college and university education. In every province post-secondary education was so expanded that it became a commonplace rather than a rare privilege. This had two results for the arts. First, it trained many artists, both in the literature departments and in specialized departments such as fine arts, film and the performing arts. Second, it trained audiences. Hundreds of thousands of Canadians were given their first exposure to serious art within a college or a university setting. Of these, a substantial number emerged with an interest in the arts that will likely continue all their lives. There are still not enough of them to provide a mass audience for the performing arts, or mass readership for many Canadian books, but there are enough that their presence is felt in all parts of our cultural life.

Immigration: During this same period, Canadian immigration maintained a remarkable pace; on an average, about 150,000 persons a year came to Canada. A considerable number of these became artists—in film, poetry, the graphic arts, the performing arts. A great many more were conditioned by European and other traditions to see the arts as part of their lives.

These three factors have produced a new situation for the Canadian artist: no longer is he or she condemned to obscurity. There is now the chance of an audience, and the chance (though still a slim one) of a fairly good income. But still, the story of

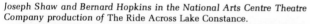

Joseph Shaw and Bernard Hopkins in the National Arts Centre Theatre Company production of The Ride Across Lake Constance.

The art of photography in its infancy is relived at Sherbrooke Village, NS.

the arts in this country is a story of struggle, and perhaps that is the most Canadian of all aspects of Canadian culture.

Canada has seen itself, from the beginning, as a country which must struggle to exist. This was as true for Ukrainian settlers in Manitoba in 1910 as it was for the pioneers of New France along the St. Lawrence shores in 1710. Each small success was measured against the overwhelming power of nature—the difficult landscape, the vast distances, the harsh winters. In the 1970s Canadian existence is still a struggle, though of a different kind. The struggle for unity within the country and independence in the world remain central themes of Canadian thought. Culture naturally reflects the essence of society, and if the historic essence of our society is struggle it should be no surprise that in our time the artists of Canada have tended to see their lives in terms of struggle rather than triumph.

When Margaret Atwood wrote her book about themes in Canadian literature (*Survival*, Anansi, 1972), it touched deeply the artists and intellectuals of English Canada, not only because it identified one important strain in our literature but also because that strain is the one closest to their own lives and their own hearts.

The people involved in Canadian culture now find it difficult to believe that they have *had* their good years, that now government support for the arts must slow down because, in a period of economic constraint, all government activity is slowing down.

This is hard to accept, but all the signs are that it must be accepted. The great flowering that began with Centennial Year may now be ending, giving way to a time of consolidation and slower growth, a time when the successes and failures of the last decade can be absorbed and assessed, a time when plans can be made for another period of expansion at some point in the future.

ROBERT FULFORD

The Performing Arts

The arts of dance, theatre, opera and music in Canada have grown to the point where it is impossible for a survey of this size to do justice to the year in review. A study done for the Ontario Arts Council says that 46 per cent of Canadians attend performing arts events. To mention even most of the high points of the year would be to present a text as dense with proper names as the "begat" genealogies of the Bible.

Fortunately there are now many sources of detailed news and reviews of the performing arts. *Opera Canada* has moved out from under the sponsorship of the Canadian Opera Company and speaks with even more authority to an international readership. *Performance, Performing Arts in Canada* and *That's Show Business* are lively showcases in the field, and for serious students there are the volumes of *The Canada Music Book*. Other more specialized periodicals such as *The Canadian Composer* and *Coda* are lively and informative, and a look under the appropriate headings of the *Canadian Index of Periodical Literature* will show that Canada's

Sonia Vartanian, David La Hay, Mannie Rowe and Maniya Barredo *of Les Grands Ballets Canadiens in the world premiere of* Lignes et Points.

general-interest magazines are helping to spread the good news about the arts in Canada. Canadian libraries usually have copies of these and of the annual reports of federal, provincial and some municipal arts-support agencies.

More readily at hand are CBC-Radio's arts programs and the entertainment pages of the daily newspapers across the country. Arts coverage in the dailies has grown broader and more knowing recently, a trend that has survived the Canadian tendency to talk things to death.

The most thoughtful reviews and biggest ads go to performances by major visiting companies and orchestras and to the more important Canadian organizations into which the Canada Council and provincial and municipal arts-support agencies put most of their funds. This is no small contingent. Over 60 organizations received grants to produce plays alone, according to the Canada Council's *1974-75 Annual Report,* a number which has since swelled. Some of the organizations are big, and others may consist of only a few permanent hands. What sets them apart is that they are recognized in the performing arts community for the outstanding quality of their work and for their importance to their cities or regions and, in some cases, to the country as a whole.

But the newspapers list a great number of other activities in the performing arts. As reporters are sent out to little league hockey games, so they also report concerts, plays and dance programs in school auditoriums and church basements that are the heart and soul of the arts for the performers and for their teachers, friends and relations. Community orchestras and established amateur theatres attract a good deal of attention in some areas, and many of the subsidized organizations began in this way. Although the coffee-house has suffered a decline, new and sometimes highly talented folk and rock artists may rub shoulders with more seasoned talent at university pubs, upgraded beer halls or rented halls as well as at the brave survivors of the coffee-house era.

The value of what can loosely be called "non-professional" arts activities by no means ends at preparing good audiences for the professionals. In recent years many smaller groups, particularly in theatre, have brought about a revolution in the performing arts. Many of them were stimulated during the heyday of the Opportunities for Youth and Local Initiatives Programs and have now joined, sometimes uneasily, the ranks of groups subsidized by arts councils. They have brought a new and salutary emphasis on Canadian and experimental work or on regional or social questions.

Dance

Ballet, like opera, is one of the most expensive of art forms. A new trend has been for smaller, very professional groups to sprout up around the country. They are usually called "chamber" or "concert" ballet companies, and new names to watch for are Ballet Ys of Toronto, which made its formal debut at the National Arts Centre in September 1975, the Entre-Six Company in Montreal, and the Alberta Ballet Company in Edmonton.

Like the "big three", these new companies have serious money worries, but they are surviving and attracting audiences. They have the advantage of great mobility and have offered many opportunities to Canadian choreographers.

The major ballet companies, the National Ballet of Canada in Toronto, the Grands Ballets Canadiens in Montreal and the Royal Winnipeg Ballet in Winnipeg, introduced a number of contemporary classics to their repertoires during the year, a brave undertaking in a field where expenses are high and audiences tend to be set in their ways.

As has become the custom in recent years, a number of Canadian companies and individuals in dance received honours at home and abroad. Veronica Tennant became the first dancer to be received into the Order of Canada, and Karen Kain was acclaimed in Paris during her guest stay with Roland Petit's company. Brian Macdonald attracted much attention among balletomanes when, concurrently with the Prime Minister's visit in Cuba, he set his ballet *Time Out of Mind* with the National Ballet of Cuba. The Royal Winnipeg Ballet performed in Israel with Valeri and Galina Panov as guest artists.

Theatre

Canadian plays have made their way into all but a few of the bigger regional companies, and continue to be the mainstay of the smaller experimental groups. At the same time, the Touring Office of the Canada Council has helped many theatre groups show their work across the country, while most of the larger groups and many smaller ones have been invited to Ottawa by the National Arts Centre. At the same time, newspaper and magazine critics have shown more awareness of theatre developments outside their own regions. The result has been to shake some complacencies and perhaps to prepare the way for unforeseen new developments.

Two bright new companies recently bounded noisily out of Newfoundland. Codco made them laugh on the island and had them holding their sides in Philadelphia as well as in mainland Canada; the small group has been called the funniest and most subtle spontaneous theatre ever to appear in this country. The Mummers is another small Newfoundland group that shakes up our usual ideas about theatre; no Canadian company has had a surer touch in making local people understand themselves better.

At the other end of the country, the Playhouse Theatre of Vancouver has become the very model of a modern regional company. Their 1975-76 season evoked everything from contemporary shock in Peter Shaffer's *Equus* to something like

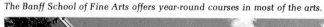
The Banff School of Fine Arts offers year-round courses in most of the arts.

Candace O'Connor, Wensley Pithey, Alexandra Bastedo and Lynne Griffin in the Shaw Festival production *of* The Admirable Crichton.

vintage tears in Dumas' *Camille,* and their New Stage series included four new Canadian productions, most with a local focus.

In Quebec, the Théâtre du Nouveau Monde paved the way for its 25th year at the centre of French Canadian theatre with a 1975-76 season that included a classic Molière, a translation of Eugene O'Neill's *The Emperor Jones,* and the original satirical revue, *Marche, Laura Secord.* Another sign of the theatrical vitality of Quebec was the sudden rise of the Compagnie Jean Duceppe, built by the man who has become perhaps the best loved theatre person in the province since Gratien Gelinas.

A knowledgeable theatre person called it a quiet year . . . but the hitherto conservative resident company of the National Arts Centre had Ottawa rocking with controversy over its production of Peter Handke's *The Ride Across Lake Constance.*

The winner of all the controversies has been the theatre-going public, who now have more and better attractions in more places than ever before.

Moe Koffman in concert on Nepean Point, Ottawa.

Opera

All opera companies have money worries. Yet this most opulent of art forms continues to grow in Canada, even to flourish. As well as the long-established Canadian Opera Company in Toronto, with its vigorous and imaginative touring program of Canada and the US, there are professional companies in Vancouver, Calgary, Edmonton and Winnipeg, and the Guelph Spring Festival in Ontario has been producing an exciting opera each year.

Canada continues to produce many exceptionally good opera singers, and it is the Guelph festival which has come up with the most striking means of improving the quality of its productions with home-grown talent. Not only did Canadians fill all the lead roles of its 1975 production of Handel's *Acis and Galatea,* but the role of chorus was taken by the Festival Singers of Canada, one of the finest choral groups in the world.

As a result of a seminar of professional opera people it sponsored in 1975, the Canada Council has prepared the *Opera Registry of Canada,* a listing of singers, conductors, designers and other professionals to help companies find the right Canadian for the right job.

Music

Music is everywhere. It is almost as universal as speech. It is pure mathematics, in a sense, and pure instinct in another.

The relations between different kinds of music are closer than one might think. For example, the Canada Council spends most of its funds for music to help major orchestras, but it also granted $4,000 so that Humphrey and the Dumptrucks of Saskatoon could compose a country and western opera called "Cruel Tears". Rock and jazz composers share many problems with composers of what is called, for want of a better term, "non-pop" music.

The growth of Canadian orchestras over the past dozen years has been a triumph for musicians and audiences alike. The symphony orchestras of Toronto, Montreal and Vancouver are recognized as being among the best in the world. In the National Arts Centre Orchestra, Mario Bernardi has helped develop a "new" kind of smaller orchestra of the very highest quality, and in Hamilton the symphony has been able to offer a wide variety of music to many different audiences by breaking down on occasion into a number of smaller groups of musicians. There is a network of good community orchestras and a growing number of fine contemporary and chamber music groups. The Association of Canadian Orchestras has 52 member orchestras, 27 of them in Ontario alone.

Of course, growth brings headaches. Hardly a day passes in which there is no newspaper story about the financial crisis of one Canadian orchestra or another. Another problem has been that our orchestras have not been able to find enough good Canadian-trained ensemble players. We seem to be able to train fine soloists—particularly singers and pianists—but not enough boys and girls of the orchestra. Late in 1975 the Canada Council commissioned the eminent musician Helmut Blume to study what might be done to correct the situation.

The Canadian Opera Company's production of Louis Riel, *with Bernard Turgeon in the title role.*

Films

It became apparent in 1976 that Canadian films were receiving more and more acclaim and recognition internationally. Increasing numbers of Canadian films — both French and English — were being lauded and were receiving prizes at film festivals around the world. A Canadian film production company, Crawley Films Limited of Ottawa, won the coveted "Oscar" award for the best feature-length documentary film of 1975. The film, entitled "The Man Who Skied Down Everest", was the first Canadian production to be so honoured at the Academy Awards presentations in California.

At home, however, the banner of Canadianism did not attract individuals to the theatres; in fact, that ingredient often tended to work against success of the product at the box-office. Nevertheless, the more professional a production was, and the more closely it matched the technical excellence of its counterparts abroad, the more Canadian audiences loved and accepted it.

The trend in 1976 was to make films more for the international market and hope for good distribution. This was the only way film-makers could hope to survive economically, and it was still much easier to receive acceptance for artistic endeavour outside Canada.

Most films can be a success at the box office if they happen to fit whatever mould is in vogue. Those that do not follow a traditional pattern find the going more difficult. During the past year, the government realized that the latter type of film could still make an artistic or cultural contribution that would be significant to a limited audience, and that such films should therefore be funded. One of the major problems to be solved was the lack of a network in Canada to promote films that did not meet the expectations of the commercial theatre marketplace.

The exodus of performers out of Canada continued in 1976. In order to make a living, artists who stayed became jacks-of-all-trades. They could not work in the film media alone; many performed in films, on the stage and in nightclubs, and also did freelance work on television to make ends meet. Although an adequate salary could be made by this method in Canada, many of the more successful performers and technical artists felt they had reached a plateau and had to leave Canada in order to progress financially and artistically.

For these reasons, the Department of the Secretary of State commissioned a research study of both public and private sectors of the film industry. Its prime objective was to define comprehensive profiles of the structure and operation of the film industry as a whole. It looked at production, distribution, exhibition and marketing, as well as the behaviour of the Canadian artistic community. Completed in 1976, the report provided an objective rationale for new policy developments, such as amendments to the mandate of the Canadian Film Development Corporation (CFDC), and identified new areas of concern with options for change. It arrived at a definition of what the film industry in Canada was really about, taking into consideration theatrical, non-theatrical and television film production.

In 1976, the advisory committees established by the CFDC functioned as very sensitive liaison instruments between government and the film industry. They put their viewpoints forward aggressively, and were able to focus on the wavelengths of those branches of government concerned with the development of policy.

The CFDC also encouraged producers to approach distributors before they began work on a film. Distribution companies have always said: "Make a good film and we will distribute it". The CFDC wanted producers and distributors to sit down together to discuss exactly what a "good film" meant to the distribution company, so that completed films would be accepted for marketing and distribution.

The Secretary of State Department wanted the CFDC to be in a position to fund not only feature films, but also short films and films for television. At the same time the corporation invested its money more judiciously in 1976 in order to reach an increasingly larger audience.

Existing co-production agreements with Italy, France and Great Britain were used with success in 1976. Arrangements to obtain similar co-operation with the Federal Republic of Germany and possibly Ireland were explored during the year.

Yuichiro Miura preparing for his historic run in The Man Who Skied Down Everest.

Agreement was reached with Famous Players Limited and Odeon Theatres (Canada), whereby both have undertaken to play a minimum of four weeks of Canadian feature films in their respective theatres across Canada. The CFDC was instructed to report quarterly on the performance of this plan to the Secretary of State, and the film industry was given access to these reports in order to ensure its capacity to participate in the review process.

Cabinet approved the establishment of a National Film Archive within the Public Archives of Canada. Its main function will be to select, acquire and conserve all film and sound recordings (film, videotape and radio) that are of enduring historical, social or cultural value; another of its tasks will be to consolidate the archival activities of the Canadian Broadcasting Corporation and the National Film Board.

In 1976 Canadian films made great inroads at international film festivals. It now remains for the government in Ottawa, in co-operation with the provincial legislatures, to continue to develop policies designed to stimulate, promote and rationalize the Canadian film industry.

Broadcasting

At its annual convention in April 1976 the Canadian Association of Broadcasters, the trade association representing private commercial broadcasters, celebrated its 50th anniversary. It is a mark of the speed of broadcasting's development in Canada

A television control room.

that station operators felt the need for such an association only four years after the first commercial broadcasting licences were issued in 1922. Indeed, the association's founding in 1926 came only seven years after XWA in Montreal, or CFCF as we know it now, began broadcasting.

The development of radio broadcasting in the 1920s and 1930s is being parallelled in the 1970s by the speed of growth of cable television. When the first community antennas were constructed 25 years ago, their purpose was to provide or improve reception in remote communities or neighbourhoods where reception by means of the individual householder's rooftop antenna was unsatisfactory or impossible. By 1976, the Canadian Cable Television Association, the cable TV trade association, could talk about more than nine million Canadians watching television via cable.

This rapid development has made Canada a world leader in cable television technology. Between 1971 and 1975, cable television penetration of the Canadian market increased from 25 per cent, a figure that was already high in comparison with other countries, to 40 per cent. In some cities, such as Sherbrooke, London, Vancouver and Victoria, more than 85 per cent of the population live in homes that subscribe to cable television service.

Table 1. Cable television by subscribers and by province, August 31, 1974

Province	Subscribers	Households		Systems licensed[1]
		Number wired	Subscribers %	
Ontario	1,229,681	1,774,650	69	121
Quebec	496,360	1,091,025	45	141
British Columbia[2]	414,904	489,757	84	68
Alberta	177,804	354,514	50	20
Nova Scotia	104,680	143,295	73	21
Manitoba	100,740	172,861	58	6
New Brunswick	25,365	44,651	57	14
Saskatchewan	10,253	13,080	78	4
Newfoundland	310	310	100	1
Prince Edward Island	..	..	..	2
Total	2,560,097	4,084,143	63	398

Source: CRTC Annual Report 1975-76 (Supply and Services Canada, 1976) Table 15.
[1] Systems licensed are as of August 31, 1975; the figures represent systems in operation.
[2] British Columbia includes Northwest Territories and Yukon Territory, each of which is served by one system.
.. Figures too small to be expressed.

As Canada entered the 1970s, its population centres were linked by microwave and coaxial-cable circuits that were ample for the needs of network broadcasting and for the exchange of programs between one region and another. In national and regional terms, the facilities of Canadian broadcasting stations, together with those of the film and recording industries, had the potential to produce national and regional program material for the radio and television systems to distribute.

However, broadcasting coverage has only recently begun to extend throughout the North and certain sparsely populated regions of Canada. Population distribution has made such expansion difficult.

The advent of satellite communications, with the launching of Anik in 1972 and the Communications Technology Satellite in 1976, has provided the technical solution to the problem of extending broadcast coverage to remote and sparsely populated areas. In the North, this technical victory conquers only half the problem. Because life in northern communities is different from life in southern Canada, these communities require different radio and television content; therefore, the next step for broadcasting in the North is to continue the work begun by the Canadian Broadcasting Corporation (CBC) developing program formats and resources to serve the needs of the communities and people who live there.

Almost since the beginning of the television age the possibility of pay TV has been much discussed. On June 2, 1976, the Minister of Communications set down three basic requirements for pay television in Canada. It must provide programming that does not duplicate what is already offered by conventional telecasters, and that does not siphon off programming from the existing telecasting system. It must ensure the production of high-quality programs that Canadians will watch. It must ensure that programs are produced in Canada for international sale.

Later, in June 1976, the Canadian Radio-television and Telecommunications Commission (CRTC) called for submissions on the form and function of an organization to assemble, produce or acquire programming for distribution to pay television in English and in French on a national or regional basis.

In this process of submission and public hearing about pay television, the CRTC and the Canadian broadcasting industry have been setting out to deal with a new element in the balance between east-west and north-south lines of communication. The advent of each new development in communications technology — canals, railways, aircraft, radio, films, television, cable television — has demanded new Canadian responses to resist the economic and geographic pressures toward north-south lines of communication that would inevitably be dominated by the much larger American transportation and transmission systems.

Canadian broadcasting legislation and regulation set out frankly and deliberately to prevent this from happening in the realm of radio and television. Although it has been a focal point of controversy, successive Conservative and Liberal governments have strengthened and reinforced this goal of broadcasting legislation.

The current statute, the Broadcasting Act of 1967-68, enunciates the national policy that the Canadian broadcasting system shall be owned and controlled by Canadians so as to safeguard, enrich and strengthen the cultural, political, social and economic fabric of Canada; and it stipulates that all Canadians are entitled to broadcasting services in English and in French as public funds become available. The Act then empowers and directs the CRTC to "regulate and supervise all aspects of Canadian broadcasting with a view to implementing the broadcasting policy" set forth in the legislation.

These principles find specific expression in the CRTC regulations governing Canadian content. At least 30 per cent of the recordings broadcast by Canadian AM radio stations are required to be Canadian, and specific commitments about the use of Canadian material are written into the licences of individual FM stations. Television stations and networks are required to maintain a minimum of 60 per cent Canadian programming in their schedules. Cable television systems are required to give priority to local and regional Canadian television stations in assigning channels to the program services that they distribute. There are also requirements concerning the deletion of commercial announcements from the signals of American stations that cable systems include in their distribution, and in 1976 the CRTC began to bring in regulations aimed at increasing the proportion of Canadian-produced commercial messages carried on Canadian radio and television stations.

Table 2. Broadcasting stations, as of March 31, 1976

Station	Originating station[1]			Rebroadcasters[2]			Total
	English	French	Multi-lingual[3]	English	French	Multi-lingual[3]	
Television	77	25	—	543	96	1	742
FM radio	75	18	9	45	26	1	174
AM radio	279	82	10	247	81	1	700

Source: *CRTC Annual Report 1975-76* (Supply and Services Canada, 1976) Tables 10, 11 and 12.
[1] Originating station: originates, in whole or in part, a daily program schedule.
[2] Rebroadcasting station: rebroadcasts program schedule of another station.
[3] Multilingual: all languages other than English and French.
—Nil or zero.

The Canadian Broadcasting Corporation (CBC)

The CBC is a publicly owned corporation established by the Broadcasting Act to provide the national broadcasting service in Canada. Created in November 1936, it reports to Parliament through the Secretary of State, while responsibility for its policies and programs lies with its own directors and officers. It is financed mainly by public funds voted annually by Parliament; these are supplemented by revenues from commercial advertising — mostly on television, since CBC radio is almost completely non-commercial.

The CBC's head office is in Ottawa. The operational centre for English services is in Toronto, and there are several regional production centres across the country. The operations of the French services are centred in Montreal, with local stations at other points in Quebec and in most other provinces.

The corporation's facilities extend from Atlantic to Pacific and into the Arctic Circle, and include both French and English networks in television, in AM radio and in FM stereo. A special northern radio service broadcasts in English, French, several Indian languages and Inuktitut, the language of the Inuit; northern television is also beginning to introduce some programming in Inuktitut.

In both radio and television, CBC networks are made up of some stations owned and operated by the corporation, which carry the full national service, and some privately owned affiliated stations, which carry an agreed amount of CBC programming. In many small or isolated locations there are relay or rebroadcast transmitters that carry the national service but have no staff or studios to produce local programs. CBC transmission methods include leased channels on the Canadian space satellite Anik.

Radio Canada International, the CBC's overseas shortwave service, broadcasts daily in 11 languages and distributes recorded programs free of charge for use by broadcasters throughout the world. The CBC Armed Forces Service, in co-operation with the Department of National Defence, provides recorded and shortwave radio programs for Canadian military bases abroad. In other international activities, the CBC sells programs to other countries, is a frequent winner of international program awards and belongs to several international broadcasting organizations. The corporation maintains offices in London, Paris; New York and Washington, and news bureaus in Moscow and the Far East.

CBC schedules are varied, reflecting the principles set out in the Broadcasting Act that "the national broadcasting service should be a balanced service of information, enlightenment and entertainment for people of different ages, interests and tastes, covering the whole range of programming in fair proportion." Program content is largely Canadian—about 70 per cent in television and usually more in radio—with a selection of programs from other countries.

CBC gives continuing support to Canadian artists and performers through the broadcast of Canadian music, drama and poetry, the commissioning of special works, the sponsorship of talent competitions and the presentation of Canadian films. It produces a variety of recordings, audiotapes and books from some of its program material.

A production of La Belle Hélène *on the CBC French television show* Les Beaux Dimanches.

King of Kensington, *a popular situation comedy on the CBC English television network.*

Visual Arts

The visual arts in Canada appear to be in a state of vigorous health. A reliable barometer of activity in this area is the quality and quantity of exhibitions in public galleries and museums — and these continued unabated through 1976. The year witnessed the revival of a phenomenon that has become increasingly rare in contemporary museological practice; prompted in part by such special manifestations as the Olympic Games in Montreal and by the United Nations Habitat conference on low-cost indigenous housing in Vancouver, the large-scale survey show was once again in fashion. In Montreal, the Royal Canadian Academy organized Spectrum Canada, a major invitational exhibition coinciding with the Olympic Games and embracing such contemporary means of expression as film, photography and video as well as the more traditional forms of fine art. Following the Games, the Montreal Museum of Fine Arts, which opened in May after an extensive $10 million renovation and expansion, mounted another large-scale national juried exhibition of contemporary Canadian art. A similar form of national pulse-taking was also organized by the Vancouver Art Gallery to coincide with Habitat.

The year witnessed several noteworthy retrospective shows by major Canadian artists. In Ottawa, the National Gallery of Canada mounted a solo exhibition of the work of Guido Molinari, the leader of Montreal's school of Plasticiens. In Toronto, Jack Bush, the 65-year-old dean of Canada's colour-field painters, was also honoured with a major retrospective at the Art Gallery of Ontario. Other senior artists whose work was seen in major travelling shows included Roy Kiyooka (organized by the Vancouver Art Gallery), Graham Coughtry (the Robert McLaughlin Art

Portrait de Louis-Joseph Papineau 1836 by *Antoine Plamondon.*

Gallery in Oshawa, Ont.), and Takao Tanabe (the Norman Mackenzie Art Gallery, in Regina, Sask.). Contemporary Canadian was represented internationally in 1976 when, after having lain dormant for four years, the Venice Biennale was revived; the Canadian pavilion there was devoted to the work of a single Canadian artist, Greg Curnoe, of London, Ont.

Earlier in the year, the Museum of Modern Art in New York organized a select show of the work of Michael Snow, the Toronto artist and film-maker, which included a retrospective of his experimental films. A further significant exposure of Canadian art organized under the auspices of the Department of External Affairs was an exhibition culled from the collection of the Canada Council Art Bank; consisting of the work of Molinari, Paterson Ewen, Gershon Iskowitz, Claude Breeze, John Meredith, Charles Gagnon and Ron Martin, it was destined for an extended international tour to Japan, Australia and Western Europe.

Publishing

Over the past years, and particularly in 1976, Canadian books have found a receptive market across the nation. In fact, the market in Canada for Canadian books has steadily increased and, over a specific period of time in 1976, Canadian books outsold foreign publications on a per-title basis.

The trend for government in 1976 was not to increase its involvement in the industry, but to determine how to use its intervention more effectively and efficiently to the benefit of Canadian publishing houses.

Distribution of the final product always has been and still is seen as a major problem by Canadian publishing houses. Government officials have met a number of times with publishers and distributors to discuss the development of a common national distribution service. This would be supported by government, since it would alleviate the problem of getting Canadian periodicals and paperbacks into outlets in communities where they are now rarely, if ever, accessible.

The government is revising the Canadian Copyright Act, but in the interim relevant sections of the Customs Tariff and the Copyright Act are being enforced to prohibit the importation of foreign editions of Canadian books for which copyright is held in Canada, or of foreign titles for which the licence to reproduce the title in Canada is held by a Canadian publisher. In either case, the Canadian publisher must make application for enforcement and must prove an entitlement to protection as the legal copyright holder or licensee for reproduction purposes.

The government is also reviewing all proposed new entries into the publishing industry in Canada and projected takeovers of Canadian publishing enterprises by foreign interests under the terms of the Foreign Investment Review Act.

In 1976, Parliament passed legislation which amended Section 19 of the Income Tax Act. The effect of this section as it stood had been to accord to certain foreign

A bookstore at Bayshore Shopping Centre, near Ottawa.

Early printing methods in use at the reconstructed Upper Canada Village at Morrisburg, Ont.

magazines the benefit of tax deductions for advertising costs, which was otherwise reserved for Canadian magazines and denied to all other foreign periodicals. Whether the passage of the amended Act has led to a greater viability and economic success for the Canadian periodicals industry is yet to be determined, but this type of action has been successful in the case of the business press in Canada, which has experienced substantial economic improvement since 1965 when it was afforded this type of shelter.

Over the past few years, the French-Canadian periodicals market has remained stable, with readers indicating a preference for weeklies rather than magazines. Although certain French-language-only magazines such as *Nous* have attained some success in Quebec, the subscription and sales figures show that this market has remained steady in 1976, and no growth was in evidence outside the province.

Great anxiety exists about the availability and variety of Canadian textbooks for Canadian schools. The Task Force on Book Publishing is conducting a study of the education market, particularly its economics and market patterns. That part of the study relating to the English language market was completed in 1976; the French language market will be studied in 1977. It is hoped that it will soon become more feasible for Canadian publishing houses to produce Canadian textbooks by Canadian authors to a much greater degree than formerly.

Analysis of the Canadian publishing industry in Canada in 1976 indicated that a light exists at the end of the tunnel. A healthy, viable Canadian publishing industry is certainly possible, given greater co-operative efforts in the industry as a whole, both with the private sector and with government.

Museums and Galleries

During the last decade, Canada has witnessed a dramatic increase in museum activity. Extensive financial support for galleries, museums and museum programs flows from all levels of government, in keeping with growing public interest in the preservation of Canada's natural, historic and artistic heritage. This widespread interest was made clear in a recent and important study, *The Museum and the Canadian Public*, by the Department of the Secretary of State.

Since 1965 the number of museums in Canada has almost doubled, so that there are now over 1,000 in operation. The number of museum workers has also expanded enormously and training programs in museology have proliferated as a result of initiatives taken by major institutions, national and provincial associations, and universities and colleges.

The vast majority of Canada's museums are local community institutions reflecting the history of man and nature in their immediate area, and art galleries responding to the needs of local artists. Above these stand the major institutions of the country: the four national museums in Ottawa, the provincial museums of Alberta and British Columbia, the Art Gallery of Greater Victoria, the Vancouver Art Gallery, the Glenbow–Alberta Institute in Calgary, the Winnipeg Art Gallery and Manitoba Museum of Man and Nature, the Art Gallery of Ontario and the Royal

The Alexander Graham Bell Museum at Baddeck, NS, part of a National Historic Park.

Ontario Museum, and the Montreal Museum of Fine Arts. As a result of the National Museum Policy, 25 of these museums are drawn together as partners in a network of associate museums, and they receive specially allocated federal funds to encourage programs of extension and travelling exhibitions.

A significant contribution to Canada's museum scene has also been made by major outdoor museum complexes, such as the restored and recreated gold rush town of Barkerville in British Columbia, Heritage Park in Calgary, Alberta, Upper Canada Village and Black Creek Village in Ontario, and Kings Landing Historic Settlement in New Brunswick.

An important component of Canada's museum community is the Canadian Museums Association, founded in 1947 to serve the country's institutions and those who work in them. From its head office in Ottawa, with its publications, seminars, conferences and museological resource centre, it promotes professional practice among museum employees and aids communication and the spread of information within Canada's healthy museum community.

National Museums of Canada

In 1968 the National Museums Act incorporated the four national museums under one administration known as the National Museums of Canada, to increase their capacity to serve a greater public. The deliberations of museum directors from across the country early in 1971 led to the announcement in March 1972 of a new National Museum Policy, and the National Museums Corporation was given the responsibility of implementing it.

Basic to this new policy was the concept of the "democratization" and "decentralization" of Canada's cultural heritage. Key features included the establishment of an Associate Museum network of 25 museums, including the National Museums of Canada, in which activities, collections and standards of member museums are raised to the same professional level, and within which exhibits may be exchanged. National Exhibition Centres have been set up in areas not served by museums, and a Museumobile Programme has been established to take specially designed exhibits to areas where, because of inadequate facilities, collections could not previously be exhibited. The National Museums Corporation has embarked on a vigorous publications program to better inform the public of the role of the corporation and the work of the museums.

The National Museum Policy also provides for such essential services as: an Emergency Purchase Fund to buy cultural objects; the Canadian Conservation Institute in Ottawa, with two regional branches and more planned; a computerized National Inventory; and the training of museum professionals.

The National Museum of Natural Sciences. The National Museum of Natural Sciences consists of the divisions of Botany, Invertebrate Zoology, Vertebrate Zoology, Mineral Sciences, Palaeontology, Interpretation and Extension, and the Canadian Oceanographic Identification Centre. The museum is engaged in almost 70 major research projects undertaken by its staff members or associated scientists from universities and other outside organizations, and provides financial assistance, facilities and field work for several National Research Council postdoctoral fellows. Special service units are continuing to serve the identification needs of research, survey and environmental agencies throughout Canada.

Striking examples of the costumes of the Northern Plains Indians, circa 1890.

A major renovation of the Victoria Memorial Museum Building, which is shared by the National Museum of Natural Sciences and the National Museum of Man, is gradually being completed. Audio-visual presentations, visitor-operated displays, drawings and models, as well as thousands of specimens from the museum collections, have been used in the four permanent exhibit halls entitled The Earth, Life Through the Ages, Birds in Canada and Mammals in Canada. A Special Exhibits Hall displays temporary and travelling exhibits from the museum and other sources. Exhibits of Plant Life, Animal Life and Animal Communities are in preparation on the third and fourth floors.

The public lectures, film presentations and special interpretive programs offered by the museum have become increasingly popular with school classes and the general public. Popular publications, a school loans service of educational resource materials and a program of travelling and temporary exhibits make examples of our national heritage more accessible to Canadians across the country.

The National Museum of Man. The National Museum of Man collects, preserves, interprets and displays artifacts and data of the cultural and historical heritage of Canada's varied population.

For this work the museum is organized in the six divisions listed below.

The Archaeological Survey of Canada conducts archaeological rescue excavations on sites about to be destroyed or damaged by development.

The Canadian Centre for Folk Culture Studies has the country's largest archive of folk culture materials, which represents some 40 ethnic and cultural groups.

The Canadian Ethnology Service conducts comprehensive research on native and Métis cultures. Its Urgent Ethnology Programme is expanding yearly to study as many of the rapidly changing and disappearing cultures as possible.

The Canadian War Museum is concerned with research, exhibits and publications in military history, and houses an extensive collection of memorabilia ranging from military art to tanks.

The Communications Division plans and co-ordinates the museum's exhibition and education programs. The division provides a wide range of school loans, including the multi-media "Museum Kits", publishes educational materials and provides interpretive tours of the museum for school groups, while travelling exhibitions bring the treasures of Canada's heritage to people from coast to coast.

The History Division carries out studies of Canadian society and material culture since the beginning of European colonization. These studies are currently being published in a series of booklets and accompanying slide packages entitled "Canada's Visual History". Another program, a policy of saving packages from consumer products and everyday objects on today's market, will ensure the museum of their availability years from now.

The museum has nine stimulating exhibit halls in the Victoria Memorial Museum building, in addition to those in the Canadian War Museum building. They include: "Immense Journey", an orientation gallery; "Canada Before Cartier", the story of prehistoric Canada; "The Inuit", the people of the North; "People of the Longhouse", a portrait of the Iroquois; "The Buffalo Hunters", a study of the Plains Indians; and "Children of the Raven", the life of the Northwest Coast Indians. Two more permanent halls — origins and development of folk culture, and Canadian history — are near completion. A temporary exhibit hall houses the museum's travelling exhibitions and shows from other institutions.

The National Gallery of Canada. The function of the National Gallery since its incorporation in 1913 has been to encourage public interest in the arts and to promote the interests of art throughout the country. Under this mandate, the gallery has increased its collections and developed into an art institution worthy of international recognition.

The gallery's planning for the future emphasizes promoting the understanding of works of art. Another aspect of future planning came closer to realization in 1975 with the launching of the first stage of a two-part architectural competition for the design of a new National Gallery building.

There are more than 18,000 works of art in the gallery. The collections have been built up along international lines, and give the people of Canada an indication of the origins of their traditions. The collection of Canadian art, the most extensive and important in existence, is continually being augmented; over 60 per cent of all new acquisitions since 1966 have been Canadian. There are many Old Masters, as well as a growing collection of contemporary art, prints and drawings and diploma works of the Royal Canadian Academy.

Visitors to the gallery are offered an active program of exhibitions, lectures, films and guided tours. The gallery's reference library, which contains more than 46,000 volumes and periodicals on the history of art and other related subjects, is also open to the public.

The interests of the country as a whole are served by circulating exhibitions, lecture tours, publications, reproductions and films prepared by the National Gallery staff. The gallery promotes interest in Canadian art abroad by participating in international exhibitions and by preparing major exhibitions of Canadian art for

A female cougar and two cubs mounted in a life-like display in the National Museum of Natural Sciences.

showing in other countries. It also brings important exhibitions from abroad to be shown in Canada.

Major exhibitions at the National Gallery during 1975-76 included "High Victorian Design", "Donald Judd", "Photographs from the Collection", "The Calvary at Oka", "Seven Paintings by James B. Spencer", "Some Canadian Women Artists", "Recent Acquisitions of European Prints", and "El Dorado: The Gold of Ancient Colombia". The Gallery's National Programme organized and circulated 21 exhibitions, including 12 new ones, throughout Canada and abroad to 64 bookings in 31 cities.

The National Museum of Science and Technology. The National Museum of Science and Technology, the newest of the four National Museums, challenges over three quarters of a million visitors a year to climb, push, pull or just view its definitive collections. An additional quarter of a million annually visit the National Aeronautical Collection at Rockcliffe Airport.

The exhibit halls contain displays of ship models, clocks, communications equipment, old and new agriculture machinery, and aviation history. There are numerous examples of milestones in Canada's history of ground transportation, from sleighs and carriages to locomotives and horseless carriages, and the Physics Hall, with its skill-testing experiments and "seeing puzzles", delights young and old alike.

In the National Aeronautical Collection more than 90 aircraft illustrate the progress of aviation from primitive to present times and the importance of the flying machine in the discovery and development of Canada. Its collection of aircraft engines is one of the world's largest.

Educational programs on general or topic-oriented subject matter for all age groups are developed and conducted by a staff of tour guides. During the summer months a steam train makes a return trip from Ottawa to Wakefield, Quebec, giving everyone a taste of a bygone era.

The museum's newly opened observatory houses Canada's largest refracting telescope, which is used for evening educational programs. Resource material is available from a 10,000-volume library that places special emphasis on a retrospective collection relating to Canadian aviation.

The museum also designs and builds exhibits that are sent on tour throughout Canada, and artifacts are exchanged with museums in Canada and abroad.

Libraries and Archives

Libraries

Libraries have existed in Canada since the early 18th century. Legal, theological, university and society libraries were in existence before 1850; after 1850 business and industrial libraries appeared, along with tax-supported public libraries. The period of greatest growth for all types of libraries has been in the years since World War II.

Because Canada is a federal state and libraries fall under provincial jurisdiction, there is no unified national library system. The public library systems of the provinces, though varying in detail, are alike in being supported by local and provincial funds (except for the Yukon Territory and the Northwest Territories, which are federally funded) and co-ordinated by a central library agency.

Public libraries feel they have a responsibility to be community resource centres open to all, in addition to being sources of print and non-print materials for the pleasure, information, or education of their users. This belief has led to the libraries' greater involvement in providing information on community organization, services and facilities, etc. Along with this greater involvement has come a growing trend toward taking the public library to those who cannot or do not come to it; senior citizens, shut-ins, prisoners, and the physically and economically handicapped use special materials, services and facilities provided by public libraries. People whose mother tongue is neither English nor French find that many libraries now provide foreign-language materials, often with the assistance of the Multilingual Biblioservice of the National Library, which assembles collections of books in selected languages and lends them to provincial libraries for circulation throughout their areas.

There are perhaps 10,000 school libraries in Canada now, as distinct from unorganized classroom collections. The emphasis in this type of library has shifted from the use of printed materials alone to use of a wider range of information sources, such as films, recordings, tapes, slides and kits. As a result, school libraries are becoming multi-media "resource centres".

College and university libraries went through a period of very rapid expansion in the 1960s and early 1970s, but growth is now slowing down. These libraries have been very active in applying automated techniques to library procedures in order to enable them to handle their rapidly increasing work-loads efficiently. They have also sought ways to co-operate in automation, in collection rationalization and in sharing resources. In these efforts they have had support from the National Library, which has conducted or sponsored a number of studies of particular relevance to academic libraries — studies of library collections (e.g., of law materials and government documents), of inter-library loans and of automated systems suitable for library use or for the development of bibliographic networks.

Special libraries — those serving companies, associations, institutions such as museums and hospitals, and government departments and agencies—now number about 1,000. Among them, the government libraries tend to be the largest, especially the provincial legislative libraries. Quebec also has the Bibliothèque nationale du Québec. Some federal government libraries are de facto resource

The library towers over the University of Calgary campus.

libraries in their subject fields for the whole of the country, but in general special libraries serve only authorized users from their sponsoring organizations.

At the national level, the scientific resource library for Canada has been the National Science Library, which is now combined with the National Research Council's Technical Information Service to form the Canada Institute for Scientific and Technical Information (CISTI). CISTI's services to the scientific research and industrial communities include, in addition to its back-up serials and monograph collection, a computer-based selective dissemination of information (SDI) service, a companion on-line search service (CAN/OLE) and publication of a union list of scientific serials held in Canada.

The National Library of Canada, which specializes in the social sciences and humanities and in Canadiana of all kinds, discharges many national responsibilities. In accordance with the National Library Act of 1969, it administers the legal deposit regulations, publishes the national bibliography, *Canadiana,* and maintains union catalogues from which libraries and researchers can find out where in Canada specific works are held. It also assigns International Standard Book Numbers (ISBN) for Canadian publishers. It provides the SDI service for the humanities and social sciences, and makes one-time, on-line searches of a number of data bases available to libraries and individuals for a minimal fee. It has taken a leading part in plans for network co-ordination on a national scale, particularly national bibliographic networks.

In Canada, librarians are trained at the universities. Seven postgraduate schools offer master's degrees in library science, and two, at the universities of Toronto and

The North York Public Library, Toronto, Ont.

Western Ontario, also offer doctoral programs. In addition, post-secondary courses for the training of library technicians are available in community colleges in many parts of the country.

Archives

The increasing popular interest in history has had an important influence on archives in Canada. Numbers of users have increased and the nature of the clientele has changed. Academic historians now comprise less than 50 per cent of the users of archives. In the last five years the per capita expenditure on archives has doubled.

Expansion has been accompanied by significant developments in professional associations. Regional associations have been formed in the Atlantic, Toronto, Prairie and Pacific regions, the Association des archivistes du Québec has several hundred members and an independent Association of Canadian Archivists has replaced the former Archives Section of the Canadian Historical Association. Co-operation between archives and archivists is also promoted by such national projects as the Public Archives of Canada diffusion program, the Union List of Manuscripts in Canadian Repositories, a new computer-produced edition of which has been published recently, and a union list of maps.

Records management continues to be a matter of major concern to national, provincial, city and university archives. In both records management and archives, considerable attention is given to such media as microforms and machine readable records. The Public Archives of Canada has established a National Film Archives and a Machine Readable Records Division.

International relations in the archives field are becoming more important. In 1974, Canada was host to the International Round Table on Archives and the Archives Section of the Pan-American Institute of Geography and History. Agreements for the exchange of archivists were reached with the USSR and Australia, and staff members of foreign archives come to Canada for training in archives administration, records management, micro-technology and conservation.

Cultural Exchanges

A world phenomenon since World War II has been the manner in which culture has assumed a major role in the conduct of relations between countries. The "cultural explosion" Canada has experienced in the same period has enabled us to become a significant participant in the international cultural scene. The development of Canadian cultural relations with other countries is entrusted to the Secretary of State for External Affairs.

The history of formal External Affairs involvement in cultural matters dates only from the early 1960s. Informal cultural exchanges had been effected previously through various Commonwealth organizations and other international institutions. Similar links had been forged with the French-speaking world abroad. The government has now established formal cultural exchange arrangements with a number of countries, notably those from whom significant proportions of the Canadian population were descended, and now allocates a substantial budget annually to cultural exchanges.

The objectives of this expansion of Canadian cultural relations include the desire to reflect on the world scene the growing creativity and accomplishment of Canadians, and to increase the number of opportunities for members of the Canadian artistic and academic community to perform or teach abroad. Exchanges are also designed to support foreign policy objectives.

Cultural projection abroad may conveniently be divided into two types of programs: one involving the exchange of persons and the other concerned with artistic dissemination.

Programs involving the exchange of persons have, among other objectives, the goals of: bringing leaders in the Canadian artistic and academic communities into contact with persons in similar fields in foreign countries; creating bonds of understanding and channels of academic and scientific co-operation that can help avoid duplication in research, while allowing the most productive use of international experience; and encouraging the development of creative talent and leadership in the Canadian artistic and academic community by offering broader and more challenging international opportunities.

Academic exchanges include programs of university scholarships, inter-faculty exchanges and support of Canadian participation in international conferences. In addition, other programs make provision for exchanges of non-academic delegations of Canadian experts or professionals in socio-cultural fields such as architecture, urban studies, environment and public service, and for youth exchanges of young technicians and summer workers. Other cultural exchanges bring foreign artists and critics to Canada for working visits and assist Canadian authors, composers and artists invited to work or perform abroad.

A large part of the cultural relations budget of the Department of External Affairs is devoted to artistic dissemination—the support of travelling art exhibitions, film weeks and performance tours which illustrate Canada's achievements in the arts. Programs in this field include support of Canadian participation in international cultural festivals, gifts of books to foreign universities and research centres, and reciprocal literary prizes. Over the past several years the department has sponsored tours by the National Arts Centre Orchestra, the Toronto Symphony, the Montreal Symphony and the Vancouver Symphony, and all the major ballet companies have been supported in foreign tours. Small ensembles of folk, popular and country music artists, dancers, classical musicians and actors have been sent around the world. Major exhibitions of contemporary art have toured extensively, including collections of the Group of Seven sent to Russia and Canadian landscape paintings seen in China; works from the Art Bank of the Canada Council have toured throughout the US and Europe. For the US Bicentennial Year the department sponsored a number of special events; one of the major activities was a festival of Canadian Performing Arts held at the Kennedy Center in Washington.

The Department of External Affairs also has a rapidly expanding program to promote the teaching of Canadian subjects in universities and institutions abroad, in the expectation that students who profit from these courses will go on to reach positions of influence in government, business, journalism and the academic community of their countries, where their understanding of and sympathy for Canadian aspirations and points of view will profit Canada. For some years, External Affairs has assisted the Association for Canadian Studies in the US and has seen a steady increase in the number of Canadian subjects taught in US universities. A similar program exists in the United Kingdom where, in October 1975, the Secretary of State for External Affairs inaugurated a chair and centre for Canadian Studies at Edinburgh University. An Association of Canadian Studies in France was established at a Canadian Studies Conference held in Bordeaux in March 1976. Direct support for Canadian Studies programs is under way or planned for France, Belgium, Germany, Italy and Japan.

Rug hooking at Upper Canada Village, Morrisburg, Ont.

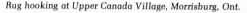

Governments and Cultural Policy

Private and Public Responsibilities

All Canadians live their cultures, but very few of them discuss the subject very much. When they do, they usually regard culture primarily as a personal affair. While certain kinds of government support are welcome, any attempt by any government to determine the substance of cultural life would be inconsistent with Canadian values.

Nevertheless, members of the public demand certain kinds of cultural services from their governments. There seems to be increasing public interest in cultural expressions that illuminate the reality of Canada and Canadians. The problems are complicated by the cultural diversity of the population, the decentralization of public authority and the openness of Canada to cultural currents from Europe, the United States and other parts of the world. The resources available from the market and from private patronage, while important, are inadequate to the task; it is recognized that public authorities must also play a part.

Thus cultural policies in Canada are characterized by a search for acceptable ways in which governments may support cultural development and the production and enjoyment of the arts, without imposing official values, control or censorship.

Governments as Proprietors

By historical accident or considered decision, governments own a great deal of property of cultural importance to Canadians. Holdings range from national monuments like the Parliament Buildings, to the most representative collections of Canadian painting, to the records of obscure 19th century parish priests. From this role as proprietor have emerged important institutions like the provincial and federal archives, historic sites and monuments services, and important art galleries and museums operated at all three levels of government. In short, governments are the predominant collectors and exhibitors in the country.

The responsibilities of proprietorship have been recognized in a number of ways. Collections have been steadily expanded and diversified. Facilities are being improved and interpretation services strengthened so that public holdings may be more readily available and meaningful to the public.

In building construction, governments at all three levels have been prepared to give some weight to aesthetic as well as functional considerations. This extends beyond architectural design to include the use of works of art both in exterior landscaping and in furnishing. Recently there has been a new interest in renovating heritage buildings, either for their historic purposes as was the Kingston City Hall, or for new uses such as government office space.

As proprietors, governments have also been prepared to construct and operate physical facilities for exhibition and performance. Over the past 15 years, there has been quite remarkable progress in building theatres and concert halls. Virtually all the major urban areas, and many smaller centres as well, are now reasonably adequately equipped.

It is striking that investment in cultural goods and facilities for the enjoyment of the public is not limited to any single level of government. One finds libraries,

Fine food from the restaurant of the National Arts Centre, displayed on one of the centre's terraces.

concert halls, art collections and heritage buildings owned and made available by municipalities, as well as by the provincial and federal authorities. Numerous co-operative arrangements have developed between governments to strengthen the services offered and to assist with financing, especially of capital costs. Federal grants to provincial governments and municipalities have been important, especially in building facilities for exhibition and the performing arts; provincial grants to municipalities are essential for the construction and operation of public libraries, cultural centres and many programs offered at the local level. In some provinces, very substantial lottery revenues are allocated to municipal capital expenditure on cultural and recreational facilities.

Underwriting Creativity

Apart from purchasing some of their work for collections or other public purposes, governments took it for granted until the middle of this century that creative people would make it on their own. No substantial expenditures were regularly devoted to the support of people rather than the purchase of product.

The report of the Massey-Lévesque Commission in 1949 marked the turning point, when it became apparent that flourishing cultural life in Canada simply could not be sustained by market revenues, private benevolence and artists living in poverty. Since that time governments have recognized, albeit hesitantly, that it is appropriate for some public funds to underwrite painters, dancers, musicians and other artists, and the companies within which some of them work. Even now, very few professional artists approach income levels regarded as normal in other professions, but the current level of creative expression in Canada is in some measure a reflection of government support.

Several techniques are used to channel public funds to artists in a rational way, without constraining or attempting to control the direction of their work. A number of arts councils have been established separate from the normal government structure. The Canada Council, which is the chosen instrument of the federal government, is a statutory foundation, or public trust, that is expected and required to make its own decisions without direction from any authority apart from its legislation. Several provincial governments use this pattern, with modifications to meet regional requirements.

The arts councils, in turn, are guided by advice from the creative community itself, and typically rely on recognized practising professionals in a given discipline to advise on the best distribution of the available funds. There are seldom enough funds to meet the need and very hard choices must be made; the system is designed to identify excellence as objectively as possible.

Governments as Educators

In a broad sense, all education policy is cultural policy. The schools are the most important cultural institutions of Canadian society. Education is a provincial responsibility administered largely at the municipal level; the subject is accordingly diverse, complex and locally oriented, and the paragraphs that follow can suggest only a few general characteristics.

School programs in Canada have always recognized the importance of the arts as an element in general education. Schools have been teaching literature for as long

School choirs can develop an appreciation of music that lasts a lifetime.

as there have been schools; in many jurisdictions, the current tendency is to increase the stress on contemporary works, particularly on Canadian writing. Music is also well established in almost all jurisdictions, and many schools offer programs in the visual arts.

Recently there appears to have been increasing concern, reflected both in policy and in student interest, with theatre arts, television and films. Television has appeared both as a teaching aid and as a subject of study, and there have been many interesting and rewarding innovations in the use of video technology by students as an additional medium of cultural expression.

In co-operation with school boards, and often with the financial support of other levels of government, many performing arts companies mount presentations to school audiences and associate student companies with their principal endeavours. In addition, many professional companies and community groups offer weekend theatre for young audiences.

Governments as Regulators

Following public opinion, governments have generally avoided any conscious interference with the arts and the cultural life of the community, treating artists and cultural organizations like ordinary private or corporate citizens. Nevertheless, significant regulatory policies have been established in a few defined areas. Space permits only two or three examples.

Governments provide the legal context for artistic production (through legislation respecting copyright and other property rights, for example), and tax policy is designed to favour the arts and other cultural activities by providing tax exemptions for private donations to arts organizations. Sometimes they have also been prepared to intervene to compensate for the economic disadvantage Canadian producers suffer beside foreign competition that can achieve very low unit costs through access to large international markets.

Many provincial and municipal governments have recently shown active interest in legislation designed to protect privately owned heritage buildings and neighbourhoods from demolition or intensive modification. Here again, regulatory policies are often coupled with incentives to encourage the restoration and reanimation of the cultural legacy received from earlier generations.

Governments as Producers

Apart from a few special cases like the National Arts Centre Orchestra, governments have preferred not to assume managerial responsibility, even indirectly, for artistic performance or the production of cultural works; the work of the artist or company, although often intended for the public, is in the private sector. Where government presence exists, it is intended to be unobtrusive, supportive and neutral.

One striking exception to the foregoing is radio and television broadcasting, where the limitations of the technology, the economics of the industry and the character and scale of the country have dictated a mixed public and private system. However, even in the public sector, governments have chosen to operate through

In 1975 the CBC English network produced a documentary special on the life of Emily Carr.

statutory corporations in order to preserve official detachment from program content, and both public and private sectors are regulated by a separate commission which has no operational responsibilities.

As cultural institutions, the broadcasting enterprises are second in importance only to the schools, and indeed some people would rank them first. One could scarcely over-estimate the cultural significance of the radio and television networks of the government-owned CBC, which now serve almost all of Canada in both English and French. At the same time, an important recent development in public sector broadcasting has been the establishment of some provincial educational television services; these are normally operated through statutory corporations, and complement the CBC and private services with programming designed for school use, for pre-school children and for adult learners.

In conclusion, the cultural policies of Canadian governments are probably a rough reflection of the cultural characteristics, aspirations and priorities of the Canadian population. Since the population is diverse, dispersed and pluralistic, the policies are equally diverse and sometimes perhaps even contradictory. Like the country itself, cultural policy is a mosaic rather than a melting-pot.

Education

The beginnings of the post-industrial society are upon us. As Daniel Bell and others have suggested, the creation of a service economy and the pre-eminence of professional and technical occupations characterize the structure of a post-industrial society.[1] Thus the problem of producing the required professional and technical manpower is one that education must face.

A second major problem of modern-day education lies in the area of learning. If one stops to consider that children today leave elementary school with what is, in many ways, more knowledge than the greatest philosophers of ancient times accumulated, then the problem is evident. The extremely high input of data and basic information in today's society has created a need for new methods of instruction. Attempts to arrive at a solution are hampered by the fact that western society values individualism, which creates a demand for greater flexibility in teaching methods.

To solve these problems, an important step has been taken in Canada through the development of an array of educational structures at the tertiary, or post-secondary, level. Further steps include those at the elementary and secondary levels, where programs are being structured around such innovations as non-graded systems, promotion by subject and the elimination of departmental examinations, with an emphasis on continuous evaluation. New teaching methods include the use of educational aids such as closed circuit and educational television, tape recorders and overhead projectors to facilitate and enrich the learning process of individual students.

At the same time, there has been a concomitant need for an increase in professionalism of the teaching staff at all educational levels. In part, this has resulted in a shift of teacher-training programs to universities, with an accompanying decrease in numbers of teachers' colleges in Canada.

Educational Jurisdictions

Under the British North America Act, Section 93, the provinces are generally responsible for education, except for federally-sponsored schools for Indian and Inuit students, for children of servicemen in Europe and for inmates of federal penitentiaries. In addition the federal government helps finance tertiary education in the provinces, participates in informal education and makes grants for research personnel and equipment.

Provincial autonomy has resulted in the development of distinctive educational systems in the various provinces. There are, however, certain similarities. Each province and territory has established a department of education, headed by a minister who is a member of the Cabinet and administered by a deputy minister who, as a public servant, advises the minister and administers legislation relating to education. Each department of education is engaged in supervising the quality of

[1]Daniel Bell. "Notes on the Post-Industrial Society," *The Public Interest* (Winter 1967 and Spring 1968).

An Inuit teacher instructs a kindergarten class at Repulse Bay, NWT.

educational systems, certifying teachers, providing financial assistance to school boards and determining courses of study and lists of textbooks.

In some provinces the original department of education has been changed, to create a second government department dealing exclusively with post-secondary education; provinces with two departments concerned with education are Alberta, Manitoba, Ontario and Saskatchewan, while Quebec has established two directorates within its department of education, one concerned with universities and the other with colleges.

Elementary and Secondary Education

Administration

The provinces have delegated considerable responsibility for operating publicly controlled elementary and secondary schools to locally-elected or appointed school boards whose authority is determined by legislation. These boards are responsible for building and maintaining schools, hiring teachers and preparing budgets. With decreases in the degree of centralization in most provinces, local authorities exercise greater control in setting year-end examinations in the final year or years of secondary school and in determining the curriculum and textbooks to be studied.

A most important change in the last decade has been the restructuring of local education administrations through the creation of larger school districts operating larger schools. Enlarged administrative units ensure that all areas in a province have similar levels of education, and larger schools, being more solvent, are in a better position to provide the necessary teaching and administrative personnel and up-to-date educational equipment.

Following the recommendations made by the Royal Commission on Education and Youth in 1964, school districts have been consolidated in Newfoundland. The 300-odd denominational boards were reduced to 35 districts — 12 Roman Catholic school districts, 21 integrated Protestant boards and one each for the Pentecostal and Seventh Day Adventist denominations. In Prince Edward Island some 300 local units have been integrated into five regional boards. The trend in Nova Scotia is also toward the consolidation of small educational units, and New Brunswick has replaced its 422 school districts with 33 enlarged districts.

In Quebec, legislation enacted in 1961 created large units of administration for secondary school education. The number of elementary school boards was reduced from 1,100 in 1972 to 175 in 1975.

As a result of legislation in the late 1960s, significant administrative reorganization occurred in Ontario. Thousands of small units, administered by three-member boards of trustees, were replaced by enlarged county boards of education integrating elementary and secondary school operations. Large cities have been exempted from this reorganization and are allowed to administer their own school systems. Most Roman Catholic school administrations have been integrated within these county boards, although separate schools have the option of whether or not to join. In 1975 there were 92 school boards for the elementary schools, including 58 Roman Catholic and two Protestant separate school boards.

In all four western provinces districts have been consolidated. In fact, Alberta and British Columbia were the precursors of this trend toward amalgamation. Since 1937, the school districts' authority in Alberta has to a large extent been assumed by enlarged school divisions (aggregations of designated school districts) and counties are gradually superseding divisional organizations. In the mid-1940s, British

The Nakasuk Elementary School at Frobisher Bay, NWT, was built to an experimental design for large buildings in the Arctic.

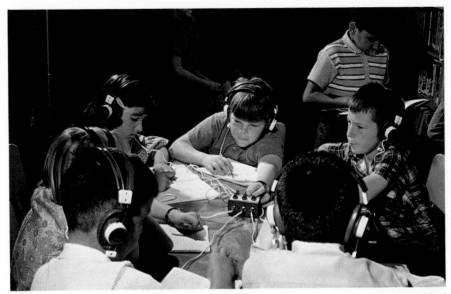

The extremely high input of data and information in today's society has created a need for new methods of instruction.

Columbia reduced the number of school districts from 650 to 74 large administrative districts. In the 1960s school administration in Manitoba was reorganized. In Saskatchewan, recommendations regarding implementation of consolidated school districts are being considered.

School Organization

Kindergarten classes are offered in all but two provinces, Prince Edward Island and New Brunswick. The other provinces provide this education to five-year-olds in the publicly controlled school system. However, it should be noted that these services are found predominantly in the larger urban centres. Throughout Canada there are increasing numbers of nursery schools and kindergartens for children from three to five years of age that are privately operated.

The traditional organization of elementary and secondary schools has been grades 1 to 8 in elementary and 9 to 12 in secondary. Modifications on this particular arrangement have come through the introduction of junior high schools. Junior highs have developed in all provinces except Newfoundland, Quebec and Saskatchewan, and generally include grades 7, 8 and 9, with senior high schools providing grades 10, 11 and 12 (and 13 in Ontario).

Most secondary schools offer technical and commercial subjects as options in the academic curriculum. Vocational, technical and commercial secondary schools, at one time located only in large cities, are now an integral part of the whole school system in many provinces. An increasing number of composite schools offer optional programs in academic or technical subjects, such as agriculture, home economics and commerce, allowing more flexibility for individual interests and capabilities.

A key change in the last few years has been the increasing tendency toward non-graded or continuous-progress school organizations, which allow students to advance at their own rate. Many provinces are in the process of developing innovative approaches in handling non-graded school systems.

The Atlantic provinces are accelerating the development of a school organization emphasizing promotion by subject rather than by grade, using a "credit" system. Nova Scotia has in addition introduced a program allowing secondary school students with high academic standing to carry one or more extra courses.

In Quebec, programs with graduated options and promotion by subject are increasingly emphasized.

Ontario is also proceeding with a "credit" system. In the secondary schools, implementation of this policy is leading to increasingly flexible individual program scheduling, optional diversified courses and promotion by subject.

The western provinces are also encouraging a less rigid classification by grade. In Saskatchewan the traditional 12 grades have been replaced by four divisions, each consisting of three years of school for a student making normal progress. In Divisions I and II, the principle of non-grading with continuous evaluation and flexible promotion has been adopted; Division III programs have been designed to accommodate the special problems of the young adolescent. The newly developed programs stress more flexibility, which makes allowance for individual differences. Students are encouraged to discover facts and think for themselves; at the core of these divisions is the belief that students should develop values, skills and ideas or concepts, rather than learn by rote.

Since 1969, Nova Scotia has made provision for individuals with incomplete formal high school education to obtain secondary school accreditation by passing a series of tests prepared by the Commission of Accreditation of the American Council on Education. Similarly, Alberta now allows adults who have upgraded their education through informal learning and adult education courses to obtain a secondary school diploma.

The trend toward giving French-language instruction in the elementary grades of publicly controlled schools has accelerated in many provinces. In addition, recent legislation in Ontario allows French-speaking students to receive their entire elementary and secondary education in French. Similarly, in 1970 Manitoba passed legislation which allows schools to teach in French; this same legislation also provides for the instruction of students in other languages at the elementary and secondary levels.

Education systems in the Northwest Territories and the Yukon Territory are geared primarily to fulfilling the needs of the local population, chiefly the Inuit, Indian and Métis living in isolated settlements. In the Northwest Territories, responsibility for education was moved from the federal Department of Indian and Northern Affairs to the new Territorial Department of Education. The official transfer occurred in the Mackenzie District in April 1969 and in the Franklin and Keewatin districts in April 1970. The Territorial Department of Education is continuing the progress made by the federal government in providing a far-flung, modern and solidly based school system, and it has begun constructing numerous new schools and developing new curricular materials relating to the cultural

Introducing live quail to the classroom brings studies of nature alive.

backgrounds of the students. Apart from that, the schools in the Northwest Territories have chosen to follow the programs of Alberta and Manitoba.

The majority of schools in the Yukon Territory have always been classified as public and have been administered directly by the Yukon Department of Education in Whitehorse. The Yukon Territory has chosen to follow the British Columbia school curriculum, although the program is adapted to incorporate material relevant to the heritage of the native peoples.

The fact that the Northwest Territories and the Yukon Territory are facing the challenge of preparing their students to compete in contemporary Canadian society is clear, as more children are enrolled in school and more are staying in school longer and completing grade 12.

Enrolment

Enrolment of students at the elementary and secondary levels in public schools in the 1950s and 1960s showed a fairly rapid increase because of the high postwar birth rate in Canada. At the elementary level, a decrease in enrolment was first noticed in 1971-72, and the decline is now starting to affect secondary school enrolment. The downward trend is expected to prolong itself in future years because of a continuing decline in the birth rate since the mid-1960s.

102 CANADA 1977

Enrolment in the public elementary and secondary school system declined from a total of 5,418,854 in 1974-75 to an estimated 5,335,140 in 1975-76, a decrease of 1.5 per cent. Quebec continued to lead this trend, with a decrease of 5.9 per cent in its total enrolment.

At the pre-elementary level, the enrolment in 1975-76 shows an increase of 3.6 per cent over last year, apparently because of the addition of more facilities. Throughout Canada the total elementary enrolment is estimated to have declined 4.6 per cent from 1974-75 to 1975-76; Quebec showed the most dramatic decrease, 6.5 per cent. It is estimated that total enrolment at the secondary level should decrease by 1.2 per cent, mainly as a result of the sharp drop of 8.1 per cent expected for Quebec, as the other provinces do not yet show a tendency to decline.

Table 1. Public elementary and secondary school enrolment[1], 1974-75 and 1975-76

Province or territory	Year	Pre-elementary	Elementary[2]	Secondary[2]	Special classes	Total
Newfoundland	1974-75	12,512	81,058	59,030	5,414	158,014
	1975-76	12,322	80,180	59,610	5,656	157,768
Prince Edward Island	1974-75	—	14,962	13,014	173	28,149
	1975-76	—	14,384	13,335	131	27,850
Nova Scotia	1974-75	14,307	97,085	89,756	3,132	204,280
	1975-76	14,583	93,520	91,448	3,055	202,606
New Brunswick	1974-75	—	84,677	80,878	995	166,550
	1975-76	—	82,682	81,325	992	164,999
Quebec[3]	1974-75	92,554	639,481	608,989	82,461	1,422,485
	1975-76	92,160	597,816	559,366	89,335	1,338,677
Ontario	1974-75	170,441	885,564[4]	938,484	—	1,994,489
	1975-76	176,122	837,815	947,302	33,399	1,994,638
Manitoba	1974-75	15,983	106,334	102,607	4,628	229,552
	1975-76	17,014	103,090	103,219	4,804	228,127
Saskatchewan	1974-75	11,465	105,050	103,937	3,724	224,176
	1975-76	13,160	100,912	103,576	3,325	220,973
Alberta	1974-75	14,423	205,316	207,155	5,283	432,177
	1975-76	17,831	202,596	212,575	6,352	439,354
British Columbia	1974-75	35,470	241,669	257,814	6,622	541,575
	1975-76	37,066	235,773	259,461	10,377	542,677
Yukon Territory	1974-75	—	2,713	2,142	48	4,903
	1975-76	—	2,731	2,183	61	4,975
Northwest Territories	1974-75	688	7,663	4,153	—	12,504
	1975-76	691	7,685	4,120	—	12,496
Canada[3]	1974-75	367,843	2,471,572	2,467,959	111,480	5,418,854
	1975-76	380,949	2,359,184	2,437,520	157,487	5,335,140

[1] Includes separate schools. Excludes enrolment of private schools (213,500 in 1974-75), of schools operated by the federal departments of Indian and Northern Affairs (32,800) and National Defence (4,600 overseas) and of schools for the blind and the deaf (3,884).
[2] Elementary is defined as grades 1 to 6 and secondary as grades 7 to 13.
[3] Data for Quebec are preliminary, hence also the total for Canada.
[4] Includes special education, grades 1 to 8.
—Nil or zero.

Teachers

The number of teachers in the public elementary and secondary schools did not change significantly over the last two years, a decrease of only 0.3 per cent being expected.

Vocational and Technical Education

In the last decade there has been a rapid development of vocational and technical education in Canada. For the purposes of this article, vocational education includes all training (the great majority of cases not requiring a complete high school education for entrance) for occupations requiring varying degrees of skill, normally taking less than one year to acquire, and in the performance of which greater emphasis is placed on manipulative skills and predetermined procedures than on the application of ideas and principles.

Vocational training is available in publicly operated trade schools and similar institutions, in private trade schools and business colleges, in provincially registered apprenticeship programs, in publicly supported training-in-industry programs for employees and in on-the-job training programs introduced as a measure to offset unemployment. Institutions similar to public (provincially operated) trade schools include adult vocational centres, trade divisions of community colleges, and schools for specific occupations such as nursing aid schools, forestry schools, and police and firefighter training establishments. Not included in this discussion are vocational and composite high schools; while in some provinces the courses offered in these secondary schools continue to provide training leading to employment, changing aims and school organization have made the distinction between academic and vocational students less and less recognizable.

In instances where applicants do not have the required academic background to proceed with vocational training, there are upgrading courses to bring trainees to the required educational level. Many vocational centres also offer language training for those who do not have the proficiency in either English or French to receive instruction in a vocational course. Short "orientation" courses that guide trainees into the proper skill areas and help them brush up prerequisite skills are also made available.

Adult Continuing Education

There is a wide array of educational opportunities for adults in Canada today. Many school boards, trade schools and adult vocational centres, institutes of technology, community colleges and universities offer courses during the day or evening. The provincial departments of education provide home study courses and educational television programs, while other government departments provide a variety of extension services. Non-profit organizations also offer community interest courses, and many professional associations encourage their members to participate in professional development or special certificate courses which they sponsor.

The range and availability of courses has had its impact on participation. Enrolments in programs conducted by public educational institutions increased by approximately 165 per cent from 1960-61 to 1970-71. In 1974-75, approximately 1.5

million adults enrolled in courses to complete formal studies, to upgrade vocational skills or to develop new hobbies and interests.

Tertiary Education

The past decade has witnessed an extraordinary increase in enrolment in the tertiary level of education, an increase which has surpassed the elementary-secondary rate of growth during the same period. This educational level has two main sectors: the non-degree-granting institutions, encompassing community colleges and other related institutions, teachers' colleges and diploma schools of nursing; and degree-granting institutions, including universities and affiliated colleges. Over the decade the increase in enrolments was especially marked in the universities and community colleges, although at present there is a shortfall in enrolment in the former.

Several factors contributed to this continuing significant growth. The main ones are the higher retention rates in secondary schools and the high birth rates in the postwar years, which resulted in increases in enrolments at the elementary-secondary level and culminated in a rise in numbers at the tertiary level. Other factors are the growing diversification of types of post-secondary institutions and programs that cater to individual interests and abilities, and the supposition that education beyond the secondary level is a path to increased social mobility.

Community Colleges and Related Institutions

Community colleges have developed to meet the need for various types of programs for students seeking post-secondary education in other than the university sector. Enrolments in these institutions are rapidly increasing because of the community colleges' flexible open-door policies. Further, the need for semi-professional personnel in a system that is rapidly moving toward a service economy has recently stimulated increased enrolments.

Most colleges are provincially supported and exercise various degrees of autonomy. High school graduation is a prerequisite for entrance to post-secondary programs, but where this is lacking many colleges provide a qualifying year. In addition, or alternatively, some institutions permit older applicants without the necessary qualifications to attend classes as "mature" students.

Although community colleges are not degree-granting institutions, some do offer the junior years of a university program, from which graduates may apply for admission to the senior years at a university. Principally, however, they offer diploma or certificate programs which lead directly to a career in applied arts, business or a wide range of highly skilled technical occupations. Most programs require two or three years for completion, but a few may be completed in one year and even fewer may take up to four years. Generally speaking, certificates are granted for completion of one-year programs, and diplomas for the longer programs.

Provincial Systems of Community Colleges. In the Atlantic provinces, community colleges include: the College of Fisheries, Navigation, Marine Engineering and Electronics and the College of Trades and Technology in Newfoundland; Holland College in Prince Edward Island; an agricultural college, a teachers' college, Cape

The one-room school house has become a thing of the past.

Breton College, an institute of technology, a marine institute, a land survey institute and a federal Coast Guard College in Nova Scotia; and the New Brunswick Community College and a forest ranger school in New Brunswick. The New Brunswick Community College was recently established, and comprises eight campuses, including the former New Brunswick and Saint John institutes of technology.

In Quebec, the Collèges d'enseignement général et professionnel (CEGEPs), offering three-year terminal technical studies and two-year academic programs (a prerequisite for entrance to university), were inaugurated in the mid-1960s following recommendations of the Royal Commission on Education. This new college system incorporated a variety of post-secondary institutions, including many normal schools, diploma schools of nursing and institutes of technology. In addition to the 35 CEGEPs, some of which are multi-campus institutions, many private colleges, whose numbers vary from year to year, are approved for public instruction at the post-secondary level.

In Ontario, colleges of applied arts and technology (CAATs) were established in 20 regions in 1965. They are oriented to providing vocational and technical education. Other institutions in this sector include the Ontario College of Art, the Toronto Institute of Medical Technology, the Canadian Memorial Chiropractic College, four colleges of agricultural technology and a school of horticulture. In 1974-75 there were 56,000 students enrolled in the CAATs and other related institutions.

Manitoba set up a community college structure in 1969, redesignating the Manitoba Institute of Technology and Applied Arts and two vocational centres as the

Red River, Assiniboine and Keewatin Community Colleges, respectively.

The province of Saskatchewan has 12 community colleges, one technical institute and two institutes of applied arts and science. The community colleges, created in 1975, are designed to offer credit and general interest programs to residents on a part-time basis. The colleges have no campuses, buildings or classrooms; instead they rent existing facilities in their respective regions. The institutes located in Moose Jaw, Regina and Saskatoon provide vocational and technical programs for full-time students.

In Alberta there are two institutes of technology, eight community colleges, two agricultural and vocational colleges and three private church-related colleges. A third agricultural and vocational college at Vermilion became part of Lakelands College at Lloydminster in 1975; this latter college, one of the eight mentioned above, is operated jointly by the Alberta and Saskatchewan governments. The two institutes of technology and the two agricultural and vocational colleges offer only career programs at the post-secondary level, but the community colleges offer university transfer programs as well. The three private colleges offer university transfer programs only.

Table 2. Full-time enrolment in tertiary education, 1974-75[1]
(preliminary data)

Province	Community colleges and related institutions[2]		Teachers' colleges	Non-university sector— diploma schools of nursing[4]	Universities and affiliated colleges
	Technical programs[3]	University transfer programs			
Nfld.	1,094	—	—	767	5,987
PEI	666	—	—	176	1,343
NS	1,206	164	517	803	17,249
NB	641	—	—	546	10,501
Que.	41,905	61,841	—	8,436	70,693
Ont.	47,797	—	—	8,078	150,136
Man.	1,627	—	—	1,165	17,694
Sask.	1,294	56	—	999	13,579
Alta.	10,072	2,193	—	1,826	30,064
BC.	7,059	8,135	—	1,387	30,569
Canada	113,361	72,389	517	24,183	347,813

[1] Includes enrolments in: the non-university sector (including post-secondary courses in community colleges and related institutions); teachers' colleges (outside the universities); diploma schools of nursing; and the university sector (including universities and affiliated colleges).
[2] Related institutions include a number of private colleges—e.g., the Nova Scotia Agricultural College and the Ontario College of Art.
[3] Students in RN diploma programs have been excluded.
[4] Includes students enrolled in hospital schools of nursing and those enrolled in RN diploma programs in community colleges.
—Nil or zero.

In British Columbia there are 14 regional or community colleges, an institute of technology and two private colleges; the Vancouver School of Art is part of the Vancouver Community College. The majority of students attending community colleges are enrolled in university transfer programs, which enable students in regions remote from the lower mainland and Victoria to acquire their junior years of university closer to home. Four of five recently opened colleges and the two private colleges offer university transfer programs only. On the other hand, the British Columbia Institute of Technology offers career programs only; students may enter the second year of programs at this institution having completed the first year of an articulated career program at a community college in their region.

Schools of Nursing

Most diploma programs of nursing, which prepare graduates for certification as registered nurses in the provinces in which they will practise, have now been transferred from hospital schools to community colleges; hospital schools no longer exist in Quebec, Ontario or Saskatchewan. While most training in the other western provinces in 1974-75 took place in hospital schools, nursing diploma programs were available in community colleges as well. Only in the Atlantic provinces was training carried out exclusively in hospital schools.

There are also schools of nursing located in universities where students work toward a bachelor of science in nursing or an equivalent degree. Graduates of these programs are also eligible for registration, but they have an added advantage in entering teaching or administrative posts.

In many instances the transfer of diploma programs to community colleges has reduced the duration of training from three to two years. In Quebec, however, the program still requires three years for completion.

In autumn 1974 the total enrolment in diploma programs at hospital schools and community colleges was 24,183. This shows little change from the 24,050[2] enrolled in 1973, but a drop of almost 10 per cent from the peak enrolment of 26,545 in 1970.

Teacher Training

Until recently only teachers at the secondary level were required to have university degrees. Teachers for the elementary schools were trained in teachers' colleges, or normal schools. Over the past few years, however, the requirement for public school teachers in Canada to have university degrees has been introduced, and now the requirement is almost universal. In September 1975 only one teachers' college, in Nova Scotia, remained; during the previous year four operated in Ontario; as recently as 1973, 13 teachers' colleges—one in Nova Scotia, two in New Brunswick, two in Quebec and eight in Ontario — were in existence.

From 1972 to 1973 the number of students in teachers' colleges dropped by 60 per cent, from 3,255 to 1,304; from 1973 to 1974 there was a further drop of 60 per cent to 517 students, all attending the Nova Scotia Teachers' college.

[2]Revised upward from the preliminary figure of 22,949 shown in *Canada 1976*.

University Education

By definition, a university is a post-secondary educational institution which has degree-granting powers. The number of such institutions has risen to over 60 in the 1970s. In addition, there are significant numbers of colleges affiliated with universities.

Most Canadian universities provide instruction in English, but there are also a number of French degree-granting institutions and some bilingual institutions such as the University of Ottawa and Laurentian University in Sudbury. Institutions range in size and number of faculties from those with full-time enrolments of less than 1,000 students and one faculty to universities with more than 10,000 students with numerous faculties offering a comprehensive range of programs.

Depending on the province, a student must have a junior or senior matriculation certificate from a secondary school in order to gain admission to courses leading to a first degree. Many universities now require or suggest, in addition, that applicants write specified aptitude tests. The length of programs varies from three to four years for a pass bachelor's degree to five years or longer for a professional degree in medicine, theology, architecture or law. The master's degree program following the bachelor's degree requires one or more years of study and intensive research after completion of the master's degree courses.

For the second straight year there was an increase in full-time enrolment in degree, diploma and certificate programs in universities; preliminary figures indicate an increase of 4.7 per cent in 1974-75 over the previous year. A significant feature of this is the continued increase in women enrolled in these programs, up to 41.1 per cent in 1974-75 from 39.3 per cent in 1973-74.

Financing

Expenditures on education in 1972-73, 1973-74 and 1974-75 are shown in Tables 3 and 4, by level of education and by source of funds respectively.

Table 3. Expenditures on education, by level of education
(thousand dollars)

Level	1972-73	1973-74	1974-75[1]
Elementary and secondary			
Public	5,452.3	6,112.8	6,907.8
Private	172.7	200.1	247.5
Sub-total	5,625.0	6,312.9	7,155.3
Post-secondary			
Non-university	573.0	656.5	790.6
University	1,867.8	2,029.9	2,374.3
Sub-total	2,440.8	2,686.4	3,164.9
Vocational	603.4	635.9	682.5
Total	8,669.2	9,635.2	11,002.7

[1] Preliminary figures.

Table 4. Expenditures on education, by source of funds
(percentage)

Source of funds	1972-73	1973-74	1974-75[1]
Governments			
Federal	10.9	10.2	9.5
Provincial	60.6	60.7	63.5
Municipal	20.5	20.2	18.7
Sub-total	92.0	91.1	91.7
Fees and other	8.0	8.9	8.3
Total	100.0	100.0	100.0

[1] Preliminary figures.

The federal contributions shown in Tables 3 and 4 do not include transfers to the provincial governments for post-secondary education or for the minority language program. If these federal transfers are considered, then the adjusted contributions for the three years would be, respectively: federal, 23.0, 22.1 and 21.4 per cent; and provincial, 48.5, 48.8 and 51.6 per cent.

Federal government expenditures on education, apart from transfers for post-secondary education and the minority language program, consisted of the following items in the 1973-74 fiscal year:

Elementary-secondary education	
Indian and Eskimo schools	157,600,000
Department of National Defence	28,700,000
University-sponsored research and military colleges (including capital items)	181,800,000
Student aid (including cost of loans and aid given by the Canadian International Development Agency)	164,500,000
Manpower (vocational) training	401,200,000
Other expenditures	112,900,000
Total	1,046,700,000

A lecture hall at the University of Waterloo.

The University of Saskatchewan at Saskatoon.

Since expenditures by school boards for elementary and secondary education comprise the largest portion of education cost, the details by source of funds and by province are shown in Table 5.

Table 5. Expenditures of school boards in 1973[1] and 1974[2] calendar years
(thousand dollars)

Province or territory	Year	Local taxation	Provincial government	Federal government	Fees and other	Total
Newfoundland	1973	3,530	78,362	289	22,689	104,870
	1974	1,076	112,023	6,443	4,565	124,107
Prince Edward Island	1973	—	20,872	62	136	21,070
	1974	—	29,170	—	80	29,250
Nova Scotia	1973	63,928	86,377	1,037	1,923	153,265
	1974	64,661	99,357	764	1,252	166,034
New Brunswick	1973	—	105,857	—	—	105,857
	1974	—	122,782	—	—	122,782
Quebec	1973	553,403	870,858	6,280	110,334	1,540,875
	1974	474,000	1,101,785	9,380	28,185	1,613,350
Ontario	1973	779,878	1,222,431	7,838	40,142	2,050,289
	1974	885,389	1,332,796	8,644	34,805	2,261,634
Manitoba	1973	100,007	117,746	855	1,694	220,302
	1974	111,173	129,993	1,364	5,726	248,256
Saskatchewan	1973	86,800	100,691	4,280	3,421	195,192
	1974	92,260	115,319	4,920	2,297	214,796
Alberta	1973	165,389	252,911	8,299	8,131	434,730
	1974	190,211	282,165	9,700	11,691	493,767
British Columbia	1973	177,365	297,863	9,609	17,050	501,887
	1974	236,677	334,733	6,594	16,187	594,191
Yukon Territory	1973	—	8,187	3	54	8,244
	1974	—	7,784	—	58	7,842
Northwest Territories	1973	—	24,460	—	59	24,519
	1974	296	20,785	—	148	21,229
Canada	1973	1,930,300	3,186,615	38,552	205,633	5,361,100
	1974	2,055,743	3,688,692	47,809	104,994	5,897,238

[1] Revised figures.
[2] Preliminary figures.
—Nil or zero.

Post-secondary education accounts for the second-largest amount of educational expenditures. Table 6 shows these expenditures for 1973-74 and 1974-75 by type of post-secondary education and also by source of funds.

Table 6. Expenditures on post-secondary education by type of education and source of funds, 1973-74 and 1974-75[1]

(thousand dollars)

Province or territory	Year	Type of education			Source of funds			
		University	Non-university	Total	Federal[2]	Provincial	Municipal	Fees and other
Newfoundland	1973-74	45,758	6,744	52,502	4,910	41,274	—	6,318
	1974-75	48,451	7,934	56,385	6,078	43,726	—	6,581
Prince Edward Island	1973-74	9,661	2,077	11,738	809	7,161	—	3,768
	1974-75	8,557	2,628	11,185	878	8,826	—	1,481
Nova Scotia	1973-74	73,280	10,151	83,431	8,428	56,984	—	18,019
	1974-75	93,784	11,456	105,240	9,595	74,385	—	21,260
New Brunswick	1973-74	49,052	5,424	54,476	5,693	39,082	—	9,701
	1974-75	61,118	4,441	65,559	5,841	48,463	—	11,255
Quebec	1973-74	440,579	290,881	731,460	67,255	540,604	4,396	119,205
	1974-75	548,278	356,172	904,450	73,114	669,756	449	161,131
Ontario	1973-74	861,647	221,632	1,083,279	107,498	757,342	514	217,925
	1974-75	971,372	251,886	1,223,258	119,127	862,553	3,077	238,501
Manitoba	1973-74	101,591	7,638	109,229	13,085	78,871	47	17,226
	1974-75	124,567	9,167	133,734	14,790	98,194	52	20,698
Saskatchewan	1973-74	74,229	9,299	83,528	11,235	58,685	—	13,608
	1974-75	83,809	10,670	94,479	9,869	68,307	—	16,303
Alberta	1973-74	164,993	46,448	211,441	24,243	158,850	32	28,316
	1974-75	186,514	62,325	248,839	23,500	187,621	29	37,689
British Columbia	1973-74	170,911	44,139	215,050	33,832	150,143	4,337	26,738
	1974-75	208,158	61,254	269,412	33,904	195,040	2,463	38,005
Undistributable[3]	1973-74	38,209	12,094	50,303	50,143	160	—	—
	1974-75	39,654	12,730	52,384	52,216	168	—	—
Canada	1973-74	2,029,910	656,527	2,686,437	327,131	1,889,156	9,326	460,824
	1974-75	2,374,262	790,663	3,164,925	348,912	2,257,039	6,070	552,904

[1] Preliminary.
[2] Excludes federal transfer payments to the provinces.
[3] Includes Yukon Territory, Northwest Territories, overseas and undistributed expenditures.
— Nil or zero.

Leisure

Industrialization and technological progress in Canada have led to high rates of productivity. This in turn has resulted in shorter work weeks, longer paid vacations, earlier retirement and hence more time for leisure and recreation.

Definitions of leisure are numerous and reflect a variety of views. Leisure can be simply defined as those groups of activities undertaken in "non-work" time. Leisure has also been described as that group of activities in which a person may indulge of his own free will: to rest, to amuse himself, to add to his knowledge or skills, to enhance his personal, physical and mental health through sports and cultural activities, or to carry out unpaid community work. However, many definitions of leisure exclude activities such as sleeping, eating, commuting to and from work, household duties and personal care. Formal programs of continuing education may be regarded as personal improvement or maintenance just as much as sleeping or eating, and therefore may also be excluded from leisure activity. On the other hand, it can be argued that the allocation of all non-work time is at the discretion of the individual and therefore any part of it is potentially time available for leisure. Nevertheless most people would agree there is a basic minimum time required for sleeping, eating and personal care that cannot in any sense be regarded as being available for leisure activities.

Despite the fact that there is no precise agreement on what constitutes leisure, there is agreement on a core of activities. These are activities that offer recreation or give pleasure to the participants. Examples would be playing tennis or taking a walk in the park. There are instances of activities that may be regarded as undesired household tasks in some circumstances, yet pleasurable recreational activities in others; such tasks might include mowing the lawn, cooking, dressmaking or house painting. Thus, recreation and leisure may be regarded as qualitative terms which are valued differently according to personal tastes and inclinations. These may vary not only between persons but in different circumstances for the same person.

There is a reciprocal relationship between work and leisure. Longer working hours mean less time for leisure. Additional work time normally provides additional income, while additional leisure time typically leads to increased expenditures. The distribution of time between work and leisure is theoretically a matter of choice, but in practice most employed persons as individuals have only limited freedom in determining how long they work. This is because working hours and holidays in Canada are normally fixed, either by employers or as a result of collective bargaining, according to current legislation and accepted norms. As a result, Canadian workers are typically committed to working a fixed number of hours a day and days a week.

The normal work week in Canada is from 35 to 40 hours, spread over five working days. Most employees receive at least 10 paid holidays annually and a two-week annual vacation, which is usually extended to three, four or more weeks after several years of service with the same employer. Allowing for weekends, paid holidays and annual vacations with pay, most employed persons in Canada have at least 124 days free from work each year. The net amount of non-work time available to Canadians depends also on the proportion of the population in the labour force and whether or not they are employed or seeking employment. Those outside the

Canoeing on Lake Waskesieu in Prince Albert National Park, Sask.

labour force are by definition non-working and therefore have more free time at their disposal. Typical of these are persons who have retired early or are elderly.

Events and Attractions

Every year, in all parts of Canada, events and attractions draw large numbers of vacationers and travellers seeking diversion, excitement and relaxation. Events such as the Quebec Winter Carnival and the Calgary Stampede promote or celebrate historical, social or cultural occasions. On the other hand, attractions can be either natural or man-made physical features of a permanent nature that provide facilities for displaying distinctive architectural or geographic qualities or for recreational or cultural activities. In this category are museums, parks, mountains and city night-life; specific examples would be a natural phenomenon like the tidal bore on the Petitcodiac River at Moncton, New Brunswick, or a man-made attraction such as Lower Fort Garry in Selkirk, Manitoba.

Outstanding events take place in each province and territory. One of the oldest sporting events in North America is Newfoundland's annual regatta, held in St. John's. Prince Edward Island's capital city, Charlottetown, features Country Days and Old Home Week, with musical entertainment, agricultural and handicraft displays, harness racing and parades. Nova Scotia events include Highland Games in the centres of Cape Breton, while in New Brunswick there are a variety of festivities related to the province's fishing resources, such as the Shediac Lobster Festival and the Campbellton Salmon Festival.

In Quebec attractions include Man and his World, Montreal's permanent cultural and ethnic exhibition, and the Sherbrooke Festival de Cantons which features "Québécois" shows, horse-pulling, soirées and gourmet cuisine. Drama festivals in Stratford and Niagara-on-the-Lake are examples of happenings in Ontario.

Western Canada's events reflect its cultural diversity and pioneering heritage. A national Ukrainian festival is held in Dauphin, Manitoba, and a Bavarian festival, in Kimberley, British Columbia. Pioneer Days are celebrated in Saskatoon, Saskatchewan, and Banff, Alberta, has its Indian Days.

Special events are held each summer in the North. In Yellowknife, Northwest Territories, a Midnight Golf Tournament is held each year late in June. In Dawson City, Yukon Territory, the discovery of gold in 1896 is celebrated on Discovery Day in August by raft races on the Klondike River and by dances, sports and entertainment relating to the period.

Recreation

The types of leisure activities undertaken vary widely according to the age, sex, income and occupation of the individual. A survey by Statistics Canada in 1972 of leisure-time activities showed that in a series of selected physical recreational activities, walking was the most popular of all, followed by swimming, hunting and fishing. In recent years bicycling has become increasingly popular with adults and

Sand skiing at Tadoussac, Que.

The midway at the Canadian National Exhibition in Toronto.

families in many parts of Canada. In 1972, close to 12 per cent of the adult population indicated that they went bicycling regularly.

Every year more Canadians discover the pleasures of winter sports. Survey results have shown that in the winter months, the sports that have the most participants are indoor skating, snowmobiling and both downhill and cross-country skiing. The recent growth of trail and cross-country skiing in the winter has to some degree paralleled the growth of bicycling in the summer months. Non-professional hockey is a traditionally popular Canadian sport in which many young people take part regularly. Curling is also a favourite indoor winter sport in most parts of Canada. Other common leisure-time activities of Canadians include home handicrafts, bowling, and attendance at movies, sports events, musical performances, exhibitions, fairs and the theatre.

All levels of government play an active role in enriching the leisure time of Canadians, and several federal agencies have major programs related to leisure. Among these is the Fitness and Amateur Sports Branch of the Department of National Health and Welfare. It is mainly responsible for outdoor recreation and physical fitness programs and carries out a number of programs aimed at encouraging citizens of all ages to take part in physical fitness activities. It provides financial and consultative assistance to recreational agencies such as the YMCA, boys' clubs, Scouts, Guides and youth hostels. It also assists Canada's native people in increasing their participation in sports and recreation.

The responsibilities of Environment Canada encompass various facets of recreation, including sports fishing, the conservation of migratory game birds, the provision of interpretive centres on wildlife and the construction and maintenance of wharf facilities for small recreational craft.

The Ministry of State for Urban Affairs is responsible for co-ordinating all federal programs that have an impact on urban areas, including open-space recreation. For the area in and around Ottawa–Hull, the National Capital Commission plays an important role in conserving and developing space for outdoor recreation. The facilities it provides include the Gatineau Park, an area of 357 km² (square kilometres) similar to a national or provincial park, a system of scenic driveways and bicycle paths, and a greenbelt of land forming a semi-circle of recreational land to the south of Ottawa; it also maintains the longest outdoor skating rink in the world, on the Rideau Canal during the winter, and rents out garden plots in the greenbelt during the summer.

The cultural and artistic aspects of recreation are primarily the responsibility of the Secretary of State. This department supports the visual and performing arts and a variety of cultural activities in which it encourages citizens to participate.

Camping on Baffin Island, NWT.

Kejimkujik National Park, NS.

Parks Canada

National Parks

Canada's national parks system began with a 26 km² reservation of land around the mineral hot springs in what is now Banff National Park. From this nucleus, the system has grown to include 28 national parks that preserve more than 129 500 km² of Canada's natural areas.

Canada's national parks reflect the amazing diversity of the land. The program now extends from Terra Nova National Park, on the rugged eastern coast of Newfoundland, to Pacific Rim National Park, where breakers pound magnificent Long Beach on the west coast of Vancouver Island, and from Point Pelee, Canada's most southerly mainland point, to Auyuittuq National Park on Baffin Island.

There is at least one national park in each province and territory. The mountain parks of British Columbia and Alberta, among the oldest in the system, are noted for their craggy peaks, alpine lakes and meadows, glaciers and hot springs.

At Waterton Lakes National Park, which together with Glacier National Park of the US forms an international park, the mountains rise dramatically from the prairie, without the usual transitional foothills. Aspen and spruce forests contrast with the surrounding flat farm land in Elk Island National Park, Alberta. Prince Albert National Park, Saskatchewan, displays three floral zones — boreal forest, aspen parkland and prairie; within the park's boundaries are hundreds of lakes, streams, ponds and bogs. In Riding Mountain National Park, situated on the summit of the Manitoba escarpment, northern and eastern forests and western grasslands form a diverse landscape which shelters a broad variety of plant and animal life.

There are four national parks in Ontario—Georgian Bay Islands, Point Pelee, St. Lawrence Islands and Pukaskwa. La Mauricie in the Laurentian Mountains and Forillon on the historic Gaspé peninsula are located in Quebec.

Seven national parks in the Atlantic provinces conserve areas of acadian and boreal forest, harsh sea coast and sandy beaches, and the lake-dotted interior of Nova Scotia.

There are now four parks located partially or completely above the 60th parallel of latitude. Wood Buffalo National Park, which straddles the Alberta–Northwest Territories border, is home to the largest remaining herd of bison on the continent. Kluane, in the Yukon Territory, contains Canada's highest peak, Mount Logan, while in Nahanni National Park the spectacular Virginia Falls of the South Nahanni River plunge 90 m (metres) to the valley below. On Baffin Island, Auyuittuq, which in Inuit means "the place that does not melt", is Canada's first national park above the Arctic Circle.

The magnificent scenery and numerous recreational possibilities of the national parks attract visitors year-round, whether to sightsee, hike, mountain-climb, swim, fish, ski or snowshoe. Interpretive programs include guided walks, displays, films and brochures that explain the natural history of the park regions.

National Historic Parks and Sites

To preserve Canada's past, the National Historic Parks and Sites Branch of Parks Canada commemorates persons, places and events of national historic importance in the development of Canada. Since 1917, when Fort Anne in Nova Scotia became the first national historic park, more than 80 major parks and sites and over 650 plaques and monuments have been established at significant sites.

Sites are selected on the basis of their cultural, social, political, economic, military or architectural importance, and include major archaeological discoveries. Two finds in Newfoundland are the ancient Indian burial ground at Port aux Choix and the Norse settlement at L'Anse aux Meadows, believed to have been occupied about 1000 AD.

Many historic parks and sites recall the early exploration of Canada and struggles for its possession. Cartier-Brébeuf Park in Quebec City marks Jacques Cartier's first wintering spot in the New World, and is, in addition, the site of the Jesuit order's first residence in Canada.

The pursuit of furs led to extensive exploration of Canada and construction of many posts and forts to expand and protect the fur trade. Such posts include Port Royal, the earliest French settlement north of Florida, Fort Témiscamingue, a strategic trading post in the upper Ottawa Valley region, and Fort Prince of Wales, the most northerly stone fort in North America. Lower Fort Garry, near Winnipeg, has been restored to recreate a 19th century Hudson's Bay Company post. Here one can see women baking bread and spinning and weaving fabric at the "Big House", and a blacksmith at work in his shop. Furs, once the mainstay of Canada's economy, hang in the loft above the well stocked sales shop, which was the hub of fort activity.

Military fortifications that have been protected as national historic sites range from the massive Fortress of Louisbourg on Cape Breton Island, built by the French

Fortress of Louisbourg National Historic Park, NS.

in the 18th century to protect their dwindling colonial possessions, through a series of French and English posts along the Richelieu and St. Lawrence rivers, to Fort Rodd Hill on Vancouver Island, site of three late 19th century British coastal defences.

The fur-trading posts of Rocky Mountain House in Alberta, Fort St. James in northern British Columbia, and Fort Langley, British Columbia, where the province's salmon export industry also began, recall the expansion of trade and settlement in the West. The orderly development of western Canada was due in large part to the North-West Mounted Police, who are commemorated at Fort Walsh, Saskatchewan, first headquarters of the force.

The major route to the Klondike Gold Rush is being marked and protected by the Klondike Gold Rush International Historic Park. In Dawson City, boom town of 1898, buildings such as the Palace Grand Theatre and the Robert Service Cabin, as well as the paddlewheeler *S.S. Keno,* have been restored, while others are in the process of restoration or stabilization.

Province House in Charlottetown, Prince Edward Island, a national historic site, continues to serve as the legislative chambers of the province. The childhood homes of two of Canada's prime ministers, Sir Wilfrid Laurier and William Lyon Mackenzie King, have also been protected. Bellevue House National Historic Park in Kingston, a superb example of the "Tuscan Villa" style of architecture, was once occupied by Sir John A. Macdonald.

An historic venture of the 20th century is commemorated at the St. Roch National Historic Site. The RCMP vessel *St. Roch,* skippered by Sgt. Henry Larsen, was the first ship to conquer the Northwest passage in both directions, and is now restored to her appearance in 1944 when she entered Vancouver harbour on the completion of her return voyage through the passage.

Agreements for Recreation and Conservation

A new program entitled Byways and Special Places was introduced in 1972; this program is now called Agreements for Recreation and Conservation (ARC) to more precisely reflect its purposes. A long-range program, ARC will include projects carried out by all levels of government, private organizations and individuals. It is based on the concept of "linear corridors" following waterways or land byways, including both natural and historic areas and recreational facilities.

The four main components of ARC are historic waterways, wild rivers, historic land trails and motor trails.

Historic waterways. Canada's waterways were major avenues of exploration and transportation used by the native peoples, the pioneers, the early entrepreneurs and the military. The first ARC agreement, known as the Canada—Ontario Rideau—Trent—Severn (CORTS) agreement, was signed with the Government of Ontario in February 1975, and provides for the development of a waterway which accommodates a variety of recreational activities along a transportation route important in the historical development of Canada.

Wild rivers. Many of Canada's rivers contain long stretches as yet unharnessed for industrial purposes. ARC is making an inventory of such rivers, assessing them for recreational potential and seeking to preserve parts of these river systems in their natural state.

Historic land trails. A series of land trails, portages and military routes, often interconnected with historic waterways, will provide opportunities for hikers, cyclists and travellers on horseback to rediscover the history of Canada.

Motor trails. For the motorist tired of high-speed freeways, low-speed motor trails will offer alternative routes through the countryside, with access to picnic areas, campgrounds, recreational areas, nature trails and, wherever possible, national and provincial parks and historic sites.

Spruce Woods Provincial Park, Man.

Baker Lake Provincial Park, NB.

Provincial Parks

Most provinces have set aside vast areas of land for the conservation of the natural environment and the enjoyment of residents and visitors. Provincial parks total about 298 600 km², which when added to the area of the national parks bring the total federal and provincial parkland available to more than 1.6 ha for each resident of Canada.

Some of the oldest parks in Canada were created by the provinces. In Quebec, the provincial government's concern for the conservation of the caribou in 1895 led to the establishment of Laurentide Park, of which one boundary is only 48 km north of Quebec City. In Ontario the first park was Algonquin, created in 1897, which covers an area of 7 540 km² and extends to within 240 km of the city limits of both Toronto and Ottawa; this park, like many of the others in Ontario and the other provinces, features camping, canoeing and sport fishing.

In 1974 the total number of visits to provincial parks was estimated at over 50 million and the total number of nights spent by campers was about nine million.

In addition, provincial governments administer a variety of recreational programs, manage natural resources, hunting and fishing, and provide recreational facilities, both directly and through municipal programs.

Tourism

Tourism affects the lives of all Canadians. It has an impact on our lifestyle and provides a change of pace from contemporary social pressures. It also contributes to national unity by increasing understanding among people of different regions of the country.

Tourism is a major earner of foreign exchange for Canada and, given the propensity of Canadians to travel abroad, our travel income from visitors is a key plus value in our international balance of payments. At the same time, tourism is a significant generator of domestic spending. It has a considerable impact on consumption, investment and employment, and is a source of substantial tax revenue for governments; it also spreads its benefits widely across Canada, playing a prominent role in helping to alleviate regional socio-economic disparities.

According to the World Tourism Organization, global tourism in 1975 involved 213 million international arrivals (up 2 per cent from 1974), and these travellers spent an estimated $31.9 billion in their countries of destination (up 10 per cent from 1974). In the world context, Canada ranked eighth in 1975 in terms of international travel receipts and third in terms of international travel spending by its residents.

Domestic travel by Canadians increased 48 per cent by volume over the four years 1971-74, and 84 per cent by value in the same period. This rate of growth for travel by Canadians inside their own country was just double the rate of growth of the spending in Canada by visitors from abroad, which rose 42 per cent during 1971-74.

Despite the energy situation, inflation and world-wide economic recession, tourism was a business worth $8.5 billion to Canada as a whole in 1975, an amount equivalent to about 5.5 per cent of the gross national product. The spending of Canadians travelling within Canada amounted to nearly $6.7 billion, much the greater part of our tourism over-all. The balance of $1.8 billion was earned from spending in Canada by visitors from abroad — our fifth largest source of foreign exchange after autos and auto parts, crude petroleum, wheat and wood pulp.

Visitors from the US numbered 34.6 million, down 1.7 per cent from 1974. Non-resident travellers from countries other than the US numbered 1.3 million, an increase of 8.9 per cent over 1974. Of this number 892,400 came from Europe, while arrivals from the United Kingdom, the largest source of tourists after the US, totalled 379,700. Visitors from other major tourist-producing countries included 138,000 from the Federal Republic of Germany, 90,400 from Japan, 85,200 from France, 65,300 from the Netherlands, 45,400 from Italy and 41,500 from Australia.

The value of tourism spending in Canada should not, however, be measured solely in terms of the $8.5 billion direct travel expenditure. Subsequent rounds of spending spread throughout the economy and create additional business.

For example, when a traveller rents a hotel room, he contributes in the first instance to the gross margin of the hotel owner. Part of this margin will be paid out to employees in the form of wages. These wages will subsequently be spent to the benefit of the owner of a corner store, for example; the money will then pass to the

Cloud-enshrouded mountains in Kluane National Park, Yukon Territory. ⟶

wholesaler who supplied the goods purchased, and then to the manufacturer, who in turn probably purchases his raw materials from another Canadian firm, and so on. Counting this "multiplier" effect, the total contribution of tourism in the GNP could be as high as $15 billion in 1975.

Tourism also generated the equivalent of 800,000 jobs across Canada in 1975 — about 7 per cent of the labour force. It involved governments at every level and almost 80,000 individual private enterprises of diverse kinds, such as transportation companies, accommodation operators, restaurateurs, tour wholesalers and operators, travel agents, operators of activities and events, and trade associations.

Another important feature of travel consumption in Canada is the low import content of the products consumed. As travel is predominantly service-oriented, travel spending is on goods and services with a relatively high domestic labour content. Furthermore, the goods purchased by tourists are usually home-produced —food and drink by Canadian farmers and processors, and souvenirs by Canadian craftsmen, for example.

The growth of tourism in Canada is no accident. Canada possesses many basic tourism assets. It has an enviable location at the crossroads of the northern hemisphere and adjacent to the world's most affluent travel market. It is endowed with an abundance of open space, for which world demand is sure to intensify. Its northern territories constitute one of the world's few remaining tourist frontiers. It possesses immense supplies of a most precious recreational resource—water—and of a most promising one — snow. The variety, quantity and quality of Canada's wildlife compare favourably with those of any country. Its scenic, cultural and ethnic diversity add to its travel appeal, as do its heritage buildings and the developing attractions of its major cities.

Above all, Canada enjoys a world-wide reputation for friendliness and hospitality. But the growth of tourism also reflects the efforts of 10 provincial tourism departments and two territorial tourism departments, the services and promotion effected by the thousands of businesses catering to Canadian tourism, and the work of the Canadian Government Office of Tourism.

Receipts and payments on travel between Canada and other countries, 1971-75
(million dollars)

Country	1971	1972	1973	1974	1975[1]
United States					
Receipts	1,092	1,023	1,160	1,328	1,324
Payments	898	919	1,073	1,196	1,558
Balance	+194	+104	+87	+132	−234
Other countries					
Receipts	154	207	286	366	481
Payments	550	545	669	782	953
Balance	−396	−338	−383	−416	−472
All countries					
Receipts	1,246	1,230	1,446	1,694	1,805
Payments	1,448	1,464	1,742	1,978	2,511
Balance	−202	−234	−296	−284	−706

[1] Preliminary estimates.

Science and Technology

Canada's gross expenditure on research and development (GERD) in 1973-74 approximated $1.4 billion. This placed Canada sixth down the list of the 24 member countries of the Organization for Economic Co-operation and Development (OECD) in terms of total expenditures on these activities. Expressed as a proportion of gross national product, Canada's GERD was 1.1 per cent, a figure exceeding 15 other OECD countries but exceeded by eight.

The average annual rate of growth of Canada's expenditure on research and development (R&D) was over 18 per cent in the period from 1963 to 1967. It declined to 8.5 per cent from 1967 to 1969, and to 5 per cent from 1969 to 1971. Between 1971 and 1973, R&D funding grew at an annual rate of 9.5 per cent. In common with the United States, France and the United Kingdom, Canada has experienced a marked levelling-off in the support of science and technology since the period of rapid growth in the early 1960s.

Over 40,000 scientific, technical and operational personnel were engaged in R&D in Canada in 1973-74.

Science Policy

"A nation needs a comprehensive and consistent policy for the support and advancement of science, because there are more opportunities to advance science and technology than there are resources available to exploit them all. Government authorities who are subjected to continuing requests for support from industry, universities, scientific institutions, individual scientists, graduate students and international scientific organizations, as well as from consumers of science within various departments and agencies of government itself, need guidance on how to allocate their funds and their trained manpower. The purpose of a national policy for science is to provide such guidance." (OECD, 1963.)

This was probably the first contemporary definition of science policy. It was written by a group of advisers to OECD of which the late Dr. E.W.R. Steacie, then President of the National Research Council, was a member. In the intervening years governments everywhere have struggled to adjust their structures, methods and policies to accommodate the increasing influence of science and technology on all aspects of life. Cognizant of the arguments and experiences of other countries, but faced with the complex circumstances of our vast, relatively thinly populated land, Canada has gone through similar arguments and has experimented in its internal organization to achieve an understanding of how government and science should interact. A period of intensive study in the latter half of the 1960s and the early 1970s has resulted in a great variety of useful reports sponsored principally by the Science Council of Canada and by the Senate Special Committee on Science and Technology. The latter in particular, in its three-volume report (1971-73), advocated the substantial reorganization of government institutions to meet the challenges of the 1970s.

The Ministry of State for Science and Technology

The Ministry of State for Science and Technology, created in 1971, encourages the development and use of science and technology in support of national goals, through the formulation and development of appropriate policies.

Canada needs policies for science to ensure that scientific tools will be available. Grants in aid of research through the National Research Council, the Medical Research Council and the Canada Council are an expression of a policy for science that is aimed at generating and maintaining national research capability.

Policies are also needed for the use of science, to help Canada achieve non-scientific aims using scientific tools. The maintenance of research laboratories by science-based government departments (such as Energy, Mines and Resources, National Health and Welfare, Agriculture, and Environment) is an expression of a policy for the use of science. The recently instituted Make-or-Buy policy, whereby federal departments are required to purchase new research requirements from non-government research facilities where possible, was designed to enhance the capability of Canadian industry to perform research. This is another example of a policy for the use of science, in this case to reach economic goals.

The integration of science into public policy formulation is a relatively new development, and is the third element of science policy. Mechanisms that the Government of Canada is using to bring science into policy include the recruitment of both natural and social scientists into the federal public service at the policy level, and the use of consultative mechanisms such as Royal Commissions and Task Forces.

Canada's competitive position in higher-technology manufactures depends on the use of new technology in industry.

The Science Council of Canada

The Science Council, a quasi-independent body that advises the government on science policy by the publication of reports on subjects of current importance, published its 10th Annual Report in June 1976. During the same year it published a report on *Technology Transfer: Government Laboratories to Manufacturing Industry*. It also released two background studies, *Energy Conservation and Northern Development and Technology Assessment Systems*. Volume 2 of *Issues in Canadian Science Policy* and Volume 1 of *Perceptions*, a new Science Council series on population issues, were also published.

Science and Technology in Government

Total expenditures on science and technology by the Canadian government were estimated to have reached $1,350 million in 1975, or 5 per cent of the total federal budget. This represented an increase of 13 per cent over the preceding year. The natural sciences received 78 per cent of this amount, and the human sciences 22 per cent. Some 64 per cent of the expenditure of $1,350 million was devoted to R&D. The remainder covered other scientific activities such as seismic and magnetic surveys and the collection and dissemination of data and statistics.

In 1975 the National Research Council spent more on R&D than any other federal department or agency. Its estimated R&D expenditure of $139 million represented 16 per cent of the government's R&D budget. Government spending on related scientific activities in 1975 was mainly attributable to Environment Canada and Statistics Canada, which together were responsible for half the total expenditure in this category.

Government expenditures are generally classified under 11 headings: (1) general government services, (2) foreign affairs, (3) defence, (4) transportation and communications, (5) economic development and support, (6) health and welfare, (7) education assistance, (8) culture and recreation, (9) fiscal transfer payments, (10) public debt and (11) internal overhead expenses.

In 1975, government expenditures on scientific activities totalling $1,350 million fell under nine of these headings. The greatest part of science expenditures was related to economic development and support, with transportation and communications and health and welfare close behind.

The National Research Council (NRC), a federal body, operates a complex of laboratories in Ottawa and a network of laboratories across the nation pursuing basic and applied R&D in the natural sciences and engineering. Trisectoral collaboration, R&D efforts and projects performed jointly by industry, university and government are NRC's current priorities. NRC laboratories are active in the full spectrum of the natural sciences. NRC is also a granting body providing funds to Canadian university scientists, doctoral and post-doctoral scholarships and fellowships to university students, and grants to industries through the Industrial Research Assistance Program (IRAP) to stimulate R&D in the industrial sector.

Science and Technology in Canadian Industry

Canada's competitive position in higher-technology manufactures remains a serious concern. A number of factors, such as restraints caused by inflation and recession, the tendency of foreign-owned companies to perform R&D in the home country, insufficiency and conservatism of venture capital sources, and limited domestic markets, combine to produce this situation.

The federal government has a number of programs designed to provide incentives to industry to perform R&D. Among these, the Make-or-Buy program shows promise of becoming a most effective mechanism to stimulate R&D in the industry sector and to promote an increased innovative capacity. The program is aimed at producing a more even balance in the ratio of government in-house R&D to that of private industry, through contracting-out to industry R&D related to departmental missions; it also provides for interim financing of unsolicited industry proposals

An experiment in Calgary, Alta., aims to determine the value of sulphur as a sub-base for street pavement.

that are related to departmental research requirements. A recent evaluation of three years of the program's operation indicates that, while still far from its goal, it has begun a definite shift from government to industry R&D. The evaluation also produced evidence of the emergence of a new kind of industry in Canada — small-to-medium "knowledge-based" companies with a strong engineering and science orientation. These companies, it is felt, will be of great importance in development of the new technologies Canada will require in achieving its national goals in the fields of energy, space, oceanography, environmental monitoring, resource conservation and development, transportation and housing. Expenditures on industrial R&D in 1974 amounted to some $564.7 million, of which some $84.2 million came from government grants and contracts.

University Research

Direct federal aid for research in Canadian universities in 1975 was estimated at $150 million, an increase of 5.5 per cent over 1974. Of this total, $18 million went to the social sciences, 19.5 per cent more than in the previous year. In line with its previously announced decisions, the government thus continued to maintain a growth differential in favour of the social sciences. The three major research councils — the National Research Council, the Medical Research Council and the Canada Council — distributed 72.3 per cent of federal grants for university research. Indirect support in the form of graduate and postgraduate scholarships and fellowships amounted to an additional $19 million, bringing the total to $170 million in 1975.

Federal government support has traditionally been given to individual scientists on the basis of scientific excellence, rather than to institutions. Federal grants have not normally paid the salaries of scientists or much of the overhead cost. Consequently the provincial governments, in their financing of the universities, pay a very substantial but indefinable share of the costs of scientific research as well as the costs of teaching. Increasing efforts are being made to estimate this contribution, but no figures are yet available.

Many aspects of the government support of university research are currently under review. Among these are: the means of research support, whether by grant or contract; the mechanisms of financial support, both federal and provincial; the extent of overhead payments; the uniformity of treatment of the universities by various federal and provincial departments and agencies; and, finally, the relationship of government expenditures on university research to various government objectives.

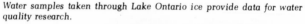

Water samples taken through Lake Ontario ice provide data for water quality research.

Science and Technology in International Affairs

Canada has agreements with several countries for co-operation in science and technology. These often provide for the exchange of scientists for limited periods, for co-operative scientific projects and for the exchange of information. Even without formal agreements, regular bilateral meetings may be held or scientific missions exchanged. A network of science counsellors in Canadian embassies plays a key role in establishing and maintaining these relationships.

Canada plays a significant role in the plenary committees on science and technology of OECD, the North Atlantic Treaty Organization (NATO), the Economic Commission of Europe (ECE), the United Nations (UN) and the Commonwealth. The NATO Science Committee met in Canada for the first time in its history in September 1974. The work of those international groups, such as the Club of Rome, that endeavour to apply scientific techniques to the clarification of global problems is also followed very closely. Canada has played a substantial role in the creation and support of the International Institute of Applied Systems Analysis in Vienna, which is devoted to the development and application of systems analysis and modelling.

Canadian scientists participate widely in international conferences on specialist scientific and technological subjects, and Canada frequently hosts such meetings.

Scientific Activities

The following are some of the highlights of Canadian research, development and other scientific activities in major areas of national interest.

Agricultural Research

Over 50 per cent of agricultural research in Canada is conducted by Agriculture Canada, which employs over 900 scientists at about 50 establishments located from coast to coast. Agriculture faculties at universities comprise the second major research group. Private industry and provincial departments were minor contributors in the past, but now are becoming more significant. At all establishments there are probably 2,000 scientists involved, although many of them devote only a portion of their time to agricultural research.

The broad traditional areas of crop production, animal production and soils still receive the bulk of the research effort; however, in recent years there has been increasing emphasis on food processing. In addition, agricultural scientists are now becoming involved in research directed at protection of the environment, an activity frequently conducted in collaboration with other agencies at the provincial, federal and international levels.

In crops research, plant breeding is a major activity. New varieties are selected for such traits as higher yield, better product quality, resistance to disease and insects, and shorter season. In the past one or two years, at least a dozen new cereal varieties, several new forage legumes and grasses, and some new oilseed varieties have been licensed. Plant breeders have also made dramatic progress in altering the chemical composition of rapeseed, which is our major oilseed crop; erucic acid, which was a major component of rapeseed oil, has been eliminated from new varieties, as have glucosinolates, which interfered with utilization of the meal. New varieties of a number of fruits and vegetables have also been released, including potatoes, cucumbers, tomatoes, apples, peaches and cherries.

The other major activity in crops research is the development of better means of protection against insects, diseases and weeds. Chemical pesticides are one of the major means of plant protection, but scientists have reduced the number of sprays required by timing them so that they are applied when they are most effective. Biological methods of control have also been developed; such methods include use of insects to control other insects and weeds, and of pheromones and sterile male techniques to disrupt insect reproduction. The integration of chemical and biological controls reduces both costs and the risks of environmental pollution. In addition, engineers have developed spray equipment to reduce drift and achieve more effective application.

In animal production, breeding projects are under way with sheep, swine, poultry and cattle, largely conducted by Agriculture Canada. The department has one of the largest research projects on dairy cattle breeding in the world, a project designed to test the feasibility of exploiting hybrid vigour in dairy cattle. At the present time, the dairy cattle industry relies heavily on a single breed, the Holstein.

Three British breeds, Hereford, Angus and Shorthorn, have long been the basis of Canada's beef production. In the last decade, ranchers have imported various other European breeds for crossbreeding purposes. Agriculture Canada has a large breeding project to test and assess the value of these imported breeds when crossed with the traditional British breeds.

When grains are in surplus supply, they are used extensively for growing and finishing beef cattle. Now that grain prices have risen, researchers are developing methods of achieving the same rate of gain and adequate finish by substituting processed forages. Increased attention is also being paid to the utilization of waste products, such as straw, wood, poultry manure and industrial waste in the feeding of ruminants. Part of the stimulus for this research comes from pressures to reduce environmental pollution. In swine, poultry and sheep production, emphasis is being placed on the development of more efficient integrated production systems.

Research on animal diseases is conducted by the Health of Animals Branch of Agriculture Canada and by staff at three veterinary colleges. Methods for the early diagnosis of disease and for parasite control are being developed, and a blood-typing service is operated for cattle breeders. Several Canadian commercial companies are in the business of embryo transplantation in cattle, which permits the more rapid increase of high-quality stock; a scientific first in this area was the development by Agriculture Canada scientists of a method of sexing embryos at 14 days of age. Other achievements have been the production of an antigen for the early detection of Aleutian disease in mink, and the isolation for the first time of the organism responsible for scrapie disease in sheep.

In food processing, the Food Research Institute in Ottawa has developed an economical method for producing a high-protein food product from whey, while two commercial companies are conducting research on the extraction of food components from a high-protein oat variety developed at Ottawa. Continuing programs are concerned with characterizing Canadian foodstuff source materials, improving the quality of meats and dairy products, and developing new food products.

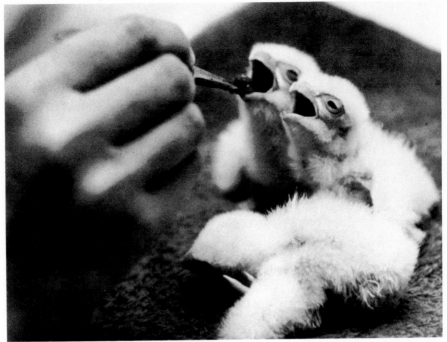

Young peregrine falcons are hand-fed at a captive breeding facility. The goal of such programs is to replenish wildlife stocks.

Soils research is concerned with basic work on soil reactions, on a soil survey to provide information on the soil resources of Canada and on fertilizer practices for various crops. Land capability studies are becoming increasingly important because of urban encroachment on prime agricultural land and the looming world food shortage.

Concern for environmental quality is a new thrust in agricultural research. Scientists are monitoring rivers, streams and lakes for contamination with soil nutrients, animal wastes and pesticide chemicals. Food products are carefully checked for freedom from chemical residues. Analytical methodology to permit this monitoring is continually under development.

Environmental Research

Atmospheric Environment Research: Pollutants such as freons and supersonic transport exhausts affect the stratosphere, especially the ozone layer, and lead to potentially harmful effects on human, animal and plant life. Important stratospheric constituents are being measured by the Atmospheric Environment Service of Environment Canada to establish the current unperturbed stratospheric photochemical balance and to verify photochemical reaction rates needed for input to models of stratospheric behaviour. These models indicate that the effects of pollution are not negligible.

Climatic trends that may gravely affect agricultural production and other environmental factors bearing on human welfare are also being analyzed to discover the basic physical processes required to make long-term predictions of climate.

A comprehensive system for environmental prediction through forecasts of ice masses and ice floes and weather elements is operating to support many activities going on in the Arctic, especially oil drilling in the Beaufort Sea, and is still being developed. New powerful techniques of data assimilation and numerical prediction are in operation at the Canadian Meteorological Centre, and improvements are still being made. Advanced computer methods for processing satellite data are producing very high quality photographs of weather systems for use at Canada's main weather centres.

Methodologies are being developed for conducting air quality environmental impact assessments of major industrial developments and of energy production and transportation activities, in order to provide information relevant to land use planning and air pollution control strategy that would minimize any adverse effects.

Fisheries and Marine Programs: Bounded by three oceans and having the longest coastline of any country in the world, Canada conducts an extensive range of scientific programs aimed at probing the secrets of the seas and their vast and valuable resources. Responsibility for Canadian fisheries, oceanographic and hydrographic research is entrusted to the Fisheries and Marine Service of Environment Canada.

(a) Fisheries: Programs of fisheries research directly supporting national and international fisheries activities are conducted from Fisheries and Marine Service research stations located in coastal and inland areas across Canada. These programs

Conservation and management of such commercially important resources as the west coast salmon fishery depend on scientific studies.

are designed to add to the fundamental knowledge of Canada's vast living marine and fresh-water resources. Life history, population and behaviour studies provide a sound scientific basis for the conservation and management of some marine plants, such as phytoplankton and seaweeds, and of the commercially important fisheries, including those for lobster, crab, shrimp, oyster, scallops, clams, marine mammals, salmon, cod, flounder, halibut, herring and capelin. Studies on fish and shellfish diseases and fish predators, and research on fish genetics, physiology and behaviour are also important, the latter with a view to improving fish culture and farming methods, and fish farm and hatchery stocks. In addition to these basic studies, new fishing grounds and new species for exploitation are sought, and experiments in improving fishing methods are undertaken.

The aquatic environment program takes in studies of the marine and fresh-water environments of aquatic organisms in order to learn more about primary and secondary productivity and the occurrence of ocean and fresh-water life of importance to man. Considerable importance is placed on increased research efforts associated with the prediction, abatement and elimination of pollution, including the effects of fresh-water and marine eutrophication. Investigations are also conducted into the distribution and physical and chemical characteristics of major ocean currents and the physical and biological structures of large ocean areas, including the ocean bottom, where concentrations of fish and other aquatic life occur. Ocean climate and ocean weather as they affect the distribution of fish and other living organisms, as well as the vertical and horizontal distribution of nutrient matter and the cycle of energy and life in the seas, are regularly observed and correlated.

(b) Oceanography: A principal objective of oceanography is to contribute to the understanding, exploitation and management of renewable and non-renewable ocean resources. To achieve this, a broad spectrum of programs is conducted in coastal and deep ocean waters to examine the physical, chemical and biological processes that, in combination with atmospheric interaction, govern much of the sea's behaviour. This work has given new insight into key areas such as the productivity and sensitivity to pollution of our marine waters. It also helps support fisheries and ocean legislation, provides a basis for marine information and advisory services, and assists in expressing Canada's position in international forums dealing with the health and use of the world's oceans.

Programs are centred mainly in three regional establishments: the Bedford Institute of Oceanography at Dartmouth, NS, the Institute of Ocean Sciences at Patricia Bay, BC, and the Canada Centre for Inland Waters, Burlington, Ont. The Marine Environmental Data Service in Ottawa acquires, records and disseminates oceanographic data on a world-wide basis.

Visible benefits of the research programs are apparent in the growing level of scientific and technological expertise in the marine sciences and in marine-oriented production and services in Canada. This development has been marked by close co-operation between government and private enterprise. A typical example is the Canadian Ocean Data Buoy System, currently undergoing sea trials prior to incorporation in an observational network that will aid long-range weather forecasting. Another case in point is the Beaufort Sea Program, undertaken early in 1974; this was a major marine environmental assessment program related to the possible environmental impact of off-shore exploration for oil and gas in the southern Beaufort Sea.

Considerable emphasis is given to the control of pollution at sea and development of legislation dealing with our continental shelves. The recently proclaimed Ocean Dumping Control Act permits Canada to manage an activity that was largely unregulated in the past, and also permitted ratification of an intergovernmental agreement to control and monitor dumping of substances at sea.

(c) Hydrography: The Canadian Hydrographic Service publishes nautical charts to ensure the safety of navigation on Canada's coasts, the major inland water routes and the adjacent oceans. One thousand charts, 16 sailing directions and annual tide tables are published. Multidisciplinary surveys are carried out jointly with the Department of Energy, Mines and Resources, and over 200 natural resource maps showing magnetics and gravity data and the surficial geology of the continental margin have been published. Canada is a member of the International Hydrographic Organization and has published three small-scale charts in the International Chart Series; also in production are the first four sheets of the International Bathymetric Chart of the Oceans.

Environmental Protection Service Research: The Wastewater Technology Centre in Burlington is charged with the conception, development and implementation of technical development programs related to water pollution control of industrial and municipal waste waters across Canada. Studies are made and field demonstration projects are conducted at industrial sites.

Current projects on the treatment of municipal waste waters include: the development of systems for the removal of nutrients, particularly phosphorus and nitrogen; the application of physical/chemical or biological waste-water treatment systems to small communities; the de-watering, handling and disposal of sewage sludges by incineration or by application to agricultural land; and investigations of existing sludge disposal sites for heavy metals and polychlorinated biphenyls (PCBs). For the treatment of industrial waste waters, current projects include; development and demonstration of a physical/chemical treatment process for removing arsenic and cyanide from gold mining and milling waste waters; biological removal of nitrogen from various industrial waste waters, removal of toxic metals from metal-bearing waste waters, removal of radioactive products from industrial waste waters and the leachability of radioactive materials from uranium mine tailings; study of the parameters influencing the de-waterability of various industrial sludges; and the evaluation of the effect of various treatment processes on the toxicity of various organic chemical plant effluents.

The Environmental Emergency Branch is studying cold-weather environmental problems, such as drilling blowouts in the Arctic, winter pipeline spills, dyking of storage facilities in the North and spills in ice-infested water. The branch is also involved in technology development work for controlling and cleaning up accidental pollution. It tests, evaluates and develops oil-spill counter-measures equipment, materials and techniques; this program includes the use of skimmers, booms, pumps and remote sensing systems. Work is also under way on various oil-spill treatment agents, such as absorbents, biodegraders, combustion agents and chemical treatments, and on the analysis of counter-measure requirements for specific high-risk and sensitive areas.

The radio collar being attached to this drugged polar bear will provide data to aid efforts to protect the species.

Environmental Management Service Research: Research in this arm of Environment Canda is undertaken by the Canadian Forestry Service (CFS), the Canadian Wildlife Service (CWS), the Inland Waters Directorate and the Lands Directorate.

The CFS has taken a leading role in establishing a task force to monitor large-scale aerial forest spraying operations in Quebec and New Brunswick. This task force is co-operating with the provinces in assessing possible environmental side effects of spraying operations in 1976. Successful experiments to evaluate satellite (Landsat) imagery for forestry purposes have led to a large remote-sensing contract, which in turn is expected to yield better procedures for resource inventories and environmental monitoring projects. The CFS has also fostered large-scale operational tree-breeding programs in Nova Scotia, Quebec, Ontario, Alberta and British Columbia that will provide faster-growing, superior trees to help offset predicted wood shortages.

Among many other important forestry research ventures are programs for improving the urban environment by introducing the concepts of urban forestry, for establishing modified forestry operations calculated to safeguard the environment, and for abating air, water and land pollution caused by forest industries.

The CWS is continuing its efforts to protect rare and endangered birds such as the whooping crane and the peregrine falcon. Attempts are being made to breed a new whooping crane population in Idaho using eggs from Wood Buffalo National Park.

CWS also hopes to increase falcon numbers by raising birds in captivity and releasing them into the wild. Research in the Northwest Territories has covered population studies on the Peary caribou and barren-ground grizzly bear, species regarded as being especially sensitive to the disturbances associated with oil and gas exploitation in that area.

Other significant work includes monitoring the effects on songbirds of aerial spraying for spruce budworm, researching the impact of toxic chemicals in Lake Ontario on the reproduction of herring gulls, photographically enumerating breeding colonies of lesser snow geese and Ross' geese in the western Arctic, and determining habitat and reproduction requirements of white-fronted geese.

Most of the Inland Waters Directorate's research program takes place at the Canada Centre for Inland Waters, Burlington, Ontario. The remainder is undertaken in Ottawa, Winnipeg and Vancouver. Research is concerned with water quality and water quantity problems.

Water quality research provides a basis for setting water quality objectives. Specific projects include: eutrophication and nutrient dynamics at work in the Bay of Quinte and Lake St. George; toxic substances research covering bacterial degradation of PCBs, and asbestos detection and removal; sedimentation research; and investigations of ground-water contaminants, particularly radio-isotopes.

Water quantity research covers measurements of stream-flow and ice movement, physical exchanges at the air/water (ice) interface, and forecasting of the physical effects of water and ice on the environment. Specific projects include: bank and bed stability at northern river crossings; studies of Arctic lakes; glacier coring for interpreting climatic history and predicting future trends; models of river and shore processes such as erosion and ice scouring; and work on an oil and ice boom for oil-spill clean-up procedures.

Land classification and land use change are the principal subjects of the Lands Directorate's current research activities. Land classification research is directed toward establishing better methods of surveying and classifying land according to ecological characteristics, use capabilities and present use. Such techniques are used in major resource investigations to determine land development potential and environmental management requirements. There is also research emphasis on satellite imagery and high-altitude aerial photography for land resource surveys and land use monitoring systems. Land use change at the fringes of urban centres is another important area of investigation; this work covers rural-to-urban conversion around centres with 25,000 or more people.

Energy, Mines and Resources

Mining and Metallurgical Research: The Canada Centre for Mineral and Energy Technology at the Department of Energy, Mines and Resources (EMR) has undertaken a $4 million, five-year program to improve the stability of open-pit slopes. The objective of this project is to reduce the cost of producing minerals from open pits by synthesizing research data into engineering systems for the design and support of the sloping walls. This could reduce the excavation of mine waste, which is the largest cost element in open-pit mining; the successful completion of this project could save the mining industry $50 million annually.

Extensive R&D efforts are being directed at solving problems posed by the low-grade petroleum deposits in the oil sands of the Athabasca region of western Canada.

A major area of R&D is the mining of coal in the mountainous areas of western Canada. The severely folded and faulted coal seams restrict the use of conventional coal-mining techniques and create difficult ground support problems. Spontaneous combustion in coal exposed to the atmosphere is complicating both cost recovery and the mine working environment. R&D is being undertaken by government and industry to resolve these problems.

By far the largest and most comprehensive R&D is taking place with respect to the oil sands of the Athabasca region of western Canada. These low-grade deposits of petroleum present a multitude of problems, from their removal from the ground and separation of the oil from the sand to the use of the product. One company alone has a program that will cost $1,000 million. The NRC's Division of Chemistry has developed a process of spherical agglomeration for recovering oil from tar sands such as the Athabasca's.

The Canada Centre for Mineral and Energy Technology has developed a blue-flame domestic oil burner that is expected to save up to 10 per cent in fuel consumption and is non-polluting. This burner is undergoing extensive trials and should be available commercially in the near future.

The production of steel is vital to the development of all sectors of the Canadian economy, including energy. There are three separate R&D projects that are attempting to circumvent the need for the blast furnace and the dependence on coking coal. One steel company has developed the SL/RN rotary kiln process for the direct reduction of iron ore. Another is operating a pilot plant at Niagara Falls, Ont., on a rotary kiln process, also for direct reduction of iron ore. The Canada Centre for Mineral and Energy Technology has successfully demonstrated a process called the Shaft Electric Reduction Furnace (SERF), which utilizes the waste gases from an electric reduction furnace to preheat and pre-reduce iron ore.

Two mineral processing companies have co-operated on a multi-million dollar, multi-year project to develop a hydro-metallurgical method for the commercial production of copper. This technique would avoid the atmospheric pollution that now typifies copper smelters, and thus be environmentally acceptable. Moreover, the process would recover sulphur, rather than emitting it to the environment. The successful commercialization of this process would give Canada a strong position in copper production in an era when environmental concerns are forcing restrictions on the traditional smelters.

Fuels: The refining of Canada's low-grade crude oils and bitumen sands is complicated by the presence of organically-combined traces of nickel and vanadium, and of 5 per cent sulphur, which must be removed. The Canada Centre for Mineral and Energy Technology has developed a high pressure hydro-cracking process that eliminates much of the nickel and vanadium and produces a low-viscosity product that would make a suitable feedstock for refineries.

Research on the chemical composition of Athabasca bitumen has resulted in the development of improved analytical techniques that have proved their value in detecting oil spills and "fingerprinting" crude oils. This capability has revealed differences in Canadian cretaceous oils of the tar belt. The extent of thermal maturation of the crude oil determines the possibility of its extraction from the terrain. This promises to be a useful tool for oil exploration in the Arctic and off-shore on the east coast.

Energy Research: Current expenditures of $113 million in 1975-76 on energy R&D by the federal government are distributed approximately as follows: nuclear energy, 75 per cent; oil and gas, 9 per cent; energy conservation, 7.5 per cent; transportation and transmission, 4.5 per cent; coal, 2.5 per cent; renewable energy resources, 1.5 per cent.

In 1976-77 the federal government allocated $10 million, in addition to the normal budget, to increase energy research and development activities in six priority areas: energy conservation, $1.8 million; oil sands and heavy oils, $1.5 million; coal production and utilization, $2.5 million; nuclear fuel resources, $1.1 million; energy transportation and transmission, $1.7 million; and renewable energy such as solar, wind and geothermal energy, $1 million. Additional energy R&D funding is also anticipated in the areas of environmental studies, biomass energy, health and safety programs, tidal energy, fossil fuels resource assessment and socio-economic energy research.

Most of the R&D on nuclear energy is conducted by the Crown agency, Atomic Energy of Canada Ltd. (AECL), although this agency also funds considerable amounts of R&D in industries and universities. AECL's current major thrust is in support of its CANDU (CANada Deuterium Uranium) nuclear power reactor system and associated heavy water plants. Successful operation of the Pickering generating station and of both the Port Hawkesbury and the Bruce heavy water plants has convincingly demonstrated the commercial viability of the CANDU system. Much of AECL's R&D in improved equipment, components and materials for CANDU reactors is done in collaboration with Canadian industry.

The success of the Canadian reactor system has no doubt had some influence on the recent British decision to choose a similar type of reactor for its new power program. The British authorities have already declared their intention of seeking substantial co-operation with Canada during the development of that project.

1. Marcasite on Calcite
   (Montreal, Que.)
2. Fossil Coral (near Arkona, Ont.)
3. Celestite in Limestone
   (Amherstburg, Ont.)
4. Selenite (Winnipeg, Man.)

Private industry and the utilities play a major role in R&D on oil, gas and hydropower (notably in pipeline transportation, thermal electric conversion, hydropower development and electrical-industrial equipment), which compensates for lesser federal funding in these areas.

Several provincial governments support research councils or foundations that are involved to some degree in energy R&D activities. The largest performer is Alberta Research, with an energy science and technology budget in 1974-75 of about $2.4 million. Alberta has initiated a five-year, $100 million research program on in situ production of deep oil sands. Alberta has also approved a joint program with Environment Canada on Alberta Oil Sands Environmental Research, involving a shared expenditure of $40 million over 10 years. Most of the other energy R&D in Alberta is concentrated on conventional oil, gas and coal research.

Within the federal government, the Department of Energy, Mines and Resources is concerned with the determination of reserves of oil and gas, mainly in the frontier areas. The Department of Industry, Trade and Commerce (ITC) is playing an important role funding R&D on the development, production and processing of energy resources, and it is by far the predominant department in transportation and storage R&D, mainly for oil and gas.

ITC and NRC are major contributors to transmission R&D. Environment Canada is predominant in environmental management (especially of oil and gas pipelines).

Remote Sensing: The Canada Centre for Remote Sensing (CCRS), a part of the Department of Energy, Mines and Resources, collects, processes and disseminates data derived from aircraft- and satellite-borne sensors for the management of Canada's environment and natural resources. The data are applied to a wide variety of disciplines, including agriculture, forestry, geology, oceanography, glaciology and ice reconnaissance. The four aircraft used for remote sensing are operated and maintained by two companies on contract to the CCRS.

The centre's satellite receiving station in Prince Albert, Saskatchewan, receives data from two American earth resources satellites, Landsat-1 and Landsat-2, and one weather satellite, Noaa-3. A new satellite receiving station in Shoe Cove, Newfoundland, was scheduled to begin operating in October 1976. It will receive data from the Landsat and Noaa satellites, and will supplement the services provided by the station in Prince Albert, which receives data for all of Canada except Newfoundland and the east coast. The data received are processed into images at a special facility in Ottawa. These images are distributed throughout Canada by the National Air Photo Library.

Communications and Space Research

Total government expenditure on space research in 1976-77 has been estimated at $55 million. Government departments with a direct interest in space research and activities are Communications, Environment, Transport, National Defence, and Energy, Mines and Resources; the National Research Council is also involved in space research. Domestic satellite communications service is provided by Telesat Canada, a company owned by the federal government and by the Trans-Canada Telephone System. Teleglobe Canada, a Crown corporation, provides overseas communications service.

Data received from aircraft- and satellite-borne sensors are processed into images at the CCRS facility in Ottawa, Ont.

Canada's newest satellite, called Hermes, was designed and built by the Communications Research Centre of the Department of Communications; this experimental communications technology satellite (CTS) was launched in January 1976 by the United States. It is the world's most powerful telecommunications satellite in orbit.

Hermes, or CTS, will be used by 19 experimenters from government, industry and institutions to perform 25 experiments, primarily technological. Hermes may well become the forerunner of a series of new high-powered satellites operating at virtually interference-free frequencies, receiving and transmitting two-way video, audio and data signals. The ground stations used with Hermes have antennas ranging in size from one to three metres, making them the smallest now in service and just a step away from terminals that may be mounted on rooftops. The small ground stations are made possible by Hermes' high power; less powerful satellite systems require much larger dish antennas.

The Department of Communications, along with the Ministry of Transport, is participating in an international aeronautical satellite (Aerosat) program designed to develop the use of satellites for international air traffic control. Aerosat is a joint effort by the European Space Agency (ESA), Canada and the United States. Major contracts for construction of the geosynchronous satellite for air traffic control communications over the North Atlantic were to be awarded in November 1976. Funding, ownership and user participation have been calculated at 47 per cent US, 47 per cent ESA and 6 per cent Canada, rates based approximately on the GNP of each participant.

Canada's first satellite, Alouette, was launched in 1962 and made Canada a pioneer in the use of satellites in scientific research. This satellite and its successors, Alouette II and ISIS I and II, contain experiments to study the properties of the upper atmosphere and of electronic devices such as antennas in that environment. Alouette I went out of service after 10 years of useful life, and the Alouette II satellite was placed in a standby "mothball" status on June 3, 1973, after seven and a half years of extensive and valuable data acquisition. ISIS I and II are still in good health and are providing extensive scientific data to scientists from the eight countries that are participating in the analysis of the data.

The National Research Council, whose activities include operation of the Churchill Rocket Range, spent about $17.5 million in 1976-77 and is the project manager for delivery of a remote manipulator system (RMS) to the United States as part of the National Aeronautics and Space Administration (NASA) space shuttle program. Spar Aerospace Ltd., Toronto, is the prime contractor for the RMS, which is like a long mechanical arm to be used to take satellites out of the space shuttle's cargo area and place them in orbit or pull them out of orbit for repair. The space shuttle, with a payload capacity of 29 500 kg (kilograms), will be launched like a rocket, orbit like a spacecraft and land like a large aircraft.

The Canada Centre for Remote Sensing's receiving station in Prince Albert, Saskatchewan, has been converted for use as a tracking station for Landsat, an American remote sensing satellite (formerly Earth Resources Technology Satellite). The data received are processed into image form at a special facility in Ottawa. These images are distributed throughout Canada by the National Air Photo Library. A contract was awarded to MacDonald-Dettweiler Ltd. for a semi-mobile earth receiving station, and an agreement was signed with ISIS Ltd. of Prince Albert to process and market data for Canadian users. One of those users is Environment Canada, which is developing applications of data from Landsat and spent about $3 million in 1976-77 toward this end.

Telesat Canada announced that it had awarded a contract for a fourth satellite in its Anik series, to be launched in 1978. The Anik system was inaugurated in January 1973 by a telephone call from Ottawa to Resolute Bay via Anik I. By the end of that year a second satellite, Anik II, was also in orbit, and a third was launched in 1975. The three satellites are performing satisfactorily, exhibiting only slight anomalies not expected to have any major effect on their longevity or usefulness. The satellites have an estimated useful life of six years.

Teleglobe Canada spent about $3 million in leasing channels on communications satellites and about $5 million for improving the ground station network.

The Department of National Defence spent about $2.5 million on its space activities, the principal one of which is through its commitment to NORAD. The Department of Industry, Trade and Commerce spends about $2 million a year in support of the country's aerospace industry.

Medical and Health Research

Biomedical research in Canada is carried out primarily in laboratories located in the universities and their affiliated hospitals. The major part of the financial support for the direct operating costs of this research is provided by the federal government through grants or contributions to investigators whose salaries are, by and large, paid from university funds. Voluntary agencies such as the National Cancer Institute of Canada, the heart foundations, the Arthritis Society and others that derive their monies from public campaigns are providing an increasingly significant share of the support for research in the health sciences. The share provided by provincial governments has also grown in recent years.

In 1975 some 2,048 investigators received research grants from the various funding agencies. Their work ranged from the development of reading machines

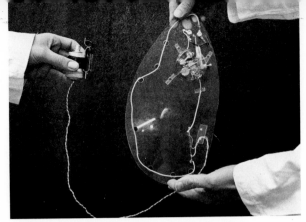

Testing a heart pacemaker at Health and Welfare Canada.

for the blind, through clinical trials of drugs thought to be useful in the prevention of strokes, to research of the most fundamental kind related to the immunology of transplantation. The two federal bodies with primary responsibility in the field of health research are the Medical Research Council, whose main function is the support of university-based research in the health sciences, and the Research Programs Directorate of the Department of National Health and Welfare, which is concerned particularly with studies relating to the biology of populations, the delivery of health care and the alteration of lifestyles in order to prevent disease.

The Department of National Health and Welfare also carries out research in central laboratories of its own. Research in the department's Health Programs Branch has seen the development of a preparation for the slow release into the body of the anti-tuberculosis drug isoniazid, permitting larger doses to be given to Inuit, among whom the risk of tuberculosis is greater. There has been substantial progress in field trials of rubella vaccines and increased activity in the study of mental and physical rehabilitation problems.

Northern Research

Canada has long recognized the contribution research makes to the socio-economic development of the North. Moreover, the Canadian north has some unique characteristics that are of particular interest to the scientific community.

Because of this, the Department of Indian and Northern Affairs has designed certain long-term measures to encourage and support northern research. The training of graduate students is assisted by special grants administered by the department. In addition, under its Northern Science Resource Centres Program the department operates the Mackenzie Delta Science Resource Centre at Inuvik and the Eastern Arctic Science Resource Centre at Igloolik to accommodate scientists from government, universities and industry. Plans are being made for science resource centres at Whitehorse in the Yukon Territory and at Yellowknife and Resolute Bay in the Northwest Territories.

These measures do not, however, meet the need for research to support development programs or to obtain specific information required to support the regulatory and administrative responsibilities of the department. For these purposes substantial short-term programs of applied problem-oriented research have been organized, such as the environmental-social program, the northern pipelines program, the Beaufort Sea project, oil-spill studies, waste disposal studies, and regional socio-economic studies.

Communications

The existence of Canada as a political and social entity has always been heavily dependent upon systems of east-west communications. This is the historical reason for development of the routes of the voyageurs, coast-to-coast railways, telegraph and telephone systems, broadcasting services, airlines, microwave networks, the Trans-Canada Highway and a domestic communications satellite system. These systems, counter-balancing the strong north-south pull of continentalism, have been essential for the economic development of Canada, for transmitting and disseminating information and for expression and sharing of social and cultural values.

Telecommunications make possible virtually instantaneous transfer of information in any form between all parts of the country. They help bridge distance — an obstacle to national trade and commerce — and provide prospects for reducing regional disparities and developing the Canadian north.

Television, radio, telephone, telegraph, teletype, facsimile and other means of communications have become part of our daily life. By January 1, 1975, the number of telephones in service in Canada had reached 12,454,331 (about one phone for every two people). Ninety-eight per cent of households now have radios and 97 per cent have television sets. Cable television, a medium that may provide a variety of services in the future, including two-way communications, is now wired into more than 2.5 million Canadian households (about one in three). Radio operating licences in force in Canada at the end of the fiscal year 1974-75 numbered nearly 400,000.

In most countries outside North America, telecommunications services are provided by the state. In Canada, these services are provided by a mixture of investor-owned companies and government agencies. The industry comprises telephone and telegraph companies, broadcasters and cable operators, and manufacturers of telecommunications equipment. Operations of telecommunications carriers are generally licensed and regulated by either federal or provincial authorities.

Broadcasting transmitting and receiving undertakings are federally regulated. Telecommunications carriers under federal jurisdiction include Bell Canada, British Columbia Telephone Company, CNCP Telecommunications, Telesat Canada, Teleglobe Canada and four relatively small telephone or telegraph companies. All other telecommunications common carriers are provincially regulated.

There were about 937 telephone common carriers by the end of 1974, ranging from big corporations serving millions of telephones to small co-operatives, mainly in Saskatchewan. However, the eight member companies of the Trans-Canada Telephone System (TCTS) account for more than 90 per cent of total subscribers. Much of the long distance communications in Canada travel by their two nation-wide microwave routes.

Other telecommunications services are provided by a variety of carriers. CNCP Telecommunications, specializing in business communications, offers services such as telegraph and telex. Telesat Canada, jointly owned by the Canadian government and the common carriers, operates the domestic satellite communications system consisting of three Anik satellites and an associated ground network.

The Telesat transmitting-receiving antenna at Frobisher Bay, NWT.

Teleglobe Canada (formerly the Canadian Overseas Telecommunications Corporation), a Crown corporation, provides Canada with telecommunications to the rest of the world through cables and international telecommunications satellites.

The federal Department of Communications is responsible, both nationally and internationally, for the development and efficiency of communications in Canada and for the long-range planning of Canada's communications. It carries out research in the field of telecommunications and manages the radio-frequency spectrum in Canada. This latter function requires development of regulations, technical standards, radio-frequency plans and assignment criteria. It includes: technical evaluation of applications to use radio frequencies, licensing of radio stations and technical certification of broadcasting undertakings; inspection and monitoring of radio stations to ensure adherence to regulations and standards; and gathering of information for spectrum planning purposes.

A score of groups ranging from provincial governments to native peoples' associations are shaping the satellite communications services of tomorrow in a unique program of social and technical experiments using the department's Communications Technology Satellite (CTS), which was launched on January 17, 1976. The aim of the CTS experiment is to test the technology and applications of a new breed of high-powered orbiting transmitters to meet the needs of the 1980s. About 80 per cent of the $63 million expenditure on this, the world's most powerful communications satellite, went to Canadian industry.

There has been a rapid upsurge in the purchase and use of two-way radio in the general radio service (GRS), or citizen's band as it is frequently called. This trend shows no sign of slowing and it accordingly will lead to a greater congestion of the radio frequency spectrum, a limited resource.

A $19 million contract for construction of Canada's fourth commercial satellite for domestic telecommunications, to be launched in 1978, was announced by Telesat Canada in December 1975. About 35 900 km above the earth, Telesat's first three satellites have facilities for relaying 10 colour television channels or up to 9,600 simultaneous telephone circuits. All Canada is within their range; distance and isolation are removed as obstacles to communications for government, business, industry, science and technology.

Teleglobe Canada is the Canadian signatory to the International Telecommunication Satellite Organization (Intelsat) and operates earth stations at Mill Village, NS, and Lake Cowichan, BC. In 1976 it expanded its facilities to accommodate the demand for international telephone, telex and telegraph during the Olympic Games held in Montreal in July 1976. A transportable earth station was erected on Mount Royal to transmit two simultaneous television channels to Europe via the Intelsat satellites stationed 35 900 km over the equator.

A CNCP electronic Telex exchange.

This TCTS *communications command centre monitors the telephone networks for technical problems.*

The Trans-Canada Telephone System (TCTS) was expected to have Direct Dialing Overseas (DDO) in service in Vancouver by September 1976, making Vancouver the first Canadian city to have this service. In the next three years, Victoria, Edmonton, Calgary, Toronto, Ottawa, Montreal, Quebec City and Halifax are scheduled to be hooked up for DDO.

The Standard Network Access Protocol (SNAP) is the standard of a new TCTS Datapac network. Datapac was the first to provide packet switching for commercial use in Canada; it allows information to be put in standard-size packets for data transmission and gives the format in which data can be transmitted. Approval of standards for such universal packet-switching data networks by the UN's International Consultative Committee on Telephone and Telegraphs in March 1976 means that various data networks can now be interconnected.

Companies belonging to TCTS have started to plan and construct provincial service co-ordination centres where the networks are monitored. If one circuit is broken in an emergency it is reported instantly, and another route may be found. In this way, downtime in telecommunications — with its increasingly intolerable costs — is minimized. Such centres are now in New Brunswick, Quebec and Ontario. Another is planned for Manitoba.

Canada Post and CNCP Telecommunications have extended their Telepost service to the public. Telepost features next-day delivery and gives Canada Post electronic mail for the first time; it is also linked with the US Mailgram network. The Infodat network, a digital service provided by CNCP, has expanded to 30 servicing locations.

CNCP plans to introduce a nation-wide digital data switching network called Info-Switch, which will offer both circuit and packet switching.

The first leg of Double DUV (Data-Under-Voice) went into operation in June 1975. Double DUV is an improved method of sending data communications over the existing microwave network and is based on a new transmission technique that transmits digital data in a portion of the microwave radio spectrum below the frequencies normally used for voice telecommunications. The existing service from Montreal to Winnipeg was expected to reach from Halifax to Vancouver by spring 1977.

One of the federal government's top priorities in telecommunications is extending access to basic communications to all Canadians, particularly those living in isolated or rural parts of the country. At the other extreme — in Canada's urban centres — the demand for access to good communications grows while the radio frequency spectrum becomes more congested. Use of the spectrum can be expanded by going to higher frequencies than those occupied now or by more efficient use of existing frequencies. This places demands on government to carry out research in opening up higher frequency bands and setting policy on allocation of frequencies. Use of frequencies between 10 and 20 GHz are expected to grow dramatically in the next decade.

There is an evident and growing tendency for many formerly distinct systems of electronic communications to become interconnected. One important symptom of this development is the rapid integration of computers and communications, the economic benefits of which are already being exploited.

Federal policy is that communications should be developed with regard for its impact on Canadian social and cultural values, the economy and the quality of life.

Telephone wires carry communications beside the Trans-Canada Highway near Wawa, Ont.

Mail delivery by letter carrier was increased to 5,236,834 points of call in 1974-75.

The Postal Service

At the end of the 1974-75 fiscal year, 8,655 postal facilities were in operation. Mail delivery by letter carrier was increased by 153,810 points of call, making a total of 5,236,834 points on 11,968 full-time and 459 partial letter-carrier routes; there are now 281 post offices providing letter-carrier service. Improvements continue to be made in the frequency and quality of service to isolated or remote communities where mail transportation is normally provided by air.

The coding and mechanization program began in 1972 with the goal of achieving more efficient handling of first class mail. Automated electronic equipment is capable of sorting first class mail at speeds of from 20,000 to 30,000 pieces an hour by use of the postal code. By the end of 1975 it had been installed in Ottawa, Winnipeg, Regina, Saskatoon, Edmonton, Calgary and Saint John, NB. Toronto and Vancouver facilities were expected to hook up to the national network in 1976, and all of the 26 cities that account for 85 per cent of domestic mail will have automatic high-speed mail sortation by 1978.

Other new machinery currently being introduced is capable of sorting flats, or oversize mail, at speeds of up to 6,000 pieces an hour. Since first class parcels and small packets are already being machine-sorted, this means that now virtually all classes and kinds of mail can be sorted mechanically.

Canada Post was charged with the responsibility of helping to raise funds for the 1976 Montreal Olympic Games. In addition to a number of commemorative stamps, a series of semi-postals was issued, together with a unique program of stamp sculptures in gold, silver and bronze. Several other Olympic-related products were also offered in post offices across the country in support of Olympic funding.

The National Postal Museum, located in Ottawa, is constantly adding to its unique collection of philatelic and historical items, and in its first year attracted more than 20,000 visitors from inside and outside Canada.

The Olympics

The Games of the XXI Olympiad have passed into history, leaving Canadians with a new pride of achievement and a reawakened interest in amateur sport and physical fitness. In 1976 the finest young athletes in the world came to Canada to compete with one another in the spirit of friendship and true sportsmanship. Those who had the opportunity to witness or take part in the sports activities over the last two weeks in July gained exciting insights into the Olympic movement and shared the unity of spirit that prevailed through the great quadrennial festival of world youth.

With the staging of the 1976 Olympic Games, Canada assumed an active role in a tradition that began in 776 BC and continued for a thousand years until the Christian Emperor Theodosius banned them in 393 AD because he considered them a pagan festival. The tradition was revived 1,500 years later when French fitness enthusiast Pierre de Coubertin succeeded in having the first Games of modern times staged at Athens in 1896.

Montreal's bid to host the Games of 1976 was accepted by the International Olympic Committee (IOC) at a meeting in Amsterdam on May 12, 1970. Following established Olympic protocol, the IOC entrusted the organization of the Games to the Canadian Olympic Association; COA then delegated its mandate to a special organizing committee, which quickly adopted the nickname COJO, the acronym for Comité organisateur des Jeux olympiques, its title in French.

National teams marching into the Olympic stadium for the opening ceremony.

The main site of the Games, with the Olympic Village in the foreground.

The sports program adopted for the Montreal Games was the official IOC list of 21 sports, with some slight variations from the program of the 1972 Munich Games. On the program were track and field, archery, basketball, boxing, canoeing, cycling, equestrian sports, fencing, football (soccer), gymnastics, handball, field hockey, judo, modern pentathlon, rowing, shooting, swimming (including diving and water polo), volleyball, weightlifting, wrestling and yachting. The main variation in the sports program was the inclusion of women's competition in basketball, handball and rowing.

Sports Facilities

One of COJO's first decisions was to choose Maisonneuve Park as the main site of the Games. One of the city's major green spaces, the park already contained a 50-ha (hectare) section that had been earmarked for Olympic purposes for half a century; the Maurice Richard Arena and the Maisonneuve Sports Centre, which housed a gymnasium and swimming pool, had already been built there in the hope that they would one day be used for the Olympics.

The Olympic Park section was redeveloped, leaving only the Maurice Richard Arena to be used for boxing preliminaries and wrestling and the Maisonneuve Sports Centre for wrestling; the latter was renamed the Pierre Charbonneau Sports Centre to honour an original member of the Organizing Committee who died in 1975. Added were a stadium-pool-tower complex, a velodrome, underground parking north and south of the stadium, training and warmup areas, and landscaping. Another addition was a station for the métro rapid transit system, which was extended northeastward prior to the Games and which carried up to 45,000 persons an hour to and from Olympic Park during July.

Despite work stoppages and an unusual construction technique, the stadium complex and velodrome were completed in time to become favourites of both competitors and spectators. Prefabricated elements were post-tensioned into place to permit the domed roof of the velodrome to span 190 m (metres) without intermediate supports and the cantilever roof of the stadium to overhang all the seating by 50 m. There is not a pillar or support anywhere to interfere with the view of the spectators. The roof of the swimming centre is similar to that of the velodrome, and both are covered with a latticed superstructure with double-paned acrylic openings through which daylight bathes the interiors.

Construction of the tower, which was to have been the outstanding architectural feature of the stadium complex, was suspended before the Games, to be completed later. This tower is to be used as a mast from which cables will be fastened to the ring circling the top of the stadium to permit a membrane covering to be lowered and enclose the stadium. When completed the tower will also house 18 floors of sports facilities.

The stadium was the site of the most ancient of Olympic sports, the track and field events that were the bases of competition in the original stadium at Olympia 2,600 years earlier. It also was the site of the equestrian team grand prix jumping and of 11

The Olympic Basin, built for the rowing and canoeing events.

The new Olympic Yachting Centre at Kingston, Ont.

association football matches, including the winners' and losers' finals; the 42.195-km (kilometre) marathon and 22-km walk started and finished there. It was also there that the impressive opening ceremony and the sad and moving farewells of the closing ceremony took place.

The swimming events, including diving and water polo, took place in the swimming centre, while the velodrome was home to the track cycling events and the judo matches.

Five other major construction projects provided facilities for the Games. The city of Montreal, which undertook the erection of the stadium, pool and velodrome in Olympic Park, also built the Olympic basin for rowing and canoeing and three competition sites outside the city. The fifth major element was the Olympic Yachting Centre at Kingston.

The basin is on Notre Dame Island and extends 2 188 m alongside the St. Lawrence Seaway canal approaching the St. Lambert lock. With its 10,000 permanent grandstand and bleacher seats supplemented by grassy banks where another 20,000 spectators could stand or sit, the basin was one of the most popular of the Olympic sites, only minutes from downtown Montreal by car or métro.

Another popular site in a natural setting was the equestrian centre at Bromont, 65 km from Montreal in the Eastern Townships. Despite the distance, large crowds attended the equestrian and modern pentathlon events in their lush setting.

Two other rural competition sites were the archery centre at Joliette, developed next door to the popular Joliette Archery Club 60 km from Montreal, and the L'Acadie shooting range, developed at the Montreal Anglers and Hunters Inc. sports centre 40 km away.

The major facility away from Montreal was the Olympic Yachting Centre at Kingston, Ontario, a major facility that will be used by generations of sailors taking

156

CANADA 1977

part in international regattas on Lake Ontario. Portsmouth Harbour, a commercial harbour in the days of sailing ships, had fallen into disrepair. It was dredged and completely rebuilt by the federal government in time for the Olympics; new harbour walls were constructed, and the breakwater was extended by a revolutionary A-frame structure of steel pipe driven into the harbour floor and faced with concrete slabs weighing 18 t (metric tons).

The land bordering the harbour was obtained with financial assistance from the Ontario government and prepared to receive the Olympic Yachting Centre, a building designed by a consortium of Kingston architects and financed by COJO. The main body of the two-storey building is a steel space frame structure of prefabricated steel sections assembled on site. The lower floor contains offices, a large lobby and a measuring room for the inspection of hulls, sails and spars. A grass-covered ramp leads to the second-level promenade deck, which contains a restaurant overlooking the marina and competition areas in the lake outside.

From the outset, the Games organizers were determined to use existing facilities as much as possible. With the concurrence of the IOC and sports federations they settled on these: Montreal Forum, home of the Canadiens of the National Hockey League, where all the gymnastic events and the finals in basketball, boxing, handball and volleyball were played; Etienne Desmarteau Centre, a new municipal sports facility, where basketball preliminaries were played; Claude Robillard Centre, another new sports facility built by the city especially for the Games, where some of the handball preliminaries and water polo preliminaries were played; the St. Michel Arena, still another municipal facility, where the weightlifting events were staged; Paul Sauvé Centre, a privately owned sports complex, where the volleyball preliminaries were played; the University of Montreal winter stadium, where the fencing events were staged; and Molson Stadium at McGill University, where the field hockey matches were played.

Several out-of-town facilities were used for the association football and handball tournaments. With 13 teams entered in the football tournament, some of the matches up to and including the quarter finals were played at Varsity Stadium, Toronto, at Lansdowne Park, Ottawa, and at the Sherbrooke Stadium; the semifinals were played at Varsity and Olympic stadiums, the final at Olympic Stadium. Eighteen teams competed in the handball tournament, and preliminary matches were played at the Laval University physical education centre in Quebec City and at the Sherbrooke Sports Palace.

The Olympic Village

A major obligation imposed by the IOC on an Olympic organizing committee is to "provide an Olympic Village for the men and one for the women so that competitors and team officials can be housed together and fed at a reasonable price. The Village shall be located as close as possible to the main stadium, practice fields and other facilities".

The Olympic Village for the Montreal Games was developed as a pyramidal apartment complex in the Municipal Golf Course section of Maisonneuve Park, 800 m from the stadium. Set in three hectares of parkland, with another 30 ha of

Queen Elizabeth and Prince Andrew visiting the Games with Mr. Harold Wright, President of COA.

park extending beyond, four half-pyramids rise 20 storeys above a plateau over-looking Olympic Park. Three of the half-pyramids comprised the men's village and the other was for the women athletes.

The 989 apartments in the four buildings and large areas of floor space in what are now commercial sections of the ground floor levels were subdivided into compact sleeping modules to accommodate the athletes. A host of other facilities and programs were available for their recreation, and a broad international menu satisfied their dining needs.

Media Coverage

More than two billion people around the world were able to follow the XXI Olympiad at home via the press, radio and television.

A central press centre was established in the same building as COJO's administrative offices to provide accredited news writers and commentators from around the world with all the facilities they required to get coverage of the Games to their various publications. Other press centres were established at each competition site and press sections were reserved in the seating at all venues.

Much more complex arrangements had to be made for the reporters, commentators and technicians covering the Games for radio and television. The Olympic

Radio and Television Organization had been set up by the CBC as host broadcaster to cover the Games completely, to make its audio-visual coverage available to networks around the world and to provide visiting broadcasters with the means of sending their own comments and pictures to home audiences. Main headquarters for that operation was the former CBC headquarters on Dorchester Boulevard and another was the International Broadcasting Centre on Cité du Havre, part of the Expo 67 complex. Each competition site also had its own facilities. The technical equipment amassed for this operation included 89 colour cameras, 19 videotape recorders and 15 slow-motion VTRs, as well as the great lengths of transmission lines and the monitors and other equipment required by the television reporters at 700 commentator positions. Signals were transmitted across the Atlantic and Pacific oceans by satellite.

Arts and Culture at the XXI Olympiad

An important offshoot of the Games was the stimulation given the visual and performing arts in Canada by the month-long Olympic Arts and Culture Program organized by COJO. The program was offered as a national arts and culture festival involving performing arts groups, individual artists and craftsmen from all parts of Canada. Although the main events were centred in Montreal, where the big exhibitions were displayed and five theatres were busy daily with performances, Ottawa and Kingston also shared in the events.

The Montreal Games gave a number of Canadian designers an opportunity to participate on a scale reminiscent of the remarkable contributions made by Canadian designers.

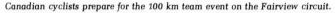

Canadian cyclists prepare for the 100 km team event on the Fairview circuit.

1. Canada's Greg Joy winning the silver medal in the high jump.
2. John Wood of Canada winning the silver medal in the canoe event.
3. Michel Vaillancourt on *Branch County* won the silver medal for Canada in the grand prix individual jumping.

dian designers to Expo 67. Graphics and design became one of COJO's earliest concerns and the team it enlisted quickly produced what was adopted as the official emblem of the Games, the five Olympic rings surmounted by a stylized "M"; designed to fit within the dimensions of a square, it served as the keystone for the entire graphics program of the Games. Red and white, the colours of the Canadian flag, were the official colours of the Games, and the remaining rainbow colours were used in such areas as the sign system, identification, coding and decoration. The pictograms used to identify the different sports were basically those developed for the Munich Games in 1972, with some modifications for greater clarity. The metric system was adopted to support the government's metric program.

The uniforms used by hostesses and guides as well as other COJO and Games officials were designed by four leading costume designers. The COA had other uniforms designed for members of the Canadian team taking part in the Games.

Finances

The 1976 Olympic Games were launched with a determination that they should be self-financing and prove that any Olympic Games could be self-financing. Although that ideal fell short of its mark because of such factors as the surge of inflation that swept across much of the world in the middle 1970s, the techniques that were developed to create revenue were remarkably successful and still may provide a pattern for underdeveloped countries to follow in the staging of future Olympiads.

The two main sources of revenue for the Montreal Games were the national lottery, with million-dollar first prizes, and the sale of Olympic silver and gold coins, both supported by the federal government. Between them they produced enough to cover practically the whole of the pre-inflation budget for the Games.

Both programs benefited amateur sport in general, as well as the Olympics. Five per cent of gross lottery ticket sales in each province went to the appropriate sports agency in that province to finance the training of amateur athletes; the amount ran into millions of dollars in the provinces where sales were highest. The allotment for amateur sport from coin sales was 3 per cent of the face value of the coins sold in other countries, and the allotment went to the country's Olympic committee; in Canada the money went to the Olympic Trust, the financial arm of the COA which provides funds for the training of athletes.

Less spectacular revenue was generated from the sale of special issues of Olympic stamps, from the sale of more than four million tickets to Olympic sports events and from strictly-controlled sale of the privilege of using the Games symbols.

Although the results are not all in yet, economic surveys conducted at varying periods before the event indicated that the XXI Olympiad generated in excess of $2 billion in added economic activity in Canada. The economic benefits included increased revenue from income and sales taxes as well as reduced unemployment costs. At the same time, the growing merchandise trade and revenue from the Games was expected to reduce the deficit on trade in goods with other countries to $4.8 billion in 1976 from $5.5 billion in 1975.

The Games brought upwards of 100,000 persons a day to Canada, and they were accommodated in hotels, motels, tourist rooms, rooms in private homes and

Flags of the nations competing in the equestrian events.

campsites arranged for them by a special agency set up by the Quebec government and known as the Quebec Lodging Bureau. Prices and quality of premises were controlled and, for the most part, the board made hosts of new friends for Canada.

The Olympic Spirit

One of the most exciting aspects of the XXI Olympiad outside the arenas of competition was the arrival of the Olympic flame. The fire was ignited from the sun's rays on the altar of Zeus at Olympia, borne to Athens by a relay of runners, and there transformed into electrical particles for transmission by satellite to Ottawa to be reconstituted as fire by means of a laser. That was the beginning of an event that caught the imagination of the world. In Canada the fire was borne by another relay of runners to Mount Royal in Montreal, where it rested the night before the Games. Its arrival by another relay of torchbearers for the opening ceremony at the Olympic Stadium highlighted the drama of the occasion with its direct link with the ancient birthplace of the Games.

Special visitors to Montreal were the 1,200 young men and women in their late teens from countries around the world who came to share life and experiences with one another at the International Youth Camp, a standard feature of the Olympic Movement. These were young people who could not qualify for places on their countries' Olympic teams but who were active in sports and community affairs and who could make their own contributions to the Olympic spirit.

External Relations

Foreign policy goals

Canada's foreign relations make possible or facilitate many of the everyday activities of Canadians. The businessman who produces for export, the consumer who relies on imports, the graduate student who enters a foreign university under a scholarship exchange, the tourist whose travel abroad is simplified by internationally-accepted passport and civil aviation practices — all take it for granted that Canada's position in the world will not change suddenly in a manner inimical to their interests.

The protection and promotion of Canadians' collective interests abroad involves the activities of more than 20 federal government departments and agencies. The Department of External Affairs co-operates with other departments to assist their international programs, while ensuring that the actions of all departments are consistent with Canadian policy goals.

Foreign policy objectives reflect national priorities as perceived and pursued by government. Unlike domestic policy objectives, however, the objectives of foreign policy are unlikely to be achieved without the co-operation of other governments. Some foreign policy objectives are long-term and involve the welfare of all Canadians — the preservation of Canadian security, for example. Others are short-term and involve more particular interests, such as co-operation with the United States to improve the quality of water in the Great Lakes.

A review of foreign policy published in 1970 identified six major themes of national policy at home and abroad. These are to foster economic growth, safeguard sovereignty and independence, work for peace and security, promote social justice, enhance the quality of life and ensure a harmonious natural environment. The character of Canadian foreign policy at any time is determined by the pattern of emphasis given to these policy themes, as well as by the constraints and opportunities that external and internal circumstances may suggest. In general, the government seeks to emphasize what Canada can do best in the light of the resources available.

Canada and the United States

Canada's relationship with the United States is clearly its most important one. It is a varied and complex relationship, and differences and frictions can and do occur from time to time. However, the basic character of the relationship between the two peoples and governments is very much one of friendship and of constant effort at mutual understanding and co-operation.

Canada and the United States continue to co-operate closely on defence questions. The Permanent Joint Board on Defence, for example, has met regularly since 1940. In 1975, the North American Air Defence (NORAD) Agreement was renewed, transferring full responsibility for control of Canadian airspace to a Canadian command centre.

The two countries co-operate closely in resolving environmental questions of mutual concern. A principle instrument of this co-operation is the International

Canada's Bicentennial gift to the US was the book Between Friends, *and Prime Minister Pierre Trudeau presented a copy to President Gerald Ford.*

Joint Commission, established in 1909 by the Boundary Waters Treaty. The IJC is a unique approach to international environmental co-operation.

Canada and the United States are each other's best customers. The United States provides the market for about two thirds of Canada's exports, while Canada takes approximately one fifth of the exports of the US. There is also great interdependence in the financial field, with large US investments in Canada and substantial Canadian investments in the United States. Canadians have become keenly aware of the magnitude of this economic relationship.

The world trend is discernibly in the direction of interdependence in the economic realm, in science and in technology. For Canada, inevitably, interdependence is likely to mean an even more complex relationship with the US. The balance of benefits of such a trend for Canada may well be substantial, but a major consideration in interdependence with such a large, powerful country is its effect on Canada's separate identity.

Upon reviewing Canada's relations with the US it appeared that the choices open to Canada fell into three broad categories: Canada could seek to maintain more or less the same relationship with the US, with a minimum of policy adjustment; we could move deliberately toward closer integration with the US; or we could pursue a comprehensive, long-term strategy to develop and strengthen our economy and other aspects of our national life and, in the process, reduce the present Canadian vulnerability to political and economic events in the US. The "Third Option" was adopted.

This policy does not entail protectionism or isolationism. On the contrary, it really means a greater involvement for Canada in the rest of the world. It is certainly not anti-American. The effort to diversify relations means that Canadians seek not to supplant but to supplement their relations with the US. Canada's purpose is to strengthen our world position in order to create a better-balanced, more reciprocal and thus healthier relationship between two independent partners.

Implementation of the Third Option policy requires application of a broad range of policy instruments in a number of sectors. In the international realm, efforts are being made to broaden the spectrum of markets to which Canadians have access and to diversify cultural relations by building on the multiplicity of Canada's cultural roots. The two most important targets of Canada's diversification effort are Europe and Japan.

New Directions

Europe

Canada's relations with Europe are founded on deep-rooted historical, linguistic, ethnic, cultural and social affinities. The vast majority of Canadians are of European extraction, and many of the more recent immigrants maintain strong ties with their countries of origin. Canada's economic links with Europe, and particularly with Britain, have been traditionally close, though in recent years they have tended to diminish in relative importance.

However, the European Community is Canada's most important trading partner after the US and presents obvious opportunities for Canada in its search for alternatives to complement its close economic relationship with the US. In March 1976, following two years of preliminary consultation, Canada and the European Community entered into the formal negotiation of a framework agreement for economic and commercial co-operation — otherwise known as the "contractual link". The agreement, the first of its kind to be concluded between the European Community and an industrialized country, is intended to promote industrial co-operation through the expansion of two-way trade, two-way investment flows, intercorporate links, and science and technology exchanges. The agreement will provide for regular consultations and will be non-preferential.

Canada's efforts to develop relations with the European Community as a distinct entity have been paralleled by efforts to strengthen bilateral relations with its individual members and with non-member European countries.

European stability is vital to the assurance of world peace. Through its NATO membership, Canada contributes to peace and security in Europe by helping to maintain a deterrent to conventional and nuclear attack. NATO is the best forum available to Canada for consultation and joint action with the 13 European member states, not only in the military and political but also in the economic, social, scientific and environmental spheres. Canada is also participating in the negotiations that began in Vienna in October 1973 between members of NATO and the Warsaw Pact nations aimed at mutual and balanced force reductions in Central Europe.

Canada participated fully in the two years of negotiations that led in August 1975 to the Final Act of the Conference on Security and Co-operation in Europe, signed in Helsinki by the political leaders of the 35 participating states. This document, which marks a significant step forward in the process of détente, is the groundwork

Prime Minister Trudeau visited Cuba in 1976. He and Premier Fidel Castro addressed a crowd of 20,000 in Cienfuegos.

for expanded co-operation between East and West in the fields of economics, the environment and science and technology. The Final Act enunciates general principles of interstate relations and also provides a basis for increased human contacts and the freer movement of information and ideas amongst the participating states. As a party to this agreement, Canada consolidated its ties with Europe as a whole and set the course for improving its established relations with Eastern Europe.

Asia and the Pacific

With the development of modern transportation and communications, Canadians have become increasingly aware of their position as a Pacific as well as an Atlantic nation. The countries of Asia and the Western Pacific include some of the most highly-industrialized and wealthiest countries of the world, such as Japan,

Australia and New Zealand, and some of the poorest and least-developed, such as Indonesia and India. Canada has established a valuable trading relationship with the former group and has played a major role in assisting the latter.

Japan, Canada's third most-important trading partner, is very important to Canada's goal of diversifying its external relations. Efforts continue to increase the manufactured and upgraded content of Canadian exports to Japan. But the relationship between Canada and Japan is much broader than trade. The two countries are expanding co-operation in political, economic, cultural, scientific, technological and other fields. Matching and complementary programs for the development of Japanese studies in Canada and Canadian studies in Japan have been initiated.

The Sino-Canadian relationship as a whole reflects Canada's belief that the co-operation and participation of the People's Republic of China are essential to peace and stability in the Asian and Pacific regions and in the world at large. Exchanges with China in the fields of industry, science, medicine, culture, education and sports continue to expand, and Sino-Canadian trade has increased and diversified.

Relations with the Rest of the World

Exchanges between Canada and Latin America have been increasing and diversifying. Canada has a permanent observer mission to the Organization of American States and is a member of the Inter-American Development Bank, the Pan-American Health Organization and the Inter-American Institute for Agricultural Sciences, as well as the UN Economic Commission for Latin America. Canada extends development assistance to Latin American countries, on a bilateral basis and through such multilateral bodies as the World Bank and the Inter-American Development Bank.

Canada's major concerns in the Middle East are to achieve a just and lasting peace to end the Arab-Israeli conflict and the development of Canadian relations with countries in the region, in particular commercial relations. Canada has followed a policy of balance and objectivity toward the Arab-Israeli dispute. It holds the view that Resolution 242 of the UN Security Council, November 1967, offers a valid framework upon which to base the negotiations required to achieve a settlement of the dispute. Respect for the sovereignty of Israel and every other state in the Middle East is a condition for an enduring peaceful settlement. Canada supports the right of the Palestinian people to participate in negotiations affecting their future. Canada has contributed to the maintenance of the cease-fire that followed the war of October 1973 by providing a contingent of 1,100 troops to serve with UN peacekeeping/observer forces.

Canada's bilateral relations with Africa have been strenghtened in recent years by increased development assistance, expanded economic and commercial ties, and the common search for social justice in southern Africa. The establishment of cultural, academic and scientific relations with the African countries has only recently begun.

The present relations between Canada and the Commonwealth Caribbean have evolved from historical ties. Common association in the Commonwealth has contributed to mutual understanding through shared traditions, institutions and values. Trading relations with several countries have been close, and have been

Secretary of State for External Affairs Allan MacEachen took time out during his tour of the Middle East to visit Egypt's Pyramids and the Sphinx.

supplemented by considerable Canadian commercial interests and investment in the area. In recent years, communication has increased through movement of large numbers of tourists, students, businessmen and immigrants between the West Indies and Canada. The Commonwealth Caribbean receives the highest per capita disbursements in Canada's aid program.

Multilateral Diplomacy

The preceding paragraphs have dealt with Canada's bilateral relations — relations with individual countries. Achieving Canada's national aims also requires

Prime Minister and Mrs. Trudeau with Israel's Prime Minister Yitzhak Rabin at a dinner in Jerusalem.

multilateral activity — that is, participation in organizations and conferences in which many or most of the other countries of the world are represented and that have as their goal the solution of particular problems.

Multilateral diplomacy is particularly important to the achievement of Canada's aim of developing and strengthening its economy, as there are several international forums dealing with international economic issues. Canada is actively participating in the multilateral trade negotiations in Geneva; the most comprehensive negotiations yet undertaken, they cover tariffs, non-tariff barriers and other measures that impede or distort international trade in industrial and agricultural products. Canada has also played an influential role in the negotiations on international monetary reform conducted under the sponsorship of the International Monetary Fund, and is a founding member of the International Energy Agency established under the auspices of the Organization for Economic Co-operation and Development. Canada works through the International Atomic Energy Agency for the application of nuclear power to peaceful pursuits.

Three international organizations are of special interest to Canada—the UN, the Commonwealth and the French-speaking community.

The United Nations (UN)

Canada has worked diligently to make the UN an effective instrument for international co-operation and to improve its capacity to discharge its Charter responsibilities. The activities of the organization touch on almost every aspect of Canada's foreign policy aims.

Economic questions have attracted increased attention at the UN in recent years. The developing countries make up more than two thirds of its membership, and they exhibit considerable solidarity in UN forums in the promotion of a new world economic order more favourable to them. Canada recognizes the need for changes in international economic relations to reduce disparities between rich and poor nations, at the same time realizing that there exist, and will continue to exist, practical restraints upon the extent to which progress can be made in the short and medium terms. The consensus of all interested parties, both industrialized and developing, is in Canada's view an essential condition for the effective implementation of UN resolutions on economic matters.

Canada has participated in all major UN peacekeeping operations, and in mid-1976 military personnel were serving the UN in this capacity in the Middle East, in Cyprus and in Kashmir. Canada will consider requests to participate in such ventures when they hold the promise of contributing to peace and stability.

Canada plays an active role in efforts in the United Nations and other forums, such as the Conference of the Committee on Disarmament (CCD), to develop effective agreements to prohibit, limit or control the use of armaments, particularly nuclear weapons and other weapons of mass destruction.

A number of conferences organized under UN auspices have dealt with matters of special importance to Canada. At the Law of the Sea Conferences, for example, there have been lengthy and arduous negotiations to draw up a comprehensive and viable treaty on the law of the sea.

Canada participates in all of the specialized agencies of the UN, one of which, the International Civil Aviation Organization, is located in Montreal. Canada also contributes the ninth-largest share of the regular annual budget of the UN; since 1946, Canada has contributed over $700 million to the UN family of organizations.

The Commonwealth and the French-speaking Community

As the colonies within the British Empire achieved self-government and independence, similarities of language, habits, institutional traditions and working methods convinced many national leaders that maintaining some form of association would be valuable. The fruit of that belief is the modern Commonwealth. The shared values and traditions of this association facilitate consultation among governments in a confidential and informal atmosphere that is missing in more complex international organizations. The Commonwealth is able to transcend the differences of ideology, race, region and economic conditions, and to bring a global, multiracial perspective to bear on matters that concern its members and the world at large.

The biennial meetings of Commonwealth heads of government and the annual meeting of Commonwealth finance ministers attract wide public attention. The public is less aware of the programs of functional co-operation and the specialized exchanges that take place regularly under Commonwealth auspices — among parliamentarians, academics, educators, scientists, journalists, broadcasters, health officials and youth leaders. Of the over 50 conferences held each year, about half are organized by non-governmental Commonwealth organizations. Recent meetings held in Canada include the Commonwealth finance ministers and law

ministers, the Commonwealth Air Transport Council and the 23rd Commonwealth
Parliamentary Conference. In 1978 Canada will be host to the 11th Commonwealth
Games in Edmonton, Alberta, which will bring together over 50 teams of young
athletes in friendly competition. The 12th Congress of Commonwealth Universities
and the second General Conference of the Commonwealth Council for Educational
Administration will also be held in Canada.

To demonstrate abroad the bilingual aspect of Canadian society, the federal
government fosters the broadening and strengthening of ties with La Francophonie
—an association of countries that are entirely or partially French-speaking. Canada
plays a very important role in multilateral organizations such as the Agency for
Cultural and Technical Co-operation, the Conference of Ministers of Education and
the Conference of Youth and Sports Ministers of francophone countries.

The provinces are invited to take part in the work of joint commissions and in the
implementation of Canadian government aid programs on the bilateral level. On
the multilateral level, in addition to participation by New Brunswick, Ontario and
Manitoba in some activities of the Agency for Cultural and Technical Co-operation,
the federal government and the government of Quebec have agreed on an arrangement under which the latter has been admitted as a participant in the agency's
institutions, activities and programs. The federal government also gives its support
to various private French-speaking associations that have a Canadian origin or have
a large Canadian participation, either through annual subsidies or by contributing
to the Canadian participation at conferences and seminars.

Federal-provincial Aspects of International Relations

The Canadian provinces have an obvious interest in the international aspects of
matters for which they have domestic responsibility. The Department of External
Affairs maintains close liaison with the provinces to facilitate their international
programs while ensuring a consistent Canadian foreign policy.

Provincial participation in international conferences and in the work of international organizations on subjects of interest to the provinces is assured by including
provincial officials in Canadian delegations and by canvassing provincial governments for their views on the positions and attitudes that the Canadian government
might adopt on these subjects internationally. The federal government assists
provincial officials by making arrangements and appropriate appointments for
provincial visits abroad and by co-ordinating visits of foreign dignitaries to the
provinces. During the negotiation of formal agreements between Canada and other
countries, consultations take place between the federal government and the provinces if the terms of such agreements touch on provincial or joint federal-
provincial fields of jurisdiction.

Projecting Canada's Image Abroad

The Department of External Affairs conducts a public affairs program in liaison
with other federal departments and agencies involved in the cultural and information fields, as well as with the provinces, with organizations and with individuals.

The basic aims of the program outside Canada are to foster in influential circles an awareness of Canada's distinctiveness and culture and an appreciation of Canadian positions on international issues.

This program relates to the collective aims of Canadians in two ways — by creating a favourable climate of opinion for the achievement of foreign policy objectives and by satisfying the growing demand by Canadians that their cultural and academic communities receive international exposure and experience.

Public affairs activity is greatest in the US, Western Europe, Japan and the USSR, reflecting the importance of these areas to Canada. Canada has general cultural or exchange agreements with Belgium, France, the Federal Republic of Germany, Italy and the USSR, and specialized reciprocal programs with a number of other countries. Canadian cultural centres have been established as permanent showcases in Brussels, London and Paris.

Information activities include the promotion and distribution of publications and films about Canada and Canadian foreign policy, exhibits, speaking appearances, media relations and response to inquiries. Cultural activities include assistance to tours abroad by performing arts groups and exhibitions of Canadian art, donations of Canadian books to foreign university and public libraries, and exchanges with other countries of scholars and language teachers and young people pursuing academic, technical and professional studies.

There is also a public affairs program within Canada, whereby information about the department and foreign policy formulation is provided to Canadians.

Flags decorated the site of Habitat Forum, held in Vancouver, BC, in conjunction with the UN Conference on Human Settlements.

the economy

Economic Trends in Canada, 1975-76

In 1975 the Canadian economy registered its worst performance in more than 20 years. The volume of goods and services produced failed to increase. Moreover, this "no-growth" performance in 1975 followed a year of slow growth in 1974, when the economy had also failed to make full use of its productive resources. Consequently, by the end of the year 1975 the Canadian economy was operating substantially below its capacity levels — representing a loss in income and output approaching $12 billion a year and resulting in an unemployment rate of over 7 per cent.

The annual rate of inflation, while decelerating slowly, remained at approximately 10 or 11 per cent, taking the year 1975 as a whole. The deficit on the current account of the balance of international payments jumped to $5.1 billion from a level of $1.6 billion in 1974—a huge increase that was financed by heavy borrowing from abroad. The exchange value of the Canadian dollar remained high, buoyed up by this capital inflow, with effects on costs and prices that tended both to encourage imports and to discourage exports. The position of the government sector in the economy (all levels of government combined) swung around from a surplus of $1.9 billion in 1974 to a deficit of $4.6 billion in 1975, creating major financing problems

The Shell Canada oil refinery in Oakville, Ont.

for governments. And the rate of increase in wage and salary costs continued to outpace those in the United States by a wide margin at a time of declining productivity in Canada, posing a threat to Canada's ability to compete internationally.

These adverse developments must be viewed against the background of the world recession of 1974-75 that affected all of the major industrialized countries — the most serious economic slump since the Great Depression of the 1930s. The effects of this recession were felt in Canada in a variety of ways, but primarily in a sharp drop in the volume of exports as world demand for Canadian export products declined. At the same time Canadian business firms, in company with those of other industrialized countries, had become heavily overstocked with inventories following the world-wide commodity boom of 1973 and early 1974; they responded by massive liquidation of inventories in 1975 in an attempt to restore more balanced stock-to-sales positions. This was a major factor contributing to the recession in this country, as it was in other countries. In addition, the succession of oil price increases administered by the Organization of Petroleum Exporting Countries, while less serious for Canada than for the big oil importers, created conditions that reduced demand for products of the Canadian economy — in part directly, but mainly through its effects on the economies of Canada's major trading partners.

Thus, Canada's economic difficulties in 1975 were related in part, though by no means entirely, to the pattern of international developments. However, the world recession of 1974-75 now appears to have come to an end, with the US economy leading the way into recovery in 1976. The upturn in Europe and Japan so far has been less decisive than in the US, but recovery is also proceeding in these areas. Current assessments are for a steady but, by past standards, rather slow recovery. Consequently, the prospects for the Canadian economy in 1976 were much improved over the previous year. Exports were expected to provide a basic prop under the recovery in Canada and inventory liquidation, which dragged down the growth of output in 1975 and which had almost run its course by early 1976, was not operating as a negative factor. Over-all, it seemed likely that Canada's real gross

Welding pipes for heating and plumbing installations in apartments and commercial buildings.

national product — the volume of goods and services produced — would grow by about 5 per cent in 1976.

While such a rate of growth would be a great improvement over the performance of 1974 and 1975, it would do no more than barely match the potential growth rate of the economy. Thus, even if a 5 per cent growth rate was achieved in 1976, this would have done nothing to close the production gap that had opened up, nor would it have brought down the rate of unemployment. To begin to close the gap and to reduce unemployment, a rate of economic growth in excess of 5 per cent a year will be needed. Given the rather slow recovery expected in the international economy and very real concerns about the rate of inflation in Canada, such a prospect probably lies beyond the year 1976.

Inflation

Canadians are now engaged in a new experiment with a program of anti-inflation controls. No one yet knows how successful this program will be in curbing the

A worker guides a steel beam into place at the construction site of a new department store.

inflation with which the economy is afflicted. As the economy recovers productivity performance will improve, and this should have the effect of gradually reducing the pressures of unit labour costs. In addition, international inflation has subsided perceptibly; for the area covered by the 24-country Organization for Economic Co-operation and Development (OECD), the annual rate of increase in consumer prices was 9.1 per cent in January 1976, compared with 13.4 per cent in the year 1974 and 10.6 per cent in the year 1975.

The controls program should have the effect of somewhat moderating increases in costs and prices in 1976. It should be noted, however, that close to one half of the items included in the consumer price index are exempt from the controls program — agricultural commodities, energy products and imports. Each of these has the potential for substantial increases in 1976.

In a recent report, the OECD forecast that the consumer price index in Canada would rise by about 9¼ per cent in 1976, compared with about 11 per cent in 1975. Reducing the rate of inflation to acceptable levels in Canada is going to be a long and difficult process.

ROBERT CROZIER

Natural Wealth

Agriculture

Farming is carried on in all provinces of Canada and in a limited way in a few areas of the Yukon Territory and the Northwest Territories. Although there are exceptions, especially in the Peace River area of Alberta and British Columbia, farms are for the most part scattered within a 320 km (kilometre) strip along Canada's southern boundary. There are currently about 310,000 farms, some in the western wheat and beef production area covering thousands of hectares.

Average farm size has increased from 185 ha (hectares) in 1971 to about 200 ha in 1976. Originally settlement in eastern Canada was planned on the basis of 40 ha per farm and farms in western Canada were laid out in 64 ha parcels; today there is a considerable range in size in all farming regions. As the number of farms has decreased most of the land has been added to the farms that remain, with the consequence that current farm areas are usually multiples of 40 or 64 ha.

There are about 70 000 000 ha of land in agriculture in Canada, of which some 40 000 000 ha are improved and used for intensive production; the unimproved land is generally unsuited for cultivation and used mainly for grazing purposes, although in some regions much of this type of land is covered with bush and forest. Although the amount of land used in agriculture has slightly decreased in recent years, the amount of improved land has remained relatively constant. Because of climatic restrictions and present economic circumstances, very little additional land is likely to be brought into agricultural production in the near future.

Approximately 5 per cent of Canada's labour force is employed in farming. Although there has been a slight increase recently, the agricultural work force steadily declined in the years before 1974. The disappearance of farm labour as rural populations migrated to developing urban centres resulted in extensive mechanization of agriculture. As a consequence of this and of the relatively rapid acceptance of new technology by farmers, productivity per worker increased in agriculture at a more rapid rate than in non-agricultural industries. From 1960 to 1974 the output per worker in agriculture increased by 95 per cent, compared with a 39 per cent increase per worker in other industries. The average current output of one farm worker provides food for about 50 people.

Farms that are owned and operated by farm families dominate the agricultural picture in all parts of Canada. Only about 2.1 per cent of farms are incorporated and approximately 1.9 per cent are family farm corporations. About 5.6 per cent of farms are operated as partnerships, many of which include individuals who are closely related. In the last census, 69 per cent of farm operators owned the land they operated, 26 per cent partly owned and partly rented their farm land, and 5 per cent operated only rented land.

Although farming takes place in every province, 79 per cent of Canada's farm land is in the Prairies; this is reflected in farm income figures. In 1974 total net farm income was about $3,400 million, distributed as follows: British Columbia, $163 million; the Prairie provinces, $2,223 million; Ontario, $541 million; Quebec, $344 million; and the Maritime provinces, $128 million. The total capital value of farm real estate, livestock and machinery in 1974 was estimated to be $36,049 million.

There are many types of farms in Canada, but most may be roughly classified as one of the following: grain, dairy, livestock (excluding dairy), combination grain and livestock, and specialty crops. Specialty crops include fruits, tobacco, potatoes, sugar beets and vegetables.

Grain and oilseeds constitute 62 per cent of the value of exports. Although Canadian agricultural products are exported to many parts of the world, the European Economic Community countries are Canada's most important export market. Agricultural exports account for over 12 per cent of the total value of all Canadian exports, and agriculture provides about 2.7 per cent of gross national product.

Besides providing an abundance of food, agriculture benefits the country in many other ways. Transportation charges resulting from the movement of agricultural products provide revenue to Canada's railway companies, shipping companies and port facilities. The processing of farm products and the manufacture of farm machinery, equipment, fertilizers and other supplies sold to farmers contribute to industrial employment. Farm operators are also an important market for building materials, petroleum products, electric power, veterinary services and other necessities. At the rural retail level, many people depend on farmers' purchases of goods and services for their livelihoods.

Field Crops

Spring wheat was grown on more than 7 700 000 ha of the Prairies in 1975. Historically, wheat has contributed significantly to the Prairie economy in particular and to the Canadian economy as a whole. Farm cash receipts for wheat in 1975

Irrigation systems pump water from BC rivers to otherwise dry and unproductive land near Kamloops.

Hay baled in the new circular fashion, near Westbourne, Man.

amounted to $2,463 million, an increase of $429 million over 1974. Wheat is also a significant contributor of foreign exchange for Canada; in 1975, 10 740 000 t (metric tonnes) of wheat were exported — over 75 per cent of the total crop.

However, wheat is not the only grain grown in Canada; oats and barley (particularly in the Prairies) and corn (in Ontario) are essential to the Canadian livestock industry. In 1975 Prairie farmers grew 12 450 000 t of oats and barley and total Canadian production of these grains amounted to 13 860 000 t.

The oilseeds—rapeseed, flaxseed, soya beans and sunflower seeds—make up the third major type of field crop. These crops are processed to produce vegetable oils for human consumption or industrial use and high-protein meal for livestock feed. Production of rapeseed, flaxseed and sunflower seed is centred in the Prairie provinces, that of soya beans in Ontario. In 1975 there were 1 620 000 ha planted to rapeseed, 570 000 ha to flaxseed, 157 800 ha to soya beans and 25 000 ha to sunflower seeds. Production amounted to 1 640 000 t of rapeseed, 445 000 t of flaxseed, 367 000 t of soya beans and 30 000 t of sunflower seeds.

Outside the Prairies, field crop production is more diversified. The degree of emphasis placed on livestock production influences the kinds of field crops grown and the proportion of land devoted to forage crops, pasture and feed grains. In Ontario, grain corn is an important crop for livestock feed as well as for industrial uses; in 1975, production amounted to 3 320 000 t. Grain corn is also becoming increasingly important in Quebec. Besides grain corn, Ontario also produced 8 960 000 t of fodder corn in 1975.

Although it is raised in relatively small areas, tobacco has a high cash value. Most of Canada's tobacco production is centred in Ontario, but some takes place in Quebec and a smaller amount in the Maritimes. Winter wheat and vegetables are other important sources of income for Ontario farmers.

Horticultural Crops

The fruit and vegetable industry is an important part of the agricultural and food distribution sectors of the economy. Fresh and processed fruits and vegetables account for more than one third of the quantity of all food consumed in Canada. There are over 25 fruit and vegetable crops grown commercially in Canada. The annual farm value of these crops in 1974 amounted to $564 million.

By far the most important fruit crop grown in Canada is the apple, which accounts for over 43 per cent of the value of commercial Canadian fruits. Commercial apple orchards are found in Nova Scotia, New Brunswick, southern Quebec, Ontario and the interior of British Columbia, particularly in the Okanagan Valley. Tender tree fruits — pears, peaches, cherries and plums — are also grown in Ontario, with the most important concentrations in the Niagara region and in Essex County. These fruits, as well as apricots, are also grown on a large scale in the southern part of the Okanagan Valley in British Columbia.

In addition to tree fruits, strawberries and raspberries are cultivated commercially in the Maritimes, Quebec, Ontario and British Columbia. On land near urban areas many such operations are being rapidly converted from the traditional farm harvesting to "pick your own" harvesting. British Columbia fruit growers also produce loganberries commercially in the Lower Mainland and on Vancouver Island. Grapes are grown in the Niagara District of Ontario and in the Okanagan Valley of British Columbia; grape production has increased 11 per cent since 1970, reflecting the increasing acceptance of Canadian wines during that period. The native blueberry is found wild over large areas in Canada and is harvested in commercial quantities in the Atlantic provinces and Quebec; a cultivated crop is grown in British Columbia.

The production of field-grown vegetables in Canada is seasonal. During the winter when no domestic vegetables are being harvested, except in greenhouses, supplies of most fresh vegetables are imported from the US. During the growing season a varying percentage of domestic requirements are met from Canadian crops. Some vegetables are exported from Canada, particularly to a few large centres of population in the US close to the border.

Potatoes are the most important of the vegetables produced in Canada. Production slightly exceeds consumption and normally about 5 per cent are exported. Potatoes are produced commercially in all provinces except Newfoundland, with the Maritimes accounting for nearly 50 per cent of Canadian production. Soil and weather conditions combine to make regions within the Maritime provinces ideal potato growing areas.

The processing industry plays an important part in the marketing of Canadian-grown fruits and vegetables. Over the years factories have been built in most of the important growing regions and considerable portions of the fruit and vegetable crops are canned, frozen, or otherwise processed each season, especially asparagus, beans, peas, corn and tomatoes. In recent years the importance of freezing has been increasing. Most vegetables for processing are grown under a system whereby the processor contracts annually with each grower for certain amounts.

Over the past several years the processing of canned tender tree fruits has declined considerably and imports have increased rapidly; in 1974 this situation continued with respect to imports, while the total weight of tender fruit processed

Potatoes are the major source of income from field crops in Prince Edward Island and New Brunswick.

in Canada increased. Over the past 25 years the weight and value of exported vegetables has varied considerably, but there is a slight upward trend. However, in the same period vegetable imports have doubled.

In 1974 the supply of domestic and imported fruits and vegetables remained relatively unchanged from 1973. The per capita domestic disappearance of all fruits for 1974 of 117.26 kg (kilograms) fresh equivalent weight was marginally lower than in 1973, but remained above the five-year (1969-73) average of 114.30 kg. Of this total 56.33 kg per capita were fresh, 1.20 kg were frozen, 25.82 kg were canned, 4.65 kg were dried and 28.50 kg were made into juice; jams, jellies and marmalades accounted for 0.68 kg per capita and unspecified uses for 0.07 kg. The per capita disappearance of vegetables (excluding potatoes) was 56.59 kg in 1974, and this represented an increase from the five-year (1969-73) average of 51.71 kg. The total included: 37.62 kg of fresh vegetables; 12.73 kg of canned vegetables; 4.70 kg of frozen vegetables; and 1.53 kg otherwise used.

Including potatoes and mushrooms there were 244.99 kg of fruit and vegetables available per capita for consumption in Canada in 1974.

The farm value of greenhouse industry sales jumped from $85.2 million in 1973 to $105.3 million in 1974; the production of greenhouse tomatoes and cucumbers alone accounted for 16 per cent of industry sales. However, the benefits of this growth were somewhat off-set by the fact that fuel and other costs also rose; the average fuel expenditure per farm jumped 44 per cent. The total area operated under glass and plastic in the greenhouse industry increased only marginally.

In 1974, nurseries had a total revenue of $87 million, an increase of 29 per cent from 1973. Approximately 39 per cent of this represents growers' sales of traditional fruit and nursery stock, and 35 per cent was earned by supplying the increasing demand for contracted services.

Sugar beets are grown commercially in Quebec, Manitoba and Alberta, and beet sugar factories are located in these provinces. In Quebec commercial production is centred in the St-Hilaire area of the Eastern Townships. Alberta (where sugar beets are grown under irrigation) produces the largest crop.

Maple syrup is produced commercially in Nova Scotia, New Brunswick, Quebec and Ontario. In 1974 Canada produced 7 960 000 litres of maple syrup, 137 t of maple sugar and 156 t of maple taffy. The bulk of the crop comes from the Eastern Townships of Quebec, a district famous in both Canada and the US as the centre of the maple products industry. Virtually all of the maple syrup we export goes to the US. Much of the syrup sold in Canada is marketed in one-gallon (4.55 litres) cans direct to the consumer from the producer, but a considerable amount of both sugar and syrup is sold each year to processing firms.

In 1974 Canada produced 7 960 000 litres of maple syrup, most of which came from sugar bushes in Quebec.

Honey production was marginally greater in 1975 than in 1974. Honey is produced commercially in all provinces except Newfoundland, and honey bees are kept in some districts for the added purpose of pollinating certain fruit and seed crops. Yields naturally vary to some extent from year to year, but Alberta is consistently the largest producer, supplying 30 per cent of Canada's honey crop in 1975. To facilitate storage, shipment and uniformity of quality, large quantities of Canadian honey are pasteurized. Beekeepers' marketing co-operatives are active in several provinces. In 1974 Canada exported 3 175 000 kg of honey valued at $3.7 million, down substantially from the 7 303 000 kg exported in 1973. Exports went mainly to Britain and the US.

Livestock

Preliminary estimates for 1975 indicate that total cash receipts from farm produce were $9,790 million, of which $4,782 million came from livestock and animal products. Cattle (including calves) and pig sales in 1975 amounted to $1,778 million and $894 million respectively. Cash receipts from the sale of sheep and lambs in 1975 increased to about $14.7 million.

On July 1, 1975 the number of cattle and calves on farms in Canada (not including Newfoundland, which had 7,138 head at the time of the June 1, 1971, Census) was estimated at 15,260,000, up 2 per cent from 14,948,000 on July 1, 1974. This was a record high for total cattle at that time of year. Beef cows, estimated at 4,375,500, were up 2 per cent, while beef heifers were up 3 per cent to 1,578,700 from 1,538,100 on July 1, 1974. Steers were up 5 per cent, while calf numbers showed a modest increase of one per cent.

Inspected slaughter of cattle in 1975, as reported by Agriculture Canada, was up 12.2 per cent to 3,337,687, while calf slaughter showed a dramatic increase of 73.6 per cent, moving from 392,811 in 1974 to 682,094 in 1975.

Agriculture Canada also reports that exports of slaughter cattle (90 kg and more) to the US amounted to 112,063, an increase of 1372.0 per cent from 8,167 head in 1974, while feeder cattle (90 kg and more) increased 285.0 per cent from 10,109 in 1974 to 28,762 in 1975.

The weighted average price per hundred kilograms of A1 and A2 steers at Toronto was $21.31 in 1975 — below the 1974 price of $22.39.

On July 1, 1975, pigs on farms (not including Newfoundland, which had 14,639 at the June 1, 1971, Census) numbered 5,254,000, down 18 per cent from July 1, 1974. Pigs slaughtered in federally inspected plants during 1975 totalled 7,656,334 according to Agriculture Canada, a decrease of 14.4 per cent from 1974. The decreased slaughter resulted in increased prices, making the weighted average price at Toronto $30.49 per hundred kilograms for Index 100 hogs, up from $22.81 in 1974. Agriculture Canada reports that total exports of dressed pork were up almost 4 per cent to 43 224 933 kg in 1975 from 41 749 013 kg in 1974.

The sheep and lamb population of Canada (not including Newfoundland, which had 9,384 at the June 1, 1971, Census) declined to 702,300 by July 1975 from 764,200 in July 1974, a drop of 8 per cent. The West showed a drop of 5 per cent; the East a drop of 12 per cent. Federally inspected slaughter of sheep and lambs, as reported by Agriculture Canada, showed a very slight increase to 186,566 head in

Table 1. Estimated meat production and disappearance, 1974 and 1975

Animal	Year	Animals slaughtered No.	Meat exports t¹	'000 lb.	Production t¹	'000 lb.	Domestic disappearance t¹	'000 lb.	Per capita consumption t¹	lb.
Beef............	1974	3,629,300	26 064	57,461	906 789	1,999,106	965 820	2,129,247ʳ	43.0	94.7
	1975	4,069,900	20 325	44,808	993 773	2,190,873	1 058 993	2,334,656	46.4	102.3
Veal............	1974	615,800	2	2	35 115	77,415	35 561	78,397ʳ	1.6	3.5
	1975	1,008,800	2	2	55 463	122,273	55 513	122,385	2.4	5.4
Pork............	1974	10,289,300	41 810	92,174	611 100	1,347,230	610 300	1,345,468ʳ	27.1	59.9
	1975	8,358,300	40 682	89,687	494 613	1,090,424	501 549	1,105,716	22.0	48.4
Mutton and lamb............	1974	424,300	57	126	8 240	18,167ʳ	25 790	56,857ʳ	1.1	2.5
	1975	423,500	85	187	8 205	18,090	29 591	65,237ʳ	1.3	2.9
Offal............	1974	—	—	—	58 824	129,683	37 761	83,248ʳ	1.7	3.7
	1975	—	—	—	59 364	130,873	35 419	78,084	1.5	3.4

¹Metric tonnes.
²Included with beef.
ʳRevised figures.
—Nil or zero.

Table 2. Per capita disappearance of meats on a cold dressed carcass weight basis

Year	Beef		Veal		Mutton and lamb		Pork		Offal		Canned meat		Total	
	kg²	lb.	kg²	lb.	kg²	lb.	kg²	lb.	kg²	lb.	kg²	lb.	kg²	lb.
1935	24.3	53.6	4.4	9.8	2.7	6.0	17.8	39.3	2.5	5.5	0.7	1.5	52.5	115.7
1940	24.7	54.5	4.9	10.8	2.0	4.5	20.3	44.7	2.5	5.5	0.6	1.3	55.0	121.3
1945	29.7	65.4	5.6	12.4	2.0	4.3	23.9	52.8	2.5	5.6	1.5	3.3	65.2	143.8
1950	23.0	50.8	4.3	9.4	1.0	2.2	24.9	55.0	2.2	4.9	2.3	5.1	57.8	127.4
1955	31.3	69.1	3.8	8.4	1.2	2.6	22.3	49.2	2.4	5.3	1.9	4.2	63.0	138.8
1960	31.8	70.0	3.1	6.9	1.3	2.9	23.9	52.6	2.2	4.8	2.9	6.4	65.1	143.6
1966¹	38.1	84.0	3.1	6.9	1.8	3.9	21.3	47.0	1.6	3.6	1.9	4.2	67.9	149.6
1967¹	37.7	83.2	3.2	7.0	1.9	4.2	24.7	54.5	1.8	3.9	2.1	4.7	71.4	157.5
1968¹	38.6	85.1	3.1	6.8	2.2	4.9	24.3	53.5	1.7	3.7	2.1	4.7	72.0	158.7
1969¹	38.8	85.6	2.3	5.1	2.3	5.0	23.3	51.4	1.7	3.8	2.1	4.6	70.5	155.5
1970¹	38.3	84.4	2.1	4.6	2.1	4.6	26.6	58.7	1.5	3.4	2.1	4.7	72.8	160.4
1971¹	40.5	89.2	2.1	4.7	1.5	3.3ʳ	31.0	68.3ʳ	2.0	4.4	...	...	77.1	169.9
1972	42.0	92.5	1.6	3.5	2.1	4.7ʳ	27.7	61.0ʳ	1.9	4.1	...	...	75.2	165.8
1973	41.6	91.8	1.4	3.1	1.7	3.7	26.1	57.6	1.6	3.6	...	...	72.5	159.8
1974	43.0	94.7	1.6	3.5	1.1	2.5	27.2	59.9	1.7	3.7	...	...	74.5	164.3
1975	46.4	102.3	2.4	5.4	1.3	2.9	22.2	48.4	1.5	3.4	...	...	73.7	162.4

¹ Intercensal revision.
² Kilograms.
ʳ Revised figures.
... Figures not available.

1975, as opposed to 185,077 in 1974. Exports of sheep and lambs to the US were up to 2,937 in 1975 from 803 in 1974. Imports of slaughter sheep and lambs increased from 28,872 in 1974 to 51,608 in 1975.

Dairying

July 1, 1975 estimates place the number of milk cows in Canada at 2,132,500. During 1975 they produced 8 017 222 000 kg of milk. Although the dairy industry is important in every province in Canada, production is concentrated in the more densely populated regions of Quebec and Ontario. These two provinces accounted for 74.5 per cent of the country's milk supply in 1975.

The most important manufactured dairy products were butter, cheese, concentrated milk products and ice cream mix; approximately 63 per cent of the total milk supply was used this way. Fluid milk sales accounted for 31 per cent and farm use made up the remaining 6 per cent. Farm use figures include milk fed to livestock, farm home consumption and, previous to 1974, farm-made butter.

Dairy farms have been decreasing in numbers but increasing in size during the past decade. In the census years of 1961, 1966 and 1971 there were, respectively, 309,000, 222,000 and 145,000 farms reporting milk cows. The principal dairy breeds in Canada are Holstein, Ayrshire, Guernsey and Jersey. During 1975, the farm value of milk production was approximately $1,444 million; the farm value of milk used in factories was $758 million and that for fluid sales $619 million.

Dairy cattle in the stock yards at Kitchener, Ont.

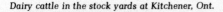

Table 3. Milk production and utilization, by regions, 1974-75

Region	Year	Total milk production		Milk used for dairy factory products		Fluid milk sales		Milk used on farms	
		t	'000 lb.	t	'000 lb.	t	'000 lb.	t	'000 lb.
Maritimes	1974	329 863	727,224	134 158	295,767	175 870	387,728	19 835	43,729
	1975	348 420	768,137	151 289	333,536	176 595	389,326	20 536	45,275
Quebec and Ontario	1974	5 650 485	12,457,186	3 694 911	8,145,885	1 667 468	3,676,137	288 106	635,164
	1975	5 975 533	13,173,794	4 036 738	8,899,483	1 625 077	3,582,682	313 718	691,629
Prairies	1974	1 182 534	2,607,042	620 013	1,366,895	403 778	890,179	158 743	329,968
	1975	1 199 178	2,643,737	661 306	1,457,931	400 217	882,328	137 655	303,478
British Columbia	1974	462 725	1,020,135	141 693	312,380	298 256	657,543	22 776	50,212
	1975	494 089	1,089,281	166 401	366,852	299 796	660,938	27 892	61,491
Totals, Canada	1974	7 625 607	16,811,587	4 590 775	10,120,927	2 545 372	5,611,587	489 460	1,059,073
	1975	8 017 220	17,674,949	5 015 734	11,057,802	2 501 685	5,515,274	499 801	1,101,873

Table 4. Summary of supply and disposition of poultry meat and eggs, 1975

	Total poultry meat[1]		Fowl[1]		Chicken[1]		Turkey[1]		Goose[1]		Duck[1]		Eggs		
	'000 kg	'000 lb.	'000 kg	'000 lb.	'000 kg	'000 lb.	'000 kg	'000 lb.	'000 kg	'000 lb.	'000 kg	'000 lb.	'000 kg	'000 lb.	'000 doz.
Stocks at January 1	40874	90,110	2 350	5,181	15787	34,804	22220	48,987	88	195	428	943			5,086
Production	406542	896,263	30613	67,489	285229	628,815	85989	189,572	955	2,105	3757	8,282			444,925
Imports	12874	28,383	554	1,221	9266	18,935	2 353	5,187			702	3,040			12,092
Total	460290	1,014,756	33517	73,891	310282	682,554	110562	243,746	1043	2,300	4887	12,265			462,103
Exports	3 112	6,861	121	267	2063	4,549	536	1,181	392	864	—	—			10,681
Stocks at December 31	22054	48,620	2 504	5,520	7181	15,832	12 109	26,696	3	6	257	566			4,291
Eggs used for hatching															24,061
Domestic disappearance	435 124	959,275	30892	68,104	301038	662,173	97 917	215,869	648	1,430	4630	11,699			423,070
	kg	lb.	kg	lb.	kg	lb.	kg	lb.	kg	lb.	kg	lb.			doz.
Per capita consumption	19.1	42.1	1.4	3.0	13.2	29.0	4.3	9.5	0.03	0.06	0.23	0.51			18.5

[1]Eviscerated weight.
— Nil or zero.

The foothills area of southwestern Alberta produces prime beef cattle.

Poultry and Eggs

A high degree of specialization and concentration has been developing recently in the production of poultry and eggs, particularly in the egg, broiler chicken and turkey industries. The egg industry itself, for example, is further specialized into fields such as hatching eggs, started pullets and shell eggs for the table, and over 80 per cent of eggs are produced by about 5 per cent of producers. The production of broiler chickens and turkeys has comparable features, and a few very large enterprises account for most of the geese and ducks produced in the country.

An egg packing plant near Regina, Sask.

The producers of eggs, turkeys and broiler chickens operate within the constraints of supply-management programs directed by provincial producer marketing boards. The activities of egg producers and turkey producers at the provincial level are co-ordinated by national agencies (the Canadian Egg Marketing Agency and the Canadian Turkey Marketing Agency, respectively), which operate under federal government charters.

Furs

Fur statistics have been collected and published annually since 1920. For the 1974-75 fur season the reported harvest of pelts was 4,355,250, a 13 per cent increase from the 3,841,196 pelts harvested in 1973-74. The value, however, decreased to $41,536,994 from the 1973-74 figure of $52,069,417. The value of wildlife pelts in 1974-75 was $24,949,708, or 60 per cent of total pelts; the value of pelts produced by fur farms decreased from $19,321,892 to $16,587,286 for the 1974-75 season.

Table 5. Number and value of pelts produced by kind, 1973-74 and 1974-75

Kind	1973-74			1974-75		
	Number	Value $	Average value $	Number	Value $	Average value $
Wildlife						
Badger	5,134	110,507	21.52	3,626	56,990	15.72
Bear:						
Black or brown	4,261	221,134	51.90	3,585	114,635	31.98
Grizzly	27	7,550	279.63	20	5,249	262.45
White	546	618,024	1,131.91	548	347,706	634.50
Beaver	431,071	9,072,632	21.05	357,732	5,990,920	16.75
Cougar	40	3,233	80.82	33	3,404	103.15
Coyote or prairie wolf	87,139	3,169,119	36.37	44,366	1,416,512	31.93
Ermine (weasel)	55,968	57,463	1.03	88,098	81,011	0.92
Fisher or pekan	12,566	613,347	48.81	10,163	463,739	45.63
Fox:						
Blue	208	4,909	23.60	207	4,226	20.42
Cross and red	63,321	2,650,470	41.86	43,103	1,450,227	33.65
Silver	533	24,406	45.79	429	13,827	32.23
White	53,415	1,727,350	32.34	31,913	593,249	18.59
Not specified	17,674	859,465	48.63	13,563	429,575	31.67
Lynx	35,372	3,071,387	86.83	20,648	2,331,933	112.94
Marten	62,356	907,428	14.55	47,598	538,250	11.31
Mink	68,425	1,143,721	16.71	63,083	688,792	10.92
Muskrat	1,434,871	3,728,490	2.60	1,762,589	4,519,164	2.56
Otter	18,016	739,146	41.03	15,258	629,655	41.27
Rabbit	15,308	5,719	0.37	8,353	3,595	0.43
Raccoon	73,442	1,075,603	14.65	81,504	1,015,354	12.46
Seal:						
Fur seal—North Pacific[1]	9,169	432,860	47.21[2]	7,543	344,312	45.65[2]
Hair seal[3,4]	130,496	1,789,748	13.71	157,472	3,074,246	19.52
Skunk	867	1,283	1.48	596	862	1.45
Squirrel	183,309	151,700	0.83	469,093	336,755	0.72
Wildcat	4,129	225,095	54.52	3,425	133,235	38.90
Wolf	5,088	230,090	45.22	5,510	246,957	44.82
Wolverine	1,242	105,646	85.06	1,090	115,328	105.81
Sub-total	2,773,993	32,747,525	...	3,241,148	24,949,708	...
Ranch-raised[5]:						
Fox	1,395	137,254	98.39	1,545	162,024	104.87
Mink	1,065,808	19,184,688	18.00	1,112,557	16,425,262	14.76
Sub-total	1,067,203	19,321,892	...	1,114,102	16,587,286	...
Total	3,841,196	52,069,417	...	4,355,250	41,536,994	...

[1] Commonly known as Alaska Fur seal. The value figures are on the net returns to the Canadian government for pelts sold.
[2] The gross average realized price per pelt sold was $97.46 in 1973-74 and $66.83 in 1974-75.
[3] Includes data for the Maritime provinces.
[4] Hair seal data are based on calendar years 1974 and 1975, except for the Northwest Territories which are on a fur year ending June 30.
[5] Ranch-raised data are based on calendar years 1973 and 1974.
... Not applicable.

A fishing fleet near Prince Rupert, BC.

Fisheries

After several years of steadily declining catches, Canada's fish harvest in 1975 gave the first indications of a stabilizing trend, together with the promise of a resurgence of the nation's oldest primary industry.

Total landings in Canada in 1975 amounted to 965 000 t, compared to 969 000 t in 1974. Returns to fishermen from the catch totalled $278 million, 4 per cent less than in the previous year.

However, the value of Canadian exports of fishery products continued to rise, with the 1975 total provisionally estimated at $450 million, up by $15 million over 1974. Following the trend of previous years, some 82 per cent of Canadian exports went to the US and to European countries.

Intensive efforts were made by the federal government during the year to assist the Atlantic Coast groundfish fishery and other distressed sectors of the industry by means of various support programs. At the same time Canada continued to push for international recognition of the need to establish a viable balance between fishing effort and the state of the resources. Forceful representations at sessions of the International Commission for the Northwest Atlantic Fisheries resulted in sizable reductions in the catch quotas allocated to foreign countries that fish the heavily-exploited fishing grounds off Canada's Atlantic Coast.

Lobster catches increased substantially in 1974.

Canada also played a major role at UN Law of the Sea negotiations, seeking support of a change in international sea law whereby coastal states would be given the authority to manage fishery resources off their own coasts. In anticipation of an extension of Canadian jurisdiction in the foreseeable future, Canada took action during the year to conclude fishing agreements with countries that have substantial fisheries off our coasts.

Landings on the Atlantic Coast totalled 797 000 t, or basically the same volume as the previous year. In the course of five years, Atlantic Coast landings have declined by more than 370 000 t. A series of factors, such as severe ice conditions and a strike that paralyzed the Newfoundland trawler fleet, affected the level of landings. However, heavy exploitation by foreign fleets remained the most serious problem.

Catches of cod and flatfish accounted for the largest declines over the previous year. However, ocean perch landings of 100 000 t represented a 15 per cent increase over 1974, and lobster, scallop and shrimp catches all increased substantially.

A drastic drop in salmon catches was the main factor in the over-all decrease in Pacific Coast landings, the 1975 total of 123 000 t entailing a $30 million reduction in landed value for Pacific Coast fishermen. Halibut landings, however, increased by 1 400 t over 1974.

The market value of all Canadian fisheries products in 1975 is estimated at $640 million, a decline of some 5 per cent. Canned fish production was approximately 20 per cent lower than the previous year, almost entirely because of the reduced salmon catch.

The number of commercial fishermen in Canada remained relatively stable at approximately 58,500, of which some 67 per cent were located on the Atlantic Coast and 20 per cent on the Pacific Coast; the remainder were engaged in the inland fisheries. The size of the fishing fleet operating in the sea fisheries was approximately 35,000 vessels.

Forestry

Canada's forests are among her greatest renewable resources. Stretching across the continent in an unbroken belt 966 to 2 092 km wide, they provide raw material for the great lumber, pulp and paper, plywood and other wood-using industries so vital to the country's economy. In addition, the forests of Canada control water run-off and prevent erosion, shelter and sustain wildlife, and offer unmatched opportunities for human recreation and enjoyment.

Forest land — that available for producing usable timber — covers more than 320 Mha (megahectares). The total volume of wood on these lands is estimated at 193 404 000 000 m³ (cubic metres), of which four fifths is coniferous and one fifth deciduous.

Three quarters of Canada's productive forest area is known as the Boreal Forest; it stretches in a broad belt from the Atlantic Coast westward and then northwest to Alaska. The forests of this region are predominantly coniferous, with spruce, balsam fir and pine the most common species. Many deciduous trees are also found in the Boreal Forest; poplar and white birch are the most widespread.

The Great Lakes–St. Lawrence and Acadian regions are south of the boreal region. Here the forests are mixed and many species are represented. Principal conifers are eastern white and red pine, eastern hemlock, spruce, cedar and fir. The main deciduous trees are yellow birch, maple, oak and basswood.

Entirely different in character is the coastal region of British Columbia. Here the forests are coniferous, and because of a mild, humid climate and heavy rainfall very large trees are common — 61 m tall and more than 2 m in diameter. This region

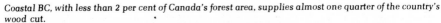

Coastal BC, with less than 2 per cent of Canada's forest area, supplies almost one quarter of the country's wood cut.

contains less than 2 per cent of the country's forest area, but supplies almost one quarter of the wood cut. Species are cedar, hemlock, spruce, fir and Douglas-fir.

The coniferous forests of the mountainous regions of Alberta and the British Columbia interior are mixed; distribution and characteristics of species depend on local climate, which ranges from dry to very humid. Production in this area has expanded rapidly in recent years, with the establishment of many new pulp mills.

The only true deciduous forests in Canada occupy a relatively small area in the southernmost part of Ontario, which is predominantly an agricultural district.

Ownership and Administration of Forests

Eighty per cent of Canada's productive forest land is publicly owned. Under the British North America Act, the various provincial governments were given the exclusive right to enact laws regarding management and sale of public lands within their boundaries, including the timber and wood on those lands. In the northern territories, which contain only about 8 per cent of the country's productive forest land, the forests are administered by the federal government.

For many years the policy of both federal and provincial governments has been to retain in public ownership lands not required for agricultural purposes. In some of the older settled areas of Canada, however, a high proportion of land is privately owned, especially in the three Maritime provinces, where nearly two thirds of the productive forest area is owned by individuals and companies. Thus, the administration and protection of most of Canada's productive forest area is vested in the various provincial governments, which make the forests available to private industry through long-term leasing and other arrangements.

Forest Industries

The forest industries group includes: logging; the primary wood and paper manufacturing industries, which use roundwood as their chief raw material; and the secondary wood and paper industries, which use lumber, wood pulp, basic paper, etc., as raw materials to be converted into numerous wood and paper products. This group of industries accounted for approximately 15.8 per cent of all Canadian exports in 1975, down from 17.6 per cent in 1974 mainly because of a large decrease in the quantity and value of lumber exported to the United States.

Logging. Production, consisting of sawlogs, veneer logs, pulpwood, poles and other roundwood products, dropped from an all-time high of 1 438 000 000 m³ in 1973 to 1 379 000 000 m³ in 1974. Sawlog production decreased substantially, from 968 000 000 m³ in 1973 to 853 000 000 m³ in 1974; this was partially offset by a 13 per cent increase in pulpwood production east of the Rockies. British Columbia was hardest hit, with production dropping from 701 000 000 m³ in 1973 to 600 000 000 m³ in 1974.

The value of exports of roundwood increased substantially, from $31 million in 1973 to $49 million in 1974. Exports of sawlogs, logs and bolts more than tripled in both quantity and value in 1974.

This red pine forest near Cobourg, Ont., was planted only 40 years ago. ➡

The value of shipments by the logging industry in 1974 was $2,733 million, up from $2,494 million in the previous year as a result of increased unit values rather than of quantities shipped.

In 1974, 50,733 people were employed in logging, an increase of about 2 per cent over 1974; wages in 1974 were $601 million, compared to $513 million in 1973.

Sawmills and Planing Mills. This industry is particularly dependent upon the general economic condition of the country and the state of foreign markets, particularly the market in the US. In spite of a slight increase in domestic residential construction starts in Canada and the US, the lumber market continued to fall throughout most of 1975. Lumber production in Canada declined about 16 per cent to an estimated 2 690 000 000 m³ in 1975 from the 3 216 000 000 m³ recorded in 1974. Exports of Canadian lumber dropped 21 per cent from 1 954 824 000 m³ in 1973 to 1 545 922 000 m³ in 1974. The long-term trend toward increased size of individual sawmills and toward more complete automation is continuing, particularly in the interior of British Columbia where the sawmill industry is becoming more and more integrated with the pulp and paper industry.

Other Wood Industries. This group includes the shingle mills, veneer and plywood mills and particleboard plants which, like the sawmills and pulp and paper mills, are primary wood industries. It also includes the secondary wood

The manufacture of pulp and paper has been Canada's leading industry for many years.

A ranger look-out watches for forest fires near Crows Nest Pass in BC.

industries that further manufacture lumber, plywood and particleboard into flooring, doors, sashes, laminated structures, prefabricated buildings, boxes, barrels, caskets, woodenware, etc. In 1974 the veneer and plywood industry, the single most important of this group, accounted for $462,998,000 in shipments of goods of own manufacture and paid their manufacturing employees $111,879,000 in salaries and wages.

Table 6. Principal statistics of the pulp and paper industry, 1971-74

Item		1971	1972	1973	1974
Establishments	No.	142	141	146	147
Employees	No.	79,397	78,969	80,085	86,203
Salaries and wages	$'000	745,608	808,869	884,242	1,097,108
Value of shipments of goods of own manufacture	$'000	2,832,267	3,127,821	3,790,939	5,703,192
Value added—manufacturing activity	$'000	1,272,551	1,374,129	1,803,889	3,033,697
Pulp shipped	'000 t	5 823	6 698	7 199	7 603
	'000 tons	6,419	7,383	7,936	8,381
	$'000	878,132	976,147	1,301,486	2,205,290
Paper and paperboard shipped	'000 t	10 831	11 656	12 213	12 853
	'000 tons	11,939	12,848	13,463	14,168
	$'000	1,751,847	1,925,194	2,252,280	3,225,962
Newsprint exported	'000 t	7 074	7 350	7 617	7 846
	'000 tons	7,798	8,102	8,396	8,699
	$'000	1,084,282	1,157,509	1,285,928	1,721,768

Newsprint from New Brunswick mills being loaded for market in Great Britain.

Pulp and Paper. The manufacture of pulp and paper has been Canada's leading industry for many years. Although it is not growing as quickly as some other manufacturing industries in Canada, it still ranks first in employment, in salaries and wages paid, and in value added by manufacture. The manufacturing value added by this one industry accounts for 2.1 per cent of the total gross national product and it contributed 12.8 per cent to the total value of domestic exports in 1974 (10.6 per cent in 1973). Canada is the second largest producer of wood pulp in the world (19 678 161 t in 1974) after the US (43 743 541 t), and the largest exporter. It is by far the largest producer of newsprint, 8 710 418 t in 1974, which is close to 40 per cent of the world total.

Although the pulp and paper industry is engaged primarily in the manufacture of wood pulps and basic papers and paperboard, it also produces converted papers and paperboards, and even chemicals, alcohol and other by-products. More than 60 per cent of the wood pulp manufactured in 1974 was converted in Canada to other products, particularly newsprint. The rest was exported.

Quebec has the largest share of Canada's pulp and paper industry, accounting for 32.3 per cent of the total value of production in 1974. It is followed by British Columbia with 28.7 per cent and Ontario with 19.7 per cent.

Paper-converting Industries. These include asphalt roofing manufacturers, paper box and bag manufacturers, and other paper converters. In 1974 this group had 501 establishments (503 in 1973), employed 45,072 persons (43,053 in 1973) and paid $428,656,000 in salaries and wages ($364,092,000 in 1973); the value of factory shipments set a new record of $1,974,246,000 ($1,480,089,000 in 1973). In contrast to the basic pulp and paper industry, the paper-converting industries are dependent primarily on the domestic market.

Minerals and Energy

Minerals

Canada is richly endowed with mineral wealth; it ranks among the world's largest producers of minerals. A great deal of the country's history is closely entwined with mineral exploration and development, beginning with Frobisher's search for illusory gold in the 16th century. Coal in Nova Scotia and iron ore in Quebec were discovered and later mined in the 17th and 18th centuries. The Geological Survey of Canada, founded in 1842, encouraged the collection of information about Canada's minerals. In the next decade came the first gold rush — to Barkerville in the Cariboo district of British Columbia — and silver, zinc and lead were subsequently found in the Kootenay district. Crews blasting a roadbed for the Canadian Pacific Railway in northern Ontario first revealed the riches in copper and nickel to be found there. The most famous event in Canadian mining history was undoubtedly the Klondike gold rush of 1896, but more significant have been the discoveries in the 20th century of cobalt, silver, uranium, asbestos and potash, among other minerals, as well as more copper, nickel and iron ore.

The remarkable progress of the Canadian mining industry since World War II is shown by the increase in value of mineral production from $499 million in 1945 to $13,403 million in 1975. A measure of the importance of mining to the Canadian economy may be found in the following figures. In 1973 expenditures by mining and exploration companies (excluding the petroleum and natural gas industry) for exploration, development, capital costs and repairs were greater than $1,254 million; over $7,000 million worth of mineral products were exported — over one

The Great Canadian Oil Sands complex at Fort McMurray, Alta.

quarter of Canada's export trade; more than 100,000 Canadians were employed in the industry; and about 300 mines were operating. Cities such as Sudbury, Ont., and Trail, BC, depend almost entirely on the mineral wealth in the surrounding area, while Toronto and Calgary are financial centres for the mining and oil industries, and many people employed in these cities depend on mining for their livelihood.

The value of production of Canadian minerals increased to $13,403 million in 1975, from $11,711 million in 1974 and $8,370 million in 1973. Metallic minerals accounted for 36 per cent of the value of Canadian mineral production in 1975. In order of importance, the principal metallic minerals produced in Canada were nickel, copper, iron ore, zinc, gold, silver and lead. Headed by crude oil and natural gas, mineral fuels accounted for 51 per cent of the total value of production. Non-metallic minerals and structural materials accounted for 13 per cent. The main structural materials were cement, sand and gravel, and stone; the non-metallic minerals group was dominated by potash, followed by asbestos, elemental sulphur and salt. The leading mineral commodity in 1975 was crude oil, with a production value of $3,781 million, up from $3,522 million in 1974 and $423 million in 1960.

Nickel production in Canada in 1975 amounted to 244 782 t valued at $1,109 million, a decrease from 269 035 t valued at $975 million in 1974. Most of Canada's nickel was mined in the Sudbury, Ont., region by The International Nickel Company of Canada Limited and Falconbridge Nickel Mines Limited.

Copper production in 1975 amounted to 724 053 t, valued at $1,017 million; the figures for 1974 were 821 380 t and $1,403 million. Canada ranks fourth in the production of copper in the non-Communist world. The major producing provinces were British Columbia (241 310 t), Ontario (265 166 t) and Quebec (117 806 t).

Iron ore production in 1975 amounted to 44 800 000 t (worth $923 million); in 1974 it was 46 800 000 t (worth $724 million). Zinc production was 1 083 000 t, valued at $895 million in 1975; in 1974, 1 127 000 t worth $867 million were mined.

The Iron Ore Company of Canada's open pit mine at Carol Lake in Labrador.

A uranium mine at Elliot Lake, Ont.

Natural gas production continued at a high level, with an output of 87 065 000 000 m³ worth $1,730 million. Production in 1974 was 86 239 000 000 m³ ($724 million); in 1960 it was only 14 810 000 000 m³ ($52 million).

Natural gas by-products (propane, butanes and pentanes plus) remained in seventh place among Canada's most important minerals. In 1975, production amounted to $768 million, up from $654 million the previous year.

Asbestos production in 1975 was 1 036 912 t valued at about $267 million. Seventy-five per cent of the asbestos produced in Canada came from the province of Quebec; the rest came from British Columbia, the Yukon Territory, Newfoundland and Ontario. Canada produces over 40 per cent of the world's total supply of asbestos and is the world's leading producer.

Cement was the most important structural material produced in Canada, with about two thirds of the production coming from Ontario and Quebec.

Among the minerals of previously lesser importance whose production has increased significantly in the past few years are potash, molybdenum, elemental sulphur, gold and coal.

The value of Canadian potash production increased from less than $1 million in 1960 to $347 million in 1975, as a number of mines were opened in Saskatchewan between 1962 and 1970. About 95 per cent of the world's potash is used as fertilizer.

Canada is second only to the US among the producers of molybdenum. The value of production increased from $1 million in 1960 to $69 million in 1975, with over 90 per cent of the Canadian production coming from British Columbia.

Elemental sulphur production decreased from 5 000 000 t in 1974 to 4 100 000 t in 1975, while the value rose to $89 million from $69 million. Natural gas is the major source of elemental sulphur in Canada, so its production is in direct proportion to

Adgo, the second well drilled from an artificial island in the Beaufort Sea, discovered oil and gas.

natural gas production regardless of the price of sulphur. Nearly all sulphur is transformed into sulphuric acid, of which one half is used in the manufacture of fertilizers.

Although gold production decreased slightly to 52 067 kg in 1975 from 52 826 kg in the previous year, its value rose to $276 million from $264 million in 1974, because of increases in the world prices.

Coal production increased slightly from 21 300 000 t in 1974 to 24 000 000 t in 1975, with its value increasing from $303 million to $576 million.

Table 7. Canada's mineral production by class, 1965-75
(million dollars)

Year	Metals	Non-metals	Fossil fuels	Structural materials	Total
1965	1,908	327	1,045	434	3,714
1966	1,985	363	1,152	481	3,980
1967	2,285	406	1,234	455	4,380
1968	2,493	447	1,343	440	4,722
1969	2,378	450	1,465	443	4,736
1970	3,073	481	1,718	450	5,722
1971[r]	2,940	501	2,014	507	5,963
1972[r]	2,956	513	2,368	571	6,408
1973[r]	3,850	615	3,227	674	8,366
1974[r]	4,821	895	5,202	793	11,711
1975[1]	4,812	929	6,854	807	13,403

[1]Preliminary estimates.
[r]Revised figures.
Figures may not add to totals owing to rounding.

Table 8. Canada's mineral production, by province, 1973-75

Province or territory	1973[r] Value $'000	%	1974[r] Value $'000	%	1975[1] Value $'000	%
Newfoundland	374,506	4.5	448,473	3.8	568,212	4.2
Prince Edward Island	1,680	—	1,454	—	1,540	—
Nova Scotia	61,719	0.7	80,251	0.7	96,688	0.7
New Brunswick	163,550	1.9	213,519	1.8	251,393	1.9
Quebec	926,083	11.1	1,192,440	10.2	1,142,457	8.5
Ontario	1,852,875	22.2	2,429,530	20.8	2,339,449	17.5
Manitoba	419,214	5.0	486,249	4.1	533,189	4.0
Saskatchewan	510,313	6.1	790,330	6.7	826,536	6.2
Alberta	2,764,142	33.0	4,518,383	38.6	6,000,849	44.8
British Columbia	975,699	11.7	1,155,787	9.9	1,223,915	9.1
Yukon Territory	150,667	1.8	171,538	1.5	228,898	1.7
Northwest Territories	165,489	2.0	223,050	1.9	189,477	1.4
Total	8,365,938	100.0	11,711,004	100.0	13,402,603	100.0

[1] Preliminary estimates.
[r] Revised figures.
— Too small to be expressed.
Figures may not add to totals owing to rounding.

Steel production is one of the industries depending on Canada's mineral wealth.

Table 9. Canada's mineral production, by kind, 1974 and 1975

Mineral	1974		1975[1]	
	'000	'000	'000	'000
Metallics				
Antimony......................	..	..	..	..
Bismuth	111 kg	245 lb.	37 kg	81 lb.
Cadmium	1 241 kg	2,736 lb.	1 217 kg	2,682 lb.
Calcium.........................	476 kg	1,050 lb.	375 kg	826 lb.
Cobalt...........................	1 564 kg	3,447 lb.	1 338 kg	2,949 lb.
Columbium (Cb₂O₅)	1 920 kg	4,23% lb.	1 685 kg	3,714 lb.
Copper	821 380 kg	1,810,834 lb.	724 053 kg	1,596,263 lb.
Gold	53 kg	1,698 troy oz	52 kg	1,674 troy oz
Indium	8 kg	259 troy oz	..	..
Iron ore	46 784 t	51,571 tons	44 829 t	49,415 tons
Iron, remelt..................	..	..		
Lead	294 268 kg	648,750 lb.	338 439 kg	746,130 lb.
Magnesium	5 957 kg	13,133 lb.	4 501 kg	9,922 lb.
Mercury	483 kg	1,064 lb.	..	..
Molybdenum	13 942 kg	30,736 lb.	12 435 kg	27,414 lb.
Nickel...........................	269 071 kg	593,199 lb.	244 782 kg	539,652 lb.
Platinum group	12 kg	384 troy oz	13 kg	430 troy oz
Selenium.......................	272 kg	600 lb.	304 kg	670 lb.
Silver............................	1 332 kg	42,810 troy oz	1 216 kg	39,101 troy oz
Tanéalum......................	199 kg	438 lb.	179 kg	395 lb.
Tellurium......................	56 kg	124 lb.	36 kg	80 lb.
Tin................................	324 kg	714 lb.	283 kg	623 lb.
Tungsten (WO₃)............	1 614 kg	3,558 lb.	1 355 kg	2,987 lb.
Uranium (U₃O₈)............	4 350 kg	9,591 lb.	5 557 kg	12,251 lb.
Zinc..............................	1 127 008 kg	2,484,628 lb.	1 083 005 kg	2,387,617 lb.
Non-metallics				
Asbestos........................	1 644 t	1,812 tons	1 037 t	1,143 tons
Barite............................	..	..	..	..
Feldspar........................	—	—	—	—
Fluorspar	..	..	..	..
Gemstones	4 kg	8 lb.	..	..
Gypsum.........................	7 225 t	7,964 tons	5 674 t	6,255 tons
Magnesitic dolomite and brucite...............	..	..	..	..
Nepheline syenite	560 t	617 tons	472 t	520 tons
Nitrogen........................	..	..	..	..
Peat	369 t	407 tons	347 t	383 tons
Potash (K₂0)	5 776 t	6,367 tons	4 850 t	5,346 tons
Pyrite, pyrrhotite..........	49 t	54 tons	19 t	21 tons
Quartz	2 506 t	2,762 tons	2 323 t	2,561 tons
Salt	5 447 t	6,004 tons	5 156 t	5,683 tons
Soapstone, talc, pyrophyllite..............	86 t	95 tons	67 t	74 tons
Sodium sulphate	638 t	703 tons	495 t	546 tons
Sulphur in smelter gas.	663 t	731 tons	704 t	776 tons
Sulphur, elemental.......	5 033 t	5,548 tons	4 061 t	4,476 tons
Titanium dioxide, etc...	..	..	..	..
Mineral fuels				
Coal..............................	21 352 t	23,536 tons	24 494 t	27,000 tons
Natural gas...................	86 239 137 m³	3,045,506 Mcf	87 064 658 m³	3,074,659 Mcf
Natural gas by-products..............	18 028 m³	113,304 bbl	17 577 m³	110,468 bbl
Petroleum, crude..........	97 819 m³	614,777 bbl	83 589 m³	525,342 bbl

Table 9. Canada's mineral production, by kind, 1974 and 1975 (concluded)

Mineral	1974		1975[1]	
	'000	'000	'000	'000
Structural materials				
Clay products (bricks, tile, etc.)	..	..	..	..
Cement	10 375 t	11,436 tons	9 764 t	10,763 tons
Lime	1 823 t	2,009 tons	1 714 t	1,889 tons
Sand and gravel	214 629 t	236,588 tons	204 080 t	224,960 tons
Stone	88 437 t	97,485 tons	88 088 t	97,485 tons

[1] Preliminary estimates.
.. Figures not available.
— Nil or zero.

Petroleum and Natural Gas

The petroleum industry is Canada's leading mineral producer; it extracted about $6,278.5 million worth of hydro-carbon products in 1975, an increase of 28.1 per cent over 1974. Crude oil, Canada's most important mineral, contributed $3,781.1 million (83 600 000 m³) to this total. Production of natural gas, now Canada's second leading mineral, accounted for $1,729.6 million (87 065 000 000 m³) and pentanes, propane and butanes for $767.8 million (17 600 000 m³). In addition, elemental sulphur is a very valuable by-product of gas-processing plants.

Pipeline construction near Upsala, Ont.

Alberta accounted for 90 per cent of all production, Saskatchewan for 6 per cent, British Columbia for 3 per cent and all the other provinces for one per cent.

Due to increases in the cost of natural gas, the value of exports in 1975 increased dramatically. Natural gas exports amounted to 26 886 800 000 m³, a decline of 1.2 per cent from 1974, but their value was $1,092.2 million, an increase of 121.2 per cent. Crude oil exports in 1975 of 4 1 800 000 m³, down 21 per cent from 1974, had a value of $3,051.5 million, a decrease of 10.4 per cent over the $3,406.8 million in 1974. Imports of crude oil amounted to 47 400 000 m³.

To help redress a situation in which western Canadian crude oil was being exported at relatively low prices while eastern Canada had to rely on expensive foreign crude oil, the federal government applied an export tax November 1, 1973. The proceeds from this tax subsidize eastern Canadian consumers.

Total sales of refined petroleum products were 92 200 000 m³ in 1975, including 34 400 000 m³ of motor gasoline, 29 400 000 m³ of middle distillates, 15 700 000 m³ of heavy fuel oils and 12 800 000 m³ of lubricating oils and grease, asphalt and other products.

The need to move oil and natural gas to many parts of the continent has led to the development of large pipeline systems as a major form of transportation. In 1975 the transportation of crude oil and its equivalent, liquefied petroleum gases, and of refined petroleum products amounted to 114.9 million pipeline cubic metre kilometres, down 15.3 per cent from 1974; that of natural gas amounted to 89 705 779 million pipeline cubic metre kilometres, an increase of 2.9 per cent.

In 1974 the total operating and capital expenditures of the petroleum industry amounted to $3,456.9 million. The industry has made great efforts to find new reserves and increase its production of hydro-carbon products since 1961, when its investment was only $716.2 million. In 1974 geological and geophysical work accounted for $241.5 million of the total; $217.0 million was spent on acquiring land or leases; $621.6 million was spent on exploratory and development drilling; $364.9 million was spent on capital additions; $463.0 million was spent on field, well and natural gas plant operations; and $1,548.9 million was spent on royalties, taxes and other miscellaneous expenditures. Seventy-three per cent of all expenditure, amounting to $2,515.4 million, was in Alberta; 9 per cent was in the Northwest Territories, the Yukon Territory and the Arctic islands; 6 per cent was in British Columbia; and 9 per cent was in Saskatchewan.

The energy crisis of 1973 brought about a much greater awareness that the use of energy, particularly oil and gas, was growing faster than the rate at which new resources were being found. Canada is fortunate in that it is one of the few countries in the world that is self-sufficient in energy. Canada has proven reserves of conventional crude oil to last approximately 12 years, and enough natural gas to last 25 years at current rates of consumption. However, the long-term oil and natural gas supply depends on harnessing the vast reserves of "synthetic" crude oil in the Athabasca tar sands and in finding more reserves in the frontier areas of Canada. Great Canadian Oil Sands Limited has the only plant now operating in the tar sands area, but several other consortiums are planning similar operations. The Athabasca tar sands contain an estimated 47 734 000 000 m³ of synthetic crude oil recoverable by mining or thermal processes, although only some 955 000 000 m³ are recoverable using present technology. Along with this development is the increasing emphasis being placed on exploratory work in the Arctic and off-shore areas, and on studies on the optimum method of transporting any energy form that may be found.

Coal

Production of coal in Canada increased 18 per cent in 1975, from 21 352 000 t in 1974 to 25 222 000 t. Excluding subvention payments, the preliminary value of coal production increased 93 per cent to $585,600,000. This dramatic increase in value resulted from a strong demand for coal, coupled with increased production costs. New contracts calling for greatly increased prices were negotiated with the Japanese steel producers who, as Canada's main export customers, accounted for approximately 95 per cent of all coal exports.

The Elkview coal preparation plant at Sparwood, BC.

Table 10. Production of coal, by province, 1974 and 1975

Province	Type of coal	1974		1975[1]	
		Metric tonnes '000	Short tons '000	Metric tonnes '000	Short tons '000
Nova Scotia..........	Bituminous	1 279	1,410	1 656	1,826
New Brunswick ...	Bituminous	376	415	418	461
Saskatchewan	Lignite	3 485	3,842	3 549	3,912
Alberta..................	Sub-bituminous	5 075	5,594	5 958	6,568
	Bituminous	3 396	3,743	4 061	4,476
	Total Alberta	8 471	9,337	10 019	11,044
British Columbia..	Bituminous	7 740	8,532	9 580	10,560
Total......................		21 351	23,536	25 222	27,803

[1] Preliminary estimates.

Electricity

Canada's electric power development has grown steadily since the beginning of this century. The country's total generating capacity has increased from a modest 133000 kW (kilowatts) in 1900 to approximately 62925000 by the end of 1975.

Although water power traditionally has been the main source of electrical energy in Canada, and still is, thermal sources are becoming more important and this trend is expected to continue. The choice between the development of a hydro-electric power site and the construction of a thermal generating station must take into account a number of complex considerations, the most important of which are economic. The heavy capital costs involved in constructing a hydro-electric project are offset by maintenance and operating costs considerably lower than those for a thermal plant. The long life of a hydro plant and its dependability and flexibility in meeting varying loads are added advantages. Also important is the fact that water is a renewable resource. The thermal station, on the other hand, can be located close to areas where power is needed, with a consequent saving in transmission costs; however, pollution problems at these plants are an undesirable factor.

The marked trend toward the development of thermal stations, which became apparent in the 1950s, can be explained to some extent by the fact that in many parts of Canada most of the hydro-electric sites within economic transmission distance of load centres have been developed, and planners have had to turn to other sources of electrical energy. Although recent advances in extra-high voltage transmission techniques have given impetus to the development of hydro power sites previously considered too remote, thermal stations will probably be the more important of the two sources in the long run.

Water Power Resources and Developments. Substantial amounts of water power have been developed in all provinces except Prince Edward Island, where there are no large streams. The resources of Newfoundland are estimated to be considerable; topography and run-off favour hydro-electric power development. In fact, the hydro-electric site now being developed at Churchill Falls in Labrador will, with its

5 225 000 kW capacity, be the largest single generating plant of any type in the world. The water power of Nova Scotia and New Brunswick, small in comparison with that of other provinces, is none the less a valuable source of energy; the numerous moderate-sized rivers provide power for the cities and for the development of the provinces' timber and mineral resources.

Quebec is richest in water power resources, with over 40 per cent of the total for Canada, and has the most developed capacity. Even this considerable figure could double if plans for the development of a number of rivers flowing into James Bay become a reality; this development could result ultimately in an additional 10 000 000 kW. Another significant development is Hydro-Québec's Manicouagan – Outardes project, which when completed will produce 5 517 000 kW on the two rivers; already some 3 900 000 kW are installed. At the moment, the largest single hydro-electric installation in Quebec is Hydro-Québec's 1 574 260 kW Beauharnois development on the St. Lawrence River.

In Ontario, almost all of the sizable water power potential within easy reach of demand centres has been developed, and planners are looking to more remote sites. Most of the hydro-electric power produced in the province comes from Ontario Hydro, the largest public utility in Canada. Its chief stations are on the Niagara River at Queenston, and have a total generating capacity of 1 804 200 kW.

Manitoba is the most generously endowed of the Prairie provinces, with immense potential on the Winnipeg, Churchill, Nelson and Saskatchewan rivers. In Alberta, most of the developments are located on the Bow River and its tributaries. British Columbia ranks second in terms of potential water power resources, and is third in installed generating capacity; current development of the Peace and Columbia rivers will provide immense power resources in the future. In the Yukon Territory and the Northwest Territories, water power is of special importance in the development of mining areas such as Mayo and Yellowknife. In the Yukon Territory most resources are on the Yukon River and its tributaries. In the Northwest Territories, the rivers flowing into Great Slave Lake and the South Nahanni River draining into the Mackenzie River have considerable potential, although they have not yet been thoroughly surveyed.

Conventional Thermal Power. Some 90 per cent of all conventional thermal power generating equipment in Canada is driven by steam turbines and the remainder of the load is carried by gas turbine and internal combustion equipment. Prince Edward Island, Nova Scotia, New Brunswick, Ontario, Saskatchewan, Alberta and the Northwest Territories depend on thermal stations for most of their power requirements. Quebec's wealth of water power has so far limited the application of thermal power to local use, and the James Bay project should maintain hydro pre-eminence. Manitoba and British Columbia both have substantial amounts of thermal capacity, but current development is still of hydro electricity.

Nuclear Thermal Power. Development of commercial electric power generation in thermal plants using the heat generated by nuclear reactors is one of Canada's major contributions to energy resource technology. This development has centred around the CANDU reactor, which uses a natural uranium fuel with a heavy water moderator; heavy water as a moderator provides a high-energy yield and facilitates the handling of spent fuel. The first experimental reactor went into use in 1962 at

Rolphton, Ont., with a capacity of 20000 kW. Since then, four major nuclear projects have been undertaken. The first full-scale nuclear plant is situated at Douglas Point on Lake Huron; it consists of a single unit, completed in 1967, with a capacity of 220000 kW. The second project is a four-unit 2 160000 kW capacity plant built at Pickering, east of Toronto; its four units came on line from 1971 to 1973. Both the Douglas Point and the Pickering plants use heavy water as a coolant. The third nuclear plant is a 250000 kW unit situated at Gentilly, Que.; it uses boiling light water as a coolant. The fourth plant is the 3 200000 kW Bruce Station in Ontario, scheduled for completion by 1978. The utilization of present nuclear plants has been hindered by a shortage of heavy water, but recently instituted programs to increase production should alleviate this shortage in the near future.

Power Generation and Utilization. In 1975 Canada's generating facilities produced 272 636 000 000 kWh of electric energy, 75 per cent in hydro-electric stations. Energy exported to the US exceeded by 7 412 000 000 kWh the energy imported, bringing the total available to Canadian users to 265 224 000 000 kWh. Average domestic and farm consumption continues to rise year by year. In 1974 it was 8 701 kWh, ranging from a low of 5 475 kWh in Prince Edward Island to a high of 10 772 kWh in Manitoba. The average annual bill for domestic and farm customers was $153.39.

The Bruce nuclear power plant near Kincardine, Ont.

Employment

The Labour Force

In 1975, the Canadian labour force averaged 10,060,000, or 61.1 per cent, of the total population 15 years of age and over. The labour force was composed of 9,363,000 employed persons and 697,000 unemployed persons. Table 1 shows the growth in the Canadian labour force during the 1970-75 period. This growth continues to be the result of increases in the population aged 15 and over and in the participation rates for the 15-to-24 age group and for women aged 25 and over. The growth in employment over the same period for persons aged 15 to 24 was 25.8 per cent; for all persons 25 and over employment increased by 15.8 per cent, while for women aged 25 and over it increased by 28.4 per cent.

Table 1. Labour force characteristics, annual averages, 1970 to 1975

Year	Population[1] '000	Labour force '000	Employment '000	Unemployment '000	Participation rate %	Unemployment rate %
1970	14,528	8,399	7,919	480	57.8	5.7
1971	14,878	8,644	8,107	538	58.1	6.2
1972	15,227	8,920	8,363	557	58.6	6.2
1973	15,608	9,322	8,802	520	59.7	5.6
1974	16,039	9,706	9,185	521	60.5	5.4
1975	16,471	10,060	9,363	697	61.1	6.9

[1] Excluding: inmates of institutions; full-time members of the Canadian Armed Forces; residents of the Yukon Territory and the Northwest Territories; and residents of Indian reserves.

Table 2. Unemployment by age and sex, and by province, annual averages, 1970 and 1975

Age and sex	1970 '000	1975 '000	Province	1970 %	1975 %
Total unemployed	480	697	Nfld.	7.2	14.2
Men....................................	315	397	PEI	8.1	8.2
Women	165	301	NS	5.5	7.8
			NB	6.3	9.9
Unemployed aged 15-24	215	331	Que.	7.0	8.1
Men....................................	134	191	Ont.	4.4	6.3
Women	81	141	Man.	5.4	4.6
			Sask.	5.1	2.9
Unemployed aged 25+	265	367	Alta.	5.1	4.1
Men....................................	181	206	BC	7.7	8.5
Women	84	160			

Table 2 shows the distribution of unemployment by principal age and sex groups over the five-year period 1970-75. The 25-and-over age group accounted for 55 per cent of unemployment in 1970, and 53 per cent in 1975. The female share of unemployment increased from 34 per cent to 43 per cent between 1970 and 1975, while the male component declined from 66 per cent to 57 per cent.

Table 2 also shows provincial unemployment rates in 1970 and 1975, and the fact that differences between provincial unemployment rates have increased.

Over the past three years Statistics Canada has developed a number of major modifications to the monthly labour force survey, to provide a more comprehensive range of information on employment and unemployment. The data for 1975 were obtained from the revised labour force survey, while data for the period 1970 through 1974 were derived by observing the relationship of data from previous surveys to those from the revised surveys throughout 1975. As a result, there are changes in the data for some of the previously published series.

Miners emerge from the cage at the Tantalum Mine at Bernic Lake, Man.

Building construction in Winnipeg, Man.

Earnings and Hours of Work

Statistics Canada obtains information on average weekly earnings, average weekly hours and average hourly earnings from its monthly survey of employment, earnings and hours. The survey covers larger companies that have 20 or more employees in any month of the year; these companies account for almost 75 per cent of the total commercial non-agricultural employment in Canada.

Average Weekly Earnings. Average weekly earnings of all employees in all of the industries surveyed were $203.33 in 1975; this was a 14.2 per cent rise from the 1974 level. The industrial gains ranged from 12.1 per cent in finance, insurance and real estate to 17.2 per cent in mining. Among the provinces, gains ranging from 12.9 per cent in Ontario to 18.2 per cent in Prince Edward Island were recorded.

Average Hourly Earnings.[1] In 1975, average hourly earnings rose 18.4 per cent in mining, 15.8 per cent in manufacturing and 17.0 per cent in construction. By province, average hourly earnings in manufacturing registered gains ranging from 12.0 per cent in British Columbia to 20.0 per cent in Saskatchewan.

Average Weekly Hours.[1] From 1974 to 1975, average weekly hours dropped 1.2 per cent in mining and 1.0 per cent in manufacturing, while they increased by 0.5 per cent in construction. Average weekly hours in manufacturing declined in all provinces except Nova Scotia, New Brunswick and British Columbia; the changes ranged from −2.1 per cent in Saskatchewan to 0.3 per cent in Nova Scotia.

[1]Data on average hourly earnings and average weekly hours pertain only to those wage-earners from whom data on hours were available.

Arranging stacks of fresh-cut lumber in a sawmill in Restigouche, Que.

Table 3. Average weekly earnings for all employees, selected industries, and industrial composite¹, by province, annual averages, 1961, 1974 and 1975

Industry and province	1961	1974[2]	1975[2]	1961 to 1975[2]	1974[2] to 1975[2]
	$	$	$	%	%
Industry					
Forestry	79.02	219.64	250.36	216.8	14.0
Mining, incl. milling	95.57	238.97	280.01	193.0	17.2
Manufacturing	81.55	185.62	213.35	161.6	14.9
Durables	88.22	198.39	227.04	157.4	14.4
Non-durables	76.17	172.86	199.91	162.5	15.6
Construction	86.93	250.30	290.99	234.7	16.3
Transportation, communications and other utilities	82.47	204.39	233.39	183.0	14.2
Trade	64.54	139.92	159.25	146.7	13.8
Finance, insurance and real estate	72.82	172.25	193.07	165.1	12.1
Service	57.87	126.08	144.51	149.7	14.6
Industrial composite¹	78.24	178.09	203.33	159.9	14.2
Industrial composite by province					
Newfoundland	71.06	168.48	196.16	176.0	16.4
Prince Edward Island	54.91	126.92	150.05	173.3	18.2
Nova Scotia	63.72	149.98	172.55	170.8	15.0
New Brunswick	63.62	154.58	181.72	185.6	17.6
Quebec	75.67	172.89	198.95	162.9	15.1
Ontario	81.30	181.43	204.83	151.9	12.9
Manitoba	73.66	162.71	186.47	153.1	14.6
Saskatchewan	74.38	160.99	188.18	153.0	16.9
Alberta	80.29	178.72	208.12	159.2	16.5
British Columbia	84.99	200.55	230.20	170.9	14.8

¹ "Industrial composite" is the sum of all industries except agriculture, fishing and trapping, education and related services, health and welfare services, religious organizations, private households, and public administration and defence. All statistics are based on returns received from employers having 20 or more employees in any month of the year.
² Data for 1974 and 1975 are preliminary.

Table 4. Average hourly earnings and average weekly hours for hourly-rated wage earners, annual averages, 1961, 1974 and 1975

Industry and province	Average hourly earnings (AHE)			Average weekly hours (AWH)			Changes in AHE		Changes in AWH	
							1961 to 1975[1]	1974[1] to 1975[1]	1961 to 1975[1]	1974[1] to 1975[1]
	1961 $	1974[1] $	1975[1] $	1961 No.	1974[1] No.	1975[1] No.	%	%	%	%
Industry										
Mining, including milling	2.13	5.50	6.51	41.8	40.4	39.9	205.6	18.4	−4.5	−1.2
Manufacturing	1.83	4.37	5.06	40.6	38.9	38.5	176.5	15.8	−5.2	−1.0
Durables	2.00	4.69	5.41	40.9	39.5	39.1	170.5	15.4	−4.4	−1.0
Non-durables	1.69	4.03	4.69	40.3	38.3	37.9	177.5	16.4	−6.0	−1.0
Construction	2.06	6.43	7.52	40.9	38.9	39.1	265.0	17.0	−4.4	0.5
Building	2.16	6.63	7.65	38.9	37.5	37.3	254.2	15.4	−4.1	−0.5
Engineering	1.90	6.05	7.30	44.8	42.3	42.4	284.2	20.7	−5.4	0.2
Manufacturing by province[2]										
Newfoundland	1.69	4.17	4.84	40.5	38.4	37.7	186.4	16.1	−6.9	−1.8
Nova Scotia	1.58	3.87	4.60	40.3	38.2	38.3	191.1	18.9	−5.0	0.3
New Brunswick	1.55	3.88	4.65	40.9	38.2	38.2	200.0	19.8	−6.6	0.0
Quebec	1.65	3.87	4.56	41.5	39.6	39.0	176.4	17.8	−6.0	−1.5
Ontario	1.94	4.54	5.18	40.5	39.2	38.8	167.0	14.1	−4.2	−1.0
Manitoba	1.67	3.95	4.62	39.7	37.6	37.2	176.6	17.0	−6.3	−1.1
Saskatchewan	1.98	4.49	5.39	39.0	37.8	37.0	172.2	20.0	−5.1	−2.1
Alberta	1.96	4.66	5.54	39.7	37.4	37.3	182.7	18.9	−6.0	−0.3
British Columbia	2.23	5.66	6.34	37.7	36.4	36.4	184.3	12.0	−3.4	0.0

[1] Data for 1974 and 1975 are preliminary.
[2] Data for Prince Edward Island are not available.

Labour Organizations

Membership in labour organizations active in Canada totalled 2,875,464 in 1975. About 71.1 per cent of the members were in unions affiliated with the Canadian Labour Congress (CLC); 6.0 per cent were affiliates of the Confederation of National Trade Unions (CNTU); 1.4 per cent were affiliated with the Centrale des syndicats démocratiques (CSD); 0.7 per cent were affiliates of the Confederation of Canadian Unions (CCU); the remaining 20.8 per cent were members of unaffiliated national and international unions and independent local organizations.

Of the total union members, 51.4 per cent belonged to international unions, chiefly AFL—CIO/CLC unions. National unions accounted for 48.6 per cent of union membership in Canada.

Twenty-three unions reported memberships of 30,000 or more in the 1975 survey. The five largest unions were the Canadian Union of Public Employees (198,900); the United Steelworkers of America (187,000); the Public Service Alliance of Canada (136,000); the International Union, United Automobile, Aerospace and Agricultural Implement Workers of America (117,500); and the United Brotherhood of Carpenters and Joiners of America (89,000).

Industry

Industrial Growth

Early in the 1960s, the Canadian economy rebounded from the relative stagnation that had marked the late 1950s. With few exceptions, the 1960s witnessed rates of growth approaching those achieved during the early 1950s. In the period from the first quarter of 1961 to the fourth quarter of 1969, real output increased by 68.6 per cent, or by an average quarterly rate of 1.5 per cent. In 1970, there was some dampening of the rate of growth, reflecting to some extent the tightened monetary and fiscal policies introduced in the previous year. The quarterly growth rate during this period was 0.5 per cent.

From the fourth quarter of 1970 to the third quarter of 1974, the rate of over-all growth, 1.3 per cent, was only slightly below the level for the 1961-69 period.

Table 1. Quarterly growth rates[1]

	1st Q 1961 — 4th Q 1969	4th Q 1969 — 4th Q 1970	4th Q 1970 — 3rd Q 1974[2]	3rd Q 1974[2] — 4th Q 1975[2]
Real domestic product	1.5	0.5	1.3	0.1
Goods-producing industries	1.6	0.1	1.3	−0.8
Agriculture	0.9	0.0	−0.5	−0.3
Forestry	1.2	−2.3	1.1	−8.4
Fishing and trapping	0.2	−1.7	−0.4	−2.4
Mining	1.4	3.9	0.9	−1.6
Manufacturing	1.7	−0.7	1.6	−1.0
Non-durables	1.4	0.4	1.2	−1.1
Durables	2.2	−1.9	2.1	−0.9
Construction	1.3	0.4	1.5	−0.8
Electric power, gas and water utilities	1.7	2.1	2.1	−0.3
Service-producing industries	1.5	0.8	1.4	0.7
Transportation, storage and communication	1.6	0.8	1.7	0.1
Transportation	1.6	1.5	1.6	−0.5
Trade	1.4	0.3	1.6	0.3
Wholesale	1.7	0.3	1.6	−0.6
Retail	1.2	0.3	1.6	1.0
Finance, insurance and real estate	1.5	1.0	1.3	1.0
Community, business and personal service	1.7	1.0	1.2	1.0
Public administration and defence	0.6	1.0	1.1	1.0

[1] Based on the terminal years compound interest formula.
[2] Data for 1971-75 based on 1970 standard industrial classification (SIC) and 1971 weight base.

A marked slowdown in activity began toward the end of 1974, and from the third quarter of 1974 to the end of 1975 the growth in real domestic product was limited to 0.1 per cent. As will be seen from Table 1, this rate of growth was considerably

An industrial gas turbine casing being machined at a plant in Mississauga, Ont.

below that experienced during the 1960s and early 1970s; it was achieved only by continued expansion in the service sector. Declines in the goods sector, especially in certain manufacturing industries, were quite sharp.

From the third quarter of 1974 to the end of 1975, the service sector showed an average quarterly rate of increase of 0.7 per cent. During the same period all sectors of the goods-producing industries declined. The two largest components, manufacturing and mining, registered declines of 1.0 per cent and 1.6 per cent respectively. In part, the decline in the Canadian economy was an extension of world-wide problems that affected all major industrialized nations. The Canadian situation was further affected by continuing high rates of inflation, unemployment and balance-of-payments problems.

Control room of Canadian Industries Limited at Bécancour, Que.

The years 1974 and 1975 were also marked by serious labour problems and Canada's strike record was one of the worst experienced by any major industrialized country. Time lost in labour disputes reached 9.3 million man-days in 1974 and increased a further 25 per cent to an estimated 1975 level of 11.5 million man-days. These losses were the highest ever recorded in Canada and resulted from prolonged work stoppages in the wood, transportation, communications, mining, construction and rubber industries.

The accompanying chart illustrates the growth since 1957 in real domestic product, with a breakdown of the goods-producing and service-producing sectors. For the period previous to 1974 the manufacturing component provided a prime thrust, particularly with the unprecedented levels of production in the motor vehicle and motor vehicle parts industries; between 1961 and 1974 these industries recorded increases of 595 per cent and 393 per cent respectively. Other industries that contributed significantly to growth in the period up to 1974 were pulp and paper, and iron and steel mills.

These same industries also contributed heavily to the declines in 1975. The latter two were affected by labour problems and recorded declines of 23.6 per cent and 9.7 per cent respectively during 1975. In the same year the motor vehicle industry declined by 1.6 per cent and the parts sector declined by 6.7 per cent, reflecting a lessening of demand in the North American market. Canada's trade position on automobile products deteriorated sharply, reaching a record loss of $2.059 billion, 26 per cent more than the 1974 deficit. The primary factor was a loss on automotive trade with the United States, in which unprecedented deficits of $1.204 billion and $1.905 billion were recorded in 1974 and 1975.

Despite labour problems and over-all depressed economic activity, the service sector of the economy continued to follow a steady growth pattern. Between the first quarter of 1961 and the third quarter of 1974 the service-producing industries

Production of a concrete pressure pipe for Montreal, Que.

showed an average growth rate of 1.4 per cent, slowing to 0.7 per cent between the third quarter of 1974 and the end of 1975. Over the entire period, particularly strong growth was recorded in the transportation sector, especially in air transport and communications.

The importance of the service sector to Canada's economic activity has continued to increase. As shown by the following table, the service-producing industries increased their share of gross domestic product in 1971 as compared with 1961. This represents a continuation of the trend apparent between 1949 and 1961, the two previous weight base periods.

	1949	1961	1971
Goods-producing industries	53.1%	44.2%	40.8%
Service-producing industries	46.9%	55.8%	59.2%
Total gross domestic product	100.0%	100.0%	100.0%

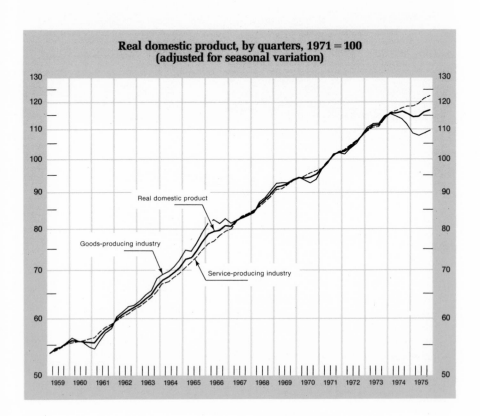

Real domestic product, by quarters, 1971 = 100
(adjusted for seasonal variation)

Distillation column of a Union Carbide air separation plant at Montreal, Que. The facility produces atmospheric gases for industrial and medical applications.

Capital Expenditures

A sustained rising income in Canada depends upon, among other things, the capacity to produce and sell goods and services. This capacity and its efficiency in turn depend largely on the amount invested in new mines, factories, stores, power generating installations, communications and transportation equipment, hospitals, schools, roads, parks and all other forms of capital that encourage the production of goods and services in future periods.

Surveys of these capital expenditures are made at regular intervals every year. On each occasion statistics are published for expenditures on housing, non-residential construction, and machinery and equipment by all sectors of the Canadian economy. Approximately 25,000 establishments are surveyed for their investment intentions. In order to approximate full coverage, adjustments are made for nonsurveyed and for non-reporting firms. In a few areas, expenditure estimates are arrived at independently on the basis of current trends and expert opinion in these fields (e.g. agriculture, fishing and housing).

Table 2. Summary of capital and repair expenditures, by sectors, 1975 and 1976[1]

(million dollars)

Sector		Capital expenditures			Capital and repair expenditures		
		Construction	Machinery and equipment	Sub-total	Construction	Machinery and equipment	Total
Agriculture	1975	519.2	1,998.1	2,517.3	724.0	2,382.4	3,106.4
	1976	553.7	2,299.0	2,852.7	771.0	2,729.6	3,500.6
Forestry	1975	88.9	97.6	186.5	120.8	203.8	324.6
	1976	93.1	91.9	185.0	132.3	214.7	347.0
Mining, quarrying and oil wells	1975	2,000.2	622.0	2,622.2	2,235.6	1,262.7	3,498.3
	1976	2,753.0	700.4	3,453.4	3,038.0	1,408.1	4,446.1
Construction industry	1975	75.2	457.2	532.4	93.3	860.1	953.4
	1976	82.9	504.0	586.9	102.8	948.3	1,051.1
Manufacturing	1975	1,536.9	3,888.1	5,425.0	1,883.7	5,833.8	7,717.5
	1976	1,596.7	4,132.9	5,729.6	1,979.5	6,297.2	8,276.7
Utilities	1975	4,146.6	3,771.1	7,917.7	4,817.3	5,248.6	10,065.9
	1976	4,705.1	3,871.4	8,576.5	5,444.2	5,500.3	10,944.5
Trade	1975	335.7	607.7	943.4	421.5	722.3	1,143.8
	1976	333.6	684.9	1,018.5	423.4	803.6	1,227.0
Finance, insurance and real estate	1975	1,475.4	187.3	1,662.7	1,567.8	221.4	1,789.2
	1976	1,486.4	217.1	1,703.5	1,579.8	253.0	1,832.8
Commercial services	1975	846.6	1,547.6	2,394.2	880.5	1,727.5	2,608.0
	1976	536.7	1,640.9	2,177.6	570.4	1,848.9	2,419.3
Institutions	1975	1,163.4	280.1	1,443.5	1,327.3	333.4	1,660.7
	1976	1,229.2	288.3	1,517.5	1,399.1	342.9	1,742.0
Government departments	1975	4,621.5	646.0	5,267.5	5,341.5	818.0	6,159.5
	1976	4,825.7	713.6	5,539.3	5,582.8	902.2	6,485.0
Housing	1975	7,084.7	—	7,084.7	8,718.4	—	8,718.4
	1976	8,613.7	—	8,613.7	10,425.2	—	10,425.2
Total	1975	23,894.3	14,102.8	37,997.1	28,131.7	19,614.0	47,745.7
	1976	26,809.8	15,144.4	41,954.2	31,448.5	21,248.8	52,697.3

[1] Preliminary actual expenditures 1975, intentions 1976.
— Nil or zero.

Information on capital spending intentions provides a useful indication of market conditions both in the economy at large and in particular industries. Since such expenditures account for a large and relatively variable proportion of gross national expenditures, the size and content of the investment program provides significant information about demands to be placed upon the productive capacities of the economy during the period covered by the survey. In addition, information on the relative size of the capital expenditures program planned, both in total and for

individual industries, gives an indication of the views managements hold on prospective market demands in relation to present productive capacity. Non-capitalized repair expenditures on structures and on machinery and equipment are also given, but these are shown separately. By including these outlays, a more complete picture is provided of all demands likely to be made on labour and materials in accomplishing the program.

Table 3. Summary of capital and repair expenditures, by province, 1975 and 1976[1,2]

(million dollars)

Province or territory		Capital expenditures			Capital and repair expenditures		
		Construction	Machinery and equipment	Sub-total	Construction	Machinery and equipment	Total
Atlantic region:							
Newfoundland	1975	548.8	179.1	727.9	625.7	338.9	964.6
	1976	652.1	187.0	839.1	740.4	362.1	1,102.5
Prince Edward Island..	1975	82.3	33.6	115.9	99.7	45.1	144.8
	1976	72.2	36.0	108.2	90.0	47.5	137.5
Nova Scotia	1975	630.4	276.5	906.9	760.0	406.7	1,166.7
	1976	758.1	292.8	1,050.9	895.5	433.4	1,328.9
New Brunswick	1975	741.9	406.2	1,148.1	854.1	542.6	1,396.7
	1976	736.8	453.0	1,189.8	859.6	598.8	1,458.4
Total, Atlantic region..	1975	2,003.4	895.4	2,898.8	2,339.5	1,333.3	3,672.8
	1976	2,219.2	968.8	3,188.0	2,585.5	1,441.8	4,027.3
Quebec	1975	5,966.8	2,982.5	8,949.3	6,918.2	4,169.6	11,087.8
	1976	6,444.7	3,179.2	9,623.9	7,477.7	4,462.3	11,940.0
Ontario	1975	7,480.9	5,551.2	13,032.1	9,004.2	7,604.0	16,608.2
	1976	8,156.7	5,983.6	14,140.3	9,796.1	8,280.9	18,077.0
Prairie region:							
Manitoba	1975	858.7	677.5	1,536.2	1,044.6	885.1	1,929.7
	1976	974.3	709.2	1,683.5	1,169.5	928.9	2,098.4
Saskatchewan	1975	884.0	858.3	1,742.3	1,079.1	1,109.7	2,188.8
	1976	1,100.6	942.3	2,042.9	1,318.8	1,227.9	2,546.7
Alberta	1975	3,331.8	1,576.3	4,908.1	3,834.6	2,037.4	5,872.0
	1976	4,262.4	1,776.4	6,038.8	4,827.1	2,309.0	7,136.1
Total, Prairie region....	1975	5,074.5	3,112.1	8,186.6	5,958.3	4,032.2	9,990.5
	1976	6,337.3	3,427.9	9,765.2	7,315.4	4,465.8	11,781.2
British Columbia	1975	3,007.2	1,408.3	4,415.5	3,524.8	2,281.4	5,806.2
	1976	3,297.7	1,479.3	4,777.0	3,892.1	2,450.4	6,342.5
Yukon Territory and Northwest Territories..	1975	361.5	153.3	514.8	386.7	193.5	580.2
	1976	354.2	105.6	459.8	381.7	147.6	529.3
Total, Canada	1975	23,894.3	14,102.8	37,997.1	28,131.7	19,614.0	47,745.7
	1976	26,809.8	15,144.4	41,954.2	31,448.5	21,248.8	52,697.3

[1] Preliminary actual expenditures 1975, intentions 1976.
[2] Capital expenditures on machinery and equipment include an estimate for "capital items charged to operating expenses", in the manufacturing, utilities and trade totals.

Pre-cast concrete components in the terminal building of the new Calgary International Airport. ➤

Provincial Expenditures

The expenditures shown for each province or territory represent the value of construction and the value of machinery and equipment acquired for use within the province or territory. Such expenditures represent gross additions to the capital stock of the province or territory, and a reflection of economic activity in that area. However, the actual production of these assets may generate its major employment and income-giving effects in other regions. For example, the spending of millions of dollars on plants and equipment in western Canada may generate considerable activity in machinery industries in Ontario and Quebec as well as construction activity in the western provinces.

It should be appreciated that there are statistical difficulties in making a precise geographic allocation of past or anticipated investment, since many business firms operating in several provinces neither record nor plan their capital expenditures geographically. As a result, it has been necessary to use approximate breakdowns in many cases. Such is the case for investment in railway rolling stock, ships, aircraft and certain other items.

Toronto, Ont.

A residence for senior citizens, located in Woodstock, NB.

Housing

The year 1975 was a notable one for housing in two ways. Production, which had slowed in 1974 and early 1975, recovered; by year-end 230,000 housing starts were recorded, thereby exceeding the government's minimum target of 210,000. The largest increases were in semi-detached, duplex and row housing which, taken together, increased from 25,955 starts in 1974 to 37,166 in 1975. Single-family housing starts increased slightly from 122,143 to 123,929, but apartment starts decreased from 74,025 to 70,361.

The other notable trend during 1975 was the shift in housing production away from more expensive housing toward the medium and lower price ranges. This emphasis had a significant effect on the residential construction industry and brought it more closely in tune with the most urgent housing needs of Canadians.

A continued effort was made during 1975 by all levels of government to increase the supply of serviced land and to stabilize land prices. The most recent amendments to the National Housing Act provide for a contribution of $1,000 to municipalities for each unit of moderate-cost medium-density housing completed. This incentive will stimulate desirable residential development, speed up approval processes and bring serviced land onto the market quickly.

Progress was also made in the fields of rural and native housing, residential rehabilitation and neighbourhood improvement. These programs, which depend for their success on the direct involvement of client groups, are growing at a steadily accelerating pace.

Sioux Lookout, located in Ontario's remote northland.

In March 1975, Parliament enacted a bill to amend the National Housing Act (NHA). The amendment broadened the Assisted Home-Ownership (AHOP) and Assisted Rental programs by making interest-reducing federal grants available to qualified home buyers or rental-housing entrepreneurs who obtained their financing through private mortgage loans; previously these grants were available only with direct Central Mortgage and Housing Corporation (CMHC) mortgages. This drew almost $750 million of private funds into new modest housing.

At the same time, the amendment allowed CMHC to acquire and lease land at favourable rates to non-profit and co-operative housing projects, offered more generous assistance to municipalities for sewage treatment projects and extended the program to trunk storm sewer systems for new residential development.

By means of a second bill, passed in December 1975, the NHA was amended again in support of the Federal Housing Action Program. By this program, the government committed itself to a target of a million new housing starts by the end of 1979, with the majority to be in the lower and medium price ranges. A million new starts would mean more than a million jobs in construction and associated activities.

The amendments approved in December also made further modifications to the Assisted Home Ownership and Assisted Rental programs. Outright grants were continued and increased under AHOP for families who need them. For the first time, however, loans that are interest-free during the first five years were made available

Mobile home park at North Kamloops, BC. →

to anyone — with or without children — who wished to buy a moderately-priced home within the local AHOP price limits; these loans have the effect of reducing monthly mortgage and tax payments to the level that would apply if the interest rate were 8 per cent. Similar arrangements can now be made with builders or owners of rental housing who are prepared to enter an agreement with CMHC regarding rents and other matters. The effect of providing assistance in this way, through repayable loans rather than subsidies and with the bulk of the mortgage financing being provided by the approved lenders, is to conserve public capital and ease the financial burden on the home buyer in the early years of ownership.

In addition to providing grants of $1,000 per unit to municipalities for low-cost medium-density housing, the bill also extended the benefits of the Sewage Treatment Assistance Program to water treatment projects required to open land for new residential development.

A single family home in Saskatoon, Sask., made available by the Assisted Home Ownership Program.

Quebec City, Que.

St. John's, Nfld.

Manufacturing

Manufacturing is the largest of Canada's goods-producing industries. Because of its importance to the growth of national productivity, its high demand for capital goods and its contribution to exports, it plays an important role in the economy.

A monthly sample survey of households produced an estimate that an average number of 1,951,000 persons were being paid salaries or wages by the manufacturing industries in 1975, compared with a total for all industries of 9,308,000.

Preliminary data from another monthly survey show that Canadian manufacturers shipped $85,101.2 million of their own products in 1975, an increase of 6.0 per cent over 1974. (By comparison, the annual average index of selling prices of manufacturing industries increased 11.1 per cent over the same period, while the annual average index of industrial production decreased 5.1 per cent.)

An exact measure of exports of manufacturers is not routinely compiled, but if exports of fabricated materials and end products are accepted as roughly equivalent to manufactured products, Canadian manufacturers did some processing on about two dollars out of every three of exports of Canadian products in 1975. Domestic exports of fabricated materials amounted to $9,796 million, compared with $10,097 million for end products. This nearly equal status indicates the importance of industrial materials produced for export.

However, the end products—roughly equivalent to highly manufactured goods, though including very small values of non-manufactured goods—have increased in value more than 14 times since 1961, when they amounted to only $706 million, while those of fabricated materials have more than tripled from a 1961 figure of $2,916 million. This is a striking reflection of the growth of those sectors of

Stockpile of sawdust and chips at a sawmill near Restigouche, Que.

Automobile production plant at Sainte-Thérèse, Que.

Canadian manufacturing producing more highly fabricated goods. For various reasons, these values are not strictly comparable with the value of over-all shipments of manufactures by Canadian factories, but they give an impression of the approximate intensity of export activity as measured by shipments. The importance of production for export would be appreciably higher if it were feasible to use a measure of the Canadian value added that is exported, as the over-all manufacturing shipments of Canadian manufacturers necessarily contain double counting of output from manufacturers supplying each other with inputs.

Most manufacturing activity in Canada is highly mechanized and Canadian factories thus constitute a large market for capital equipment. This is partly because many types of natural resource processing are inherently capital-intensive; that is, they employ a great deal of machinery, equipment and buildings in proportion to employees. Industries producing highly manufactured goods—like machinery and automobiles—are becoming increasingly important. In addition, high living standards, reflected in high wages, bring about economy in the use of workers and this often leads to increased mechanization.

In 1976, according to a survey of investment intentions, it was anticipated that the manufacturing industries would be accounting for 27 per cent of all capital expenditures by business and government for new machinery and equipment.

Coils and sheets of metal stockpiled at Westeel-Rosco Limited in Rexdale, Ont.

These expenditures represent, of course, not only the expansion of productive capacity but also some "deepening" of capital (an increase in capital per employee or per unit of product).

Increasing capital intensity of production has probably been a prime cause of the rise in productivity of each employee in the manufacturing industries. Physical output in the manufacturing industries, by man-hour worked, increased at an average rate of 4.1 per cent over the 1961-74 period.

The leading manufacturing industry in Canada in 1975, measured by the value of shipments of its own products, was motor vehicle manufacturers. With a total value of $5,757 million, this industry's shipments were approximately $536 million greater than they were in 1974, embodying the large increase due to inflation. Favourable influences on sales included a rebate offered by car manufacturers during part of 1975 and removal of the 7 per cent sales tax in Ontario, the largest domestic market, during the latter half of the year.

The second-ranking industry was petroleum refineries; their shipments of $5,431 million also reflected substantial price increases during the year. Pulp and paper

Van bodies are completely immersed and coated with primer at the Chrysler Canada Ltd. plant in Windsor, Ont.

mills had the third largest value of shipments, $5,112 million, a $227 million decrease from the previous year as a result of strikes; demand-reducing production decreased by 24 per cent in 1975. (These estimates of 1975 shipments are based on a monthly survey of shipments, inventories and orders in the manufacturing industries, and are subject to change by the results of the annual census of manufactures.) The fourth largest industry in terms of value of shipments was slaughtering and meat processing, with shipments of $3,626 million.

Four industries, in descending order of magnitude, had shipments in the $2,000 million to $3,000 million range: iron and steel mills, $2,985 million; dairy products industry, $2,574 million; motor parts and accessories, $2,537 million; and miscellaneous machinery and equipment manufacturers, $2,523 million. Ten industries, also in descending order of magnitude, had shipments of between $1,000 million and $2,000 million: sawmills, planing mills and shingle mills, $1,827 million; manufacturers of industrial chemicals, $1,810 million; miscellaneous food processors, $1,642 million; smelting and refining, $1,474 million; communications equipment manufacturers, $1,436 million; commercial printing, $1,360 million; metal stamping, pressing and coating, $1,347 million; paper box and bag manufacturers, $1,122 million; the feed industry, $1,114 million; and the bakery products industry, $1,094 million.

The largest four enterprises or groupings of companies had only 55 manufacturing establishments in 1970, but accounted for 8.9 per cent of all manufacturers' shipments, 6.8 per cent of manufacturing value added and 4.8 per cent of total

Table 4. Manufacturing statistics, selected years, 1920 to 1975

Year	Establishments	Employees	Salaries and wages	Value added by manufacture	Value of shipments of goods of own manufacture[1]
	No.	No.	$'000	$'000	$'000
1920	22,532	598,893	717,494	1,621,273	3,706,545
1929	22,216	666,531	777,291	1,755,387	3,883,446
1933	23,780	468,658	436,248	919,671	1,954,076
1939	24,805	658,114	737,811	1,531,052	3,474,784
1944	28,483	1,222,882	2,029,621	4,015,776	9,073,693
1949	35,792	1,171,207	2,591,891	5,330,566	12,479,593
1953	38,107	1,327,451	3,957,018	7,993,069	17,785,417
1954	38,028	1,267,966	3,896,688	7,902,124	17,554,528
1955	38,182	1,298,461	4,142,410	8,753,450	19,513,934
1956	37,428	1,353,020	4,570,692	9,605,425	21,636,749
1957	33,551	1,340,948	4,778,040	..	21,452,343
1958	32,446	1,272,686	4,758,614	9,454,954	21,434,815
1959	32,075	1,287,809	5,030,128	10,154,277	22,830,827
1960	32,852	1,275,476	5,150,503	10,371,284	23,279,804
1961	33,357	1,352,605	5,701,651	10,434,832	23,438,956
1962	33,414	1,389,516	6,096,174	11,429,644	25,790,087
1963	33,119	1,425,440	6,495,289	12,272,734	28,014,888
1964	33,630	1,491,257	7,080,939	13,535,991	30,856,099
1965	33,310	1,570,299	7,822,925	14,927,764	33,889,425
1966	33,377	1,646,024	8,695,890	16,351,740	37,303,455
1967	33,267	1,652,827	9,254,190	17,005,696	38,955,389
1968	32,643	1,642,352	9,905,504	18,332,204	42,061,555
1969	32,669	1,675,332	10,848,341	20,133,593	45,930,438
1970	31,928	1,637,001	11,363,712	20,047,801	46,380,935
1971	31,908	1,628,404	12,129,897	21,737,514	50,275,917
1972	31,553	1,676,130	13,414,609	24,314,751	56,234,663
1973	31,145	1,751,066	15,220,033	28,825,008	66,779,710
1974	..	1,810,000[2]	17,371,000[3]	35,267,000[4]	80,291,500[5]
1975	..	1,714,000[2]	18,855,000[3]	36,927,000[4]	85,101,200[5]

[1] Before 1952, data represent gross value of production.
[2] Based on indexes of employment published in *Employment, Earnings and Hours* (Statistics Canada Cat. No. 72-002).
[3] Estimated from current data on earnings in manufacturing.
[4] Estimated on the basis of the ratio of "value added by manufacture" to "manufacturing output" in earlier years.
[5] Based on the monthly survey, *Inventories, Shipments and Orders in Manufacturing Industries* (Statistics Canada Cat. No. 31-001).
.. Not available.
Note: Revised SIC and new establishment concept applied to data as of 1957. Further revisions made to data as of 1961.

employees. The largest 16 enterprises accounted for more than 20 per cent of manufacturing shipments. (While these data are not issued annually, figures on the size of manufacturing establishments are compiled each year.) The average size of a manufacturing establishment in 1973 was $2.1 million worth of shipments of goods of own manufacture — or about 56 persons, measured by the number of persons employed. These averages are, however, greatly affected by the large number of small establishments operated by local or regional entrepreneurs in manufacturing industries throughout Canada. Actually, 52.8 per cent of the total work force in the manufacturing industries was in establishments employing 200 or more persons. There were 145 manufacturing establishments with more than 1,000 persons employed in 1973.

The proximity of the US, the interest of foreign firms in fabricated materials for use in foreign industry, and the generally profitable character of Canadian manufacturing over many years have led to widespread investment in Canadian manufacturing by companies outside Canada. However, a special analysis of the census of manufactures for 1970 showed that Canadian-controlled firms none the less accounted for 55.8 per cent of all employees in the manufacturing industries; the proportion of value added was somewhat lower, 47.1 per cent.

The 1975 profits of incorporated companies classified as manufacturing industries amounted to 7.4 per cent of total revenue, before taxes and certain extraordinary items.

Putting the finishing touches to a complex casting, poured at a plant in Montreal, Que.

Trade

Domestic Trade

The means by which goods and services are transferred from producers to end users are usually referred to as the channels of distribution. In Canada, these encompass three distinct sectors of the domestic economy: retail trade; wholesale trade; and community, business and personal services. Businesses generally operate within one or another of these sectors, although some are active in two or all three sectors (manufacturers' sales branches and co-operatives, for example, may be engaged in either wholesaling or retailing activities).

The channels of distribution are characterized by continuous change. In retailing and services, the volume of business transacted by franchised (or voluntary group) operations is increasing rapidly. Planned shopping centres continue to proliferate in the suburbs of cities, while in the central business districts merchants are locating their stores in newly-constructed shopping malls and multi-store, multi-level building developments. The commodity mix offered by retailers is expanding in a variety of directions and the spread of businesses into new areas and types of operation (for example, from the operation of stores into mail-order retailing) continues unabated.

In the midst of such change has come a significant increase in the kinds of business that compete for the consumer dollar and in the types of specialized agencies — some of which did not even exist 10 years ago — that serve the varied needs of modern businesses. Although all sectors of the economy have shared in these developments, it is in the service trades that the greatest impact has been felt. Increases in income and leisure time have contributed to the substantial sales growth in services (as well as goods) of a recreational nature; and rising expertise in the marketing function has spurred the growing use of data processing services, market research houses, public relations firms, mailing-list agencies, and other marketing and management consulting businesses.

Retail Trade

In 1975 sales in retail locations reached an estimated $51,200 million, an increase of 14.9 per cent over 1974. During the four-year period 1972-75 for which comparable data are available, retail sales rose 50.1 per cent, chain store sales 57.7 per cent and independent store sales 44.9 per cent. The largest sales increases during this period occurred in the Yukon Territory and the Northwest Territories (74.3 per cent), Alberta (67.0 per cent) and Saskatchewan (64.5 per cent), while Ontario and Manitoba experienced the lowest rates of growth (46.7 per cent and 46.5 per cent respectively). Although Ontario and Quebec continued to account for nearly two thirds of all retail sales in Canada, their share of the retail market has been declining for many years — reaching a low of 62.4 per cent in 1975.

By kinds of business, the most substantial increase in sales for the period 1972-75 was recorded by jewellery stores (63.4 per cent), followed closely by motor vehicle dealers (63.2 per cent), family clothing stores (57.9 per cent), combination stores, which sell groceries and meat (56.9 per cent), and department stores (55.8 per cent).

In 1975 sales in retail locations reached an estimated $51,200 million.

Only one kind of business, specialty shoe stores, lost ground between 1972 and 1975, registering an 11.2 per cent decline. However, several kinds of business recorded increases that were well below average — for example, variety stores, garages, all food stores other than the combination stores, men's clothing stores and household appliance stores.

The largest shares of the retail market were held during 1975 by motor vehicle dealers, who accounted for 19.9 per cent of total sales, and combination stores (groceries and meats), with 19.0 per cent. If the sales of other food stores, used car dealers, service stations, garages and automotive accessories stores were also included, it would be found that well over half (55.1 per cent) of every dollar spent by household or personal consumers in 1975 was used to purchase food, cars or automotive services. (The inclusion of stores selling mainly clothing and footwear —other "basic necessities" of life—would only increase this total by 5.3 per cent.) The only other kind of business with a significant volume of sales was department stores; they captured 11.3 per cent of the retail market, a slight increase over the 10.9 per cent held in 1972.

Within the framework of retail trade, chain store organizations (those that operate four or more stores in the same kind of business under the same legal ownership) compete with independent retailers for a share of the consumer dollar. The market position of the chains, which has been improving slowly but steadily over the years, showed further gains during the 1972-75 period. In 1972, chain stores accounted for 40.4 per cent of total retail sales; by 1973, this figure had risen to 40.8 per cent; the following year it rose to 42.2 per cent; and in 1975 it reached 42.5 per cent. Some of this increase was due to the relatively strong growth in sales of department stores— all of which are classified as chains. If such stores were excluded from both chain and total retail sales, the market share of chain organizations would have been 33.2 per cent in 1972 and 35.2 per cent in 1975.

Between 1972 and 1975, the share of the market held by chains increased in 17 of the 28 kinds of business for which data are available (including "all other stores") and declined in only eight. Chain store organizations accounted for at least half of the total sales of: department stores, in which all firms are classified as chains (100 per cent); general merchandise stores (78.2 per cent); variety stores (75.8 per cent); combination stores, which sell groceries and meat (69.2 per cent); family shoe stores (57.4 per cent); and women's clothing stores (52.2 per cent). Kinds of business in which independent store-owners increased their market share — even if only slightly — included general merchandise stores, variety stores, motor vehicle dealers, automotive parts and accessories stores, specialty shoe stores, hardware stores, household appliance stores and florists.

Direct Selling

Retail stores account for only a part (although the largest part) of the total volume of purchases made by household or personal consumers. Other channels of distribution that completely by-pass the traditional retail outlet (for example, direct selling agencies, coin-operated vending machines and campus book stores) reported total sales of $1,515.8 million during 1974. Of this total, the direct selling activities of manufacturers, importers, wholesalers, mail-order agencies, book,

Wool from a Charlottetown, PEI mill, one of the few mills in Canada still producing 100 per cent woollen yarns.

Fruit stands along the highways of British Columbia offer a wide variety of fruits and vegetables.

newspaper and magazine publishers, and other specialized agencies accounted for $1,227.0 million, or 4.0 per cent of sales registered by comparable kinds of business in retail stores. In addition, vending machine operators reported total sales in 1974 of $227.4 million and campus book stores contributed an additional $61.3 million during the 1974-75 academic year.

The 1974 survey of direct selling in Canada showed that the largest proportion of such "non-store retailing" continues to be made by means of door-to-door canvassing. Sales of such commodities as cosmetics and costume jewellery, dairy products, newspapers and household electrical appliances, made on a door-to-door basis, accounted for 62.1 per cent of total direct selling. Sales of furniture re-upholstering and repairs, furniture, frozen foods and household electrical appliances in the showrooms and other premises of manufacturers provided an additional 17.9 per cent; mail-order sales of such goods as books, phonograph records, magazines and newspapers represented 15.8 per cent, and other channels accounted for the remaining 4.2 per cent of total direct selling.

Consumer Credit

Consumer credit refers to advances made to individuals for non-commercial purposes of cash or credit against specific purchases of consumer goods. Such advances are made under contractual sales agreements or through use of credit cards by firms that extend credit in exchange for a promise of payment at a later date — generally by instalments. Statistics on consumer indebtedness do not include fully-secured loans, home improvement loans and residential mortgages; nor do they include interpersonal loans, bills owed to doctors, dentists, lawyers, etc., and credit extended by clubs and personal service establishments.

During 1975, consumer credit outstanding reached $23,825 million—an increase of $3,259 million, or 15.8 per cent, over the level recorded a year earlier. The largest growth in balances outstanding, 37.2 per cent, was experienced by trust and mortgage loan companies, followed by Quebec savings banks' personal loans, which increased 31.8 per cent over the 1974 year-end figure. The largest share of consumer credit outstanding was held by the chartered banks, which accounted for 55.5 per cent of the total, an increase over the 52.6 per cent held in December 1974.

As shown in the accompanying table, there have been some significant shifts over the past 20 years in the "market share" of the financial and other institutions that serve the needs of consumers for credit. In 1955, sales finance and consumer loan companies accounted for 34.9 per cent, and retail vendors for 29.9 per cent, of consumer credit needs; banks and credit unions in aggregate supplied only 24.5 per cent of these needs. In 1965, the market share of retail vendors had shrunk 11.5 per cent, to 18.4 per cent, while that of the chartered banks and credit unions had risen 18.4 percentage points, to 42.9 per cent. By 1975, consumer credit held by the chartered banks and credit unions accounted for more than two thirds (69.2 per cent) of the balances outstanding, while the market shares of sales finance and consumer loan companies and of retail vendors had diminished to 12.2 per cent and 10.1 per cent respectively.

Table 1. Consumer credit in Canada: balances outstanding — selected holders — selected year-ends
(million dollars)

Credit holders/types of credit	1955	1960	1965	1970	1974	1975	Percentage change 1974-75
Sales finance and consumer loan companies:							
Instalment financing	616	886	1,198	1,136	1,169	1,152	−1.5
Cash loans under $1,500	89	392	628	525	296	252	−14.9
Cash loans over $1,500	173	100	348	1,190	1,501	1,503	+0.1
Chartered banks' personal loans	441	857	2,241	4,663	10,817	13,175	+21.8
Quebec savings banks' personal loans	2	6	16	22	44	58	+31.8
Life insurance companies' policy loans	250	344	411	759	1,066	1,157	+8.5
Credit unions and caisses populaires	174	433	813	1,493	2,762	3,243	+17.4
Department stores and other retail dealers	752	960	1,313	1,551	2,221	2,418	+8.9
Other credit-card issuers	20	43	72	186	274	338	+23.4
Public utility companies	—	—	116	181	271	330	+21.8
Trust and mortgage loan companies	—	—	—	—	145	199	+37.2
Total	2,517	4,021	7,156	11,706	20,566	23,825	+15.8

—Nil or zero.

Water freight destined for the far north at the docks of Hay River in the Northwest Territories.

Wholesale Trade

Wholesalers are primarily engaged in buying merchandise for resale to retailers, to farmers for use in farm production, to industrial, commercial, institutional or professional users, or to other wholesalers. Also forming part of wholesale trade are those who act as agents (or brokers) in such transactions, and who derive commissions from the purchase and/or sale of goods on behalf of others. In 1971, the most recent year for which data on total wholesale trade are available, Canadian wholesalers registered sales of $42,292.9 million according to preliminary census tabulations — an increase of 112.5 per cent over the comparable total in 1961.

For statistical purposes, wholesalers are grouped into five categories, the largest and most important of these being wholesale merchants. The others are agents and brokers, primary product dealers, petroleum bulk tank distributors and manufacturers' sales branches. The wholesale merchant category includes import and/or export merchants, voluntary group wholesalers, cash-and-carry wholesalers, drop shippers or desk jobbers, mail-order wholesalers, truck distributors and rack jobbers — all of whom buy and/or sell merchandise mainly on their own account. Estimated sales of wholesale merchants during 1973-75, as measured by a sample of reporting firms, are shown in Table 2.

Table 2. Estimated sales of wholesale merchants, 1974 and 1975

Trade group	Sales		Percentage change 1974-75
	1974	1975	
	$'000,000	$'000,000	
Total, all trades	43,210.2	45,377.1	+5.0
Consumer goods trades	18,866.1	20,987.0	+11.2
Automotive parts and accessories	2,529.2	2,808.5	+11.0
Motor vehicles	917.2	972.8	+6.1
Drugs and drug sundries	892.6	982.9	+10.1
Clothing and furnishings	396.2	415.9	+5.0
Footwear	96.0	92.9	−3.3
Other textiles and clothing accessories	851.3	829.4	−2.3
Household electrical appliances	897.0	993.1	+10.7
Tobacco, confectionery and soft drinks	1,342.7	1,555.6	+15.9
Fresh fruits and vegetables	751.3	795.2	+5.8
Meat and dairy products	1,083.1	1,090.9	+0.7
Floor coverings	424.3	426.3	+0.5
Groceries and food specialties	5,804.0	6,693.4	+15.3
Hardware	903.8	956.1	+5.8
Consumer goods residual	1,977.4	2,374.0	+20.1
Industrial goods trades	24,344.1	24,390.1	+0.2
Coal and coke	69.7	84.3	+20.9
Grain	4,267.3	4,278.2	+0.3
Electrical wiring supplies, construction materials, apparatus and equipment	798.2	856.7	+7.3
Other construction materials and supplies, including lumber	5,358.1	5,367.7	+0.2
Farm machinery	1,607.0	2,006.4	+24.9
Industrial and transportation equipment and supplies	3,888.5	4,496.9	+15.7
Commercial, institutional and service equipment and supplies	940.5	994.9	+5.8
Newsprint, paper and paper products	694.3	729.3	+5.1
Scientific and professional equipment and supplies	482.9	565.3	+17.1
Iron and steel	2,736.3	1,998.1	−27.0
Junk and scrap	1,024.2	614.7	−40.0
Industrial goods residual	2,477.1	2,397.6	−3.2

The relatively small increase of 5.0 per cent experienced by wholesale merchants between 1974 and 1975 (in marked contrast to the 26.8 per cent rise during the preceding year) was attributable mainly to a general weakening in sales by industrial goods dealers, who recorded a total increase during 1975 of only 0.2 per cent. Significantly rising sales were reported by dealers in farm machinery, coal and coke, scientific and professional equipment and supplies, and industrial and transportation equipment and supplies. However, these increases were almost entirely offset by the substantial declines in sales of wholesalers dealing in iron and steel and in junk and scrap metals. In the consumer goods sector, which rose 11.2 per cent during the year, the best results were registered by dealers in tobacco, confectionery and sundries, groceries and food specialties, automotive parts and accessories, and household electrical appliances.

An outdoor café in Montreal, Que.

Service Trades

Changes within the service trades can be measured best through the analysis of census data, since intercensal surveys provide only partial coverage of this large and diverse sector. In 1971, the service trades falling within the scope of the census reported total receipts (based on preliminary tabulations) of $9,407.7 million. This figure included receipts of $1,559.2 million reported by businesses in the "services to business management" group (lawyers and notaries, architects, consulting engineering services, etc.), which had not previously been surveyed in the census. In comparable terms (that is, excluding the latter kinds of business) service trade receipts rose 71.1 per cent between 1966 and 1971.

The distribution of 1971 service trade receipts by kind-of-business group was as follows (with the 1966 proportion shown in parentheses): amusement and recreation services, 10.8 per cent (9.6 per cent); services to business management, adjusted, 12.8 per cent (10.7 per cent); personal services, 9.2 per cent (13.0 per cent); and accommodation and food services, 51.6 per cent (52.2 per cent). Results in the miscellaneous services group are not comparable between 1966 and 1971 because of various classification changes that occurred during this period.

Intercensal surveys show that: since 1971 restaurant receipts increased by 30.5 per cent, to $1,980.5 million in 1975; accommodation receipts reached $1,930.7 million in 1973, of which hotel receipts amounted to $1,569.7 million, a 21.4 per cent increase over 1971; power laundries and dry cleaners reported combined receipts of $321.8 million in 1974, an increase of 36.0 per cent over 1971; and receipts of motion picture theatres and drive-ins fell to $172.7 million (including taxes) in 1974, a decline of 3.7 per cent. Other intercensal surveys carried out in the service trade sector for 1974 produced the following results: advertising agencies, $675.8 million; computer service industry, $823.0 million; consulting engineering services, $850.6 million; motion picture production, $49.6 million; and motion picture distribution (film exchanges), $87.5 million.

Table 3. Summary statistics on retail trade, 1972 and 1975
(million dollars)

	1972			1975		
	Chain stores	Independent stores	All stores	Chain stores	Independent stores	All stores
Kind of business						
Combination stores (groceries and meat) ...	4,166	2,035	6,201	6,734	2,994	9,728
Grocery, confectionery and sundries stores	244	1,276	1,520	375	1,880	2,255
All other food stores	60	660	720	87	810	897
Department stores	3,714	—	3,714	5,786	—	5,786
General merchandise stores	887	236	1,123	1,250	348	1,598
General stores	123	550	673	271	724	995
Variety stores	518	155	673	620	199	819
Motor vehicle dealers	95	6,145	6,240	126	10,058	10,184
Used car dealers	—	119	119	—	183	183
Service stations	297	1,945	2,242	704	2,598	3,302
Garages	—	445	445	—	555	555
Automotive parts and accessories stores	145	590	735	169	919	1,088
Men's clothing stores	104	412	516	179	485	664
Women's clothing stores .	294	345	639	451	412	863
Family clothing stores ...	148	320	468	320	420	740
Specialty shoe stores	30	25	55	23	26	49
Family shoe stores	163	149	312	244	181	425
Hardware stores	87	346	433	91	490	581
Household furniture stores	87	363	450	145	549	694
Household appliance stores	35	120	155	39	161	200
Furniture, TV, radio and appliance stores	102	247	349	167	311	478
Pharmacies, patent medicine and cosmetic stores	187	840	1,027	333	1,155	1,488
Book and stationery stores	33	94	127	88	104	192
Florists	7	120	127	8	163	171
Jewellery stores	101	160	261	183	244	427
Sporting goods and accessories stores	8	331	339	20	497	517
Personal accessories stores	88	431	519	166	514	680
All other stores	2,068	1,857	3,925	3,173	2,468	5,641
Total, all stores	13,791	20,316	34,107	21,752	29,448	51,200
Province						
Newfoundland	219	419	638	370	602	972
Prince Edward Island	51	105	156	93	148	241
Nova Scotia	438	664	1,102	697	922	1,619
New Brunswick	365	527	892	573	765	1,338
Quebec	2,704	5,908	8,612	4,391	8,421	12,812
Ontario	5,880	7,178	13,058	9,001	10,155	19,156
Manitoba	653	843	1,496	987	1,205	2,192
Saskatchewan	449	914	1,363	748	1,495	2,243
Alberta	1,215	1,513	2,728	2,043	2,514	4,557
British Columbia	1,777	2,210	3,987	2,779	3,160	5,939
Yukon Territory and Northwest Territories ..	40	35	75	70	61	131

—Nil or zero.

Alberta Wheat Pool Co-op elevators at Blackie, Alta.

Co-operatives

The co-operative movement in Canada goes back to the end of the last century, although most of the more than 2,250 co-operatives were established in the period 1910-30. Most co-operatives[1] are rural and agricultural (or horticultural) in character, but during the past 20 years an important development has been the growth of consumer co-operatives serving the urban population.

There are four main groups of local co-operatives serving individuals. These are: the marketing and supply co-operatives that market farmers' produce for them and

[1]This article does not cover the credit unions, insurance and recreational associations.

sell merchandise to them; production co-operatives; fishermen's co-operatives; and service co-operatives. In addition to these there are the wholesale co-operatives, whose primary function is to supply the local co-operatives.

Marketing and Supply Co-operatives

The marketing and supply co-operatives represent by far the largest section of Canadian co-operatives, both in number and in volume of business. In 1974, there were 2,274 co-operatives in Canada, of which 1,123, or 49 per cent, were marketing and supply co-operatives. These had a business volume of $4,770 million, which represented 97 per cent of total co-operative turnover.

The level of co-operative activity in both marketing and supply remained relatively static from 1932 (when the present series of statistics was started) up to the start of World War II. From then until 1970 there was a regular and steady increase in trade; since 1970 the growth in trade has been meteoric. Even as recently as 1956, the total annual turnover of marketing and supply co-operatives was barely $1 billion. It had taken 30 to 40 years to reach that mark. The doubling of turnover to $2 billion was achieved 11 years later in 1967, and a rise to $3 billion turnover was reached only six years later in 1973. The figures for 1974, the latest year available, showed that the volume of business had reached $4,770 million, an incredible increase of $1.2 billion in one year.

The 1974 figure represents an increase of 40 per cent in business over 1973, of which only a small proportion can be attributed to inflation. (The consumer price

United Co-operatives of Ontario now offer a full range of lawn and garden merchandise in addition to agricultural supplies.

index rose by 10.9 per cent during the same period.) Some of the increase was due to a true growth in the co-operative share of the market, but the major reason was the record increases in the prices of some agricultural commodities. The prime example of this is grain, which contributed $845 million of the $967 million increase in the total value of produce marketed by co-operatives.

It is in the grain industry that co-operatives are most significant. Nearly 70 per cent of all grains and seeds are handled by co-operatives, compared with about 60 per cent of dairy products and around 15 per cent of livestock, poultry and eggs.

Mention was made earlier of the increasing development of co-operatives in the consumer field. It is worth noting that in 1974 co-operatives sold $424 million worth of food products, $136 million worth of hardware, $219 million worth of petroleum and $82 million worth of building materials.

Production, Fishermen's and Service Co-operatives

The revenue of production co-operatives, which are involved mainly in livestock production, decreased in 1974 because of a reduction in livestock feeding in western Canada, where most of these co-operatives are situated. The fishing co-operatives increased their business by 12 per cent, although 1974 was not a good year for the fishing industry.

Service co-operatives had a buoyant year in 1974 in many fields. New developments occurred in transportation, housing, rural electricity and gas utilities, and one popular scheme was that for dental insurance in British Columbia.

Wholesale Co-operatives

The general upward trend in co-operative business was reflected in the revenues of the wholesale co-operatives. Over-all turnover in 1974 was $1,389 million, an increase of 33 per cent over 1973 and of 66 per cent over 1972. Most of these increases were in sales of supplies; these rose by 37 per cent in 1974, compared with the 23 per cent by which produce marketing increased during the same period.

The Consumer Price Index

The rate of change in the consumer price index (CPI), as measured by the percentage movement between annual average indexes, stood at 10.8 per cent in 1975, relatively unchanged from the 1974 increase of 10.9 per cent. While the price movements of food and clothing decelerated to some extent between 1974 and 1975, all other components of the CPI experienced higher price movements — in particular housing, up by 10.0 per cent, and transportation, which rose 11.7 per cent. The goods component of the CPI was reclassified in terms of goods and services; it increased by 10.9 per cent, based on annual averages, while the services component was up 10.7 per cent in 1975.

The consumer price indexes for cities measure the movement in consumer prices within each city, and cannot be used to indicate price level differences between cities. Between 1974 and 1975, the CPI increased in all cities, with the changes ranging from 9.6 per cent in Ottawa to 12.4 per cent in Winnipeg.

The purchasing power of the 1971 consumer dollar, which stood at 80 cents on average in 1974, declined to 72 cents in 1975.

Table 4. The consumer price index[1] and its major components for Canada, percentage change between annual average indexes

	1970 1969	1971 1970	1972 1971	1973 1972	1974 1973	1975 1974
All items	3.3	2.9	4.8	7.5	10.9	10.8
Food	2.3	1.1	7.6	14.6	16.3	12.9
All items excluding food	3.8	3.5	3.7	5.0	8.9	10.0
Housing	4.9	4.5	4.7	6.4	8.7	10.0
Clothing	1.9	1.5	2.6	5.0	9.6	6.0
Transportation	4.0	4.1	2.6	2.6	10.0	11.7
Health and personal care	4.5	2.0	4.8	4.8	8.7	11.4
Recreation, education and reading	3.5	3.3	2.8	4.2	8.7	10.4
Tobacco and alcohol	1.2	1.6	2.7	3.2	5.5	12.1

[1] Indexes prior to May 1973 incorporate 1957 expenditure weights; those from May 1973 forward are based on 1967 expenditures, except for items within the food component, which are based on 1969 detailed spending patterns.

Table 5. Consumer price indexes and major components for regional cities, percentage changes[1] between 1974 and 1975

	All items	Food	Hous-ing	Cloth-ing	Trans-porta-tion	Health and personal care	Recreation, education and reading	Tobacco and alcohol
St. John's, Nfld.	11.5	12.5	11.2	7.9	12.8	12.1	10.4	12.4
Halifax, NS	10.1	12.2	8.2	6.6	12.7	10.6	7.7	13.0
Saint John, NB	11.6	14.2	9.9	4.8	12.8	14.7	12.2	13.9
Quebec, Que.	10.2	12.9	8.9	6.4	10.4	11.0	8.3	12.1
Montreal, Que.	10.9	12.9	9.2	7.0	12.8	11.0	10.2	12.7
Ottawa, Ont.	9.6	12.6	9.1	5.6	7.8	9.8	8.6	11.9
Toronto, Ont.	10.7	13.5	9.8	4.1	11.5	12.2	10.9	10.9
Thunder Bay, Ont.	11.3	14.3	10.5	3.8	12.6	12.5	9.8	11.3
Winnipeg, Man.	12.4	13.9	12.8	5.8	15.0	11.9	9.1	12.5
Saskatoon, Sask.	11.2	13.5	11.6	6.1	11.1	9.6	12.0	9.8
Regina, Sask.	10.5	10.1	12.3	5.7	10.3	12.1	11.5	11.5
Edmonton, Alta.	10.9	10.8	11.6	5.6	13.7	11.2	8.4	12.7
Calgary, Alta.	11.3	11.1	12.4	7.3	13.5	11.7	8.4	12.6
Vancouver, BC	11.1	13.1	11.0	5.7	11.0	11.5	9.3	13.6

[1] Based on annual average indexes.

Lumber being loaded at Victoria, BC harbour.

International Trade

Canada's merchandise exports and imports reached record levels in 1975 of $33,103 million and $34,636 million, respectively, following gains of 2 and 9 per cent. After adjustment of customs totals to meet the concepts and definitions used in the system of national accounts (including the balance of payments), the relative advances still stood at 2 per cent for exports, but was close to 10 per cent for imports. The refinements included timing adjustments to certain commodity exports figures, calculation of progress payments on capital equipment, deduction of transportation charges included in some customs returns, and reduction of some values for customs duty to reflect transaction prices.

On a balance of payments basis, there was a trade deficit of $639 million in 1975, in contrast to a surplus of $1,698 million in 1974.

Exports (Customs basis)

The United States remained Canada's most important export destination in 1975, taking $21,652 million (65.4 per cent) of total exports, down somewhat from 66.0 per cent in 1974 and 67.4 per cent in 1973. Other important customers for Canadian goods were Japan, the United Kingdom and the Federal Republic of Germany. The Netherlands and Italy followed in rank in 1975; the USSR and People's Republic of China were important customers in 1973 and 1974.

Harbours

1. Halifax, NS.
2. Toronto, Ont.
3. Quebec, Que.
4. Victoria, BC.

3

4

Table 6. Commodity exports, 1973-75
(million dollars)

Commodity	1973	1974	1975
Wheat	1,221	2,065	2,001
Animals and other edible products	1,937	1,806	2,096
Metal ores and concentrates	2,000	2,376	2,231
Crude petroleum	1,482	3,420	3,052
Natural gas	351	494	1,092
Other crude inedible materials	1,192	1,503	1,576
Lumber	1,599	1,291	973
Pulp	1,082	1,889	1,827
Newsprint	1,288	1,726	1,743
Fabricated metals	2,244	2,979	2,692
Other fabricated inedible materials	2,013	2,811	2,605
Motor vehicles and parts (partial)	5,415	5,717	6,349
Other machinery and equipment	2,455	2,866	3,379
Other domestic exports	559	732	709
Re-exports	583	766	778
Total exports	25,421	32,441	33,103

Coal, coke and related products are shipped from the port of Roberts Bank, south of Vancouver, BC.

The traditional commodities in Canada's foreign trade generally retained their standing in 1975. Motor vehicles and parts represented 19.2 per cent of total exports, as compared with 17.6 per cent in 1974 and 21.3 per cent in 1973. Crude oil and natural gas accounted for 12.5 per cent in 1975, and other machinery and equipment for another 10.2 per cent. Shipments of ores, refined metals and lumber were down in 1975 due to the recessionary situation of principal markets abroad. By stage of fabrication, the proportion of manufactured goods in exports expanded sharply from 31.2 per cent in 1974 to 34.2 per cent in 1975, but was still considerably below the 36.4 per cent recorded in 1973. The share of fabricated materials fell to 31.5 per cent in 1975 from 34.8 per cent in the preceding year, while the proportion of crude materials rose slightly to 34.3 per cent.

Table 7. Exports by leading countries, 1973-75
(million dollars)

Country	1973	1974	1975
United States	17,129	21,399	21,652
Japan	1,814	2,231	2,122
United Kingdom	1,604	1,929	1,789
Federal Republic of Germany	448	557	609
Netherlands	288	396	481
Italy	298	468	479
USSR	292	32	419
Belgium and Luxembourg	286	371	381
People's Republic of China	288	439	377
France	219	324	350

Imports (Customs basis)

Some $23,560 million, or 68 per cent, of imports entered Canada from the United States in 1975. While surpassing 1974, this share was appreciably below the 70.8 per cent recorded in 1973. The United Kingdom displaced Japan in 1975 from the rank of second among major sources of Canadian imports. Venezuela and the Federal Republic of Germany followed in importance. Members of the Organization of Petroleum Exporting Countries (OPEC) such as Iran and Saudi Arabia improved their position in 1975 through the rising value of their oil shipments, as did Yemen. Purchases of Canadian goods by Venezuela and Iran also rose substantially.

Roughly half of Canada's imports in the three-year period were motor vehicles and parts, and other machinery and equipment. From 1973, crude oil more than doubled its share of total imports, to 9.5 per cent in 1975. Manufactured goods accounted for over 60 per cent of all imports, and crude materials also expanded their share. Imports of fabricated materials were comparable in 1973 and 1975.

Table 8. Commodity imports, 1973-75
(million dollars)

Commodity	1973	1974	1975
Food	1,625	2,166	2,318
Animals and other edible products	356	351	364
Metal ores and concentrates	330	397	469
Crude petroleum	942	2,646	3,304
Other crude inedible materials	745	1,029	1,315
Fabricated textiles	659	817	740
Chemical products	1,023	1,537	1,476
Fabricated metals	1,441	2,433	1,997
Other fabricated inedible materials	1,158	1,695	1,731
Motor vehicles and parts (partial)	6,081	7,094	8,137
Other machinery and equipment	6,477	8,414	9,313
Other imports	2,488	3,113	3,472
Total imports	23,325	31,692	34,636

Table 9. Imports by leading countries, 1973-75
(million dollars)

Country	1973	1974	1975
United States	16,503	21,357	23,560
United Kingdom	1,005	1,126	1,222
Japan	1,011	1,430	1,205
Venezuela	522	1,291	1,107
Federal Republic of Germany	607	767	795
Iran	133	618	758
Saudi Arabia	60	319	746
France	327	395	487
Italy	237	316	380
Australia	243	335	345

Containers at the Centennial Pier, Vancouver, BC.

Quebec North Shore Paper Company, Baie-Comeau, Que.

Balance of International Payments

The Canadian balance of international payments summarizes transactions between residents of Canada and those of the rest of the world. International transactions in goods, services, transfers and capital have an important effect on the Canadian economy and the monetary system of the country, so the balance of payments accounts form an integral part of the system of national accounts. Transactions in goods and services are also an important constituent and determinant of the gross national product (GNP), while the capital account of the balance of payments forms a sector in the financial flow accounts.

Sources of balance of payments data are as varied as the range of transactions included in each of the accounts. Considerable information originates from annual, quarterly and monthly surveys carried out by the balance of payments division of Statistics Canada. Other divisions of Statistics Canada, other government departments and the Bank of Canada all provide information concerning transactions between residents of Canada and non-residents.

In 1975 Canada's current account deficit was a record $5,074 million, almost $3.5 billion greater than in 1974. This was a major reason why the growth in the Canadian economy, as measured by the GNP in constant dollars, was recorded as a slight 0.2 per cent in 1975. The economy began emerging from a recession in early

1975, but the rate of growth on a seasonally adjusted basis was weak, with some hesitation appearing in the fourth quarter.

The seasonally adjusted balance on international transactions in goods and services has been a major contributor to this outcome; in the first quarter it showed a record deficit of more than $1.5 billion, which decreased to just under $1.2 billion in the following quarter and expanded to around $1.4 billion in the third and fourth quarters. The major factor in the larger deficit was the $800 million deficit in merchandise trade, an increase of $2.3 billion from the previous year. However, since import prices were rising more than 5 per cent faster than export prices, the shift in the balance of merchandise trade was considerably less in terms of constant dollars. As in the previous year, there were major labour disputes that had an appreciable impact on trade flows. Declines or relatively low rates of growth in economic activity in many countries also resulted in depressed levels of world trade. Canada's exports contracted in volume by about 7 per cent, while the volume of imports fell by around 5 per cent. Thus, Canada's terms of trade in 1975 were less favourable than in 1974.

A substantial increase also occurred in the deficit on services, which rose by about $1 billion. Almost half of this was attributable to an increase in net payments of interest and dividends, increasing largely as a result of capital inflows to finance the current account deficit. Payments on international travel increased by about $500 million, although receipts from international visitors to Canada offset about $100 million of this.

Capital movements during 1975 produced a record net inflow of $4.7 billion. This massive flow was $3 billion greater than in 1974. The net $3.7 billion of receipts in long-term forms was underlain by gross sales of $4.9 billion in new issues of Canadian securities. Almost $2 billion of these were delivered in the fourth quarter, a combined effect of an unusually high differential between bond yields available in Canada and abroad and of the temporary lifting of withholding tax on interest payments to non-residents on certain types of long-term corporate bonds. The main factors in the rise of $2.7 billion in the net inflow in long-term forms were an increase of nearly $400 million in the net receipts from trading in Canadian securities, a reduction of about $200 million in export credits at the risk of the Government of Canada, and offsetting movements from both a decrease of about $150 million in foreign direct investment in Canada and an increase of $150 million in retirements of Canadian securities held by foreigners.

Short-term capital movements produced a net inflow of $1 billion during 1975, an increase of about $400 million over the corresponding figure for 1974. Canadian chartered banks moved from a net increase during 1974 of about $1.3 billion in their foreign currency claims on non-residents to a net decrease of about $500 million during 1975. However, there was an offsetting movement of the same magnitude in non-bank holdings of foreign currency abroad; these had fallen by $1.6 billion during 1975, when residents were repatriating assets held abroad, but they increased by about $200 million during 1975. Transactions in money market paper produced an increased inflow of about $300 million during 1975, but this was offset by the repayment of loans or advances from non-resident banks and from parent and affiliated companies by finance companies in Canada. For the second successive year, holdings of Canadian dollar deposits by non-residents increased by the

Table 10. Canadian balance of international payments, 1973-75[1]
(million dollars)

Item	Between Canada and all countries			Between Canada and US		
	1973	1974	1975	1973	1974	1975
Current account						
Current receipts:						
Merchandise exports[2]	25,445	32,383	33,106	17,318	21,607	21,822
Service receipts:						
Travel	1,446	1,694	1,805	1,160	1,328	1,324
Interest and dividends	754	811	759	435	490	438
Freight and shipping	1,476	1,751	1,754	814	919	928
Other service receipts	1,563	1,849	2,227	810	895	917
Transfer receipts[3]	1,041	1,327	1,396	260	288	290
Total current receipts	31,725	39,815	41,047	20,797	25,527	25,719
Current payments:						
Merchandise imports	22,725	30,864	33,901	16,091	20,605	22,937
Service payments:						
Travel	1,742	1,978	2,511	1,073	1,196	1,558
Interest and dividends	2,019	2,296	2,716	1,678	1,914	2,226
Freight and shipping	1,648	1,974	2,072	862	1,038	1,094
Other service payments	2,547	3,133	3,464	1,779	2,142	2,316
Withholding tax	322	430	472	..	..	..
Transfer payments	704	783	985	155	162	175
Total current payments	31,707	41,458	46,121	21,638	27,057	30,306
Total current account balance	+18	−1,643	−5,074	− 841	−1,530	−4,587
Capital account						
Direct investment:						
In Canada	+725	+585	+425	+430	+521	+387
Abroad	−775	−675	−630	−451	−394	−261
Portfolio transactions:						
Canadian securities:						
Outstanding bonds	+31	+40	+302	−27	+15	+38
Outstanding stocks	−24	−112	+5	+20	−69	−12
New issues	+1,387	+2,437	+4,919	+1,030	+1,834	+3,393
Retirements	−781	−533	−685	−460	−446	−525
Foreign securities:						
Outstanding issues	+93	+43	+18	+73	+37	+18
New issues	−56	−27	−54	−4	−4	−11
Retirements	+15	+12	+12	+8	+8	+8
Other long-term capital transactions	−242	−734	−656	+192	+177	+179
Net long-term capital transactions	+373	+1,036	+3,656	+811	+1,679	+3,214
Net short-term capital transactions	−858	+631	+1,014	−1,123	+811	+1,656
Total net capital balance	−485	+1,667	+4,670	− 312	+2,490	+4,870
Balance settled by exchange transfers	—	—	—	+724	−1,125	..
Allocation of Special Drawing Rights[1]	—	—	—	—	—	—
Net official monetary movements	−467	+24	−404	−429	−165	..

[1] Preliminary figures.
[2] Including non-monetary gold.
[3] Including withholding tax.
··Not available.
—Nil or zero.

historically very high figure of $600 million. There was a decrease of about $400 million in all other short-term capital transactions, mainly because of an improvement of that order in the balancing item.

The current account deficit of $5,074 million, together with the capital account inflow of $4,670 million, resulted in a net decrease of $404 million in Canada's net official monetary assets during 1975. During the first half of the year the Canadian dollar floated steadily downward in terms of Special Drawing Rights (SDRs) from SDR 0.824 to a low of SDR 0.777 at the end of May. This was followed by an appreciation in value, which reached a high of SDR 0.843 in early December before closing the year at SDR 0.840, 2 per cent higher than at the end of 1974. An accompanying deterioration in the value of the Canadian dollar vis-à-vis the United States dollar lasted until August, and more than offset an appreciation in the last four months of the year that had resulted from the unusually large capital inflow. The closing rate of US 98.425 cents was still appreciably below the rate of US 100.949 cents recorded at the end of 1974.

The unprecedented shifts in Canada's international transactions in 1975 occurred against a background of international change. The course of the Canadian economy has tended to diverge from that of its principal trading partners; in 1975, this took the form of a generally slower recovery from a shallower recession than they experienced. Canada's energy position altered dramatically, with the increasing impact of changes in international and domestic prices, of reduced export authorizations and of an altered industry investment climate. Labour stoppages in transportation, in some export industries and in postal communications also had complex effects that are not easily quantifiable. As a whole, Canada's international competitive position was less satisfactory in 1975 than in 1974.

Some of these developments were reflected in a widening of interest rate differentials between Canada and other countries, which played an important part in the massive capital inflow that occurred. Other influences on capital flows included reassessments of the prospects for economic growth in Canada and abroad, the anti-inflation program and changes in tax policies. The changing pattern of international surpluses probably contributed to shifts in the mix of portfolio preferences evident in capital movements in both long- and short-term forms.

After falling slightly in the first few months of 1975 from the extremely high levels achieved in 1974, both long- and short-term interest rates exhibited a general tendency to rise during the remainder of the year. Rates in Canada were well above those abroad, and therefore Canadian borrowers obtained substantial amounts of finance from foreign capital markets.

Balance of International Indebtedness

Preliminary estimates based on available data indicated that Canada's balance of international indebtedness had reached about $43 billion by the end of 1975. Long-term foreign investment had increased by over $7.5 billion to a total of $68 billion, mainly reflecting an inflow of long-term portfolio capital and an increase in earnings accruing to non-residents. Other long-term liabilities, including non-resident equity in Canada's assets abroad, brought the total of long-term liabilities to about $72 billion. Various short-term claims on Canadians increased the total of Canada's external liabilities to over $81 billion.

Canadian long-term investment abroad increased by some $2.5 billion to about $21 billion at the end of 1975. The major elements in this increase were outflows of long-term direct investment capital, re-invested earnings accruing to Canadians from their investments abroad, export credits, and loans and subscriptions of the Government of Canada to foreign countries and international investment agencies. Short-term claims on non-residents, including resident holdings of foreign currencies and net official monetary assets, brought the total of Canada's external assets to about $38 billion.

Vegetable oil tank cars built for export to Zambia, being loaded at Halifax, NS.

Finance

Public Finance

Powers and Responsibilities of the Various Levels of Government

Canada is a federal state with a central government, 10 provincial governments and two territorial governments. Each level of government was assigned specific powers and responsibilities by the British North America (BNA) Act, which forms the written constitution of the country. This Act gives to the Parliament of Canada the right to raise "money by any mode or system of taxation" and, to the provincial legislatures, access to "direct taxation within the province in order to the raising of a revenue for provincial purposes". The BNA Act also empowered the provincial legislatures to make laws regarding "municipal institutions in the province". As a result, municipalities derive their incorporation, with its associated fiscal and other powers, from their respective provincial governments.

A direct tax is generally recognized as one that is levied on the very person who should pay it. Income taxes are the most typical example of direct taxes. However, the meaning of direct taxes has been broadened over the years to apply to various sales taxes at the retail level, where they are paid by the ultimate purchasers or users of goods and services. The federal government imposes both direct taxes, on income of individuals and corporations, and indirect taxes such as customs duties, excise taxes and manufacturer's sales taxes. Direct taxes on income are also levied by provincial governments, along with numerous taxes on sales of goods and services at the retail level. Municipalities levy real property taxes and other imposts on places of business and specific municipal services.

Organization of Government

The organization of government is not uniform from one level to another, nor is it uniform among governments at the same level. Each government operates its affairs in the manner that it finds most convenient to its resources and most suitable to the discharge of its responsibilities. The resulting differences in the organizational structures of the various governments raise problems if one seeks to compare public finance from one government to another. However, in consolidating the transactions of all levels of government to form only one governmental universe, a measure of the collective impact of government financial activities upon the general public can be obtained, as illustrated in the first columns of Tables 1 and 2.

Intergovernment Fiscal Arrangements

Fiscal arrangements between the federal, provincial and territorial governments take various forms and are governed either by an Act of Parliament or by formal agreements between such governments. Intergovernment transfer payments resulting from these arrangements are classified for statistical purposes as either general purpose transfer payments or specific purpose transfer payments, some details of which are outlined below.

The new Canadian Mint in Winnipeg, Man.

Statutory subsidies established by the British North America Act include amounts paid to the provinces, and comprise an allowance per head of population, an allowance for interest on debt and other special amounts agreed upon under terms of the union and subsequent to the union.

Under the Public Utilities Income Tax Transfers Act, the federal government remits to the provinces 95 per cent of the tax it collects from non-government-owned public utility companies that generate or distribute to the public electrical energy, gas and steam. The intent of this policy is to make available to provinces tax revenue from companies exploiting provincial natural resources.

By virtue of the Federal-Provincial Fiscal Arrangements Act, the Minister of Finance pays to a province, where applicable, a revenue equalization payment, a revenue stabilization payment, a tax revenue guarantee or 20 per cent of the federal tax under Part IX of the Income Tax Act, or enters into a tax collection agreement with the province. The most important payments are made under the equalization program; its basic philosophy is that all Canadian citizens are entitled to a standard of public services that is fairly comparable in all the various regions of the country. Thus, the federal government makes available, from its general revenue collected in all provinces, part of the nation's wealth to provinces with incomes lower than the national average income. In 1962 Tax Collection Agreements replaced the tax sharing system that had been in operation since 1952. Under these agreements, the federal government undertook to collect for the provinces their personal and corporation income taxes. All provinces except Quebec signed the agreements in respect of personal income tax, and all provinces except Quebec and Ontario signed in respect of corporation income tax.

Under the Established Programs (Interim Arrangements) Act the federal government may enter into agreements with any province that wishes to assume full financial and administrative responsibilities for certain programs in return for fiscal compensation. The province of Quebec alone availed itself of this legislation, and consequently has a larger proportion of the federal income tax field.

Government property is generally exempt from taxation by another level of government. Where the property would normally be subject to a levy but is exempt for constitutional considerations, a grant is made to a municipality or province, as the case may be, or to other local taxing authorities in lieu of the taxes the community must forego because of the exempt status of the property. These grants are classified as general purpose transfers.

The second type of transfer payments governed by federal-provincial arrangements are referred to as specific purpose transfer payments. These may take three forms: the federal government contributes financial assistance to a program administered by a province; the federal and provincial governments assume sole responsibility for the construction, administration and financing of separate as-

Trans-Canada Highway traffic on Second Narrows Bridge, Vancouver, BC.

Canso Causeway joins Cape Breton to mainland of Nova Scotia.

pects of a joint project; or the province contributes financially to a joint program administered by the federal government.

Most of the federal-provincial joint programs are in the first category. The largest such payments are made under the Hospital Insurance and Diagnostic Services Act, whereby the federal government shares the cost of specified hospital services with provinces providing hospital insurance and diagnostic services. Other large outlays are made under the Canada Assistance Plan and the Post-secondary Education Adjustment Payments; under the first program the federal government makes contributions toward the cost of providing assistance and welfare services to persons in need, while federal contributions toward the financing of part of the operating costs of the provinces' post-secondary education are made pursuant to Part IV of the Federal-Provincial Fiscal Arrangements Act.

Joint programs in the second category—those in which the federal and provincial governments accept sole responsibility for separate portions of a total project—are not numerous and are generally of a public works nature, such as irrigation projects. Programs in the third category are sporadic and few in number, and the sums of money involved are seldom large.

Most provincial government transfer payments take the form of specific purpose transfers to local entities. Among such transfers, the largest are those that contribute to elementary and secondary education and constitute a major source of funds for financing local school boards expenditures.

Table 1. Revenue of federal, provincial and local governments
(fiscal year ended closest to December 31, 1973)

Source of revenue	All governments consolidated $'000	Federal government		Provincial governments		Local governments	
		Amount $'000	Share of total revenue %	Amount $'000	Share of total revenue %	Amount $'000	Share of total revenue %
Taxes:							
Personal income taxes	13,616,120	9,225,804	36.8	4,390,316	19.6	...	...
Corporation income taxes	4,914,210	3,709,978	14.8	1,204,232	5.4	...	...
General sales taxes	6,598,816	3,590,338	14.3	3,005,904	13.4	2,574	—
Real property taxes	3,909,455	...	...	63,810	0.3	3,845,645	36.6
Customs duties	1,384,648	1,384,648	5.5	...	...	...	...
Motive fuel taxes	1,419,401	...	...	1,419,401	6.3	...	...
Health insurance premiums[1]	689,730	...	...	689,730	3.1	...	...
Social insurance levies[1]	1,524,147	1,016,620	4.0	507,527	2.3	...	...
Universal pension plan levies[2]	1,355,255	997,598	4.0	357,657	1.6	...	...
Other taxes	3,148,981	1,716,468	6.8	1,035,713	4.6	396,800	3.8
Sub-total	38,560,763	21,641,454	86.2	12,674,290	56.6	4,245,019	40.4
Natural resources	1,251,799	13,964	—	1,237,835	5.5	...	...
Privileges, licences and permits	821,740	24,155	0.1	683,143	3.0	114,442	1.1
Other revenue from own sources	7,078,768	3,422,180	13.7	2,782,450	12.4	1,143,459	10.9
General purpose transfers from other levels of government	—	—	—	1,827,404	8.1	699,059	6.7
Specific purpose transfers from other levels of government	—	—	—	3,236,411	14.4	4,297,970	40.9
Total revenue	47,713,070	25,101,753	100.0	22,441,533	100.0	10,499,949	100.0

[1]Covers contributions for workmen's compensations, unemployment insurance and vacation-with-pay schemes.
[2]Covers contributions to the Canada and Quebec Pension Plans.
...Not applicable.
—Nil or zero.

Table 2. Expenditure of federal, provincial and local governments
(fiscal year ended closest to December 31, 1973)

Expenditure	All governments consolidated $'000	Federal government Amount $'000	Federal government Share of total expenditure %	Provincial governments Amount $'000	Provincial governments Share of total expenditure %	Local governments Amount $'000	Local governments Share of total expenditure %
General government	2,916,406	1,382,044	5.7	1,078,554	4.9	455,808	4.1
Protection of persons and property[1]	4,178,242	2,529,163	10.4	748,080	3.4	900,999	8.0
Transportation and communications	4,791,817	1,708,889	7.0	1,742,334	7.9	1,340,594	11.9
Health	6,069,434	166,728	0.7	5,751,028	26.1	151,678	1.3
Social welfare	10,539,526	7,547,246	31.1	2,566,946	11.6	425,334	3.8
Education	7,303,057	331,991	1.4	2,245,620	10.2	4,725,446	42.0
Environment	1,293,479	202,547	0.8	188,398	0.8	902,534	8.0
Other expenditure	9,921,012	5,020,182	20.7	2,977,230	13.5	1,923,600	17.2
Intergovernment sales of goods and services	—	67,935	0.3	201,387	0.9	—	—
General purpose transfers to other levels of government	—	1,882,494	7.8	608,089	2.8	—	—
Specific purpose transfers to other levels of government:							
for transportation and communications	—	55,862	0.2	349,694	1.6	5,252	—
for health	—	1,784,659	7.4	41,134	0.2	386,003	3.4
for social welfare	—	562,146	2.3	234,294	1.1	27,195	0.3
for education	—	587,408	2.4	3,051,243	13.8	128	—
for other purposes	—	447,563	1.8	258,954	1.2	3,243	—
Sub-total—specific purpose transfers	—	3,437,638	14.1	3,935,319	17.9	421,821	3.7
Total expenditure	47,012,973	24,276,857	100.0	22,042,985	100.0	11,247,814	100.0

[1] Includes national defence.
— Nil or zero.

Table 3. Financial assets of federal, provincial and local governments
(fiscal year ended closest to December 31, 1973)

Financial assets	Federal government		Provincial governments		Local governments	
	Amount	Share of total financial assets	Amount	Share of total financial assets	Amount	Share of total financial assets
	$'000	%	$'000	%	$'000	%
Cash on hand or on deposit	440,277	1.1	2,582,627	12.4	549,807	12.3
Receivables	399,259	1.0	1,098,094	5.3	1,298,569	29.1
Loans and advances	23,087,791	56.5	3,566,946	17.1	5,049	0.1
Investments						
Canadian securities	14,980,702	36.7	10,547,269	50.6	1,064,202	23.8
Foreign securities	775,988	1.9	...	...	...	...
Sub-total—investments	15,756,690	38.6	10,547,269	50.6	1,064,202	23.8
Other financial assets	1,166,304	2.8	3,050,791	14.6	1,550,905	34.7
Total financial assets	40,850,321	100.0	20,845,727	100.0	4,468,532	100.0

...Not applicable.

Table 4. Liabilities of federal, provincial and local governments
(fiscal year ended closest to December 31, 1973)

Financial liabilities	Federal government		Provincial governments		Local governments	
	Amount	Share of total liabilities	Amount	Share of total liabilities	Amount	Share of total liabilities
	$'000	%	$'000	%	$'000	%
Borrowings from financial institutions	...	...	383,230	1.8	1,057,127	8.4
Payables	8,793,772	19.9	1,276,922	5.8	735,700	5.9
Loans and advances	—	—	1,384,050	6.3	—	—
Bonds and debentures	29,171,365	66.0	18,254,440	83.2	10,250,606	81.7
Other liabilities	6,209,372	14.1	642,233	2.9	505,116	4.0
Total liabilities	44,174,509	100.0	21,940,875	100.0	12,548,549	100.0

...Not applicable.
—Nil or zero.

Highway networks near Toronto, Ont.

Financial Transactions of the Various Levels of Government in the Fiscal Year Ended Closest to December 31, 1973

Tables 1 to 4 provide information on the revenue, expenditure, assets and liabilities of the various levels of government for the fiscal year that ended closest to December 31, 1973. The fiscal year concerned is the period April 1, 1973, to March 31, 1974, for the federal and provincial governments and January 1, 1973, to December 31, 1973, for most local governments.

The data are cast in the financial management statistical framework, which makes use of the financial statements of the various governments as its main source of information. This framework also standardizes government operations in order to arrive at statistics that are comparable among governments and between levels of government. As a result, the data presented differ from the related transactions reported in the financial statements of the individual governments.

Federal Government Transactions. In the period under review, the federal government derived a revenue of $25,101,753,000 and incurred an expenditure of $24,276,857,000, thus realizing a surplus of $824,896,000. Of the federal revenue, 36.8 per cent was obtained from personal income tax, 14.8 per cent from corporation income tax and 14.3 per cent from general sales tax; these three sources accounted for 65.9 per cent of the total. Social welfare, transfers to other levels of government (mostly provincial) and protection of persons and property (mainly national defence) accounted for 31.1, 21.9 and 10.4 per cent respectively (63.4 per cent collectively) of the total federal expenditure.

The financial assets of the federal government amounted to $40,850,321,000 and its liabilities to $44,174,509,000 on March 31, 1974. Of its financial assets, 56.5 per cent were in the form of loans and advances and 38.6 per cent pertained to investments in securities; 66.0 per cent of its liabilities related to bonds and debentures, and 19.9 per cent to payables.

Provincial Government Transactions. In the fiscal year 1973-74, the revenues of provincial governments amounted to $22,441,533,000 and their expenditures

Railway yards at Saint John, NB.

totalled $22,042,985,000, leaving them with a surplus of $398,548,000. The levies on personal income, general sales, motive fuel and corporation income, combined with health insurance premiums, provided 19.6, 13.4, 6.3, 5.4 and 3.1 per cent respectively (47.8 per cent collectively) of total revenues. Provincial governments also received 22.5 per cent of their revenue in the form of transfers from other governments (mainly from the federal government). Health, transfers to other levels of government, education and social welfare accounted for 26.1, 20.7, 10.2 and 11.6 per cent respectively (68.6 per cent collectively) of total expenditures.

On March 31, 1974, the financial assets of provincial governments stood at $20,845,727,000 and their liabilities at $21,940,875,000. Of their financial assets, 50.6 per cent were in the form of investments in securities and 17.1 per cent related to loans and advances, while 83.2 per cent of their liabilities were covered by bonds and debentures.

Local Government Transactions. During the fiscal year ended closest to December 31, 1973, local governments had revenues of $10,499,949,000 and expenditures of $11,247,814,000. They thus incurred a total deficit of $747,865,000. Real property taxes and transfers from other levels of government (mainly from provincial governments) produced 36.6 and 47.6 per cent respectively of total revenues. Education, transportation and communications, protection of persons and property, and environment accounted for 42.0, 11.9, 8.0 and 8.0 per cent respectively (69.9 per cent collectively) of total expenditures.

At the end of the fiscal year, the financial assets of local governments amounted to $4,468,532,000 and liabilities to $12,548,549,000. Most of these financial assets were in the form of receivables and investments in securities (29.1 and 23.8 per cent respectively), while their liabilities related mostly to bonds and debentures (81.7 per cent of the total).

Winnipeg, Man.

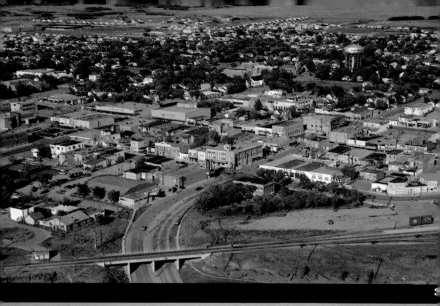

1. Saint John, NB.
2. Montreal, Que.
3. North Battleford, Sask.
4. Thunder Bay, Ont.

Banking and Savings

The Canadian monetary system is a decimal currency with 100 cents to the dollar. Currency in the form of bills is issued by the Bank of Canada. The coinage—nickel coins in denominations of one dollar, 50 cents, 25 cents, 10 cents and 5 cents, and bronze one-cent coins—is issued by the Royal Canadian Mint. At the end of 1975, Bank of Canada notes totalling $6,078 million and coins totalling $699 million were in circulation outside banks.

Although many economic transactions in Canada involve payments made in the form of Bank of Canada notes and coin, an increasing proportion of payments, and certainly virtually all large ones, are made by cheque. A cheque is an order addressed to a bank to pay a third person named in the cheque a specified amount out of the deposit account maintained at that bank by the person writing the cheque. Deposit liabilities held at the chartered banks are considered a convenient means of settling transactions and are usually thought of as money because they are generally accepted in the settlement of debts.

The banks offer three types of chequable accounts: current accounts and personal chequing accounts on which no interest is paid, and chequable savings accounts on which interest is paid. There are also non-chequable savings accounts, on which

Portage Avenue, Winnipeg, Man.

Bank of Montreal, Vancouver, BC.

the banks pay a higher rate of interest, and various types of term deposits. The banks as a group operate extensive facilities for clearing cheques drawn on one bank and cashed in another. On April 30, 1975, the chartered banks had 27,582,944 deposit accounts with an average of $2,059 in each account.

Banks

There are 10 chartered banks operating in Canada and their shares are held, for the most part, by a large number of individual Canadians. The majority of these banks have been in operation for many years, but one new bank commenced operations in July 1968 and another in January 1973. All of the banks operate under charters granted by Parliament under the terms of the Bank Act. Each of the banks has a number of branches and in the largest banks the branch network extends throughout the country. As of December 1975, the banks operated a total of 6,959 branches in Canada. By the yardstick of total assets the three largest Canadian banks were among the top 40 banks in the world in 1974.

The chartered banks are one of the major sources of financing in Canada. They also offer their customers a wide variety of other services, including facilities for obtaining foreign exchange, investing in stocks and bonds, and protecting valuables. Bank loans are made to businessmen and consumers for a variety of purposes and for varying periods of time. Most loans are relatively short-term, but in recent years there has been a quite rapid increase in longer-term loans to businesses and mortgage loans on residential property. The chartered banks are required by law to maintain cash reserves in the form of deposits with, or notes of, the Bank of Canada and may also be required to maintain secondary reserves. The Bank of Canada performs the function of a banker for the chartered banks and is empowered to make short-term advances to the banks.

Many of the chartered banks are also active in international business and provide domestic banking services in a number of other countries. The banks maintained 267 branches and agencies outside Canada, as of December 1975.

Non-bank Financial Institutions

In 1975, the assets of the banks accounted for some 60 per cent of the total assets of the major Canadian financial intermediaries. Their main competitors are trust companies, mortgage loan companies, credit unions, the Quebec Savings Bank, and sales finance and consumer loan companies. Insurance companies and investment dealers and stockbrokers also play important roles in the financial system.

Edmonton, Alta.

Toronto, Ont.

While the chartered banks remain the largest financial institutions in Canada, the postwar period has witnessed the rapid growth and development of the competing institutions. Among the fastest growing in recent years have been the 100 or so trust companies and mortgage loan companies that operate across Canada. Both types of institution accept deposits and have networks of branches. Although they compete with the banks to attract personal savings deposits, most of their funds are raised through the sale of fixed-term debentures and investment certificates. Most of the assets of both trust and mortgage loan companies are held in the form of mortgages. Trust companies also administer private and corporate pension funds and the estates of individuals, manage companies in receivership and act as financial agents for municipalities and corporations. Trust and mortgage loan companies are licensed and supervised either by the federal Department of Insurance or by provincial authorities.

Another important type of financial intermediary in Canada is the credit union, or caisse populaire as it is called in Quebec. The caisses populaires began operations around 1900 and acted mainly as savings institutions for lower income groups. Later, caisses populaires began lending to members at low cost. Unlike the chartered banks, the first of which were established in the early part of the 19th century, most of the credit unions and caisses populaires have been formed during the past 40 to 50 years. Their growth has been due in large measure to their co-operative foundation and to their local character — a striking contrast to the development of many other financial institutions.

The Bank of Canada

Canada's central bank, the Bank of Canada, is charged with the responsibility for regulating "credit and currency in the best interests of the economic life of the nation". The chartered banks are required to maintain, on a half-monthly basis, cash reserves in the form of Bank of Canada notes and deposits with the Bank of Canada equal to 12 per cent of demand deposits and 4 per cent of notice deposits. In addition, the Bank of Canada may require the banks to maintain secondary reserves consisting of excess cash reserves, treasury bills and day-to-day loans. The Bank of Canada implements its monetary policy primarily by varying the amount of cash reserves available to the banking system. An increase in cash reserves, relative to the requirement, will encourage the banks as a group to expand their loans and investments with a concomitant increase in their deposit liabilities, while a decrease in cash reserves will have the opposite effect of inhibiting the banks from expanding their activities or even of inducing a contraction in their total asset and deposit liabilities. The principal means used by the Bank of Canada to alter the level of chartered bank cash reserves over a period of time is through changes in its portfolio of Government of Canada securities.

The bank may make short-term advances to chartered banks and the Government of Canada. The minimum rate at which the bank is prepared to make advances is called the bank rate, and legislation requires that it be made public at all times. The bank acts as fiscal agent for the Government of Canada; it operates the government's deposit account through which flow virtually all government receipts and expenditures, handles debt management and foreign exchange transactions for the government, and acts as an economic and financial adviser. The sole right to issue notes intended for circulation in Canada is vested in the Bank of Canada.

Insurance

At the end of 1974, Canadians owned over $192,000 million worth of life insurance, with an average of $28,200 in force per household. Canadians are well insured compared to people in other countries.

The Canadian life insurance business consists of about 240 companies and fraternal benefit societies, over half of which are federally registered companies. The latter group of companies writes more than 90 per cent of the total business of the industry and holds assets in Canada of about $20,000 million. In addition to life insurance, most of the companies sell policies to cover expenses resulting from illness and to compensate policyholders for wages not received during illness. Insurance may be purchased from a licensed insurance salesman or through a "group" plan operated by an employer, a professional association, a union, etc.

In addition to those companies selling life insurance, about 330 companies sell property, automobile, liability and other casualty lines. The federally registered companies selling such insurance have assets in Canada of almost $3,000 million.

Transportation

Throughout Canadian history, transportation has been a necessary part of social and economic life. Exploration, fur-trading, settlement, timber trade, newsprint delivery and vacation plans, all depend on some mode of transport. The dominant means have shifted from canoe to train to motor vehicle and aircraft; dramatic changes in for-hire carriage of goods have occurred in the span of two generations. While it is estimated that railways earned over 85 per cent of Canada's freight revenue in 1930, by 1960 their share had dropped to less than half and by 1974, to just over 30 per cent. For-hire trucks, on the other hand, accounted for 2 per cent of total freight revenue in 1930, 30 per cent in 1960 and over 40 per cent in 1974.

Air Transport

In Canada, commercial air services are licensed and regulated by the Canadian Transport Commission. Registration and inspection of aircraft, licensing of personnel, operation of a variety of airports, and provision of air traffic control and other air navigation facilities are some of the services provided to civil aviation by the Canadian Air Transportation Administration of the Ministry of Transport (MOT).

The international airport terminal at Vancouver, BC.

Although Canadian air carriers perform many varied services — including crop dusting, forest fire patrol, pipeline inspection, aerial survey and construction — passenger and cargo transport is the most important. In 1975 some 562 air carriers licensed to operate in Canada transported an estimated 15 million passengers domestically and about five million on international routes. The scheduled international routes of four Canadian air carriers — Air Canada, CP Air, Pacific Western Airlines and Nordair — form a vast network connecting Canada to every continent. Canadian airlines also fly charters to destinations around the world.

Table 1. Distribution of itinerant movements[1] at MOT tower-controlled airports, by type of power plant, 1972-75

	1972		1973		1974		1975	
	No.	%	No.	%	No.	%	No.	%
Piston	1,351,175	60.5	1,584,255	61.2	1,465,022	57.7	1,833,301	61.1
Turbo-prop	234,818	10.5	235,825	9.1	234,495	9.2	246,825	8.3
Jet	547,885	24.5	661,967	25.6	734,675	28.9	781,390	26.1
Helicopter	92,042	4.1	99,720	3.9	100,837	4.0	127,471	4.3
Glider	8,834	0.4	4,858	0.2	4,512	0.2	4,412	0.2
Total	2,234,754	100.0	2,586,625	100.0	2,539,541	100.0	2,993,399	100.0

[1]A landing or take-off of an aircraft that is arriving from one airport or departing to another.

Table 2. Scheduled air passenger origin and destination journeys, top 10 city pairs, 1969-75
(thousands of passengers)

City pair	1969	1970	1971	1972	1973	1974	1975[1]
Montreal, Que. – Toronto, Ont.	586.1	674.8	685.8	758.6	915.6	965.7	955.0
Ottawa, Ont. – Toronto, Ont.	251.5	305.6	326.6	347.6	432.5	493.8	497.0
Calgary, Alta. – Edmonton, Alta.	212.9	234.8	254.8	275.3	332.2	372.4	408.0
Toronto, Ont. – Vancouver, BC	143.0	163.0	182.8	206.0	271.4	302.0	304.0
Calgary, Alta. – Vancouver, BC	141.9	166.0	179.4	201.9	247.6	275.1	292.0
Edmonton, Alta. – Vancouver, BC	122.0	139.3	144.7	170.1	217.3	246.7	256.0
Toronto, Ont. – Winnipeg, Man.	146.3	170.9	163.1	179.2	210.5	234.2	237.0
Calgary, Alta. – Toronto, Ont.	75.7	83.0	86.7	104.3	128.7	156.7	169.0
Halifax, NS – Toronto, Ont.	84.2	98.7	103.1	113.5	147.3	158.6	166.0
Thunder Bay, Ont. – Toronto, Ont.	70.0	84.5	96.5	96.6	119.6	140.2	142.0

[1]The fourth quarter component of each figure has been estimated.

Growth in civil aviation can be measured in the number of registrations for both aircraft and aviation personnel. From March 31, 1966, to December 1975, the number of civil aircraft in Canada more than doubled from 7,674 to 17,990. Licences in force for pilots of all types of aircraft, flight navigators, air traffic controllers, and flight and maintenance engineers totalled 52,496 on December 31, 1975.

Another indication of Canadian aviation activity is the number of aircraft movements recorded at airports with MOT air traffic control towers. In 1975 the 60 major airports handled 6,398,181 landings and take-offs. This represented an increase of 12 per cent over 1974, when 57 towers reported 5,692,711 movements. The total for 1975 was 46 per cent higher than that for 1970. The upward trend in tower-controlled air traffic over this period is attributable to substantial increases in both itinerant and local movements.

Table 3. Operations, operating revenue and expenses, and fuel consumption, Canadian commercial aviation, 1974 and 1975
All services (thousands)

	Trans continental and regional air carriers[1]		All other air carriers		Total all air carriers	
	1974[r]	1975	1974[r]	1975[2]	1974[r]	1975[2]
Operations						
Passengers	17,160	17,714	2,441	2,700	19,601	20,400
Passenger-kilometres	26 942 839	28 369 580	2 205 302	3 100 000	29 148 141	31 400 000
Passenger-miles	16,741,504	17,628,040	1,370,311	1,900,000	18,111,815	19,500,000
Goods tonne-kilometres	705 348	740 962	34 558	34 000	739 906	775 000
Goods ton-miles	483,124	507,518	23,670	23,000	506,794	531,000
Flight departures	394	404	677	660	1,071	· 1,060
Hours flown	564	584	1,657	1,770	2,221	2,350
Operating revenues and expenses						
Total operating revenues ($)	1,327,961	1,539,290	269,824	360,000	1,597,785	1,900,000
Total operating expenses ($)	1,269,572	1,493,187	255,644	350,000	1,525,216	1,840,000
Fuel consumption						
Turbo fuel (litres)	2 971 349	3 098 314	186 573	255 000	3 157 923	3 353 000
(gallons)	653,606	681,534	41,040	56,000	694,646	738,000
Gasoline (litres)	4 279	3 576	80 671	83 200	84 950	86 800
(gallons)	941	787	17,745	18,300	18,686	19,100

[1]Air Canada, CP Air, Pacific Western Airlines, Transair, Nordair, Quebecair and Eastern Provincial Airways.
[2]Estimated.
[r]Revised.

In 1974 Canadian air carriers transported 19.6 million passengers; in 1975 they carried an estimated 20.4 million, an increase of 4.6 per cent. Operating revenues earned by all air carriers in 1974 amounted to $1,598 million, while those for 1975 approached $1,900 million. Expenditures, reported at $1,525 million in 1974, were estimated at over $1,840 million in 1975.

Unloading supplies for the Repulse Bay Inuit Co-op store.

Trends in domestic travel are illustrated in terms of scheduled air passenger origin and destination data. Figures for air journey origins and destinations of passengers between Montreal and Toronto showed an increase of 33.5 per cent between 1971 and 1973, and an increase of 5.2 per cent between 1973 and 1975. Ottawa–Toronto passenger totals grew by 32.4 per cent between 1971 and 1973, and by 14.7 per cent between 1973 and 1975.

Railways

Historically, railways have played a central role in the political integration, settlement and economic development of Canada. In 1850, there were 106 km (kilometres) of railway in all of British North America. Eighty years later, Canada had 91 065 km of track in operation. Since then growth has been slow, with occasional declines. By 1974, 96 958 km of track were in use. Two continent-wide railways, Canadian National and Canadian Pacific, spanned 7 000 km from Atlantic to Pacific over vast stretches of rock and muskeg, flat prairie and mountain ranges to make possible the settlement of western Canada. Today, these railways offer multi-modal transportation services, with particular emphasis on the long-distance movement of bulk commodities and containers quickly, cheaply and efficiently.

Canadian Pacific is a private company, while Canadian National Railways is federally operated. Provincially operated lines include the British Columbia Railway, British Columbia Hydro's railway, Ontario Northland and GO Transit.

The development of containerized shipments, which require the co-operation of several modes of transportation and the design of smooth, efficient interchange facilities, has been one of the most significant ones for rail freight in recent years. In 1969, 27,718 railway freight cars carried 469 279 t (metric tons) of containerized

Grain elevators and railway yards at Halifax, NS.

freight. By 1972, this mode of transport had grown so rapidly that the amount of containerized freight carried had increased more than sixfold, to 2 956 385 t on 118,029 cars. For 1974 the corresponding figures were 4 065 385 t and 191,795 cars. In other words, while fewer than one in every hundred cars in 1969 carried containers, this traffic accounted for 4.6 per cent of all cars loaded in 1974. In 1975, however, containerized freight carried dropped 12.5 per cent to 3 558 082 t on 166,417 cars (13.2 per cent fewer cars than in the previous year). These declines were steeper than those reported for all car-loadings, which showed 7 per cent less tonnage and 10 per cent fewer cars loaded in 1975 than in 1974.

Revenue freight carried in 1974 increased to 246 314 822 t from the 1973 total of 241 261 903 t. The number of passengers carried increased to 24,134,040 in 1974, up 21.8 per cent from the 1973 low of 19,821,933. Reversing a downward trend that had prevailed in the industry for more than 15 years, the number of employees needed to transport these people and goods increased from the 1973 low of 124,201 to 131,908 persons in 1974.

Motor Vehicle Transportation

In 1974 the motor vehicle continued to maintain unchallenged its position as the dominant mode of transport in Canada. Registrations for all types numbered 11,002,003, up 8 per cent from the 1973 total of 10,158,440 and 72 per cent from the 1964 figure of 6,382,033. Passenger car registrations were 77 per cent of the 1974 total, numbering 8,472,224; trucks and buses, at 2,027,565, accounted for 18 per cent. Growth in net fuel sales slackened somewhat from 1973 to 1974; the 1974 figure of 30 344 million litres for gasoline was up only 4 per cent over that for 1973

(29192 million litres). Diesel fuel sales in 1974 were up 16 per cent from 1973, increasing from 3797 million litres to 4413 million litres in net sales.

Outstripping the growth in registrations, the number of motor vehicle accidents reported increased 13 per cent, from 553,146 in 1973 to 623,765 in 1974. While the number of injuries resulting from these accidents also rose slightly in the same period, from 223,777 to 229,641 (3 per cent), the number of fatalities and fatal accidents showed decreases of 6.2 per cent and 5 per cent respectively. The 6,290 fatalities in 1974 occurred in 5,204 separate accidents; equivalent figures for 1973 were 6,706 and 5,479 respectively.

The importance of the role of the motor carrier industry — both freight and passenger — in Canadian transportation is best illustrated by the fact that this industry generated $3.5 billion in operating revenue in 1974, or approximately 50 per cent of the operating revenues of all Canadian commercial carriers engaged in the transportation of freight. The economic significance of the three mutually exclusive segments of the motor carrier industry—motor carriers (freight), intercity passenger bus and urban transit — is shown in Table 4.

Wood Island Ferry from Prince Edward Island to Nova Scotia.

Highway network near Winnipeg, Man., with Red River crossing at Middlechurch.

Table 4. The Canadian motor carrier industry, 1974

	Motor carriers – freight	Intercity passenger bus	Urban transit	Total
Establishments reporting (No.)	13,186	68	82	13,336
Operating revenues ($ millions)	2,966.3	138.3	346.9	3,451.5
Operating expenses ($ millions)	2,739.1	124.2	424.2	3,287.5
Number of employees (thousands)	125.0	5.0	25.9	155.9
Pieces of equipment operated (thousands)	149.2	1.7	9.6	160.5

Historically, the motor carrier industry has been characterized by a large number of small carriers, none of which was dominant. Possibly the most important recent development has been that this statement no longer holds in 1974, since the 220 Class 1 carriers, earning more than $2 million annually, represented 50 per cent of the total operating revenue of the industry that year.

Table 5. Operating revenues of the Canadian motor carrier industry, by class of
carrier[1], 1974

Class of carrier	Motor carriers– freight		Intercity passenger bus		Urban transit		Total	
	No.	$'000,000	No.	$'000,000	No.	$'000,000	No.	$'000,000
Class 1	130	1,366.2	15	130.6	12	305.8	157	1,802.6
Class 2	380	502.0	3	2.7	16	27.2	399	531.9
Class 3	1,382	429.1	11	2.5	29	12.3	1,422	443.9
Class 4	2,398	172.9	11	0.8	4	0.3	2,414	174.0
Class 5	3,905	100.0	17	0.3	15	0.2	3,937	100.5
Class 0	4,291	396.1	11	1.4	6	1.1	5,008	398.6
Total	13,186	2,966.3	68	138.3	82	346.9	13,336	3,451.5

[1]Based on reported annual operating revenue. Class 1: over $2,000,000; Class 2: $500,000 to $1,999,999;
Class 3: $100,000 to $499,999; Class 4: $25,000 to $99,999; Class 5: under $25,000.

Water Transport

According to the results of a special profiling survey of the Canadian water
transport industry, Canadian-domiciled commercial carriers and charterers generated gross transportation revenues totalling $1.05 billion in 1974. Of this, approxi-
mately 94 per cent, or $1.08 billion, was grossed by 89 carriers earning $1 million or
more annually from water transportation operations.

Terminal and ore storage facilities at Sept-Îles, Que.

Total wage and salary expenditures on licensed and unlicensed vessel crew represented an estimated direct labour outlay of 21 per cent of total gross transportation revenue, or 21 cents out of every revenue dollar.

Of the $1.15 billion gross transportation revenue reported, the largest portion, $551 million (48 per cent), was generated by operations between Canadian ports. Canada–United States movements accounted for $229 million (20 per cent). Operations of Canadian-domiciled firms involving foreign ports accounted for $356 million (31 per cent).

International cargoes handled at Canadian ports amounted to 166 828 166 t during 1974, down 6 per cent from the 1973 total of 178 393 821 t. A total of 68 684 811 t, or 41 per cent of Canada's international trade, were handled at eight major ports: Halifax, NS; Saint John, NB; Quebec and Montreal, Que.; Toronto, Hamilton and Thunder Bay, Ont.; and Vancouver, BC.

**Gross water transportation revenue,
by type of operation, 1974**

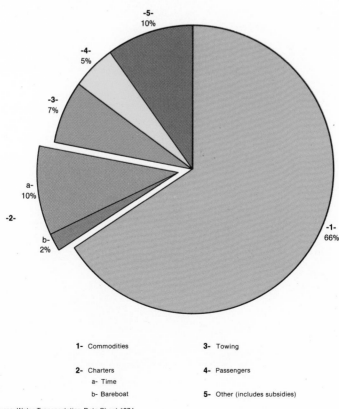

1- Commodities   3- Towing

2- Charters   4- Passengers
   a- Time
   b- Bareboat   5- Other (includes subsidies)

Source: Water Transportation Data Sheet 1974.

Villages of Newfoundland

1. Fogo.   3. Twillingate.
2. St. Anthony.   4. Port aux Basques.

governments and their services

Government

Canada is a federal state, established in 1867. In that year, the British Parliament, at the request of three separate colonies (Canada, Nova Scotia and New Brunswick), passed the British North America (BNA) Act, which "federally united" the three "to form . . . one Dominion under the name of Canada". The Act merely embodied, with one modification (providing for the appointment of extra Senators to break a deadlock between the two Houses of Parliament), the decisions that delegates from the colonies, the "Fathers of Confederation", had themselves arrived at.

The Act divided the Dominion into four provinces. The pre-Confederation "province of Canada" became the provinces of Ontario and Quebec; Nova Scotia and New Brunswick retained their former limits. In 1870, the Parliament of Canada created Manitoba; British Columbia entered the Union in 1871, and Prince Edward Island in 1873. In 1905, the Parliament of Canada created Saskatchewan and Alberta, and in 1949 Newfoundland came in.

The BNA Act gave Canada complete internal self-government, and gradually the country acquired full control over its external affairs also. It is now a fully sovereign state, except that a few (but very important) parts of its Constitution can be changed only by Act of the British Parliament. This limitation, however, is purely nominal.

The British Parliament invariably passes any amendment requested by the Canadian. The only reason the full power of amendment has not been transferred to Canada is that Canadians have not been able to agree on any amending formula.

The BNA Act gave the Canadian Parliament power to "make laws for the peace, order and good government of Canada in relation to all matters . . . not . . . assigned exclusively to the Legislatures of the provinces". To make assurance doubly sure, the Act added a list of examples of this general power. These included: defence; raising money by any kind of taxation; regulation of trade and commerce; navigation and shipping; fisheries; money and banking; bankruptcy and insolvency; interest; patents and copyrights; marriage and divorce; criminal law and criminal procedure; penitentiaries; interprovincial and international steamships, ferries, railways, canals and telegraphs; and any "works" declared by Parliament to be "for the general advantage of Canada". Amendments have added unemployment insurance and the power to amend the Constitution, except in regard to the division of powers between Parliament and the provincial legislatures, the rights guaranteed to the English and French languages, the constitutional rights of certain religious denominations in education, the requirement of an annual session of Parliament and the maximum duration of Parliament.

The Act of 1867 gave Parliament and the provincial legislatures concurrent power over agriculture and immigration (with the national law prevailing over the provincial in case of conflict); amendments provided for concurrent jurisdiction over pensions (but with provincial law prevailing in case of conflict).

Decisions by the Judicial Committee of the British Privy Council (the final court of appeal for Canada until 1949) made the examples of the "peace, order and good government" power almost swallow up the general power of which they were supposed to be examples. The general power came to mean little more than jurisdiction to pass temporary laws to meet wartime emergencies. But judicial decisions also interpreted Parliament's powers to cover interprovincial and international telephones, interprovincial and international highway traffic, and all air navigation and broadcasting.

The BNA Act established a limited official bilingualism. In debates in both Houses of Parliament, members may use either English or French; the records and journals of both Houses must be kept in both languages; Acts of Parliament must be published in both; and either language may be used in any pleading or process in courts set up by Parliament. The same provisions apply to the legislature and courts of Quebec.

In fact, the Government and Parliament of Canada, and the governments and legislatures of Quebec, Ontario, New Brunswick and Newfoundland, have extended bilingualism beyond the constitutional requirements. The whole of the central administration at the national capital, and anywhere else where there is a sufficient French-speaking or English-speaking minority, is now being thoroughly bilingualized. In 1969, Parliament adopted the Official Languages Act, which declared that English and French enjoy equal status and are the official languages of Canada for all purposes of the Parliament and Government of Canada.

Except for limited official bilingualism and certain educational rights for some religious minorities, the Canadian Constitution provides no specific protection for basic rights like freedom of worship, of the press and of assembly. Such rights are

Ottawa, Ont., Canada's capital.

protected by the ordinary law, but all of them could be curtailed or abolished by Parliament or the provincial legislatures, although such action would be contrary to the Canadian tradition. Therefore, in 1960 the Parliament of Canada adopted a Bill of Rights and the present government has proposed Human Rights legislation prohibiting discrimination in areas of federal jurisdiction.

Each provincial legislature has exclusive power over: the amendment of the provincial Constitution (except as regards the office of Lieutenant Governor, the legal head of the provincial executive); natural resources; direct taxation for provincial purposes; prisons; hospitals; asylums and charities; municipal institutions; licences for provincial or municipal revenue; local works and undertakings; incorporation of provincial companies; solemnization of marriage; property and civil rights; administration of justice (including the establishment of civil and criminal courts and civil procedure); matters of a merely local or private nature; and education, subject to certain safeguards for denominational schools in Newfoundland and Protestant or Roman Catholic schools in the other provinces. Judicial decisions have given "property and civil rights" a very wide scope, including most labour legislation and much of social security.

The Canadian Constitution

The BNA Act and amendments form the basic law of the Canadian Constitution. But they provide only a skeleton framework of government. This is filled out by judicial interpretation, by various Acts of Parliament and of the legislatures, and, most of all, by custom or "convention" — the generally accepted understandings about how the legal machinery should be worked. A person taking the BNA Act literally would think Canada was governed by an absolute monarch. In fact, the monarch's powers are exercised, as the Fathers of Confederation put it, "according to the well understood principles of the British Constitution"—that is, according to the usages and understandings which gradually transformed the British monarchy into a parliamentary democracy. These conventions Canada has inherited and adapted to suit her own needs.

The Government of Canada

The Executive

By free and deliberate choice of the Fathers of Confederation, Canada is a con-stitutional monarchy. The executive government "is vested in the Queen" of Canada (who is also Queen of Britain, Australia and New Zealand). In strict law, her powers are very great. In fact, they are exercised on the advice of a Cabinet responsible to the House of Commons, which is elected by the people.

For most purposes, the Queen is represented by the Governor General (now always a Canadian), whom she appoints on the advice of the Canadian Cabinet for a period of, normally, five to seven years. In very extraordinary circumstances, the Governor General may act on his own. For instance, if the Prime Minister dies the Governor General must choose a new one from the party with a majority in Parlia-ment, to hold office until that party can choose a new leader. Again, if a Cabinet comes out of an election with less than half the seats in Parliament, and asks for an immediate new election, the Governor General must refuse, since a newly elected Parliament must at least be allowed to meet and try to transact public business.

Except in such extraordinary circumstances, however, the Queen or the Governor General must act on the advice of the Cabinet, or, in a few cases, of its head, the Prime Minister. The Prime Minister appoints the members of the Cabinet, decides when Parliament shall meet and normally decides when a new Parliament shall be elected (though there must be an election at least every five years, unless war, invasion or rebellion makes it impossible). The Cabinet appoints the members of the Senate (the Upper House of Parliament), the judges of the superior, district and county courts, and the Lieutenant Governors of the provinces. It can annul any provincial law within one year of its passing. In the name of the Queen and the Governor General, it provides direction to the Armed Forces, appoints public servants, pardons criminals, declares war, makes peace, appoints ambassadors, makes and ratifies treaties, and makes regulations within the limits set by Acts of Parliament.

Both the Cabinet and the Prime Minister are nearly unknown to the law. The BNA

Members of the Senate and Justices of the Supreme Court listening to the recent Speech from the Throne. Madame Léger shared the reading of the Speech from the Throne with her husband, Governor General Jules Léger because of his ill health.

Act provides only for a "Queen's Privy Council for Canada", appointed by the Governor General to "aid and advise" him. In fact, this body does nothing. It consists of all Cabinet Ministers, all former Ministers, ex-Speakers of both Houses, the Chief Justice, ex-Chief Justices and various distinguished citizens appointed as a mark of honour. Its only practical importance is that it provides the legal basis for the Cabinet, which, legally, is simply "the Committee of the Privy Council".

The Cabinet consists of those Privy Councillors whom the Prime Minister invites to its meetings. In practice, this means the heads of all departments and ministries, and usually also a few ministers of state without departments or ministries. In April 1976 the Cabinet had 28 members including the Prime Minister. Usually, there is one Senator without portfolio. By custom, all ministers must have a seat in one House or the other, or get one within a reasonable time.

The Cabinet has no fixed term. It holds office until the Prime Minister dies or resigns. Sir Wilfrid Laurier's Cabinet lasted for over 15 years, Sir John A. Macdonald's second Cabinet for almost 13.

If an opposition party wins more than half the seats at a general election, the Cabinet resigns and the Governor General calls on the leader of the victorious party to become Prime Minister. The new Prime Minister chooses his Cabinet from his own party. It is customary, insofar as representation in Parliament permits, for the Cabinet to include at least one minister from every province, with the more populous provinces receiving greater representation.

The Cabinet must speak as one on all questions of government policy. A minister who cannot support that policy must resign. Each minister of a department is answerable to the House of Commons for that department and the whole Cabinet is answerable to the House for government policy and administration generally. If the Cabinet is defeated in the House on a motion of want of confidence, it must either resign office — at which point the Governor General calls on the Leader of the Opposition to form a new Cabinet—or seek dissolution of Parliament, leading to a general election; the latter procedure is generally followed nowadays.

Defeat of a major government bill is ordinarily considered a vote of want of confidence, leading to the same consequences. But the Cabinet can choose to consider any such defeat not decisive. The House then has the option of voting on a motion of want of confidence.

Only the Cabinet can introduce bills for the raising or spending of public money. Ordinary members of the House of Commons can move to reduce proposed taxes or expenditures, but not to raise them. The rules of the House allot most of its time to Cabinet business, and nearly all legislation now comes from the Cabinet. The Cabinet has the sole power to move closure, cutting off debate; and if the parties fail to agree, the Cabinet can move to fix a time-table for the various stages of a bill. But the rules are careful also to provide abundant opportunity for the Opposition to question, criticize and attack. Twenty-five days of each parliamentary year are specifically allotted to the Opposition to debate any subject it pleases, and on six of those days it can move want of confidence.

The Legislature

Parliament. Parliament consists of the Queen, the Senate and the House of Commons. The Senate has 104 members, appointed by the Cabinet: 24 from Ontario, 24 from Quebec, 24 from the Maritime provinces (10 each from Nova Scotia and New Brunswick, 4 from Prince Edward Island), 24 from the western provinces (6 each), 6 from Newfoundland, one from the Yukon Territory and one from the Northwest Territories. Senators now retire at age 75.

The BNA Act gives the Senate exactly the same powers as the House of Commons, except that money bills must originate in the Commons. The Senate can reject any bill, but rarely does. It does most of the work on private bills (such as incorporation of companies), and subjects general legislation to careful scrutiny in committee. Special Senate committees have also investigated major public problems and produced valuable reports. In April 1976 the Senate had 70 Liberals, 1 Independent Liberal, 16 Progressive Conservatives, 1 Social Credit, 2 Independents and 14 vacancies.

The House of Commons, to which alone the Cabinet is responsible, has 264 members: 7 from Newfoundland, 11 from Nova Scotia, 10 from New Brunswick, 4 from Prince Edward Island, 74 from Quebec, 88 from Ontario, 13 each from Manitoba and Saskatchewan, 19 from Alberta, 23 from British Columbia and 1 each from the Yukon Territory and the Northwest Territories. They are elected by single-member constituencies, broadly speaking in proportion to the population of each province; but no province can have fewer members in the Commons than in the Senate. The total number of members is redistributed after each decennial census. Any adult Canadian citizen (with some exceptions, such as people in jail) can vote. In April 1976 the Liberals had 139 members, the Progressive Conservatives 95, the New Democratic Party 16 and the Social Credit Party of Canada 11; there was 1 Independent member, and 2 seats were vacant.

All legislation goes through three "readings". The first is purely formal. On the

Legislative buildings of Quebec City, Que.

second, the House gives the bill "preliminary consideration" and, if satisfied, refers it to a committee, where it is dealt with clause by clause. Money bills, and such others as the House thinks fit, are referred to the Committee of the Whole, that is, the whole House, sitting under special rules facilitating detailed discussion. All other bills are sent to one of the 19 "Standing Committees" (12 to 30 members each), each of which specializes in a certain subject or subjects. The appropriate committee then reports the bill to the House, with or without amendments, and at this stage any member may propose amendments, which are debatable. Then comes third reading. If the bill passes this, it is sent to the Senate, where it goes through much the same procedure.

The Canadian Constitution would be unworkable without political parties. Yet parties are almost unknown to Canadian law — a notable example of the conventions of the Constitution. They make possible a stable government, capable of carrying its policies into effect. They provide continuous organized criticism of that government. They make possible an orderly transfer of power from one government to another. They help to educate the electorate on public affairs and to reconcile divergent elements and interests from different parts of the country.

The Liberal party has its roots in the pre-Confederation Reform parties which struggled for the establishment of parliamentary responsible government in the 1840s. The Progressive Conservative party goes back to a coalition of moderate Conservatives and moderate Reformers in the province of Canada in 1854, six years after responsible government had been won. It was broadened into a national party in 1867, when Sir John A. Macdonald, the first national Prime Minister, formed a Cabinet of eight Conservatives and five Liberals or Reformers, whose followers soon became known as "Liberal-Conservatives"; the present name was adopted in 1942. The New Democratic Party dates from 1961, when the major trade union federation (the Canadian Labour Congress) and the Co-operative Commonwealth Federation (CCF) party joined forces to launch a new party; the CCF had been founded in 1932 by a group of farmer and labour parties in the western provinces. The Social Credit Party of Canada is based on the monetary theories of Major Clifford Douglas; in 1976 all its members in the House of Commons were from Quebec.

Provincial and Territorial Government

In each province, the machinery of government is substantially the same as that of the central government, except that no province has an Upper House.

Most of northern Canada west of Hudson Bay is organized in two territories, the Yukon Territory and the Northwest Territories, which come directly under the Government and Parliament of Canada but enjoy a growing degree of self-government.

The Yukon Territory is administered by a Commissioner, appointed by the Government of Canada, and an elected Council of 12. The Commissioner in Council can pass laws dealing with direct taxation for local purposes, establishment of territorial offices, sale of liquor, preservation of game, municipal institutions, licences, incorporation of local companies, solemnization of marriage, property and civil rights, and matters of local and private nature.

The Northwest Territories are administered by a Commissioner, appointed by the Government of Canada, and an elected council of 15. The Commissioner in Council has substantially the same powers as in the Yukon Territory.

Municipal Government

Municipal government, being a matter of provincial jurisdiction, varies considerably. All municipalities (cities, towns, villages and rural municipalities) are governed by an elected Council. In Ontario and Quebec, there are also counties, which group smaller municipal units for certain purposes, and both these provinces have begun to set up regional municipalities for metropolitan areas.

In general, the municipalities are responsible for: police and fire protection; local jails, roads and hospitals; water supply and sanitation; and schools (often administered by distinct boards elected for the purpose). They get their revenue mainly from taxes on real estate, fees for permits and licences, and grants from the provinces. The total number of municipalities is now about 4,500.

The Legal System

The legal system is an important element in Canadian government. Since the British North America Act established Canada as a federal state, the Canadian legal system is somewhat complex.

The Law and Law-making

The law in Canada consists of statutes and judicial decisions. Statutes are enacted by Parliament and the provincial legislatures and are written statements of legal rules in fairly precise and detailed form. There is also a large body of case law which comes mainly from English common law and consists of legal principles evolved by the decisions of the superior courts over a period of centuries.

The English common law came to Canada via the early English settlers. It is the basis of much of the law in all provinces and territories as well as of much federal law. The province of Quebec, however, was originally settled by French inhabitants who brought with them civil law derived from French sources. Thus, in Quebec, civil law principles govern such matters as personal, family and property relations. Quebec has developed its own Civil Code and Code of Civil Procedure governing these and other matters, and has, in effect, adapted the French civil law to meet Quebec's needs.

In addition to the statutes of the federal Parliament and provincial legislatures, there is a vast body of law contained in regulations adopted by appropriate authorities, as well as in by-laws made by municipalities. This subordinate legislation, as it is called, is issued under authority conferred by either Parliament or the provincial legislatures.

Statutes enacted by the federal Parliament of course apply throughout the country; those enacted by provincial legislatures apply only within the territorial limits of the provinces. Hence, variations may exist from province to province in the legal rules regulating an activity governed by provincial law.

The main body of Canadian criminal law, being federal, is uniform throughout the country. Although Parliament has exclusive authority under the BNA Act to enact criminal law, the provincial legislatures have the power to impose fines or punishments for breaches of provincial laws. This gives rise to provincial offences — for example, the infraction of a provincial statute regulating the speed of automobiles travelling on the highways.

Most Canadian criminal law is contained in the criminal code derived almost exclusively from English sources. Criminal offences are classified under the code as indictable offences, which are subject to a severe sentence, or summary conviction offences to which a less severe sentence applies. However, the totality of statutory federal criminal law is not contained in the Criminal Code of Canada. Other federal statutes provide for the punishment of offences committed thereunder by fine or imprisonment or both. In any event, whether an offence be serious or minor, it is a fundamental principle of Canadian criminal law that no person may be convicted unless it has been proved beyond all reasonable doubt to the satisfaction of either a judge or a jury that he is guilty of the offence.

Law Reform

As society changes, as its needs and even its standards change, the law has to reflect·these changes. Therefore, many of the provinces now have Law Reform Commissions which inquire into matters relating to law reform and make recommendations for this purpose. At the federal level, the Law Reform Commission of Canada carries out this activity by studying and reviewing federal law with a view to making recommendations for its reform.

The Courts and the Judiciary

The legal system includes courts, which play a key role in the process of government. Acting through an independent judiciary, the courts declare what the law is and apply it to resolve conflicting claims between individuals, between individuals and the state and between the constituent parts of the Canadian federation.

The Judiciary

Because of the special function performed by judges in Canada the BNA Act guarantees the independence of the judiciary of superior courts. This means that judges are not answerable to Parliament or the executive branch of the government for decisions rendered. A federally appointed judge holds office during good behaviour, but is removable from office by the Governor in Council on the address of the Senate and House of Commons; in any event, he or she ceases to hold office upon attaining the age of 75 years. The tenure of judges appointed by provinces to inferior courts is determined by the applicable provincial laws. No judge, whether federally or provincially appointed, may be subjected to legal proceedings for any acts done or words spoken in a judicial capacity in a court of justice.

The appointment and payment of judges reflect the interlocking of the divided powers found in the Canadian constitutional system. The federal government appoints and pays all judges of the federal courts, as well as judges of the provincial superior and county courts, while judges of provincial inferior courts are appointed and paid by the provincial governments.

The Courts

In Canada, the power to create courts is divided. Some courts are created by Parliament—for example, the Supreme Court of Canada—and others by provincial legislatures—for example, superior courts, county courts and many lesser provincial courts. However, the Supreme Court of Canada and provincial courts are part of an integrated whole; thus, appeals may be made from the highest courts of the provinces to the Supreme Court. Generally speaking, federal and provincial courts are not necessarily given separate mandates as to the laws that they administer. For instance, although criminal law is made by the Parliament of Canada, it is administered mainly in provincial courts.

Federal courts. Federal courts in Canada include the Supreme Court of Canada, the Federal Court of Canada and various specialized tribunals such as the Tax Review Board, the Court Martial Appeal Court and the Immigration Appeal Board. These courts and tribunals are created by Parliament.

Supreme Court judges.

The Supreme Court, established in 1875, is the highest appeal court of Canada in civil and criminal matters. The Court consists of nine judges, of whom three at least must come from Quebec, a requirement added because of the special character of Quebec civil law. The conditions under which appeals are heard by the Court are determined by the statute law of Parliament. The Court entertains appeals from the provincial Courts of Appeal and from the Federal Court. It also gives advisory opinions to the federal government, when asked under a special reference procedure. Five judges normally sit together to hear a case, although on important matters it is customary for all judges of the Court to sit.

The Federal Court of Canada was created in its present form in 1970; its predecessor, the Exchequer Court of Canada, was originally created in 1875. It has two divisions, a Trial Division and an Appeal Division. This Court deals with: taxation cases; claims involving the federal government (for instance, claims against the federal government for damage caused by its employees); cases involving trademarks, copyrights and patents; admiralty law cases; and aeronautics cases. The Appeal Division hears appeals from decisions rendered by the Trial Division of the Court, as well as appeals from decisions rendered by many federal boards and agencies.

Provincial courts. Provincial courts are established by provincial legislation and thus their names vary from province to province; nevertheless, their structure is roughly the same.

Provincial courts exist at three levels. Each province has inferior courts, such as family courts, juvenile courts, magistrates' courts and small debts courts; in these courts, which deal with minor civil and criminal matters, the great majority of cases originate and are decided. With the exception of the province of Quebec all provinces also have systems of county or district courts. These courts have inter-

Legislative building in Edmonton, Alta.

mediate jurisdiction and decide cases involving claims beyond the jurisdiction of the small debts courts, although they do not have unlimited monetary jurisdiction; they also hear criminal cases, except those of the most serious type. In addition to being trial courts, county and district courts have a limited jurisdiction to hear appeals from decisions of magistrates' courts. The highest courts in a province are its superior courts, which hear civil cases involving large sums of money and criminal cases involving serious offences. Superior courts have trial and appeal levels. Appeal courts, with some exceptions, hear appeals from all the trial courts within the province and may also be called upon to give opinions respecting matters put to them, under a special reference procedure, by the respective provincial governments.

The Legal Profession

In common law jurisdictions in Canada, practising lawyers are both called as barristers and admitted as solicitors. In Quebec the legal profession is divided into the separate branches of advocate and notary. In all cases, admission to practice is a provincial matter.

Legal Aid

In recent years, all provincial governments have established publicly funded legal-aid programs to assist people of limited means in obtaining legal assistance in a number of civil and criminal matters, either at no cost or at a modest cost, depending on their financial circumstances. These programs vary by province. Some are set up by legislative enactment, while others exist and operate by way of informal agreements between the provincial government and the provincial law society. Some provide fairly comprehensive coverage in both civil and criminal matters, while others encompass only criminal offences. In some cases, federal funds are made available for the development or expansion of the programs. The purpose of all such programs is to ensure that people get adequate legal representation regardless of their financial circumstances.

The Police

Responsibility for the administration of justice in the provinces is assigned by the BNA Act to the provinces; but police forces have been created by federal, provincial and municipal governments. Responsibility for providing general police services in areas of sufficient population density and real property assessment is in the hands of municipal police forces where they exist. Municipalities that have not created their own police force use either federal or provincial police forces.

Ontario and Quebec have created provincial forces that police areas of the province not served by municipal forces. The duties of the provincial police include providing police and traffic control over provincial highways, assisting municipal police in the investigation of serious crimes and providing a central information service respecting such matters as finger-prints, criminal records, and stolen and recovered property.

The Royal Canadian Mounted Police (RCMP) is a civil force maintained by the federal government. It was originally created in 1873, under the name North-West Mounted Police, to deal with public order in what were then sparsely settled territories, many parts of which have since become provinces. The RCMP is still the sole police force in the Yukon Territory and the Northwest Territories, and eight provinces employ the RCMP to carry out provincial policing responsibilities within their borders.

The RCMP enforces many federal statutes, the most widely used being the criminal code and the Narcotic Control Act. Its members are responsible for the internal security of Canada, including the protection of government property and the safe-keeping of visiting dignitaries, and the force represents Canada at the International Criminal Police Organization (Interpol), which Canada joined in 1949.

The RCMP is also charged with the responsibility of maintaining and operating the National Police Service, the four major components of which are: the six Crime Detection Laboratories strategically located across Canada; an identification service ranging from a computerized finger-print retrieval system in Ottawa to Canada-wide field identification sections; the Canadian Police Information Centre, which responds instantaneously to nation-wide police-oriented requests; and the Canadian Police College, located in Ottawa, which provides advanced training

The Royal Canadian Mounted Police is a civil force maintained by the federal government.

courses for members of Canadian police forces.

The RCMP operates under the direction of a Commissioner and had a strength of 17,801 on February 20, 1976.

Ministry of the Solicitor General

The Ministry of the Solicitor General was established by Parliament in 1966 and given responsibility for the Royal Canadian Mounted Police, the Canadian Penitentiary Service and the National Parole Board, agencies which had formerly been under the Department of Justice.

A prime aim of the reorganization was the co-ordination of national programs for policing, penitentiaries and parole within the Canadian criminal justice system.

The ministry plays a vital role in the maintenance of law, order and the country's internal security, and has responsibility for offenders sentenced to two years or more in federal penitentiaries and for all inmates released on national parole.

The development and co-ordination of ministry policy is the responsibility of a secretariat that reports to the Deputy Solicitor General. The secretariat has branches responsible for policy planning and program evaluation, police and security planning and analysis, research and systems development, and communication and consultation.

Canadian Penitentiary Service

The Canadian Penitentiary Service operates under the Penitentiary Act and is under the jurisdiction of the Solicitor General of Canada, with headquarters in Ottawa. It is responsible for all federal penitentiaries and for the care and training of persons committed to those institutions. The Commissioner of Penitentiaries, under the direction of the Solicitor General, is responsible for control and management of the service and for related matters.

As of December 31, 1974, the federal penitentiary system controlled 51 institutions: 14 maximum, 13 medium and 24 minimum security institutions. Total inmate population was 8,830, of whom 1.66 per cent were female offenders; 40.75 per cent (including females) were in maximum security, 47.20 per cent in medium security and 12.03 per cent in minimum security institutions. New, smaller institutions are being designed to provide more rehabilitation facilities for inmates, with indoor and outdoor recreation. Plans to phase out old institutions are being worked out.

The National Parole Board

Parole granted by the National Parole Board is a conditional release of an inmate serving a sentence in a prison under federal law; the selection is made when the inmate is eligible and ready. The conditional release is designed to offer protection to the community, and there are specific obligations placed on the parolee. At the same time, the release provides an opportunity for the inmate to become reintegrated into society.

The board has 19 members, nine in the Ottawa division and two in each of five regions across Canada; the regional offices are located in Moncton, Montreal, Kingston, Saskatoon and Vancouver. Members are appointed by the Governor General in Council, nine for a maximum of ten years and the other ten for a maximum of five years. All may be re-appointed.

The board has exclusive jurisdiction and absolute discretion to grant, refuse, or revoke parole. In the cases of murderers, the board makes recommendation to Cabinet, which must approve of any such release.

The National Parole Service. In preparation for the impending integration of the National Parole Service and the Canadian Penitentiary Service, the National Parole Board has also set up regional offices for the parole service.

The service includes the operations division, for policy analysis and case preparation, the community resources division, the planning and research division, and the regional and district offices.

Citizenship

Canada was the first country in the British Commonwealth to adopt a distinct national citizenship. Since its enactment the original Canada Citizenship Act has had many revisions. A new Act introduced for debate in Parliament on October 10, 1974, is designed, among other things, to grant equality to men and women and to aliens and British subjects.

Acquisition of Citizenship

The Citizenship Sector of the Department of the Secretary of State is responsible for promoting acquisition and exercise of citizenship. To qualify for citizenship, aliens and British subjects alike must have landed immigrant status. Most adults must live in Canada for five full years from the date of landing unless they have had previous residence in Canada, in which case half of each full year of previous residence counts toward the five-year requirement. In addition to this, all adults must reside in Canada for a full twelve months prior to the date of application. Generally, applicants for citizenship must also: be able to speak either of the official languages, English or French; show evidence of good character; have a knowledge of the responsibilities and privileges of citizenship; intend to live in Canada permanently and be prepared to comply with the Oath of Allegiance. To become a Canadian citizen, an alien must apply for citizenship, appear before a Citizenship Court for a hearing, and attend a court ceremony of presentation to take the Oath of Allegiance. British subjects must also apply for citizenship, but are not required to have a court hearing or attend a presentation ceremony.

Citizenship Development

The Citizenship Sector administers a variety of programs that support participation in voluntary organizations and increase understanding among groups. Special emphasis is placed on increasing the understanding and enjoyment of fundamental human rights and reducing prejudice and discrimination related to sex, race or ethnic background.

Traffic approaching customs at the border crossing near White Rock, BC.

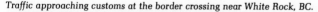

The Women's Program encourages and supports activities designed to help women acquire the knowledge and skills necessary for full and effective participation as equal citizens. It also carries out community education activities to promote greater understanding within the larger community and to encourage responsible and positive action by special influence groups to improve the status of women.

The Native Citizens' Program helps native people define and achieve their place in Canadian society by providing them with the resources to identify their needs and actively pursue their own development as Canadians. The program offers advice and technical and financial assistance to: Friendship Centres operated by native groups in many cities across Canada, which help native people from reserves and isolated areas to adjust to city life; Communications Societies, which support the development and effective use of the media by native people; and native groups working toward the recognition of basic human rights and improved lifestyles for their people.

The Multiculturalism Program encourages Canada's many different ethnic minority groups to maintain and develop their cultural heritage, to share it with others for greater inter-group understanding, and to achieve full participation in Canadian society as a whole.

The Citizens' Participation Program helps all citizens, through technical and financial assistance to their voluntary organizations, to participate in those decisions that affect the quality of their community life. The program endeavours to increase the understanding and acceptance of fundamental economic, social, cultural, civil and political rights; special emphasis is given to reducing inter-group tensions caused by prejudice and discrimination related to racial or ethnic background. The program also works with voluntary and other private organizations and with all levels of government, and assists the human rights efforts of such international bodies as the United Nations.

Manpower and Immigration

Immigration

Canada's non-discriminatory and universally applied immigration policy, administered through the Immigration Act and Regulations, has three objectives: to stimulate Canada's economic growth by admitting suitably skilled and adaptable immigrants; to reunite families; and to admit people for humanitarian reasons, as in the acceptance of refugees.

Since World War II, Canada has admitted more than 4.25 million immigrants, primarily from Great Britain, the United States, Portugal, Italy, the Federal Republic of Germany and the Netherlands. The peak years for immigration since World War II were 1957, when 282,164 persons were admitted, and 1967, when 222,876 settled in Canada. During the fiscal year 1974-75, Canada received 216,611 immigrants, an increase of 13,397 over the previous fiscal year. Britain was the major source country (41,332), followed by the United States (24,198) and Portugal (14,949).

Ontario continued to attract the greatest number of immigrants (118,865); British Columbia was second (35,544); and Quebec was third (32,433). In 1975, 77.6 per cent of the immigrants were under 35 years of age.

Anyone may apply to come to Canada. Applicants are judged by the same standards in every area of the world through a points system. There are three categories of immigrants to Canada: sponsored dependents, nominated relatives and independent applicants.

For sponsored dependents — spouses, unmarried children under 21, fiancés or fiancées, and parents or grandparents aged 60 or over — the Canadian resident assumes full responsibility for their care, accommodation and maintenance. They

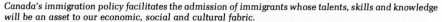

Canada's immigration policy facilitates the admission of immigrants whose talents, skills and knowledge will be an asset to our economic, social and cultural fabric.

are admitted to Canada provided they are in good health and of good character.

Nominated relatives are sons and daughters who are married and under 21 or unmarried and over 21, brothers, sisters, parents or grandparents under age 60, nephews, nieces, uncles, aunts and grandchildren, but not cousins.

An independent applicant is anyone who does not qualify for one of the above categories of relatives, or anyone else who applies for admission to Canada.

Independent and nominated applications are assessed on the factors of education, personal qualities, age, occupational skill level and occupational demand in Canada.

The Employment Visa Regulations are intended to help employers who need temporary workers. If there is no Canadian citizen or landed immigrant available for a vacant job, a non-immigrant with an employment visa may be hired. A person coming into Canada as a worker must have an employment visa that authorizes specific employment for a given period up to a maximum of 12 months. Non-immigrant workers cannot remain in Canada beyond this period, nor can they apply within Canada to have their status changed to that of permanent resident. This can only be done from their own country.

Non-immigrants visiting Canada for longer than three months are required to register at ports of entry or inland Canada Immigration Centres. Visitors cannot apply for landed immigrant status from within Canada.

A Green Paper on Immigration Policy was tabled in the House of Commons in February 1975. The four-volume document consists of policy options to be considered by Canadians as the government prepares to draft a new Immigration Act.

Manpower

The Department of Manpower and Immigration, with more than 3,000 counsellors in 450 Canada Manpower Centres across the country, offers employment services to both workers and employers.

As a result of counselling and discussion of job opportunities, a worker may be placed in employment, referred to training courses, or assisted in moving to employment in another part of the country. Employers may receive up-to-date labour market information, advice regarding training programs and information on the availability of workers. The department helps them meet their staff needs by recruiting qualified personnel from other parts of Canada through the mobility program or from other countries through the immigration program.

Canada Manpower Centres are co-ordinated by five regional offices, in Halifax, Montreal, Toronto, Winnipeg and Vancouver. All manpower programs and services are implemented through these field offices.

Services for Employers

The department's variety of services help employers obtain, train and make the most efficient use of qualified employees. Plants and industries affected by large-scale modernization and economic and technological change are assisted through the Canada Manpower Consultative Service (CMCS) to cope with resulting adjustment problems and develop constructive solutions. Management and labour are encouraged to work together. The Canada Manpower Adjustment Program, administered by the CMCS, acts as a catalyst to bring employers and workers together, to discuss changes and to formulate measures for solving any resulting problems.

During the 1974-75 fiscal year, Canada Manpower counsellors made 256,335 visits to employers as a means of familiarizing themselves with employers, personnel directors, plant superintendents and supervisors.

Under the Canada Manpower Mobility Incentive Agreements, the department pays up to one half of employers' costs involved in moving displaced employees to branch plants or to employment arranged by the employer at another company location in Canada.

The Canada Manpower Industrial Training Program (CMITP) encourages employers to: establish new training programs or improve existing ones; expand employment opportunities for unemployed workers and those with special needs who have difficulty in securing and holding a job; alleviate persistent skill shortages; prevent the lay-off of workers because of technological or economic changes; and support industrial development strategies in various regions of the country. Employers are reimbursed for the direct costs of the training and a proportion of their wage costs under the program.

In co-operation with the provinces, the department launched the three-year developmental phase of a Community Employment Strategy (CES), moving from intergovernmental discussion and organizational development in communities to concrete activities to open up employment for people who depend on transfer payments. The goals of CES are: to utilize existing resources more effectively before turning to new employment-related expenditures; and to create a coherent co-operative approach by governments and communities to the resolution of persistent problems of long-term unemployment. CES also aims at helping those who experience persistent and particular difficulty in finding and keeping permanent employment — the physically, mentally or socially handicapped.

Industries affected by modernization, economic and technological change are assisted by Canada Manpower Consultative Service to cope with adjustment problems.

The Department of Manpower and Immigration's Training-In-Industry Program helps employees to upgrade their work skills.

Services for Employees

The Canada Manpower Training Program (CMTP) is designed for workers who need training to increase their earning capacity and job opportunities. To be eligible, persons must be at least one year past the school-leaving age of the province in which they live and must have been out of school one year. A landed immigrant can also apply for training under the program, including instruction in English or French if it is necessary for employment. Living allowances are provided for those who qualify and have been referred by a Manpower counsellor. In 1974-75 the department spent a total of $401 million under CMTP institutional and industrial programs, which provided training for approximately 292,000 adults.

The Canada Manpower Mobility Program provides grants for workers whose skills are not needed in their home area, to enable them to take suitable jobs or training in other parts of the country. All adult residents of Canada who are unemployed, are about to be unemployed or are under-employed, and who have little or no prospect of finding suitable work in their own localities, may qualify for mobility assistance.

During the past few years the department has funded special job creation programs to alleviate seasonal unemployment. The Local Initiatives Program (LIP) invites Canadians to initiate and establish job-creating projects that will benefit the community. Through the Local Employment Assistance Program (LEAP) the department provides funds and technical support to job-creation projects for persons unlikely to be employed through normal labour market activity. They acquire vocational skills and learn how to cope with new or changing situations by becoming involved in the development, management and evaluation of new work experiences.

The Outreach Program develops and extends Canada Manpower Centre services and programs to persons who do not have access to them, or whose needs extend beyond normal services. Storefront offices have been established in isolated areas. In the case of co-operative arrangements with private groups and organizations that provide community employment services, special assistance may include financial support or assistance from field officers.

Labour

Labour Canada

The Acts administered by Labour Canada generally cover employment upon or in connection with any work, undertaking or business that is within the legislative authority of the Parliament of Canada, and this coverage relates to fair employment practices, labour standards, employment safety and labour relations.

The Minister of Labour is responsible for the Canada Labour Code, the Fair Wages and Hours of Labour Act, the Government Employees' Compensation Act, the Merchant Seamen's Compensation Act, the Canada Labour Relations Board and the Merchant Seamen's Compensation Board. The Minister also reports to Parliament on multiculturalism.

Labour Canada has an over-all objective to promote and protect the rights of parties involved in the world of work, a working environment conducive to physical and social well-being, and a fair return for efforts in the workplace. The department is also charged with ensuring equitable access to employment opportunities in all cases.

Labour Canada operates offices in Moncton, Montreal, Toronto, Winnipeg and Vancouver. These offices are guided by regional directors who develop and take major responsibility for implementing the range of departmental policies and programs in the field.

Several major programs and services are aimed at meeting these objectives.

Federal Mediation and Conciliation Services

Primarily concerned with the conduct of collective bargaining in federal jurisdiction industries and with related policy questions, FMCS provides conciliation and mediation services under the terms of Part V of the Canada Labour Code (Industrial Relations). The Minister will name an arbitrator in a grievance dispute where the parties cannot agree on the selection of a person to act.

Under the code, the Minister is also responsible for granting consent to refer certain complaints of unfair labour practices to the Canada Labour Relations Board, and for granting consent to complainants to institute prosecution in the courts.

Research and Program Development

Labour Data: Collects, processes and analyzes data on a number of labour-relations subjects in the national and federal jurisdiction, through surveys and other data collection systems. Information is publicly available on wages, hours of work and certain fringe benefits, collective bargaining settlements and wage developments, provisions in major collective agreements, labour organizations, and work stoppages due to strikes and lockouts.

Economic Analysis: Aids in the development of policies and programs by conducting research on appropriate and relevant trends related to the labour affairs field in the Canadian and international environment.

Conditions of Work: Develops programs and policies aimed at achieving for employees social and economic conditions that are fair to both employee and

Turbine wheels being manufactured at Lachine, Que.

employer by undertaking specific studies in areas such as wages, turnover rates, job satisfaction, "fringe benefits" and hours of work. This group also administers the Adjustment Assistance Benefit Regulations.

Rights in Employment: Develops policies and programs that aim to ensure that all individuals receive fair and equitable opportunities in obtaining employment and in advancement while employed, and fair and equitable treatment on the job; such policies and programs include those that aim to ensure compliance with Part I of the Canada Labour Code, which prohibits discrimination on the grounds of race, national origin, colour or religion. The Women's Bureau collects and analyzes data to provide relevant statistical information on working women, publicizes federal and provincial legislation concerning their status, and participates on a national and international level with organizations to make participation of women in the labour force more equitable.

Employment Relations: Develops and assists in implementing policies and programs promoting positive relationships between labour and management, by: conducting studies on various aspects of labour relations; analyzing and advising on the applicability of particular employee-employer interaction models to the Canadian context; and providing consultative services to employees and employers who wish to improve their relationship.

Occupational Health and Safety: Develops policies and programs aimed at maintaining and promoting safe and healthy working conditions. This group also administers: the Government Employees' Compensation Act, under which employment injury benefits are provided to employees who suffer occupational injuries or diseases and/or to their dependents and to persons employed by certain federal work-creating programs; and the Merchant Seamen's Compensation Act, providing employment injury benefits to seamen for accidents arising out of and in the course of their employment.

Library and Information Services: Provides two types of service to the public, a library and a legislative research service. Containing over 100,000 items, the library is the most comprehensive of its kind in Canada. The legislative research service conducts research into labour laws, their regulations and related administrative practices in all jurisdictions in Canada. Further services are provided in the answering of specific inquiries and the publication or other dissemination of informative material relating to labour legislation.

Pouring metal into shell moulds at the ductile iron foundry in Welland, Ont.

Farm implement plant at Winnipeg, Man.

International and Provincial Relations

This group is the official link between Canada and the International Labour Organization (ILO), of which Canada was a founding member in 1919. The group is responsible for co-ordinating Labour Canada's participation in international and federal-provincial organizations. It co-ordinates, with other federal departments concerned, with the provincial governments, with the major employer and worker organizations, and with the general public, all work relating to the ILO.

Policy Co-ordination

All items relating to policy matters of concern to the department in areas of economic, social and industrial relations policy are the responsibility of the Policy Coordination Group. It formulates policy options for consideration by the department, refines such policy options when they are approved by the department and presents them for interdepartmental discussion and/or Cabinet consideration.

Unemployment Insurance

The Unemployment Insurance Act was passed in 1940. Since that time the basic structure of the Act has remained unaltered, although various amendments have brought new categories of workers into the plan, and contributions and benefit rates have been raised periodically to keep abreast of changing economic conditions.

In 1968, when Parliament approved upward revisions of both contributions and benefit rates and broadened the scope of coverage, the Unemployment Insurance Commission was instructed to carry out a full-scale investigation of the program and to recommend appropriate changes in approach and structure. The Unemployment Insurance Act of 1971 was the result of extensive studies. Its basic objectives are (1) to provide assistance in coping with an interruption of earnings resulting from unemployment, including unemployment due to illness, and (2) to co-operate with other agencies engaged in social development.

During 1975, benefit payments under the Act amounted to $3,146 million.

Under the Unemployment Insurance Act of 1971 coverage is extended, effective January 1972, to all regular members of the labour force for whom there exists an employer-employee relationship. The only non-insurable employment is that which is remunerated at less than 20 per cent of the maximum weekly insurable earnings or 20 times the provincial hourly minimum wage, whichever is the lesser. Coverage, contributions and benefit entitlement cease at age 65. The number of insured persons was estimated at 8.9 million in December 1975.

Employers and employees pay for the cost of initial benefits and of administration; the employer's rate is 1.4 times the employee's rate. In 1976, the maximum weekly contribution by an employee was $3.30. The government's share is confined to the cost of extended benefits and the extra cost of initial benefits due to a national unemployment rate greater than the most recent eight-year average. There is no fund, and employer and employee contributions are adjusted yearly. The Taxation Branch of Revenue Canada started to collect contributions at the beginning of 1972. An experience-rating formula for employers may be introduced to reflect the additional expense of benefits generated by large employers who have laid off more than an average number of employees.

The duration of benefit under the new program is not determined solely by the length of time a person has worked. A claimant can draw to a maximum of 51 weeks, depending on his employment history and the prevailing economic conditions, provided that (1) he has had at least eight weeks of contributions in the last 52 and (2) he has been available, capable and searching for work. Persons with 20 or more weeks of insured earnings (called a "major labour force attachment") are eligible for a wider range of benefits that includes payments when the interruption of earnings is caused by illness or pregnancy, and three weeks retirement benefit for older workers. A claimant is not entitled to be paid benefit until he has served a two-week waiting period that begins with a week of unemployment for which benefits would otherwise be payable.

Sickness benefits are available up to a maximum of 15 weeks for persons with major labour force attachment who have suffered an interruption of earnings due to illness, injury, or quarantine (excluding Workmen's Compensation). Maternity benefits are available for a maximum of 15 weeks to women who have had a major labour force attachment. They must also have been part of the labour force at least 10 of the 20 weeks prior to the 30th week before the expected date of confinement.

Recently expanded Strathcona Refinery of Imperial Oil Ltd. at Edmonton, Alta. ➡

Great Lakes Paper Company plant at Thunder Bay, Ont.

Retirement benefit is available for three weeks. It is paid in a lump sum to major attachment claimants who are 65 years of age. In the case of those over 65, the application must be within 32 weeks of the 65th birthday, as employment weeks are no longer earned after that time. The benefit is paid without a waiting period and without regard to earnings or availability.

The benefit rate for all claims is two thirds of a person's average insured earnings in the qualifying period, to a maximum in 1976 of $133 a week and with a minimum of $20 a week. The maximum insurable earnings, and therefore the maximum benefit, are subject to annual adjustment based on an index calculated from earnings of Canadian employees. In 1976 maximum weekly insurable earnings were $200.

Income from employment in excess of 25 per cent of the benefit rate is deducted from the benefits payable. In the case of sickness and maternity, proceeds of wage-loss plans are not deducted from unemployment benefits during the waiting period but are deducted afterwards. All work-related income is deducted both during the waiting period and after the waiting period has been served.

Industry, Trade and Commerce

The Department of Industry, Trade and Commerce seeks to promote the growth of the Canadian economy by stimulating the establishment, growth and efficiency of industry, the development of export trade and external trade policies, the expansion of tourism and the travel industry, and the marketing of grains and oilseeds. To carry out its programs and meet its objectives, the department requires the services of a staff of more than 2,500, with offices in Ottawa, 10 regional offices across Canada and 88 posts in 63 countries.

Industry Development

Through its many incentive and development programs, the department offers assistance, with expert advice and information and in many cases financial help, to the Canadian businessman. The objectives of the department's programs are: to develop an efficient manufacturing and secondary processing industry to meet competition at home and abroad; to increase the domestic processing of natural resources; and to provide for a greater domestic control of the Canadian economy and ensure its future development by Canadians. The department also seeks to achieve and maintain maximum employment in Canadian industry, to increase national income and to reduce economic disparities.

Giant cranes of the new container port at Vancouver, BC.

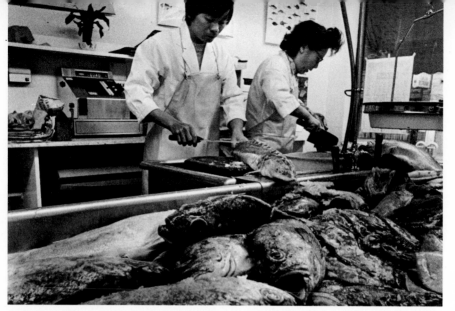

Seafood in preparation at one of Vancouver's many specialty shops.

International Trade

By providing information on export opportunities and by giving sales assistance, the department strives to increase the international market for goods and services produced in Canada. Trade arrangements are negotiated to give Canadian producers access to world markets. In addition, the department develops trade strategies, provides financial assistance and maintains Canadian trade representatives throughout the world.

Tourism

The sustained and orderly growth of tourism and the travel industry in Canada is the objective of the tourism program. To encourage both Canadians and visitors to explore Canada, the department provides information, market research and analysis, market planning and a variety of promotional campaigns in all news media. The requirements for expanding the travel industry are assessed and various programs to assist that development have been devised. A policy, planning and industry relations section of the department provides direction to the tourism program and co-ordinates the efforts of federal, provincial and private developers of the tourist industry.

Grains and Oilseeds

While the management of a system for marketing Canadian grains and oilseeds and the expansion of markets for these products comes under the Minister responsible for the Canadian Wheat Board, the Deputy Minister of Industry, Trade and Commerce is responsible for its marketing operations and for administering payments made under the program. The marketing activity is intended to complement and extend efforts by the private sector through the provision of market intelligence and financial assistance. Production guidelines are determined and initial payments for Wheat Board grains are established.

Regional Economic Expansion

While Canada enjoys one of the world's highest standards of living, its history and geography have dictated a wide disparity of economic, social and cultural well-being. Employment opportunities, per capita income, cost of living, and social and cultural services vary widely, not only from province to province, but from one region of a province to another.

The federal government has long recognized the need to reduce these disparities and has, in the past, met this need with programs such as the Prairie Farm Rehabilitation Administration (PFRA), the Agricultural and Rural Development Act (ARDA) and the Fund for Rural Economic Development (FRED). However, solutions to the long-term problems of regional disparity require not only the concerted effort of the federal government, but also co-ordination of this effort with the actions of other levels of government. For this reason, the Department of Regional Economic Expansion (DREE) was formed in 1969. The department inherited such programs as PFRA, ARDA and FRED, and was given responsibility for the newly-legislated Regional Development Incentives Act.

DREE has responded to the need for co-ordinated action with provincial governments in two ways, through a geographically decentralized organization and through negotiation of agreements with each province for concerted development action.

The department has adopted an organization with decentralized authority in each of four regions — Atlantic, Quebec, Ontario and Western. Each region is headed by an Assistant Deputy Minister responsible for planning and executing all DREE activities within the region. In addition, a DREE office in each provincial capital, headed by a Director General, is responsible for activities within the

Fort Saskatchewan, Alta.

province under the authority of the regional Assistant Deputy Minister. Thus, significant decision-making authority, in terms of both existing programs and new initiatives, rests with DREE officers close to provincial policy-makers. Sixty per cent of the total DREE staff and 70 per cent of the senior executives work in regional and provincial offices.

In 1974 DREE entered into a 10-year General Development Agreement (GDA) with every province except Prince Edward Island, where a 15-year Comprehensive Development Plan was signed in 1969. GDAs provide the framework for co-ordinated federal-provincial action to realize each province's potential for socio-economic development. Each GDA consists of a statement of mutually-agreed objec-tives, a broad strategy for development, guidelines for implementing the strategy and provision for signing subsidiary agreements, which are detailed plans of action to take advantage of specific and well-defined development opportunities.

The department's efforts, therefore, fall into three broad categories: sub-agreements under the GDAs; activities under the Regional Development Incentives Act (RDIA); and other programs such as PFRA, ARDA and FRED.

Sub-agreements

Subsidiary agreements under the GDA umbrella are widely varied, depending upon the mutually-defined objectives of the federal and provincial governments. Examples are: a sub-agreement with Saskatchewan for the development of iron, steel and related industries; one with Manitoba for social and economic develop-ment of the northern part of the province; one with Newfoundland for a com-prehensive forestry development program; and one with Quebec for expansion of industrial infrastructure. Initiatives under these agreements are financed on a cost-sharing basis by federal and provincial governments. More than 40 sub-agreements have now been signed, calling for a federal commitment of more than $800 million.

Regional Development Incentives Act

RDIA activities attempt to stimulate manufacturing investment and employment in slow-growth areas of the country. Financial incentives are offered to encourage businesses to locate in regions designated for assistance, or to expand or modernize plants already established in these regions. Since the program was introduced in 1969 DREE has helped, through more than $500 million in grants, to generate a total of $2.3 billion in capital investment and to create directly an estimated 120,000 new jobs.

Other Programs

DREE's responsibilities include a variety of other programs, most of them aimed at problems of a limited nature or in a defined area. Included in this category are the previously mentioned PFRA, ARDA and FRED programs, as well as Special Areas Agreements for certain slow-growth areas, Special Highways Agreements with New Brunswick and Newfoundland, and the Agricultural Service Centres Program. Most of these programs were launched before the formation of DREE, and many of them will, in time, be absorbed under the GDA umbrella.

Consumer and Corporate Affairs

The Department of Consumer and Corporate Affairs was established in December 1967 to bring together under one minister as much as was practical of federal law governing and regulating business in the Canadian marketplace.

The new department was assigned the role of fostering an efficient market system for the benefit of all Canadians, whether consumers, businessmen or investors. Its existence reflects Parliament's view that the competitive market system is the basis of an efficient economy and that it can be structured to operate for the good of Canadian society as a whole.

Legislation and policies administered by the department are designed to stimulate efficiency and productivity on the part of those who supply the market with goods, and to promote fair economic treatment for all concerned in commercial transactions. One result of the department's activities has been a strengthening of the concept of consumer rights and the provision of information to the widest possible consumer audience.

Yorkdale shopping centre, Toronto, Ont.

Lobster suppers at New Glasgow, PEI.

Responsibility for achieving these objectives is shared by four bureaus and the Field Operations Service.

The Bureau of Consumer Affairs develops legislative proposals and programs and provides technical guidance to field staff on a number of important consumer protection laws dealing with packaging, labelling, legal metrology and hazardous products. Its central mailing address—The Consumer, Box 99, Ottawa—provides a focal point for communication from the public on all matters of consumer concern. In addition to dealing with complaints and inquiries directed to Box 99, the bureau carries out extensive consumer information and research programs, and provides personal help at the neighbourhood level through 17 community-based and community-oriented Consumer Help Offices.

The Bureau of Corporate Affairs concerns itself with the legal framework governing the orderly conduct of business. It grants charters of incorporation to new businesses and presides over bankruptcy proceedings for insolvent companies and the licensing of trustees in bankruptcy. The bureau's bankruptcy programs have been extended to benefit low-income individuals. Liquidations are administered

Shopping centre near Quebec City, Que. ➤

Bayshore shopping centre, near Ottawa, Ont.

for a fee of $50, and even that can be waived if the debtor is unable to pay; to qualify, a debtor must have debts exceeding $500 and have a total income of less than $6,500 a year if married, and $4,000 if single.

The Bureau of Intellectual Property grants patents after ensuring that applications meet the requirements of novelty and inventiveness and do not infringe on existing patents. The bureau also registers trademarks and industrial designs, and certifies registration of applications for copyright of literary, dramatic, musical or artistic works.

The Bureau of Competition Policy administers the Combines Investigation Act, the legislation aimed at maintaining a competitive market system. Under the Act, the director has power to conduct inquiries when he has reason to believe there may have been a violation of the Act with respect to agreements, mergers, monopolies, price discrimination, promotional allowances, misleading representation as to prices, false and misleading advertising, or retail price maintenance. Results of his inquiries are sent to the Restrictive Trade Practices Commission for consideration and public report, or to the Attorney General of Canada for possible legal action. The Attorney General decides whether charges should be laid following the report of the Commission.

The Field Operations Service is responsible for a field force operating from regional offices in Vancouver, Winnipeg, Toronto, Montreal and Halifax, and from 29 district offices. It implements and enforces legislation administered by the department and ensures that it is uniformly interpreted and applied. Inspectors deal with a wide range of matters from food to textiles, from hazardous products to the accuracy of weighing and measuring devices, and include specialists in bankruptcy and false and misleading advertising. A consumer's consulting service is provided at each regional office and in more than half of the district offices.

Urban Affairs

The Ministry of State for Urban Affairs was created June 30, 1971, as a key element in the federal government's response to the challenge of rapidly accelerating urbanization.

The ministry is a policy agency designed specifically to plan, develop, foster and co-ordinate policies and programs through which the federal government can exert a beneficial influence on Canada's urban centres, in close co-operation with other levels of government and with non-governmental groups. In addition, policy-making for urban Canada is concerned with injecting urban considerations into the development and implementation of other federal policies and programs, and with fostering intergovernmental relationships to promote the co-ordination of urban policies and programs.

The historic La Salle Academy complex of Ottawa has been restored and now houses the headquarters of the Ministry of State for Urban Affairs.

Hamilton, Ont.

The ministry is actively involved in several areas:

Urban Economy. It is developing policy alternatives and program proposals for urban public finance, suggesting different ways of financing urban expansion in Canada and participating in a tri-level examination of public finance.

Urban Land and Space. The ministry is developing policy on the use of federal land holdings and is participating in its implementation. Federal land management policy is designed to harmonize planning and use of federal lands with the development goals and strategies of local communities and regions wherever possible. It is also investigating the implications of the ever-increasing consumption of land peripheral to urban centres. The ministry is co-operating with other departments and governments to determine appropriate policies to ensure that the scarce land resource is preserved and that, at the same time, the benefits of urbanization are maximized.

Urban Transportation. The ministry has developed and recommended urban transportation policies, including the National Urban Transportation Development Corporation and the railway relocation program, and is participating in implementation of the latter under an Act passed in June 1974.

It is also co-operating with the Ministry of Transport in examination of the National Transportation Act, and is offering advice on the impact of urban-city transportation policies, on national urban patterns and on metropolitan growth rates.

Under the provisions of the Railway Relocation and Crossing Act the federal government has the power to expropriate railway land, allowing cities and towns to get on with planned urban redevelopment. The program applies particularly to cities where railway facilities — tracks, yards, terminals — are obstacles to the planned redevelopment of the community. Part I of the Act permits the Ministry of

State for Urban Affairs to financially support urban planning in connection with relocation and rerouting proposed by provinces and municipalities, so that improved community services and facilities can be developed.

Urban Environment. The ministry is developing and recommending federal policies and programs to influence the form and quality of Canadian cities. It is developing plans and projects for the imaginative use of federal lands and properties as instruments for urban change and is participating in their implementation. Other efforts involve the study of conditions in the inner city areas and the preparation of a federal view on a new-communities strategy to accommodate anticipated urban growth.

Urban Information. The ministry is developing and recommending policies and programs to improve the quality of urban statistics, to provide a more complete basis for assessing the impact of federal programs on urbanization and urban areas, and for the initiation of new policy and program thrusts.

Urban Planning and Interventions. The preparation of regional plans and strategies by the provinces to guide the development of Canadian urban regions is being supported. Examples are regional planning for Vancouver, Winnipeg, Halifax, Dartmouth, Quebec City and other centres.

The beauty and charm of the old section of Quebec City, Que. attracts tourists of all ages.

Urban Institutions. The ministry is actively reviewing the relationship between the three sets of governmental institutions with jurisdictional responsibilities in urban Canada and the complexity of the broad issue of urban growth management. This involves the development of tri-level consultation mechanisms, the analysis of the capacities and resources of units of local government to be used in growth management issues, and consideration of how the federal government might, through the provinces, increase the effectiveness of local governments in this regard.

Habitat

Habitat—the United Nations Conference on Human Settlements—took place in Vancouver between May 31st and June 11, 1976. It was the culmination of more than three years of preparation by more than 130 of the United Nations member states, and the largest conference of its kind ever held in Canada.

Canada was both host and participant, and the Ministry of State for Urban Affairs was given special responsibility for co-ordinating Canada's official participation and making all the complex arrangements for a smoothly run conference.

More than 2,000 official delegates and over 10,000 non-governmental representatives from around the world attended. It was the first time in United Nations history that discussion focused on practical solutions rather than analysis of settlement problems on a world-wide scale; some 200 audio-visual presentations were shown by delegates.

One of the speakers at Habitat — the United Nations Conference on Human Settlements — held in Vancouver, BC.

Veterans Affairs

Nearly one million Canadians receive assistance from the Department of Veterans Affairs and the four agencies associated with it—Canadian Pension Commission, Pension Review Board, War Veterans Allowance Board and Bureau of Pensions Advocates. The department's services are medical treatment, welfare counselling and assistance, pensions and war veterans' allowances, and educational assistance to children of the war dead.

March 31, 1975, was the final date for the acceptance of loan applications from qualified veterans of World War II or the Korean Special Force for settlement under the full- or part-time farming provision of the Veterans' Land Act. From the passing of the Act in 1942 until December 31, 1975, loans and grants totalling $1.4 billion were made to 139,741 veterans. Of these, nearly 58,000 have subsisting purchase contracts representing repayable principal indebtedness of approximately $533 million. Within the maximum loan ceilings specified in the Act, these veterans were able to apply for additional assistance up to March 31, 1977.

The department's Treatment Services extended care to more than 27,000 veterans during the 1975-76 fiscal year, and administered a total of six hospitals and three veterans' homes.

The unveiling of a statue in Winnipeg, Man. which honours the more than 100,000 women who served in Canada's Armed Forces since the turn of the century.

In April 1975 the department sponsored "Project Italy '75", an official pilgrimage led by the Minister of Veterans Affairs to the war cemeteries of Italy and Sicily, where more than 5,900 Canadians lie buried.

The Canadian Pension Commission administers the Pension Act, which provides compensation in respect of members of the Canadian Forces who have been disabled or who have died as a result of military service, and to their families. During the year ended December 31, 1975, there were 116,158 pensions being paid to veterans and 27,005 to their dependents. The Pension Act provides that pensions be paid in accordance with the extent of the disability. As of January 1, 1976, the basic rate of pension for a single pensioner whose disability was assessed at 100 per cent was $512.54 a month. Additional pension for a wife and child would have brought this amount to $707.37.

The Pension Review Board serves as a final court of appeal for veterans, ex-servicemen and their dependents in all matters concerning disability pensions and the interpretation of the Pension Act. The board, although essentially an appellate body, may also consider new documentary evidence. In the fiscal year 1975-76 the board received 762 appeals and heard 559 claims dealing with pension entitlement and increase in assessment, concerning 854 different disabilities. The board also rendered three decisions on matters of interpretation.

The Bureau of Pensions Advocates provides counsel and free legal aid to pension applicants in the preparation and presentation of their pension claims. The relationship between the bureau and applicant or pensioner is that of solicitor and client. The bureau submitted 7,786 claims to the Canadian Pension Commission under various sections of the Pension Act during 1975-76. Pensions Advocates also presented 3,021 cases at Entitlement Board and Quantum Hearings during the year. Specialist advocates of the bureau staff at head office made 381 submissions to the Pension Review Board, which is the final court of appeal under the Pension Act.

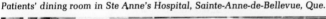
Patients' dining room in Ste Anne's Hospital, Sainte-Anne-de-Bellevue, Que.

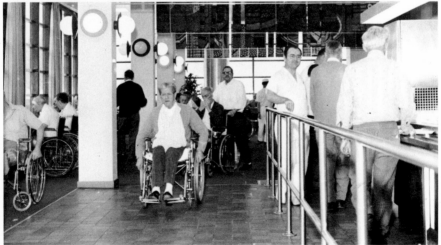

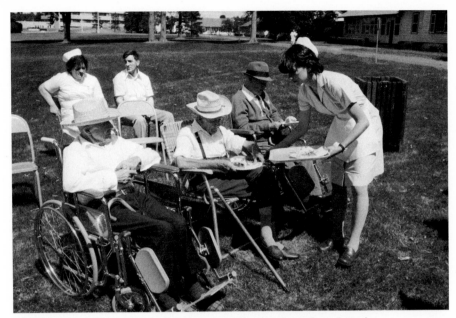

Residents of Rideau Veterans Home in Ottawa enjoy the annual strawberry festival.

The War Veterans Allowance Act was designed to provide an allowance for veterans who, because of the rigours of theatre-of-war service, were deemed to be "pre-aged", and thus were unable to support themselves and their families. Widows, orphans and dependent children of such veterans may also benefit under the terms of the Act. Similar benefits are available under Part XI of the Civilian War Pensions and Allowances Act to civilians who served in close support of the Armed Forces and performed meritorious service. The allowance is comparable to an annuity, the premiums of which the veteran has paid with his service. The War Veterans Allowance Board is a quasi-judicial body, independent as far as its decisions are concerned, which acts as a court of appeal for applicants or recipients who are aggrieved by any decision of a District Authority. As of December 31, 1975, the number of War Veterans Allowance recipients was 86,000, accounting for an annual expenditure of $160 million. The number of Civilian War Allowance recipients as of December 31, 1975, was 4,100, accounting for an annual liability of $10 million.

Of 27,000 War Veterans Allowance recipients eligible for monthly supplementation of their allowance, 26,000 received payments to meet or assist in meeting their established monthly costs of shelter, fuel, food, clothing and personal care. In addition, just under 1,200 payments were made for non-recurring needs such as housing repairs and improvements, home furnishing and equipment replacements, and similar expenses. Slightly fewer than 900 students in post-secondary education received benefits in the form of payment of tuition fees and monthly allowances under the Children of War Dead (Education Assistance) Act. More than 6,000 veterans, eligible civilians or their survivors received counselling services over extended periods to assist them in improving, stabilizing or maintaining their social or economic situations.

Health and Welfare

Health Care

The provision of health care services in Canada falls primarily within the jurisdiction of the provincial governments. Nevertheless, the federal government plays a significant role in the development of many policies and programs designed to improve the physical and mental health of all Canadians.

Provincial Responsibilities

Constitutionally and by tradition the provincial governments have the primary responsibility for health measures to prevent disease, provide treatment and maintain health. Activities such as preventive health services, hospital services, treatment services for tuberculosis and other chronic diseases, and rehabilitation and care of the chronically ill and disabled have always, therefore, depended chiefly upon this level of government. Methods of organization, financing and administration vary from province to province.

In addition to administering the hospital and medical care plans, and the mental and other types of specialized health facilities, provincial health departments supervise the provision of community health services that are delegated to the district or regional health units and city health departments. Administered by regional or city boards or councils, the health units are responsible for most of the preventive health services at the community level, including environmental sanita-

Percy E. Moore Hospital, Hodgson, Man.

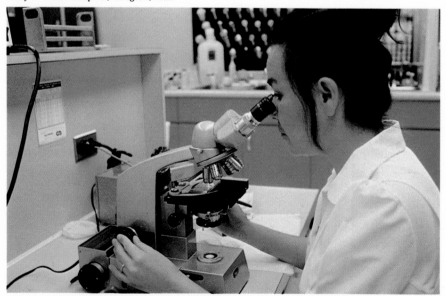

Medical Services nurse at Hobbema, Alta.

tion, control of infectious diseases and promotion of maternal and child health, mental health, and health education.

Most mental and tuberculosis hospitals and clinics are provincially operated or funded, as are special treatment centres for venereal disease, cancer, alcoholism and other specific diseases, and the public health laboratories that aid both the health agencies and practising physicians in diagnostic and control procedures. Provincial agencies are also primarily responsible for the collection and analysis of vital statistics, and for the study of epidemiological and related social and economic conditions. Other provincial programs include occupational health, nutrition, health education and pollution control, frequently in collaboration with the federal department.

Department of National Health and Welfare

Health Protection Branch: The Health Protection Branch of the Department of National Health and Welfare is responsible for protecting the public from possible risks to health from foods, drugs, cosmetics and medical devices sold on the Canadian market. Under the Food and Drugs Act, standards for safety and purity in foods are developed through laboratory research and maintained by regular and widespread programs of inspection.

Every drug manufacturer is required by law to submit information to the branch on all his products that are marketed in Canada. The branch has the authority to ban the sale of any drug that is unsafe or injurious to health. Its Drug Quality Assessment Program is aimed at producing objective evidence on the quality of the drugs already on the market and making it available to the health professions, governments and the general public.

Under the Proprietary or Patent Medicine Act the Health Protection Branch controls the manufacturing, licensing, labelling, advertising and merchandising of home remedies, which are often sold in retail outlets other than drugstores. Under the Narcotics Control Act the branch exercises control over traffic in narcotics and hallucinogens, to prevent their exportation, importation, manufacture or cultivation by persons other than those authorized by law. The branch also administers the Non-Medical Use of Drugs Program, which is designed to combat drug abuse and discourage the use or misuse of mood-altering drugs.

In the area of communicable disease control, the branch's laboratories are involved in the development and implementation of preventive, diagnostic, quality control and other measures. These laboratories also provide a reference service for identification of disease-producing bacteria, viruses and parasites.

Health Programs Branch: The Health Programs Branch is responsible for the administration of the federal aspects of Canada's two most important health programs, Hospital Insurance and Medical Care Insurance.

In 1976 the department actively participated in negotiations with the provinces to reach agreement on a new cost-sharing arrangement.

Hospital Insurance: The Hospital Insurance Program provides for a system of federal grants-in-aid to the provinces to meet about 50 per cent of the costs of specified in-patient and out-patient services, as set out in the federal Hospital Insurance and Diagnostic Services Act of 1957. Included in the insured services are: accommodation, meals, necessary nursing service, diagnostic procedures and most pharmaceuticals; the use of operating rooms, case rooms and anaesthesia facilities; and, if available, radiotherapy and physiotherapy. At present, this program covers about 99.8 per cent of the eligible population of Canada.

Medical Services nurse travels by snowmobile near Fort Chipewyan, Alta.

Federal contributions under this program do not cover the services of tuberculosis hospitals and sanatoria, mental hospitals, or institutions providing custo-
dial care, such as homes for the aged. The methods of administering and financing
the program and the provision of services above the stipulated minimum required
by the Act are left to the provinces.

Medical Care: Under the Medical Care Act, the federal government contributes to
each participating province half of the national per capita cost of insured medical
services for each insured person in that province. In order to be eligible for the
federal contribution under this program, provincial plans must: cover all medically
required services rendered by a physician; be available to all eligible residents on

Dentistry practice at Fort Smith, NWT.

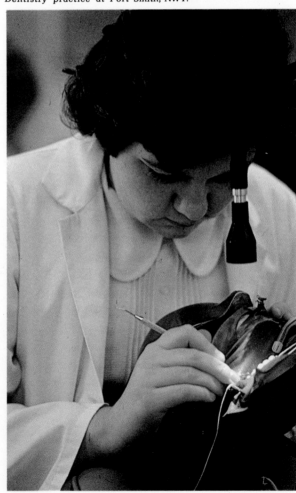

equal terms and conditions, and actually cover at least 95 per cent of them; provide coverage to persons while they are moving between provinces; and be administered by a non-profit authority.

Several methods are used by the provinces to finance their shares of the cost; for example, premiums are levied in Ontario, Alberta, British Columbia and the Yukon Territory. The characteristic mode of paying physicians is a fee for each insured service rendered. Some provincial plans also insure residents for benefits not eligible for cost-sharing by the federal government, such as the services of optometrists, chiropractors, podiatrists, osteopaths, naturopaths and dentists, and the costs of some prescribed drugs.

The Health Programs Branch also plays a major role in both development and promotion of measures conducive to optimum personal health, and the support of health research.

Medical Services Branch: This branch supplements provincial health care services and provides special public health services for registered Indians and Inuit. It is also responsible for health programs affecting all residents of the Yukon Territory and the Northwest Territories; to meet their needs it operates several hospitals and numerous other health facilities, primarily in isolated northern areas.

Other activities of the branch include the examination and treatment of immigrants and the quarantine control of persons entering or leaving Canada in order to reduce the possibility of importing or exporting certain infectious diseases. It is responsible for health services in national parks and the sanitary surveillance of interprovincial and international common carriers.

The branch also provides diagnostic services, counselling on health problems and other occupational health services for federal public servants. It acts in an

Canoe racing at Ottawa, Ont.

advisory capacity to the Ministry of Transport on civil aviation and marine medicine, operates a trans-Canada prosthetic manufacturing and fitting service, and co-operates with provinces to meet general and local disaster situations.

Long-Range Health Planning Branch: The Long-Range Health Planning Branch generates ideas and reports that provide major long-range health benefits to Canadians. The benefits include better health, lower costs and greater accessibility of health services.

Other activities of the branch are directed toward arousing a general awareness among Canadians of the avoidable risks that they impose upon their own health and toward generating concern among health administrators about the extent to which self-imposed risks contribute to sickness and death.

Fitness and Amateur Sport Branch: The Fitness and Amateur Sport Branch of the department encourages, promotes and develops fitness and amateur sport. To motivate Canadians to pursue excellence in competitive sport, the branch has established an administrative centre to house 36 national sports-governing bodies and associations. In addition to its efforts on behalf of top-calibre athletes, the branch is also striving to provide the greatest possible diversity of recreational opportunity to Canadians.

The branch co-ordinates its efforts with the provincial Directors of Sport and Recreation, and co-operates on projects of mutual interest such as the Canada Games. Special grants are made available to some provinces to assist in raising the level of sport and recreation activities.

Social Security

Federal, provincial and local governments provide a wide range of publicly funded and administered income security and social services programs, which are complemented by the activities of voluntary agencies. Income security programs provide direct cash payments to eligible recipients, and include: income insurance schemes such as the Canada and Quebec Pension Plans, Workmen's Compensation and Unemployment Insurance; income support measures such as the Old Age Security Pension, the Guaranteed Income Supplement and Spouse's Allowance, and Family Allowance programs; and social assistance provided by provincial and municipal programs. Social services programs provide some services to anyone who applies, such as crisis intervention services, information and referral services, and family planning services. They also provide specific services to designated groups, including: preventive, protective and supportive services for children; rehabilitation services to disabled persons; social integration services to persons who are, or are at a risk of being, socially isolated from community life; residential services for those needing care in an institutional setting; supportive services for the elderly; and community development services and community-oriented preventive services. The provincial governments and, by delegation, the municipalities have prime responsibility for the administration of social assistance and welfare services to persons in need.

The Canada Pension Plan

The Canada Pension Plan (CPP) and its counterpart, the Quebec Pension Plan (QPP), constitute a vehicle whereby millions of members of the work force between the ages of 18 and 70 acquire and retain, during their productive years, protection for themselves and their families against loss of income due to retirement, disability or death, regardless of where their work may take them in Canada. It is a compulsory earnings-related scheme which pays to eligible applicants retirement benefits, disability pensions, pensions for surviving spouses, orphans' benefits, benefits for the children of disabled contributors and a lump-sum death benefit. Benefits are adjusted annually to reflect full cost-of-living increases, and amendments introduced in 1975 assure equal treatment for male and female contributors and beneficiaries. In 1976 employees paid 1.8 per cent of that portion of their annual earnings between $800 and $8,300; this contribution was matched by the employers. Self-employed persons contributed 3.6 per cent on the same earnings range. Effective January 1976, the earnings ceiling of the plan ($8,300 in 1976) was increased by 12.5 per cent, and it will be increased by the same percentage each year until it catches up to the average earnings of Canadian industrial workers as published by Statistics Canada.

Old Age Security, Guaranteed Income Supplement and Spouse's Allowance

An Old Age Security (OAS) pension is payable to all persons 65 years of age and over, provided the person has resided in Canada for 10 years immediately preceding the approval of an application. Any gaps in the 10-year period may be offset if

Assisting a teacher by giving students additional help with their reading, in connection with the New Horizons Program.

the applicant has been present in Canada prior to that 10-year period and after the age of 18 for periods of time equal to three times the length of the gaps; in this case, the applicant must also have resided in Canada for at least one year immediately preceding the date on which his application for pension may be approved. The pension is also payable to persons aged 65 or over with 40 years of residence in Canada since age 18. Once a person has met the requirements in one of these three ways and has become a pensioner, he may receive payment indefinitely while living abroad if he has resided in Canada for 20 years after age 18. A Guaranteed Income Supplement (GIS) is also paid to pensioners with little or no income other than the OAS pension, the maximum supplement being paid to those whose only income is OAS pension.

The spouse of an OAS pensioner who is aged 60 to 65 and meets the same residence requirements as those stipulated for OAS is eligible for the Spouse's Allowance (SA). SA is payable, upon application, if the annual combined income of the couple was less than $6,144 as of January 1, 1976. This allowance is subject to a test of income, unlike the OAS pension and the GIS. The maximum SA is equal in amount to the OAS pension plus full GIS at the married rate, and stood at $215.68 in January 1976.

On the same date the monthly OAS pension stood at $132.90 and the maximum monthly GIS at $93.22; for a married couple, both pensioners, the maximum monthly GIS was $82.78 each. OAS pensions, maximum GIS and SA are adjusted quarterly to reflect increases in the consumer price index.

New Horizons projects
provide unique opportunities
for the elderly to develop
their talents.

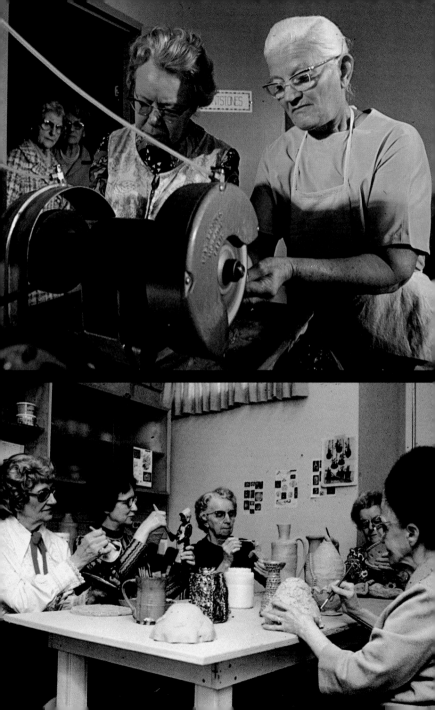

amily Allowances

A monthly Family Allowance (FA) is paid on behalf of a dependent child under
ie age of 18 to a parent (usually the mother) who is a resident of Canada, and who
'holly or substantially maintains the child. At least one of the parents must be a
anadian citizen, a landed immigrant or admitted to Canada for not less than one
ear under prescribed circumstances. FA benefits are also paid under certain pre-
:ribed circumstances to residents of Canada living abroad. The allowance is
ixable and must be included as income by the person who claims the child as a
ependent.

A monthly Special Allowance is payable on behalf of a child under the age of 18
/ho is maintained by a government, a government agency or an approved private
istitution. This allowance, which is non-taxable, may be paid directly to the
hild's foster parent at the request of the maintaining department or agency.

In 1976 the FA rate stood at $22.08. Quebec and Alberta, however, have chosen to
ary the rates; the legislation allows a province to vary the rates of the FA, provided
ertain conditions are met. Quebec and Prince Edward Island also have their own
imily allowances programs to supplement that of the federal government.

ocial Assistance and the Canada Assistance Plan

All provinces have programs that provide for social assistance to be granted to
iersons in need and their dependents. Assistance is granted on the basis of needs
ists, which take into account the budgetary requirements as well as the income and
esources of the applicant and his or her dependents. In addition to items of basic
ieed, assistance may include items of special need, non-insured health care ser-
ices and costs of homes for special care. Provision is also made for supportive
ervices such as homemaker, day-care and community development, and for pre-
entive services such as counselling, rehabilitation and adoption. These services
nay also be provided to persons likely to become persons in need without them.

Under the Canada Assistance Plan, the federal government pays 50 per cent of the
ost of providing assistance and welfare services to persons who qualify in accor-
lance with provincial law. Most provinces have discontinued the categorical
program for the blind and disabled; such persons may now receive assistance on the
iasis of need through the provincial social assistance programs under the Canada
Assistance Plan.

iervices for the Aged

Generally speaking, institutional care is available for older persons unable to care
or themselves. Although by no means organized in all areas, visiting nurse,
iomemaker, counselling, information and referral, and meals-on-wheels services,
is well as friendly visiting and housing registries, have also been established under
iublic and voluntary auspices. Low-rental housing projects have been built in
nany communities; clubs and centres to provide recreation and social activities
iave been developed.

The federal New Horizons Program affords older people the opportunity to
articipate more actively in community life. It provides grants to groups of retired

A day-care centre in Ottawa, Ont.

hobbies, historical, cultural and educational programs, social services, information services and activity centres.

Child Welfare Services

Statutory services for the protection and care of children who are neglected or who are temporarily or permanently without parental care include protection in their own homes, in foster homes or in an institution, as well as adoption services and services to unmarried parents. These programs are administered by provincial authorities or local children's aid societies.

Day-care centres are operated by local governments, voluntary associations or charitable organizations, or under commercial auspices. In addition to being licensed, they must meet the standards set by the relevant provincial government and comply with regulations relating to maintenance, safety, transportation and records.

International Welfare and Social Security

Canada actively participates in the social development activities of the United Nations through its involvement with the Economic and Social Council, the General Assembly and the Executive Board of UNICEF, as well as with numerous UN seminars and conferences dealing with social policy.

The Department of National Health and Welfare co-operates with the Canadian International Development Agency and, in conjunction with provincial departments and agencies, participates in the work of several international voluntary organizations. Canadian officials participate in the work of the International Social Security Association and the International Labour Organization.

The beauty of winter in the Laurentian area of Quebec.

Environment

Environment Canada came into being officially in June 1971 to amalgamate major federal responsibilities for the protection, preservation and enhancement of the quality of the environment and related renewable resources.

The principal objectives of the department are: administering ongoing resource programs and services; abating air, water and land pollution and preventing new environmental hazards; assessing and controlling the environmental impact of

◄— *Daisies on the southern shore of Northumberland Strait.*

Aerial application of seed and fertilizer to the ski slopes at Lake Louise in Alberta.

major developments on federal lands or involving federal funds; initiating long-term environmental protection programs; promoting and supporting international environmental and resource-management initiatives; and developing informative and educational programs.

The Minister of the Environment is assisted by a Minister of State (Fisheries) in carrying out responsibilities for fisheries and marine affairs.

Organization

Environment Canada has three principal components: Fisheries and Marine Service and Environmental Services, each headed by a senior Assistant Deputy Minister, and the Planning and Finance Service, headed by an Assistant Deputy Minister.

Responsibilities of the Fisheries and Marine Service include: the management of Canada's ocean and inland fisheries in co-operation with the provinces; fisheries and oceanographic research contributing to the management, understanding and optimum use of renewable aquatic resources and marine waters; hydrographic surveying and charting of navigable coastal and inland waters; and research in support of international agreements relating to fisheries management and marine environmental quality. The service is also responsible for the planning and ad-

Reclamation work on land disturbed by mining at the open-pit coal mines in the Crowsnest Coal Basin, BC.

ministration of some 3,000 harbours for small craft, and conducts environmental impact studies affecting coastal and inland waters.

Environmental services include the Atmospheric Environment Service (AES), the Environmental Protection Service (EPS) and the Environmental Management Service (EMS).

The Atmospheric Environment Service is concerned primarily with meteorology — the science of the atmosphere. The service provides national weather and climatological services for the public and special users. Since 1958, it has been responsible for ice services in support of navigation in Canadian waterways, coastal waters and the Arctic archipelago. It is also actively engaged in meteorological research, applied meteorology and instrument design and development.

The Environmental Protection Service develops national environmental control guidelines, requirements and regulations in consultation with the provinces and industry. The service carries out the assessment, surveillance, negotiations or enforcement necessary to obtain compliance with federal environmental legislation. It identifies and solves pollution problems, develops and demonstrates pollution control technology and serves as the focal point for all aspects of environmental protection for federal works, agencies and undertakings.

The Environmental Management Service (EMS) co-ordinates activities related to terrestrial renewable resources, their use and the impact of their use on the envi-

Lion's Gate Bridge Sewage Treatment Plant, Vancouver, BC.

ronment. It is composed of five staff directorates — Forestry, Inland Waters, Wildlife, Lands, and Policy and Program Development—concerned primarily with national environmental matters. In addition, line management operations are de-centralized in five regional directorates covering all of Canada, in an effort to provide each of the diverse regions with integrated resource management informa-tion best suited to its needs. Through its programs, EMS produces data on the quantity and quality of resources, conducts research on the methods and techniques of conservation, and plans the comprehensive utilization of renewable resources throughout the country as provided for in federal legislation. Because of its broad interests, the service plays a significant role in the consideration of the environmental effects of development projects by participating in the Environmen-tal Assessment and Review Process that applies to all federally supported projects.

The Planning and Finance Service provides an over-all framework of policy and planning advice, and co-ordinates the government's relationships respecting en-vironmental and resource matters with the provinces and other countries. It de-velops and co-ordinates a comprehensive approach to departmental science policy and research activities, and supports the over-all departmental program by assist-ing in the acquisition and deployment of resources required to meet departmental objectives. In addition, it provides financial and administrative direction to the department.

Fish caught in sampling nets are filleted and sent to a laboratory for tests of pollutant contents by the Ontario Ministry of Natural Resources.

Advisory Bodies

The Canadian Environmental Advisory Council was set up to provide advice to the Minister in four general areas: the state of the environment and threats to it; the priorities for federal or joint federal-provincial government action; the effectiveness of the department's efforts to restore, preserve or enhance the quality of the environment; and other matters which the Minister may refer to it as the need arises.

The Canadian Forestry Advisory Council reports to the Minister on specific areas of responsibility relative to our renewable resources. The Canadian Fisheries Advisory Council reports to the Minister of State for Fisheries on areas of responsibility relative to our fisheries resource. These advisory bodies review programs, assess their impact and provide links with organizations outside the government. The Councils' members include prominent Canadians from industry, the universities, the scientific community and, in the case of the Canadian Forestry Advisory Council, representatives from provincial resource departments.

The Environmental Assessment Panel manages, on behalf of the Minister, the preparation and review of formal, detailed, environmental assessments and protection statements. It defines requirements for baseline environmental studies for areas in which proposed actions are contemplated. It also provides advice and guidelines to proponents undertaking environmental assessments, and assists the proponents in the incorporation of environmental designs and procedures to implement its findings.

Although the department cannot accomplish on its own all of the necessary renewable resource and environmental tasks, owing to a division of federal and provincial jurisdictions, it can accomplish some, influence others and provide leadership.

Agriculture

The work of Agriculture Canada is carried out by seven branches and a number of special agencies under the authority of more than 35 acts of Parliament. Their activities embrace most aspects of the agricultural industry and affect all Canadians.

The Economics Branch carries out programs to improve farm income and helps obtain new markets for Canada's farm products. The Food Systems Branch plans and co-ordinates market-oriented food systems. The Health of Animals Branch is responsible for meat inspection and for animal diseases control, research and diagnosis. The Production and Marketing Branch administers legislation concerning food commodities, farm supplies and the protection of crops from pests and diseases. The Research Branch, with more than 30 establishments across Canada, conducts programs designed to solve problems of production, protection and utilization of agricultural crops and animals. The Financial and Administration Branch and the Personnel Branch provide administrative and personnel services. Like the branches, the Canadian Grain Commission reports to the Deputy Minister of Agriculture; the commission administers the Canada Grain Act, which regulates grain handling through the licensed elevator system in Canada.

Cattle feeding near Kamloops, BC.

In addition to the above, the Minister of Agriculture is responsible to Parliament for six other agencies. The Agricultural Stabilization Board assists farmers by supporting the prices of certain food commodities. The Agricultural Products Board buys, sells and imports agricultural products to maintain a healthy balance of food stocks in the country. The Canadian Dairy Commission supports the market prices of major processed dairy products. The Canadian Livestock Feed Board ensures the availability and price stability of feed grains. The Farm Credit Corporation, a Crown agency, makes loans to individual farmers and farm syndicates. The National Farm Products Marketing Council oversees the establishment and operation of national food marketing agencies.

Programs and Policies

The Animal Contagious Diseases Act—renamed the Animal Disease and Protection Act—was amended in 1975 to strengthen Canada's animal health programs, already recognized as among the best in the world. The new act provides a more equitable compensation plan for farmers whose animals are slaughtered in disease eradication programs, provides compensation for feed, bedding, fertilizer and other materials ordered destroyed in such programs, and sets out regulations for the humane care of animals in transportation. It also broadens the definition of animals to give the Health of Animals Branch authority over bees, birds and animal semen, regulates zoos and game farms for health purposes, and requires foreign ships to keep their meat lockers sealed while in Canadian waters.

The New Crop Development Fund, with an annual budget of $1 million, has provided funds to assist the development of peanuts, vinifera grapes and disease-free geraniums in Ontario, baby carrots in Quebec, sunflowers in Saskatchewan, new barley varieties in Manitoba, forage oats in Alberta, and better rapeseed varieties on the Prairies. Funds were also provided to carry out an evaluation of machinery and cropping systems for larger-scale grain crop production in Nova Scotia.

The DREAM program — Development, Research and Evaluation in Agriculture Mechanization — moved into its second year, with the Engineering Research Service awarding nearly $1 million in contracts to provincial governments, universities and private agencies for the evaluation and design of machinery to improve farm output. One of the most successful projects was the production of a small tomato harvester designed by a tomato farmer in southern Ontario.

The department continued to develop policies and programs to stabilize farm income and to relate production to national and export demands. Purchase programs, deficiency payments or subsidies were provided during 1975 to support

Corn silage from irrigated land in southern Alberta. Corn is harvested, chopped and placed in large open pits, where it is covered with plastic sheeting and allowed to ferment to provide a high protein silage for cattle feed.

Swathed harvest fields in Manitoba.

potato producers in the Maritimes, Quebec and Ontario, cherry growers in Ontario and British Columbia, apple growers in Nova Scotia, and processing-pear producers in Ontario.

The Agricultural Stabilization Act was amended to increase price support levels of cattle, sheep and hogs, industrial milk and cream, corn, soya beans, oats and barley marketed outside the jurisdiction of the Canadian Wheat Board. Prices of these commodities will be supported at not less than 90 per cent of their average market prices of the past five years, adjusted for changes in production costs.

A long-range dairy policy tying producer returns to a formula based on the consumer price index and the cost of production was announced during 1975.

External Affairs

The Department of External Affairs has three main purposes: (1) to provide information and advice to the government on foreign policy issues and to co-ordinate implementation of the government's foreign policy decisions; (2) to foster understanding of Canada and its people by other governments and nations; and (3) to provide assistance to Canadians abroad.

The headquarters of the department is in Ottawa. As of March 1976, Canadian diplomatic missions existed in 73 countries. For reasons of economy, some of these missions were accredited to more than one country, enabling Canada to maintain relations with another 68 governments.

A Canadian diplomatic post in a Commonwealth country usually has the status of high commission and is headed by a high commissioner, while a post in a non-Commonwealth country is known as an embassy and is headed by either an ambassador or a chargé d'affaires. In countries with which Canada's relations are extensive, separate consulates have also been established.

The work of an embassy or high commission is to conduct negotiations with the government to which it is accredited, to inform the Canadian government of significant developments in that country, to watch over Canada's interests, to serve Canadians in the country, and to disseminate information about Canada. A consulate has similar functions within its territory, except that it does not negotiate with the foreign government.

Canada has also established missions to advance its policies at a number of international organizations, including: the United Nations in New York and Geneva; the European Community and the North Atlantic Council, the highest authority in the North Atlantic Treaty Organization (NATO), in Brussels; the Organization for Economic Co-operation and Development and the United Nations Educational, Scientific and Cultural Organization in Paris; and the Organization of American States in Washington.

External Relations

The conduct of Canada's external relations, for which the Department of External Affairs has major responsibility, is discussed in the section on "The People and Their Heritage."

Services to Canadians

In addition to its foreign policy role, the department provides the following services to Canadians.

Consular services to Canadians abroad: In 1975, approximately 450,000 requests from Canadians for services of some kind were received by Canadian posts; 5,800 of these dealt with serious matters, such as arrest, illness, death or destitution.

Passports: In 1975, the department issued a total of 583,330 passports through its main passport office in Ottawa, its regional passport offices in Edmonton, Halifax, Montreal, Toronto, North York, Vancouver and Winnipeg, and its posts abroad. The department also issues certificates of identity and United Nations Refugee Convention travel documents to eligible non-Canadians legally residing in Canada.

Assistance in international legal matters: The Claims Section of the department's Legal Advisory Division co-ordinates the department's assistance to Canadian citizens and corporations seeking fair compensation from foreign governments for nationalization or other interference with their property. Through the Private International Law Section of Legal Operations Division, the legal profession and the public can obtain assistance with the administration of private international law, particularly with procedure pertaining to the service and authentication of documents in legal proceedings abroad and the furthering of extradition proceedings to and from Canada.

Academic relations: The department encourages a continuing dialogue between officials engaged in the implementation of foreign policy and scholars of international affairs. The Academic Relations Division operates programs to fulfil this objective, including the secondment of senior departmental officers to universities to engage in teaching, discussion and research, and speaking appearances by departmental officers in response to requests from universities and interested groups.

Access to archives: The Historical Division deals with requests from scholars studying Canada's external relations for access to departmental records, and assists them in their research when possible.

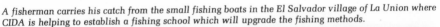

A fisherman carries his catch from the small fishing boats in the El Salvador village of La Union where CIDA is helping to establish a fishing school which will upgrade the fishing methods.

Canadian International Development Agency (CIDA)

In 1976-77 the Canadian International Development Agency, the government branch responsible for Canada's program of co-operation with developing countries, completed its first full year under the new guidelines released in the fall of 1975, which emphasized assistance for the poorest countries and the poorest sectors inside those countries. The answer to the problems of poverty and underdevelopment lies in a new concept of co-operation, in which the fully complementary and interrelated roles of concessionary financial aid, technical assistance, and trade and monetary policies are realized. This co-ordinated approach is expected to be reflected more and more in future relations between the industrialized nations like Canada and the developing world.

Canada's involvement in development assistance began with the formation of the Colombo plan to aid the newly-independent countries of Asia in 1950, and was later supplemented by programs in 1958 for the Caribbean and in 1960 for Commonwealth Africa. Programs for Francophone Africa began in 1961, and for Latin America in 1964.

Canada's Official Development Assistance allocation for the year ending March 13, 1977 was $1 billion, a figure including some unspent money allocated in previous years but not including the $25.8 million cost of administration. In 1976-77 the largest part of these funds, $585.8 million, went through bilateral (government to government) programs. Asia remained the largest recipient, at $294.4 million, while $111 million went to Commonwealth Africa, $120 million to Francophone Africa, $23 million to Latin America and $22 million to the Caribbean. The remainder of the funds was earmarked for other programs, such as emergency relief.

Canadian assistance consists of grants or loans. Loans are usually interest-free, with repayment over 50 years to begin in the 10th year; occasionally they are made at 3 per cent interest, with repayment over 30 years starting in the eighth year. The grant-to-loan ratio is about 65:35.

Bilateral co-operation takes four main forms — project assistance, food aid, commodity aid and lines of credit. Project aid, under which loans and grants are provided for specific development projects agreed on by CIDA and the developing country, is largest. This includes the provision of Canadian advisers on the projects (1,088 in 62 countries as of January 1976); at the same time, residents of countries involved are given training in Canada or elsewhere to enable them to take over and continue the projects (nearly 1,900 as of January 1976). Next in value is food aid, at $229.6 million, counting $105 million given under the multilateral program. Commodity aid is essentially a drawing account for the purchase in Canada of specific raw or semi-processed materials and fertilizer. Line-of-credit loans worth over $100 million are in effect with several countries, providing a relatively unrestricted form of credit.

Multilateral assistance—$348.5 million in 1976-77—is the second largest area of the budget. Of this, $105 million went for food aid, mostly to the World Food Programme. The second highest amount went to the International Development Association, a branch of the World Bank; Canada's contribution to the fourth replenishment of the bank's funds, covering the years 1975-77, will total $276 million. Canada is also a member of the Asian, Caribbean and Inter-American development banks, and was a moving force behind the establishment of the African Development Fund. Canada has been a major supporter of the United Nations Development Program since its inception in 1965; the 1976-77 contribution was $29 million. Canada also contributes to other UN programs such as UNICEF.

A growing part of Canada's assistance program involves voluntary agencies, churches, universities and other non-governmental organizations. CIDA subsidizes selected projects up to 50 per cent of the cost, to a total of $35 million in 1976-77. CIDA also encourages Canadian business to participate in the industrial development of Third World countries through investment in joint ventures.

Less affected than many by the high cost of oil, Canada has taken a full role in the international effort to help those countries hardest hit by current energy problems. Canada has become the largest donor of food, pledging $300 million to a special International Monetary Fund account to finance oil purchases by countries with serious balance of payments problems, extending a General Preferential Tariff to make various goods manufactured in developing countries more competitive in Canada and beginning a five-year, $230 million program for rehabilitating the Sahel region of West Africa.

Pump provided by CIDA in the Guayas Basin of Ecuador provides clean water in place of the polluted water of the coastal basin.

Canadian Executive Service Overseas (CESO)

Incorporated as a non-profit corporation late in 1967 by a group of Canadians prominent in industry and the professions, CESO functions under the auspices of the Canadian International Development Agency. One part of its assigned task is to recruit for overseas service Canadians who have a record of achievement in their chosen fields and whose personal qualities make them good communicators. The other part of the mandate is to make it known in developing countries that there are Canadians willing to share their specialized knowledge with local enterprises that are seeking to improve their contribution to the economy of their own countries.

Its system is simple and direct. The volunteer consultant having expressed willingness and ability to go abroad is on the CESO roster. When an overseas request is expressed for the service of a voluntary consultant, the roster is searched and one or more appropriate specialists are nominated by CESO. Ultimately the volunteer will have the opportunity to accept or reject the particular project and the client may accept or reject the particular volunteer. At the beginning of the 1976-77 fiscal year approximately 1,200 projects had been completed in over 44 different overseas countries. The number of projects grows at a carefully controlled rate.

It is of interest to note that here at home the Indian program, in which CESO now assists Indian bands and enterprises in collaboration with the Department of Indian and Northern Affairs, is proving most successful. The number of volunteers working with Indian bands from coast to coast on a wide variety of projects has numbered over 90 and that figure should increase in the months ahead.

Finally CESO provides the opportunity for people to extend their careers beyond normal retirement by sharing their skills and knowledge with others who can and will benefit from expert advice and guidance. CESO regards this by-product of the program as an important privilege and welcomes the opportunity to preserve the accumulated knowledge of Canadian experts through productive employment.

CESO's headquarters is in Montreal at 1010 St. Catherine Street West, Suite 420. Regional representatives are located in key centres across Canada.

Canadian University Service Overseas (CUSO)

CUSO was established in 1961 as an independent non-profit organization to provide professionally and technically qualified Canadians to meet the changing manpower requirements of developing countries. Today, in addition to placing almost 900 persons in over 40 countries, it funds, administers and staffs a wide range of projects supportive to the development efforts of those countries.

CUSO is a "middle-level manpower" program operating under the plans and priorities of the countries with which it co-operates. It is not a relief, religious or emergency aid program. CUSO has programs and projects in Africa, Asia, the Caribbean, Central and South America, and the Pacific.

Universities and colleges still play a vital role in the recruitment and initial selection of personnel for overseas assignments, through a network of 70 local committees across Canada. These committees, which operate on a voluntary basis, are usually composed of faculty and student members, returned CUSO personnel, representatives of the participating countries and members of the local community wherever possible. In addition, many committees are involved in fund-raising and development education activities. The program is administered through an Ottawa-based secretariat and regional offices both in Canada and overseas.

CUSO receives a substantial part of its finances from the Canadian International Development Agency; an equal amount is contributed by overseas governments and agencies in the form of CUSO workers' salaries and housing supplements. The balance comes in the form of contributions from individuals, corporations, foundations, community groups and provincial governments. Further support comes from Canadian universities, which provide free office space, equipment and staff manhours at the local committee level.

International Development Research Centre (IDRC)

The IDRC was created by an Act of the Canadian Parliament in 1970, when the need was recognized for a donor agency that had more flexibility than a government department to support research into the problems of developing countries. The objective of the centre has been to promote the economic and social development of those regions — particularly the well-being of their rural peoples — by research designed to adapt scientific and technical knowledge to their specific requirements.

This research is being carried out almost entirely by scientists and technologists from the countries and regions involved, in accordance with their own priorities. The role of the centre's senior staff is to help refine research proposals, recommend projects for funding, monitor their progress and disseminate the results as widely as possible. The provision of funds so that researchers in developing countries can direct their own studies and learn how to solve their own problems is possible only because IDRC, unlike government agencies, is able to offer "untied aid."

Threshing rice in the Philippines where IDRC is supporting research projects to cut down post-harvest waste.

IDRC is supporting research in Egypt to develop the best species of casuarina trees which are used as shelterbelts from desert winds and sand, allowing land to be reclaimed for cultivation.

Within a general concern for the advancement of rural peoples, there is a focus on research in four areas: agriculture, food and nutrition sciences; information sciences; population and health sciences; and social sciences and human resources. A network of information on agricultural science and technology was built, with establishment of regional centres in Costa Rica and the Philippines and of a central processing unit in Vienna, and with support of a national system in Egypt. Some 250 traditional healers in Zaïre were studied and medicinal herbs used for treatment were systematically collected with a view to integrating the healers into the government's health services. Research was carried out by Latin American architects, planners and social scientists into the provision of low-cost shelter to the urban poor of six countries, in order to recommend to their governments a set of upgraded housing policies.

Proposals are judged by such factors as: whether they fit into the priorities of developing countries; whether they are likely to have useful application beyond the country involved; whether the research will help close gaps in living standards inside these countries; whether they will make full use of local resources and people; and whether they will leave behind investments in better trained or more experienced researchers.

The centre is a public corporation with an international Board of Governors and an international staff. The chairman, vice-chairman and nine others of the 21 governors must be Canadian citizens, but the board in 1975-76 also had members from Ethiopia, Zaïre, Iran, Indonesia, Mexico, Jamaica, Britain, France, the US and Australia. The chairman was Louis Rasminsky and the President, W. David Hopper. Five IDRC regional offices have been set up, in Singapore, Bogota, Dakar, Nairobi and Beirut.

Financing has so far come entirely from the Canadian government in the form of annual grants. In 1975-76 the grant was $27 million, or 3 per cent of Canada's foreign aid budget. As of March 1976, IDRC had approved a total of 370 projects in 77 countries, a commitment of $69.9 million.

National Defence

The most significant single event affecting the Department of National Defence (DND) in 1975 was the reaching of decisions in the second phase of the Defence Structure Review (DSR).

Steered by an interdepartmental committee under the chairmanship of the Clerk of the Privy Council, the DSR had been directed by Cabinet, in November 1974, to review the tasks of the Canadian Forces, the effectiveness and optional levels of effort at which these tasks should be performed, and the organization and resources required.

The government believed this to be desirable at a time when defence budgets had been frozen for three years, and when certain critical decisions on the replacement of major pieces of equipment were required.

Phase I of the DSR had examined the various tasks related to one or more of the 15 DND objectives, which were in turn derived from national aims and policy themes. Phase II considered the range of force postures, in particular those involving fighting capability, that would be appropriate for Canada, and postulated an illustrative force model within which further detailed planning could take place. The review also highlighted the urgency of executive decisions on the purchase of new equipment that were required if certain existing capabilities were to be maintained. These involved especially the continued use of tanks and long-range patrol aircraft (LRPA).

Following consideration of Phase II of the DSR, the government reaffirmed its commitment to the four priority roles stated for the Canadian Forces in the 1971

National Defence headquarters in Ottawa, Ont. towers over the Chateau Laurier.

The cockpit of a Canadian Forces Argus plane.

White Paper, "Defence in the 70s". These are: the surveillance and protection of our sovereign territory and coastlines; the defence of North America in co-operation with US forces; the fulfilment of such NATO commitments as may be agreed upon; and the performance of such international peacekeeping roles as we may from time to time assume.

Other major decisions taken by Cabinet following submission of Phase II included: maintenance of the strength of the Canadian Forces at a level of 78,000 Regular and 22,000 Reserve Force Personnel, including a total of 2,000 men earmarked to meet current and foreseeable United Nations peacekeeping requirements; the continued maintenance in Europe of mixed army and air forces, with adequate equipment, including a modern main battle tank, to contribute to NATO's collective defence of the central region; purchase of 18 Lockheed P–3 long-range patrol aircraft (LRPA) to replace the Argus aircraft in service since 1957; and studies for the eventual acquisition of new fighter aircraft to replace the CF–104, CF–101 and CF–5 aircraft on inventory, and for a ship replacement program, which were to be considered by Cabinet early in 1976.

A significant element of the government's decision involved future funding of the Department of National Defence — namely an agreement that capital expenditures for defence were to be increased in real terms by 12 per cent each year for the next five years.

A third phase of the Defence Structure Review is under way. It involves equipment acquisition studies, such as those mentioned above, as well as consideration of the necessary infrastructure and costs required to support the Canadian Forces effectively in the future. This may result in some consolidation in headquarters, bases, and educational and logistic facilities, but only to the extent that operational capability is not impaired.

common conversion factors from SI metric to canadian imperial units

Length

1 mm	=	0.03937 in.
1 cm	=	0.3937 in.
1 m	=	3.28084 ft.
1 km	=	0.62137 mi.

Area

1 km^2	=	0.3861 sq. mi.
1 ha	=	2.47105 acres
1 m^2	=	0.000247 acres

Mass (Weight)

1 kg	=	2.204622 lbs.
1 kg	=	0.0011023 tons (short)
1 kg	=	0.000984 tons (long)
1 kg	=	32.1507 troy ounces
1 g	=	0.0321507 troy ounces
1 t	=	1.102311 tons (short)
1 t	=	0.9842065 tons (long)

Volume and Capacity

1 m^3	=	220 gal.
1 m^3	=	35.31466 cu. ft.
1 m^3	=	423.78 board feet
1 dm^3	=	0.423776 board feet
1 m^3	=	6.28982 barrels
1 litre	=	0.219969 gal.
1 dm^3	=	0.027496 bushels
1 m^3	=	27.4962 bushels

Mass in SI Metric to Average Capacity in Canadian Imperial Units for Common Field Crops

Wheat, soya beans, potatoes, peas	1 t =	36.74 bushels
Rye, flax, corn	1 t =	39.37 bushels
Rapeseed, mustard seed	1 t =	44.09 bushels
Barley, buckwheat	1 t =	45.93 bushels
Mixed grains	1 t =	48.99 bushels
Oats	1 t =	64.84 bushels
Sunflower seed	1 t =	91.86 bushels

Temperature

9/5 temperature in °C + 32 = temperature in °F

acknowledgements

Contributors

Ramsay Cook (*History*), F.R.S.C., Professor of History, York University. B.A. Manitoba, 1954; M.A. Queen's, 1956; Ph.D. Toronto, 1960. Author of *The Politics of John W. Dafoe and the Free Press* (Toronto, 1963); *Canada: A Modern Study* (Toronto, 1964); *Canada and the French Canadian Question* (Toronto, 1966); *Provincial Autonomy, Minority Rights and the Compact Theory, 1867-1921* (Royal Commission on Bilingualism and Biculturalism, 1969, in French also); *The Maple Leaf Forever* (Toronto, 1970); (with Robert Craig Brown) *Canada 1896-1921: A Nation Transformed* (Toronto, 1974); and numerous articles.

Robert B. Crozier (*Economic Trends in Canada, 1975-76*), Director of Policy Analysis, The Conference Board in Canada. Previously senior economist, Economic Council of Canada; Assistant Director, National Accounts Division, Statistics Canada. Author of *A Guide to the National Income and Expenditure Accounts* (Ottawa, 1975) and various reports in the field of economics.

Robert Fulford (*Arts and Culture*), Editor of *Saturday Night* since 1968, journalist for twenty-five years. Writes a weekly column on the arts in the *Toronto Star* and the *Ottawa Citizen* and frequently appears on CBC television and radio. Author of *This Was Expo* (Toronto, 1968); *Crisis at the Victory Burlesk* (Toronto, 1968); and *Marshall Delaney at the Movies* (Toronto, 1974).

Gordon McKay (*The Climate*), Director, Meteorological Applications Branch, Environment Canada. B.Sc. Manitoba, 1943; M.Sc. McGill, 1953. This article is an expanded version of "Climatic Resources and Economic Activity", which appears in *Canada's Natural Environment: essays in applied geography*, edited by G.R. McBoyle and E. Sommerville (Methuen Publications, Toronto, 1976).

John S. Moir (*Religion*), Professor of History, Scarborough College, University of Toronto. B.A. Toronto, 1948; M.A., 1949; Ph.D., 1954; D.D., 1975. Author of *Church and State in Canada West* (Toronto, 1959); *The Church in the British Era* (Toronto, 1972), Vol. 2 of *A History of the Christian Church in Canada*; *Enduring Witness: A History of the Presbyterian Church in Canada* (Toronto, 1974); and other books and articles.

Olav Slaymaker (*The Land*), Associate Professor of Geography, University of British Columbia. B.A. Cambridge, 1961; A.M. Harvard, 1963; Ph.D. Cambridge, 1968. Co-editor of "Mountain Geomorphology", *Tantalus*, 1972, and author of a number of articles on the physical geography of western Canada.

Dixon Thompson (introduction to *The Environment*), Associate Professor of Environmental Science, Faculty of Environmental Design, University of Calgary. B.S.c. Alberta, 1964; Ph.D. Illinois, 1970. Previously Research Assistant to the AUCC Commission on Canadian Studies and Science Adviser, Science Council of Canada. Consultant and author of a number of articles on the Conserver Society.

Photographic Credits by page number

Cover and Frontispiece. George Hunter
   3. George Hunter/Photothèque
   5. Richard Vroom
   7. Deryk Bodington
   8. Richard Vroom
  11. Malak
  13. Richard Vroom
  14. Malak
  15. Malak
  16. Canadian Government Office of Tourism
  18. J.E. Lozanski
  21. George Hunter
  22. Harold Clark
  23. Canadian Government Office of Tourism
  25. Camerique Stock Photos
  28. Audrey Giles/Photo Source Ltd.
  29. Barbara Johnstone
  31. Malak
  33. Fred Bruemmer
  34. Nova Scotia Government Information Services/Photothèque
  35. George Hunter/Photothèque
  40. Malak
  43. George Hunter
  44. Jean-Claude Grénat/Photothèque
  46. Fred Bruemmer
  47. Deryk Bodington
  51. National Capital Commission
  53. Bryce Flynn
  55. (1), (2) Bryce Flynn; (3) Ed Kucerak/Secretary of State
  56. Deryk Bodington
  58. Richard Vroom
  59. Deryk Bodington
  60. Fred Bruemmer
  62. Robert C. Ragsdale
  63. Malak
  64. Les Grands Ballets Canadiens
  66. Deryk Bodington
  67. Robert C. Ragsdale
  68. Jean Berg/Photothèque
  69. Robert C. Ragsdale
  71. Crawley Films
  72. Canadian Cablesystems Ltd.
  76. Canadian Broadcasting Corporation
  77. Canadian Broadcasting Corporation
  79. Malak
  80. Malak
  81. Malak
  83. National Museum of Man
  85. National-Museum of Natural Sciences
  87. Deryk Bodington

88. Neil Newton/Miller Services
90. Malak
92. Malak
93. A. Douglas MacPhail/British Columbia Dept. of Education
95. Canadian Broadcasting Corporation
97. Fred Bruemmer
98. Bryce Flynn
99. A. Douglas MacPhail/British Columbia Dept. of Education
101. *Vancouver Sun*
105. Malak
109. Edward Jones/Miller Services
110. Deryk Bodington
113. Deryk Bodington
114. Malak
115. Malak
116. Richard Vroom
117. Richard Vroom
119. Parks Canada
120. Barbara Johnstone
121. Malak
123. George Hunter
125. Craft Graphic Services Ltd.
127. Canadian Industries Limited
129. Deryk Bodington
130. Environment Canada
133. Environment Canada
134. George Hunter/Photothèque
137. Environment Canada
139. Dept. of Energy, Mines and Resources
141. Dept. of Energy, Mines and Resources (4)
143. Dept. of Energy, Mines and Resources
145. A.K. Cowper/Health and Welfare Canada
147. Bryce Flynn
148. Canadian National
149. Dept. of Communications
150. Bryce Flynn
151. Canada Post
152. Frank Kristian/COJO
153. George Hunter
154. COJO
155. COJO
157. Cpl. V. Johnson/Photothèque
158. François Renaud/COJO
159. (1) Claude Desrosiers/COJO; (2) Michael Wesselink/COJO; (3) Claude Desrosiers/COJO
161. Cpl. V. Johnson/Photothèque
163. Canadian Press
165. Wide World Photos
167. Dept. of External Affairs
168. Wide World Photos
171. Richard Vroom
174. George Hunter/Photothèque
175. Malak

176. Bryce Flynn
178. Deryk Bodington
179. George Hunter
181. Malak
182. Malak
186. Bryce Flynn
188. Deryk Bodington
189. George Hunter
191. E. Otto/Miller Services
192. Fred Bruemmer
193. George Hunter/Photothèque
195. Malak
196. Malak
197. Deryk Bodington
198. George Hunter
199. Chris Bruun/Photothèque
200. George Hunter/Photothèque
201. Malak/Photothèque
202. Imperial Oil
203. E. Otto/Miller Services
205. TransCanada PipeLines
207. Kaiser Resources Ltd.
210. Malak/Photothèque
212. George Hunter
213. Audrey Giles/Photo Source Ltd.
214. Bryce Flynn
217. Hawker Siddeley Canada Ltd.
218. Canadian Industries Limited
219. Canron Ltd.
221. Union Carbide Canada Ltd.
223. Malak
225. John Reeves/Genstar Ltd.
226. Malak
227. Central Mortgage and Housing Corporation
228. Ontario Ministry of Housing
229. George Hunter
230. Central Mortgage and Housing Corporation
231. Malak (top); George Hunter
232. Bryce Flynn
233. George Hunter
234. Westeel-Rosco Ltd.
235. Canadian Industries Limited
237. Hawker Siddeley Canada Ltd.
239. Audrey Giles/Photo Source Ltd.
240. Dept. of Regional Economic Expansion
241. Deryk Bodington
243. Deryk Bodington
245. Malak
247. Deryk Bodington
248. United Co-operatives of Ontario
251. George Hunter
252-253. (1), (2) George Hunter/Photothèque; (3) Paul Lambert/Photothèque; (4) George
    Hunter/Photothèque

254. Kaiser Resources Ltd.
256. George Hunter/Photothèque
257. Malak
261. Hawker Siddeley Canada Ltd.
263. George Hunter
264. George Hunter
265. Malak
269. Richard Vroom
270. Richard Vroom
271. Malak
272-273. George Hunter (4)
274. Audrey Giles/Photo Source Ltd.
275. Malak
276. Deryk Bodington
277. Barry Dursley/Photo Source Ltd.
279. George Hunter
282. Fred Bruemmer
283. George Hunter/Photothèque
284. Malak
285. George Hunter
286. George Hunter
288-289. George Hunter (4)
293. Alex Onoszko
295. Bryce Flynn
297. Malak
301. Bryce Flynn
302. Richard Harrington
304. Audrey Giles/Photo Source Ltd.
306. Deryk Bodington
307. Alec Burns/Photo Source Ltd.
308. Dept. of Manpower and Immigration
310. Dept. of Manpower and Immigration
311. Dept. of Manpower and Immigration
313. George Hunter
314. The International Nickel Company of Canada, Ltd.
315. George Hunter
317. George Hunter
318. George Hunter
319. George Hunter
320. *Vancouver Sun*
321. Sherritt Gordon Mines Ltd.
323. George Hunter
324. Malak
325. Malak
326. Malak
327. Urban Affairs Canada
328. Tom Boschler/Photothèque
329. Malak
330. Richard Vroom
331. Barbara Johnstone
332. Dept. of Veterans Affairs
333. Dept. of Veterans Affairs
334. Health and Welfare Canada

335. Health and Welfare Canada
336. Health and Welfare Canada
337. Health and Welfare Canada
338. Alec Burns/Photo Source Ltd.
339. Malak
341. Health and Welfare Canada
342-343. Health and Welfare Canada (4)
345. Miller Services
346. Malak
347. Malak
348. Deryk Bodington
349. Deryk Bodington
350. Central Mortgage and Housing Corporation
351. Bryce Flynn
352. Richard Harrington
353. Malak
354. Deryk Bodington
355. George Hunter
357. Jack Redden/CIDA
359. Jack Redden/CIDA
361. Neill McKee/IDRC
362. Neill McKee/IDRC
363. Murdoch Maclean
364. Bryce Flynn
Please note: Inquiries about photographs credited to Photothèque should be directed to the National Film Board of Canada.

Africa, relations with 166
Aged, services for 340-45
Agriculture 177-90, 352-55
−Canada 352-55
Agricultural research 131-33
Air transport 279-82
Anik 146
Appalachian region 10-12
Archives 88
Arts, the 61-95
−visual 77-78
Asia and the Pacific,
    relations with 165-66

Balance of international
    payments 257-61
Bank of Canada 278
Banking and savings 274-78
British North America
    Act 291-76
Broadcasting 72-76

Cabinet, federal 294-96
Caisses populaires 277-78
Canada Council 61, 68-69, 90, 93
−Pension Plan 340
Canadian Broadcasting
    Corporation 75-76
−constitution 31, 35, 294,
                   297, 300
−courts 300-02
−Executive Service Overseas
    (CESO) 360
−International Development
    Agency (CIDA) 358-59
−landscape 4-16
−Radio-television and
    Telecommunications Commission
    (CRTC) 74-75
−Shield 7-10

−University Service Overseas
    (CUSO) 360-61
Capital expenditures 221-26
Census of Canada 36-42
Central Mortgage and Housing
    Corporation 227-30
Child welfare 345
Churches 57-60
Citizenship 306-07
Claims, native 47-48
Climate 17-25
Coal 207-08
Collective bargaining 312
Commonwealth relations 166-67,
                   169-70
Communications 146-50
−research 142-44
Community colleges 104-07
Constitution, Canadian .. 31, 35, 294,
                   297, 300
Consumer and Corporate Affairs,
    Department of 323-26
−credit 241-42
−price index 249-50
Co-operatives 247-49
Cordilleran Region 14-16
Cultural exchanges 89-90
−policy 91-95

Dairying 186-87
Defence, National,
    Department of 363-64
Domestic trade 238-46
Drug control and abuse 335-36

Economic trends 173-76
Education 96-111
−administration 97-99
−adult 103-04
−elementary and secondary .. 97-103
−expenditures 108-11

−financing 108-11
−school organization 99-101
−statistics 97-99, 101-11
−universities 108
−vocational and technical 103
Electric power 208-10
Embassies and posts abroad .. 356-57
Employment 211-15
Energy 199-210
−research 138-42
Environment Canada 347-51
−protection of 133-38, 347-51
Eskimos. See Inuit
Europe, relations with 164-65
Exports 251-55
External Affairs,
    Department of 162-71, 356-57
−aid programs 166-67, 358-62
−relations 162-71, 356-64

Family allowances 344
Farm Credit Corporation 353
−exports 178, 254
−income 177-83, 186, 189
−legislation 352-55
−production 177-90
Federal government,
    organization of 291-98
−environment legislation 347-51
−finance 262-70
−research 128-45
−science policy 125-26
Festivals 53-55
Field crops 178-79
Films 70-72
Finance 262-73
−capital expenditure 221-26
−federal government 262-70
−federal-provincial 262-70
−municipal 262-70
−non-bank institutions 276-78
−provincial government 262-70
Fisheries 191-92
−research 134-36
Foreign policy 162
−trade 251-56

Forest industries 194-98
−ownership and administration . 194
Forestry 193-98
French-speaking community,
    relations with 169-70
Fruits and vegetables 180-82
Furs 189-90

Gas, natural 201-07
Geography 4-16
Geological Survey of Canada 199
Glaciation 4-10, 12, 15-16
Government, federal,
    organization of 291-98
−cultural policy 91-95
−expenditures, education 108-11
−municipal 298
−provincial 291-93, 298
−science and technology 128
−territorial 291-93, 298
−welfare programs 344-45
Governor-General 294-96
Grains, production of 178-79
Gross National Product
    (GNP) 173-75
Guaranteed income
    supplement 340-41

Harbours 286-89
Health 334-39
−grants 339
−research 144-45, 335-36
−services 334-39
History 27-35
Hospital insurance 336-38
House of Commons 294-98
Housing 227-31
Hydro-electric power 208-09

Immigration 308-09
Imports 255-56
Income, national 173-76
−tax 262-66
Indian and Northern Affairs,
    Department of 43-48

Indians 43-45, 47-48
Industrial growth 216-20
−research 128-29
Industry, Trade and Commerce,
  Department of 319-20
Insurance 278
−hospital 336-37
−medical care 337-38
−unemployment 340
Interior plains 10
International Development
  Research Centre (IDRC) 361-62
−payments 257-61
−trade 251-56
−welfare 345
Inuit (Eskimos) 45-48

Judiciary 300-01

Labour 211-15, 312-15
−collective bargaining 312
−earnings 213-15
−force 211-12
−legislation 312
−organizations 215
Latin America, relations with ... 166
Legislature 296-98
Libraries.................... 86-88
Livestock 183-89
Logging 194-96
Lumber 194-97

Manpower programs 309-11
Manufacturing 232-37
−statistics 236
Map........................... 4
Medical care program 334-39
−insurance 337-38
−research 144-45
−services.................. 334-39
Mental illness 334-35, 337
Middle East, relations with 166
Minerals 199-208
−fuels 199-208

−production of 199-208
Multiculturalism 53-56
Municipal government 298
−finance 262-70
Museums 81-85

National Defence,
  Department of 363-64
−Film Board 72
−Housing Act 227-30
−parks 117-120
−Research Council 126, 128, 130
Native peoples 43-48
−claims 47-48
Natural wealth 177-210
North Atlantic Treaty Organization
  (NATO) 164, 364
Nuclear power 209-10
Nursing, schools of 107

Official languages 49-53
Oil........................ 205-07
Old age security 340-41
Olympics 152-61

Pacific, relations with 165-66
Parks 117-121
Parliament................. 291-98
Pensions 340
Performing Arts 64-69
Petroleum 205-07
Pipelines, oil and gas 205-07
Police 303-04
Pollution 133-38, 347-51
Population.................. 36-42
−by age 39-40
−by province 36-39
−growth 36-42
−rural and urban 36-39
Postal service 151
Poultry and eggs 187-89
Price index, consumer 249-50
Prime Minister.. 163, 165, 168, 294-95
Privy Council 294-95